MG TF

Volkswagen Golf GTI Mk1

'67 BT24 Brabham-Repco

'68 M8A McLaren CanAm

'72 M19C McLaren F1

MEMORIES OF THE BEAR

MEMORIES OF THE BEAR

A BIOGRAPHY OF DENNY HULME

EOIN YOUNG

Haynes Publishing

First published in 2007 by HarperCollins New Zealand
First UK and US edition published in August 2007 by Haynes Publishing

A catalogue record for this book is available from the British Library

ISBN: 978 1 84425 208 4

Library of Congress control number 2006937700

Haynes Publishing, Sparkford, Yeovil, Somerset BA22 7JJ, UK.
Tel: 01963 442030 Fax: 01963 440001
Int. tel: +44 1963 442030 Int. fax: +44 1963 440001
E-mail: sales@haynes.co.uk
Website: www.haynes.co.uk

Haynes North America Inc., 861 Lawrence Drive, Newbury Park, California 91320, USA.

Front cover photo: Hulme Family Collection
Back cover photo by Gunther Swartz
Inside front cover photo by Lynton Money
Spine photo courtesy of *New Zealand Herald* and *Weekly News*
Inside back cover photo by Michael R. Hewett

Wherever possible, the author and publishers have made every attempt to
determine the ownership of photographic material used in this book.
However, it has not been possible to establish the origin and ownership of some
photographs given to the Hulme Family. If anyone has information about the
source of these photographs, please contact the Publisher in the first instance.

Cover design by Murray Dewhurst
Typesetting by IslandBridge
Printed by Griffin Press, Australia, on 100 gsm Publishers Offset

I dedicate Memories of the Bear
to memories of Selina, our daughter
and Denny's goddaughter

Acknowledgements

This book would not have been possible without the ongoing support and encouragement of my very good friends during a period of my life that was particularly difficult, for a variety of personal reasons. It is a book that I have always wanted to write, because Denny was a good friend in his racing days and although we did not see as much of each other when he went home to New Zealand, we still kept in touch. This latter period of the book looked like being the most awkward for me, and I was hugely grateful when Michael Clark stepped up and offered to research and write the final two chapters for me.

By profession, Michael is a founding partner and director of New Zealand's largest independent firm of property valuers in Auckland, but his passion is motor sport and he has honed a fascinating ability to write about his favourite racing eras, tracks, drivers and personalities in his regular columns in *New Zealand Classic Car* and on the pitpass.com website.

My thanks to the publishers of *Autosport* for allowing me to use the words I wrote with Denny after the races back in the early 1970s. I have to confess that I had forgotten many of the tales Denny recounted, or perhaps they had faded in the mists of many long and well-lubricated dinners with my journalist mates at circuits around the world.

The fact that I had forgotten some of the stories simply made writing this book on the life that Denny led all the more fascinating. I hope that others find a similar enjoyment in The Bear's memories, second time around.

It is supremely difficult to re-create an event that happened a generation ago, but Denny had a homespun way of remembering the track adventures he'd had a week earlier and being able to describe them, usually with a titter if it was fun, or a seriousness that came through when he talked about the danger of his sport in those days before it was acknowledged. Denny raced at the end of the era when danger was supposed to be part of the deal, and while he supported this view to start with, by the end of his racing days he actually led the Grand Prix Drivers' Association as their President in a push to make racing safer for drivers and spectators alike.

Phil Kerr, Denny's mentor and guide throughout his career, had been Managing Director at Brabham and then McLaren, and was always on hand to answer my questions about various aspects of Denny's life and times.

Milan Fistonic fielded my endless requests for information on races and people and places, making good use of his extensive motor racing library, and Nigel Roebuck, Alan Henry, Chris Hilton, and others always took time to assist with my many and varied questions from the other side of the world to bolster my own memories of The Bear. Donald Davidson, the ex-pat Englishman who heads the history side of the Indianapolis Motor Speedway, was always quick to assist when I needed help about some detail or other.

Pete Lyons comes in for special thanks. Pete wrote for *Autosport* and the *Autocourse* annual in the Denny days in Formula 1 and CanAm, and his history of the CanAm series was invaluable when Denny decided he wouldn't write his 'Diary' column after a race hadn't gone according to his plan. Bill Gavin accompanied Denny on that first season of 1960 in Europe and he kindly allowed me to borrow from his features written at the time. Peter (Baldric) Grant loaned me a run of *Automobile Year* and Terry Marshall let me draw on his collection of *Autocourse* annuals while I was writing the book in Christchurch, New Zealand, a world away from where it had all happened. Gavin Bain's motoring library was another constant source of loan books from which to borrow instant knowledge.

Conversion table

1 inch	25.40 millimetres
1 foot (12 inches)	30.48 centimetres
1 yard (3 feet)	91.44 centimetres
1 mile (1760 yards)	1.61 kilometres
1 pound	453.60 grams
1 stone (14 pounds)	6.35 kilograms
1 hundredweight	50.80 kilograms
1 ton (2240 pounds, 160 stone)	1.02 tonnes
1 brake horsepower (bhp)	0.746 kilowatts (kW)
1 gallon	4.55 litres
1 US gallon	3.79 litres
1 acre	0.4 hectare

Foreword Sir Jackie Stewart OBE

Denny Hulme was, to say the least, an unusual and contradictory character. My first recollection of Denny is of seeing him walking around the paddock not wearing shoes, relatively soon after he arrived to race in the UK and Europe. His barefoot attitude, informality, and his fully relaxed and what appeared to be lethargic pose and attitude towards life, was such a contrast to the Denny Hulme on the racetrack.

I raced with Denny in a variety of different formulae in the time we shared with each other. In Formula 2 he was driving with Jack Brabham in the Honda-powered Brabham, which was almost unbeatable for far too long a period. Jack himself, as the team leader, was tough opposition, but the newcomer, Denny Hulme, came as a surprise to most of us. He looked nothing like a racing driver was expected to look like, yet he went so fast and drove so well — he was certainly a contradiction.

His nickname of The Bear, which he picked up as his career developed, emerged from his sometimes very grizzly and dismissive attitude to what he felt were intrusions on his privacy and personal time, often prompted by journalists who, in Denny's words, 'would ask silly questions'. On occasions such as that, and when dealing with officials who he felt were out of order, The Bear carried his mantle in a graphic and robust style. Normally while walking up and down the paddock he had a relaxed pose, his drooping arms appearing boneless, so flexible were they. When The Bear emerged in anger, those arms would suddenly tense into what could have been the very strong and hairy paws of a great grizzly! Yet Denny Hulme was the most relaxed and gentle man that you could ever encounter. He didn't give his friendship away easily; you had to earn it. The very appearance of someone who Denny did not approve of created a reaction in the man, and he certainly didn't suffer fools gladly.

As a driver, he was one of the best in the world, although he was seldom recognised as such by those who were not his peers. Anyone who raced against Denny Hulme at close quarters, and there were few of them, knew that he had an amazing talent. Anyone who can win in Monte Carlo and at the Nürburgring, circuits that require two vastly different styles of driving, with challenges that have to be handled in a totally different fashion, has to be something special.

Denny was around just at the time when racing drivers were recognising that fitness and looking after your body created potentially better performance, both mental and physical. He was certainly no shining example for the young driver who was looking for heroes in order to follow the examples that they held to be important in furthering their career. To say the least, Denny's body seemed to constantly be in a relaxed condition. There was no apparent muscular definition. His diet might not have suited the specialists at the Mayo Clinic, but he was as strong as an ox and had amazing durability.

His regular crossings from Europe to all corners of the United States, to-ing and fro-ing to satisfy the calendars of Formula 1, Formula 2, Indy and CanAm, were exhausting, to say the least. Denny would get on to a London–Los Angeles flight wearing a polo shirt, a pair of slacks and a jacket that was always securely attached to his body by at least two buttons, scramble back into an economy-class window seat and hardly move for the entire journey, other than reading *Autosport* or *Playboy*. Most of us just seemed hopelessly affected by jetlag and time-change, and the seeming strength of The Bear was frustrating for us all.

He drove those enormously powerful and fast CanAm cars in such an elegant fashion. The comfortable and relaxed relationship he had with Bruce McLaren and the many devoted people within that team was a picture of unity, but indeed he, like all of us, suffered by such a schedule, at one time developing mononucleosis and hepatitis, which really affected him badly. He was a brave man who suffered pain and injury with tremendous fortitude. There was a very good likelihood that this was inherited from his father, such a quiet and modest man, who had been awarded the Victoria Cross.

When I was working hard — against incredible opposition — to try to revolutionise safety within motor sport, Denny Hulme was one of my strongest supporters. Denny, like myself, became the President of the Grand Prix Drivers' Association; he took the office extremely seriously and did a lot of terrific work.

Denny was not the typical caricature of a jetsetter. Although he lived in a world of glamour and speed, much travel and handsome rewards, it never seemed to change his manner of living and the values that he had carefully taken from his upbringing in New Zealand.

He seemed to be an effortless driver. He seldom made mistakes and he was fast, but more than anything else, Denny Hulme was a nice man. A truly nice man.

Author's foreword

This is a measure of Denny Hulme *déjà vu*. When I started working on this biography of Denny in 2004, I was reminded that when I wrote the introduction to *It Beats Working*, the first volume of my autobiography in 1996, I started with a lead-in that deserves repeating here. It captures the moment.

This book began at home in East Horsley, Surrey, around 4 a.m. on Sunday 5 October 1992. The telephone rang in the chill pre-dawn darkness and woke me. In my experience early morning telephone calls never bring good news: Denny Hulme had died during a 1000-kilometre touring car race at Bathurst in Australia a few hours before and the word was spreading to his friends around the world. I took in the details of how 'The Bear' had been racing a BMW in pouring rain and had a heart attack at the wheel. The car had veered to a stop against the guard railing and Denis was dead at the wheel. A racer's way to go. If you had explained it to him he would have agreed that was the way to do it.

I tried to go back to sleep but it was pointless. Heartless almost. There was too much to think about, too much of Denny to remember. I lay there numbed but wide awake now, on a flick action replay in my mind remembering the way Denny had been involved in my life through the years. He and Bruce McLaren had been, off and on, essential elements in both my life and my career. It was as though I had been able to enjoy my own personal 'Bruce and Denny' show, as their rollicking domination of the CanAm sports car race series in North America was known in the late 1960s.

I had met Denny almost by accident in the small hours of the morning after a prizegiving function following a 1960 Tasman race near Invercargill in New Zealand. I was drunk, lost, and sitting at the side of the road waiting to be rescued. The first car to stop was a Mini driven by Denny Hulme with five or six of his mates already squeezed in. Whoever I was, I could get in as well . . . if I could.

I first met Bruce McLaren in 1958 as a very junior motor racing journalist covering the New Zealand series, and was inadvertently responsible for introducing him to Patty, the girl from my home town, who later became his wife. Denny had taken me with him for his 1961 season in Formula Junior when I had only just arrived in Britain, escaping from being a bank-teller in New Zealand for the rest of my life.

Bruce hired me as his secretary in 1962 and I worked with him and the fledgling McLaren Racing team through its formative years. When my daughter Selina was born in 1971, Denny and Patty McLaren were godparents. Bruce had been killed in a testing crash at Goodwood the previous summer.

When Bruce died I vowed that I would never get close to another driver or shed tears for any bloke again. We used to talk about it on those endless shuttles back and forth across the Atlantic to CanAm races, and I'd say to Denny that, even though we were good friends, I wouldn't cry for him. I lied. In fact, the only time I had cried since Bruce's death had been one Christmas morning when news came through that Denny's son, Martin, had drowned in a lake accident near his home in New Zealand. Denny and Martin had been at Adelaide for the Grand Prix only a few months before and I spent some time with the 21-year-old, meeting for the first time in years and the first time as a man. I had been vastly impressed with him, and this made his death so much harder to accept.

It was the same with Denny. Latterly our paths would cross perhaps once a year when he stayed overnight on his way to or from a race in Europe, but we spent a week together sharing a room at Monaco during the 1992 Grand Prix, and it was to that week I looked back as I lay there trying to take on board that Denny had died.

I had just made up my mind NOT to go to the Monaco Grand Prix for the first time in 30 years because the race and the place had changed beyond belief, victim of its own popularity with costs and crowds spoiling what had been a magic atmosphere. Denny phoned from New Zealand and asked if he could share my room in Monaco. I told him I wasn't going and asked why HE wanted to go back after all this time. This was the key to the request. It was 30 years since he had won the Grand Prix. So I chased a room and the only one I could track was in a fleapit hotel high above the town in what Monaco probably regarded as France. I wasn't looking forward to the weekend. At the Imola Grand Prix a fortnight before Monaco, the Marlboro PR people were worrying that they had no guest of honour for their annual racing dinner in Monte Carlo. When I told them about Denny they were mightily relieved. I asked if they could arrange a hotel room. Absolutely no problem. So I cancelled the fleapit room and told Denny that Marlboro were picking up the tab at the ritzy Loews Hotel, right on the circuit at the old Station Hairpin. When we arrived in Monaco the first thing Denny wanted to do was find the fleapit and get our deposit back. I told him to forget it.

It was a time-warp week as though we were still knock-about Kiwis 30 years before. Some people are like that, aren't they? You don't see them for years, and yet you slot straight back in as though you'd never been apart, picking up the conversation as though you'd just slipped out of the room for a minute. We talked about old escapades long into each night. He tittered now and then, and eventually fell asleep. The Denny titter was a sort of giggling lisp with his tongue behind his top teeth. Something he did when he was amused. In the morning he'd wake up and say 'My *God*, Eoin, it's just like the old days. *Bloody* good, isn't it?' The shame of it was that it wasn't bloody good for bloody long enough.

We had arranged for a taxi to take us to the Nice airport on the morning after the race, but Denny insisted on paying the telephone bill because he had been on the phone endlessly talking to his lady friend in New Zealand and I had been doing the same at different hours talking to mine in Surrey. Denny said we'd split the bill between us. I suggested that we wouldn't because (a) my bill would have been half the size of his and (b) Marlboro would pay it anyway. Not good enough for Denny, who queued for what seemed like hours to cover the phone bill and his conscience. When he eventually came running to the taxi, tittering, I asked if he had paid the bill. He hadn't. Why not? 'Because it was six hundred quid . . . !'

Denny was pretty much a forgotten hero even at home. A Sportsman's Hall of Fame had been created in New Zealand a few months before and Denny wasn't included, although he had won the World Championship in 1967. There had never been a book on 'The Bear'. He probably would have told any prospective author that there wasn't a book in him, but in fact Alan Henry had meetings with him in our room at Monaco and they were on the point of penning an autobiography. It died with Denny.

Later, when I was in Auckland for Denny's memorial service, several people asked if I was writing a Hulme book and I resolved to explore the idea, but the ashes of enthusiasm were already growing cold in the publishing world.

Ten years down the road and at last I was given the chance to record the life and times of 'The Bear' by HarperCollins in Auckland and Haynes at Sparkford in Kent, and I am grateful for the opportunity to stroll once again down that rollicking memory lane that was international motor sport in the sixties and seventies. In the eighties and nineties huge sponsorship made drivers into multi-millionaires and the face of racing was changed forever. It seems hard to believe now that motor racing in the 'Bruce and Denny' days was hugely enjoyable. In the days of total domination by Michael Schumacher and Ferrari in the new century, Simon Barnes wrote in *The Times*: 'He is one of the great serial champions of all time and he killed his sport with his brilliance, murdered it with the thousand cuts of excellence.' Not a complaint, just an announcement in the world's most prestigious newspaper.

This story of the racing driver we knew as 'The Bear' will be about racing when there was enjoyment in equal measure to excitement, when racing was what a man did because he wanted to. Not because he wanted to be a millionaire.

Contents

1   **The Denny Hulme diaries**

The first helping of history in the Hulme family came when Clive Hulme, Denny's father, was awarded the Victoria Cross for bravery in the face of enemy action on Crete in the Second World War. Denny would inherit his dad's craggy looks, the crooked grin, a measure of intolerance of authority . . . and courage.

It was late May 1941 and the German paratroopers were being dropped on Crete in huge numbers, an airborne army fluttering down to eventually drive the British Army off the island. Sergeant Hulme performed a number of acts of gallantry, according to one report. 'At Maleme airfield he led a series of counterattacks against pockets of German paratroops, and later led his men with distinction during the counterattack at Galatos.'

It was after these skirmishes that Clive received a message to say that his brother, Corporal H.C. Hulme, had been killed. It made him further committed to kill the enemy, to avenge his brother. The Second World War had become intensely personal.

'He waited behind his withdrawing unit and shot pursuing Germans in revenge.'

During my first season touring the European Formula Junior races in 1961 with Denny, he told me how his father had delayed the Germans by gathering firearms and laying them along a roadside ditch, running up and down under cover of the ditch, firing each gun in turn and giving the impression of a defending unit instead of just one determined Kiwi. The Germans dug in and returned fire. Sergeant Hulme was winning his one-man war with the enemy. Denny also described how his father had later disguised himself in the uniform of a German parachutist he had shot, and climbed above the snipers who were pinning down a British unit. He was an anti-sniper sniper and in his element, having learned his skills as a lad at home on deer-stalking expeditions on New Zealand mountain slopes at the top end of the South Island. He was a farm labourer in Nelson when war was declared in 1939.

Denny said his father would pick off a German sniper below and immediately stand up, with his back to the slope as though looking up the hill to see where the enemy sniper was hiding. It was an instinctive move, just the sort of thing he would have done if he had been one of the enemy trying to see who was doing the killing.

'He was most renowned, however, for his work stalking snipers, which he volunteered for and carried out with coolness and determination. His courage, which amounted to recklessness, amazed his fellow soldiers. When his unit came under heavy sniper and mortar fire during the final withdrawal from Stylos on 28 May, Hulme infiltrated enemy lines and stalked and shot their snipers from the rear. In all he killed 33 snipers before himself being seriously wounded. For his "outstanding and inspiring qualities of leadership, initiative, skill, endurance and most conspicuous gallantry and devotion to duty," he was subsequently awarded the Victoria Cross.'

In his book *Where the Prize is Highest — The Stories of New Zealanders Who Won the Victoria Cross* (Collins, 1972), George Bryant set the scene in Crete that May of 1941. 'It was the invariably beautiful Mediterranean spring morning of incredibly blue skies. Wild flowers basked in the sunshine and in the clear air the noise of the sparking engines of German fighter planes and bombers, the explosions of bombs and the fast, sharp reports of machine guns and cannons rolled across the countryside and faded away in the mountains just as they had done for days now . . . '

Battalion Provost Sergeant Hulme was with a Field Punishment Centre in Platanias and his officer-in-charge told how Hulme attacked prowling Germans with considerable effect. 'Hulme used to wander about a lot — from the camp to the road was all his country. Numerous snipers in this area were dealt with by Sergeant Hulme personally. He led parties of his men from the area held by the forward positions and destroyed enemy organised parties who had established themselves out in front of our position from which they brought heavy rifle, machine-gun and mortar fire to bear on our defensive posts.'

He took a leading part in the night attack by New Zealand infantry and two British tanks to retake Galatos. General Kippenberger had ordered the attack to delay the Germans and thus save his force from disaster. 'At 8.10 p.m. the New Zealanders attacked. The men, in a surge of desperation and anger, yelling like Red Indians, charged down the main road under fire from both sides and were soon engaged in fierce fighting in the streets, gardens and in the houses, room by room. The Germans were dislodged and chased down the narrow lanes radiating from the village square.'

There were German counterattacks. 'Sergeant Hulme went forward alone, threw grenades into the school and so disorganised the defence that the British counterattack was able to proceed.'

Then came the Hulme sniper-shoot when the brigade's headquarters came under fire from German marksmen hidden among the rocks and scrub on surrounding hill faces. 'Hulme volunteered to deal with the snipers. Alone, he climbed around the snipers, took up position behind the leader and pretended to be sniping. At the right moment he shot him dead. The other snipers, four of them, hearing a shot behind them looked round. Hulme did the same, as though he too wondered where the shot could have come from. Dressed in the camouflage blouse of a German paratrooper, Hulme's deception succeeded and he started to give more thought to disposing of the rest.'

A Major Thomason, watching through binoculars, saw Hume kill two of the others in quick succession. 'The remaining two decided to pull out. One moved towards Hulme and was killed. The other was accounted for by Hulme as he appeared round the hillside.'

The evacuation of Crete had been ordered and Hulme was with an exhausted unit bedding down for the night when a party of Germans was spotted advancing out of a creek bed a quarter of a mile away. Hulme and others rushed to the top of a ridge and fired from behind a stone wall. 'Hulme, one of the first on the ridge, sat astride the wall like a cavalier on horseback and took pot shots at the withdrawing Germans.'

In the New Zealand Army battalion history covering Crete, the skirmish was officially recorded: 'One of the first to arrive and open fire was Sgt Hulme who, after the enemy had been repelled the first time, was to be seen sitting side saddle on the stone wall, shooting at the enemy down on the lower slopes. His example did much to maintain the morale of men whose reserves of nervous and physical energy were nearly exhausted.'

The Germans came back with grenades and mortars. 'Sergeant Hulme, on his own initiative, penetrated the enemy lines, killed the mortar crew of four and put the mortar out of action. From the German mortar position Hulme worked around to the left flank and killed three more snipers who were causing concern to the rearguard. This made his score of enemy snipers 33 stalked and killed.'

He was stalking what would have been his thirty-fourth sniper when he was shot through the shoulder and disabled. The wounded sergeant was ordered to the rear but 'in spite of his wound he directed traffic under fire and organised stragglers of various units into section groups'.

When Clive Hulme's VC was announced, *The Times* in London waxed lyrical: 'In the Baghdad of the *Arabian Nights* it was ordered that the story of any notable achievement should be written in letters of gold. Is gold good enough for the actions of Second-Lieutenant Upham and Sergeant

Hulme? Hulme won the VC as much by brains as by contempt for danger. The men of Talavera and Waterloo were heroically brave, but there may be some excuse for asking whether the nature of modern warfare has not raised the standard of courage to unknown heights.'

The VC citation dealt not with an isolated action but covered the whole eight days of the Crete campaign.

There was much of his dad in Denny and he spoke with pride describing the trip he and his father made back to Crete, after he had retired from Formula 1. They visited the hill villages where Clive had fought 30-odd years before, and many of the older people remembered the brave old Kiwi soldier, coming up and speaking to him as he sat having a drink with his son in the little village squares. That son had been five years old when his father had been fighting to drive the enemy out of Crete and he was immensely proud to see his dad so warmly remembered.

2 Early days

Denis Clive Hulme was born on 18 June 1936 in Nelson at the top of the South Island of New Zealand. The name is pronounced 'Hullm', not 'Hyume'. Denny would say that his father told him 'never let them knock the "l" out of Hulme'.

Clive worked on local farms as a sharemilker and a labourer; he was a strong man who had gained a name for himself as an amateur wrestler in local events.

Denny remembers his younger days on his grandmother's farm at nearby Motueka while his father was away at the war. 'That was a real wild place. I was only three or four years old, but there were some things that I remember vividly — the whole farm, the shape of it, and the old pear tree I once fell out of and knocked myself unconscious. Most of the tobacco in New Zealand was grown in the Motueka area and we used to sit among the tobacco when they picked it, little kids sitting under those giant leaves.'

As a man, Denny was an enigma, a composite person who built an image for himself as a taciturn individual and enjoyed his nickname of 'The Bear'. He could be a grizzly or a Pooh, entirely depending on his mood. He had a way with women that totally belied his bluff manner among men, and reading background stories on Denny today, you can pick the gender of the writer by the way Denny responded to questions. Priscilla Phipps was married to motor racing photographer David Phipps, and she travelled to races with him, writing profiles for books and magazines under her professional name, Elizabeth Hayward. Denny would become impatient being interviewed by males, but he had all the time in the world for a female, opening up and expanding on his answers.

I travelled with Denny to the Formula Junior races during the summer of 1961, spending endless hours on the road driving between races in Europe, but I never learned about Denny's early days until I read Hayward's profile chapter on Denny in *Motor Racing: The Grand Prix Greats*. I suppose our conversations were all blokey stuff back then. He saved the gentler stuff for a more receptive audience.

'I ran away one day, about a quarter of a mile from the house,' he told Hayward. 'I went across a swing bridge, the sort you see in African jungles, which spanned a huge river. I lay on my stomach and looked down. There were eels swimming around the bottom of the river and I watched them, for ages. I suppose I was about three and a half.' One wonders now at the recall of the little chap and whether he may have been embroidering his memories of colonial life.

'I remember they had an old fire engine on the farm which they used to drive a circular saw. I watched my grandfather sawing up the wood and wished I were big enough to help. I came along once with a big strip of bark and slung it up on the bench but it got all wrapped around the saw. My grandfather was livid; I dashed off and hid under the shed until he calmed down.

'They had big tobacco kilns there too, and a stream; and some sheep. I got knocked down by a sheep — they were big Merinos with great long horns. I was just wandering around and minding my own business when *bang!* One of them butted me and rolled me down the hill. There was a big waterwheel in the stream, too, where they used to charge the batteries, as there was no mains electricity . . .

'Before the war, Dad was a sharemilker, working on a farm. He didn't own it, maybe he just owned a herd of cows. Anyway, I nearly got drowned there when I was very small. We had to go across a stream to take the cream to the end of the road and instead of going across the bridge I decided to walk through the ford. I got swept away. Dad fished me out and turned me upside down to get all the water out, so I only had a fright. It didn't put me off the water. These are only unimportant little details, really. You are probably the first person to know about them . . .'

Hayward didn't think these details unimportant at all. She thought Denny's early days had a lot to do with his personality as an adult in the Grand Prix world. 'He is the product of a country which was *really* country,' she wrote. 'It was a country where outdoor living is considered normal and children go barefoot not from poverty but from choice and tradition.'

Denny played on his image as a loner. 'I like being alone. I like to wander about and discover nature. I never preach about it, but I'd like to go where no human being has gone — very difficult in this modern world. The best thing I've done in recent years was to make a trip with [wife] Greeta up Death Valley in America. We stopped the car in the middle of the desert and there wasn't even a vapour trail in the sky. It must have been exciting in the old days, stomping through the world looking for new places . . .'

When Denny's father was invalided out of the Army, he made a convalescent trip to Rotorua in the North Island and decided to move to the Bay of Plenty with the family — his wife Rona, Denis then six and Anita aged three.

'I remember the epic journey we had as we set off from Nelson to live in the north. We had a Morris 8 four-seater tourer. This was the first car I learned to drive. I'd already driven tractors on the farm. All the family belongings were strapped around it and on it. Most of roads were gravel then. It took us a long time to make the journey because the car kept running out of water and overheating. We had to keep going off and hunting for water to stop the radiator from boiling. We eventually made it after a day and a half.' The new Hulme family home was in Pongakawa, 10 miles from Te Puke and 25 miles from Tauranga. Denny's father was given an ex-service loan and he started a trucking business. He started with two Ford V8 trucks then bought two ex-army Chevrolets with Timken 2-speed rear ends.

The young Denny's proudest possession was his dog. 'It was a cross between a collie and a husky and he was marvellous with sheep. We boys used to go off to the river with our dogs and wade in, quite a gang of us, Maori kids as well. Sometimes we'd spend all day with no clothes on at all — it was so wild and there was no one about and I don't think our mothers worried much about us. Everyone mixed in, swimming and diving amongst the weeds, chasing eels and getting logs to float down the river. The greatest fun was when the rivers were in flood. Then we'd get the biggest logs we could find, push them into the main stream, get on them and away we would go, crashing down under bridges and swimming to the bank when we got tired and walking back again.'

Denny clearly enjoyed regaling Hayward with his Huckleberry Finn memories. 'I have seen a lot of the world from my small beginnings, and looking back I can see that my childhood did me no harm. In fact it was the sort of childhood a lot of people would love to have had — different. We had to make our own entertainment all the time, whether it were with sledges, or playing around the hills or in the rivers. We used to go home filthy, but our mothers never really gave us a growling. It was part of life out there. They expected their kids to get dirty. Over here, people are so fussy . . .'

Denny's father's main contract with his trucks was hauling sand from the beach to Rotorua, and young Denny honed his driving skills — unofficially and illegally! — at the wheel of one of the Chevrolet trucks. In 1953 the Chevs were sold and replaced with a Morris truck fitted with a Swiss Saurer diesel engine.

'Nobody knew much about diesels in those days so I got a workshop manual and learned how to maintain the engine. I also learned how to drive

— officially — and passed my driving test in a Chrysler when I was 15. At 17 I was driving heavy trucks of sheep to the sheep trains every Sunday — illegally. You couldn't get a heavy traffic licence until you were 18, but the local police tended to turn a blind eye.

'I went to school during the week, but I wasn't too bright and didn't learn much. When I was 17 they were recruiting for the Royal New Zealand Air Force and I tried to get in, but I guess they thought I was too dumb. Anyway I never heard from them after going to the recruiting office! A few days later Dad dropped a huge concrete cattle trough on his foot, snapping his Achilles tendon, and couldn't drive. As the family lived on the business, Dad said I'd better leave school and take over the driving until he was fit.'

When he turned 18 Denny went to work at a local garage, turning a one-man business into a two-man business. 'It was a small affair but we got through a tremendous amount of work, from re-bores on cars to repairing bulldozers. New parts were hard to get, so we made a lot ourselves. I worked in the garage all day and shifted sand for Dad at night. It was hard work. During my lunch break I used to drive the seven miles up to the beach, shovel six and a half tons of sand and drive back, eating an apple in the cab on the way home. I could do the whole thing in an hour and ten minutes. It took me 32 minutes to load the six-and-a-half tons of sand. Dad and I used to do it in just over 10 minutes but that was because we could pace each other.'

Denny turned this hard labour into an art form. 'To do this we had to have the right shovel handle. We used to go through a whole rack of handles to get the right spring and the right grain and the right feel. The shovel itself was always too heavy when it was new so I used to take it up to the garage and grind it to the right shape, slim it down a bit. It was amazing the difference it made to the effort. I used to feel pleased because I could load a truck on my own just as quickly as two people could in the same area.'

Like father, like son. 'Dad was strong — he used to lift two hundred-weight sacks of superphosphate and he used to shift 20 to 30 tons of sand a day.'

Anita remembers wet days at the beach when she had to lay planks under the wheels so that Denny could drive the loaded truck through the sand-hills to the road.

Sam McIntosh, a boyhood mate of Denny's, remembered one wet day when they had been loading sand and driving the truck back to Rotorua. 'We were coming down the long hill into the town and Denny suddenly shouted that he couldn't hold the thing on the brakes. The wet sand was twice the weight it usually was dry. How he drove us out of that one, I'll never know. Boy, could he *drive*! We'd actually gone on to the wrong side of the road, up on the pavement and *under* the verandah of a shop. It seemed like the best part of half a mile before he got it under control and back on the right side of the road. I was shitting myself . . .'

Sam talked of their time as lads, cycling for miles, always in bare feet. There was the day Denny was driving his father's Morris 8 Sports back from the beach at Mount Maunganui and the carburettor started misfiring. 'I had to sit out on the running board, tapping the carb to keep the thing going.' Then they had a lark with a can of lighter fluid where they'd wait just over the brow of a hill for a car to come, run across the road spilling a trail of fluid and then light it as the car approached into what looked like a wall of flame. They used to 'borrow' a railway worker's trundle jigger at Pongakawa station on Sundays and run it up and down the line . . . until they hit a cattle stop and the jigger was derailed across the line. 'What made it worse was there was a train coming a couple of miles down the line. It was heavy as hell and I was all for leaving it, but Denny had brute strength and he hauled it clear . . .'

Cars were not of major interest to the young Hulme until a friend started telling him about MGs and he decided to buy a new MG TF. He had saved about half the price of a new car when his father, impressed at Denny's hard work in the family business, offered to pay the balance on a new TF. There were three new TFs — white, red or green — on the dock in Auckland and Denny was to phone the agent with his choice of colour. He chose the red TF with disc wheels, because it was £28 cheaper than the other cars with wire wheels.

'I hitchhiked the 130 miles up to Auckland one Saturday morning to collect the car. It was still covered in grease, just as it had come from England and to me it was the greatest thing in the world. I drove it home, choosing the longest route. I'd never seen a car with a rev counter before and it wasn't until I'd done about 40 miles that I realised I'd been looking at the rev counter instead of the speedometer. I drove the car for about a thousand miles that weekend, just for the fun of it.'

Greeta remembered that she was a class ahead of Denny at Pongakawa primary school. 'In those days at school they had a saying — "chicken stealing" — if you fancied a younger boy, so I never had anything to do with Denis. He and his mates used to ride bikes to school and throw acorns at us. To me he was just a big pest, but his sister Anita was friends with my two younger sisters so I was aware what Denis was up to. We were brought up on a farm which was three miles closer to town than the Hulme family and when Denis bought the MG he used to go screaming past our place. My dad used to say "That boy's going to kill himself . . ." and he had four daughters to bring up so he wasn't very impressed with this larrikin roaring past in his sports car.'

Greeta worked in a local hardware shop as a junior office girl until she was 18, and then went away to qualify first as a Karitane children's nurse and, after a three-year course, as a registered nurse. She remembers meeting up with Denny again when she was cycling with a girlfriend in Tauranga and they passed Denny and his mate, Peter Griffin, sitting in the MG outside a milkbar. 'As we went past he called out g'day to me. I told Bonnie I'd better go back and say hello, because he'd go back to Te Puke and say that I was a snob because I hadn't talked to him. Bonnie didn't think it was a good idea, but we went back, said hello and they asked us if we were going to the dance that night. We said we were. They didn't ask to take us poor nurses, they just said they'd see us there. Denis asked me for a dance — it was rock and roll in those days — and during the course of the evening he asked if I'd like to go for a ride in his car. He went flat out and I'm sitting there thinking "I'm *not* going to be impressed here." The soft top was flapping and the gearbox was noisy and I'm telling him all the things that were wrong with his car!' She laughs now at the memory of that first ride. 'He'd had a previous girlfriend who was more in love with his car than with him and he had a bit of heartache about that, but here I was, totally different and I was pulling his car to bits . . . and he came back for more! He'd never had anyone rubbishing his car.'

He serviced the TF himself and tuned it for competition after joining the local car club and entering in races. The red TF was Denny's first step on a route that would take him to the World Championship. One day he loaned the precious MG to Anita to drive to work . . . and he came back to leave the sand lorry for Anita because he wanted to wash the MG. Anita remembers driving her father's Morris Minor and competing against Denny in the MG in local gymkhanas. 'At one event we both won our heats and Denny said "Give the prize to her because she's a girl . . ." '

Howden Ganley, who would become the 'Fourth Grand Prix Kiwi' when he raced for BRM in 1971–72 and Frank Williams in 1973, remembers seeing Denny racing the MG TF at a seafront car gymkhana at Mount Maunganui. Howden's father also raced a TF that day and they got to meet Denny, fuelling Howden's interest in motor racing. Howden started out writing freelance for the local newspaper in Hamilton and remembers meeting Denny again when he was racing the Cooper. 'I used to take photographs without a tele lens, peeping out from between the 44-gallon drums that marked the inside of corners and I remember Denny telling me I'd get run over if I got any closer . . .'

Denny: 'I used the TF on the road for nearly two years and then decided to tune the engine up and race it. I did a few hill climbs and I was quite successful, then entered at Ardmore for one of the support races at the 1957 Grand Prix meeting. It was a handicap race for MGs and I started off scratch — the last man to start — but I came home to win by about 2 seconds. I drove barefoot at that time and I was really pleased with the car; this was my first race, and it was definitely a memorable occasion.'

His next car was a new MG 'A', but he never enjoyed the same success and it went into the deal that earned him the 1958 2-litre Cooper single-seater raced by Bruce McLaren in New Zealand and subsequently raced by Merv Neil.

Greeta: 'The MG "A" was also red and he and Peter Griffin would pick me up when we were going out to dances and I always had to sit on the central armrest between them with my arm round him. I think he quite liked the boob on his shoulder. In those days you were either a tit-and-bum man or a leg man and Denis was definitely a tit man. You had to be blonde, have good boobs and be a non-smoker.' The teenage Greeta was a stunner, qualifying in all three areas.

Denny built a garage at home to work on his new racing car. 'I bought the Cooper in March at the end of the New Zealand season and wouldn't be racing until November, so I pulled it to bits, never having seen one before. I stripped the whole car *and* built a special garage for it, a proper brick one with built-in workbenches and all the tools nicely lined up. I did all the work on the car myself, including the engine, which had to have a lot done to it. It was a hell of a job. We didn't have the right sealing rings so I made some out of piston rings. When I started the engine it ran for about 30 seconds — and then seized. I took it to pieces again, made another set, and the same thing happened. The third time I got it right and I put it all back together, painted it and went racing.'

Greeta remembers Denny and his racing car being a major local attraction. 'All the local lads used to come and stand there and watch and be spectators while Denis did everything, took the gearbox off, stripped it down, took it for a run up the road. The neighbours threatened all sort of things because the racing car being tested down their country road was upsetting their milking herds. I remember coming home on leave from the nurses' home and riding a bike, riding a horse, even walking down there to see him. I think his dad was quite impressed that I bothered to do all this and then just stand there while Denis did this and that on the racing car. And then I'd go home again. But that was all that was expected of you . . .'

Since the MG 'A' had been traded for the Cooper single-seater, Denny borrowed his parents' Morris Minor for his courting visits to the nurses' home, but on one occasion when the swamp road was flooded he drove over in the big sand truck and parked it in the nurses' home car park. 'In those days we were allowed one 1.30 a.m. leave once a fortnight and a 12.30 leave once a week, and you had to sign in when you got back. The other nurses would hear the truck start up in the middle of the night and they'd all check their watches to see if you were in on time. Denis said he didn't feel so bad because another nurse's boyfriend had a huge logging truck loaded with logs and you certainly heard *that* when he was taking off in the middle of the night!'

Denny's first race with the Cooper was the 1960 New Zealand Grand Prix on the Ardmore airfield circuit near Auckland. The grid had a famous pairing at the tail. Jack Brabham was last and Denny was second-last qualifier. Brabham's Cooper had caught fire while he was leading the second heat and it looked as though Denny would score a win first time out, but his gearbox jammed and he was also a retirement. For the final, the bolts were still being tightened on the gearbox when the race started and the leaders had run five laps when Denny joined in. He finished tenth. George Lawton in a twin Cooper to Denny's was a retirement on the eleventh lap with a failed clutch.

'This was my first single-seater and the first time I drove it, I just couldn't get the hang of it. If I could have done a lap without spinning I would have probably broken the lap record, but I kept going off at the same corner and this really discouraged me — particularly as George Lawton, my chief rival, had bought the same type of Cooper and he seemed to be able to go round the corner quicker than I could without any trouble. I figured that if he could do it I could, but obviously there was a technique for taking that corner and I didn't know anything about it at that time . . .'

That year there was to be another Driver to Europe scholarship, similar to the one that had seen Bruce McLaren making his name overseas in 1958, but the organisers were unable to decide between Hulme and Lawton, both having impressed in similar cars. So both were chosen. It was later said that since Denny's father had won the Victoria Cross and George's dad was mayor of Whangarei, the judges didn't dare to cross either parent!

At Levin the following weekend there were no overseas drivers and Denny won the feature race, setting fastest lap. George was third. At Wigram, Lawton did not start and the Hulme Cooper was off song. He was running fifth when the oil pressure faded and he retired.

'George was quicker than I was,' Denny told Elizabeth Hayward in a *Road & Track* profile, 'but we got my Cooper running quite well on the rubbishy old tyres we had. We caught on to a good idea without knowing it then. Just before a race I used to get my tyres re-capped. I would go to a meeting with four brand new treads on and the rubber was obviously very fresh and very sticky which gave us an advantage in traction.'

Bill Gavin was a New Zealand journalist who would travel with the trio in Europe during the 1960 season, and in *Autosport* he wrote perceptively of Denny's early days in a 1972 backgrounder on world title contenders. 'Denny got the Cooper well sorted and won the first race of the season [at Levin] pretty much by default. But at the next meeting he led or shadowed George Lawton in the ex-McLaren car in three events, then won the fourth. This startled everybody, for Lawton had a few seasons racing behind him and his performance in '58 and '59 with Bruce McLaren's old bob-tailed Cooper sports had in almost everybody's mind earned him the Driver to Europe award, but the New Zealand International Grand Prix officials did not award it in 1959. But for 1960 Lawton was considered a certainty and it was thought that no local driver would see him off in the ex-McLaren 2-litre.

'Hulme's arrival on the scene changed all this and there was keen competition for the award from other worthwhile contenders like the late Johnny Mansel, who was attempting, and often accomplishing, the impossible with the ex-Moss 250F Maserati. Hulme was an outsider in racing circles and the fact that his father was famous as a war hero didn't really help. Clive Hulme had put up most of the money for the Cooper and he was obviously ambitious for his son. That 1960 Grand Prix was a disaster for both Denny and George Lawton as both had mechanical problems, but afterwards it was announced that both would be sponsored in Europe by the NZIGP.

'Sponsorship wasn't quite the right word for the financial aid the New Zealand Racing Team was getting from the NZIGP and Clive Hulme had to invest a great deal more money in getting Denny fixed up with a new 1.5-litre Climax Formula 2 engine.'

Travelling to Britain seemed almost as great a challenge to Denny as the challenge of racing in a professional area for the first time.

'I'd always said I never wanted to travel. I said, "Who the hell wants to go to England?" Then they asked me to come over with George and away we came . . .'

George and Denny boarded the *Rangitiki* for the trip with Feo Stanton, who would be their team manager and their mechanic. They stopped off at Pitcairn Island halfway across the Pacific to send postcards of the boat (Denny marked his cabin with an X on the card he sent to his mate Peter) and then went shopping at Panama. Greeta remembers the present he bought for her and mailed to New Zealand. 'He sent me this blue quilted box with a set of seven different pairs of knickers embroidered with each day of the week — Monday, Tuesday, Wednesday, etc — and a little heart on the side. My mother was *horrified* that a boy would send knickers to her daughter!'

Denny's racing career was about to commence. It was early 1960. Seven years later he would be champion of the world, but there were hard yards before then.

3   First seasons overseas

Denny drew attention in the paddock for his first race in Britain by climbing into his Formula 2 Cooper in bare feet. He said it never occurred to him that this was unusual. He had *always* driven in bare feet. His feet were size 10 and that caused him problems because his shoes squared across the wrong pedals in the MG TF and the Cooper in New Zealand. Plus he believed that he had a better feel of the pedals in bare feet. He had driven those big sand-laden lorries in bare feet, so what was the problem? The problem apparently was that racing drivers in Britain wore shoes and drivers who didn't were inevitably regarded as wild colonial boys. This may have been where Ken Tyrrell gathered his first opinion of Denny as a driver who wasn't taking his racing totally seriously.

Bruce McLaren loaned his Morris Minor to Denny's sister Anita and she met Denny, George and Feo off the boat train. 'Feo and George were in the back seat and I was in front with Denny. We hadn't gone a hundred yards when he pulled over and said, "You drive — I'm not driving in this country!" ' Anita and a girlfriend were on their OE (overseas experience) in the summer of 1960, and for a time Anita was an au pair in Paris. While she was in London she flatted not far from the lads, who had bought a pair of then-new Minis.

Denny and George brought their two Coopers with them from New Zealand and they were entered as the New Zealand International Grand Prix (NZIGP) Racing Team. Denny's car was chassis number F2-20-58; the Lawton car was F2-12-58.

Their first race was the Lavant Cup at Goodwood on 18 April, where Denny distinguished himself by heading Grand Prix driver Harry Schell in the British Racing Partnership F2 Cooper. Denny finished seventh, Schell (Cooper T51) eighth, Ian Raby (Cooper T43) ninth and George was tenth.

Their next race was the Norfolk Trophy at Snetterton in late April when George won and 'David' Hulme was second. They had arrived in style. *Autosport* noted: 'The two New Zealanders, having driven very well indeed on their second appearance in Europe, were left with no competition; Lawton was a lap ahead of Hulme (having taken an escape road avoiding a spinning McKee), who, in turn, was two laps ahead of David Piper's ailing Lotus in third place.'

In a combined F1/F2 field at Aintree on 30 April, Denny was tenth and George fourteenth. Denny's drive drew special mention in *Autosport*: 'One also noted the fine driving of New Zealand's D. Hulme, whose placing in such fast company was an excellent show.'

At Oulton Park they were third and fourth behind Roy Salvadori (Cooper 51) and Mike McKee (Cooper 45).

The International Trophy at Silverstone saw the death of Harry Schell when his Yeoman Credit F1 Cooper crashed in the rain during practice. *Autosport* editor Gregor Grant was still calling Denny 'David', but he didn't much mind what he was being called as long as he was winning — he finished twelfth overall and was the first F2 car home. It is interesting to note that the new Formula 1 Coopers had arrived for Jack Brabham and Bruce McLaren, and that Bruce qualified on the fifth row and Denny on the sixth. Bruce finished two places behind Denny, delayed with a broken throttle linkage.

Denny had been entered for the Formula Junior race at Monaco at the end of May in an Envoy, but the car never appeared in the principality. As a result, his first race in Formula Junior was on 29 June in the Grand Prix della Lotteria at Monza, in a BMC-powered Cooper T52 fielded by the New Zealand Racing Team. He finished second in his race heat, set fastest lap and was third in the final. Ken Tyrrell then entered him in one of his Formula Junior Coopers at Silverstone and he finished sixth.

The rough and tumble of the Formula Junior races in Italy seemed to suit Denny's competitive style. At Salerno on 24 July he won his heat and finished second in the final. At Messina on Sicily the following weekend he won his heat, set fastest lap and was second in the final.

The race at Pescara on 15 August was the high point of his season, as he was second in his race heat and won the main event, setting fastest lap. The following summer Denny drove me around the 15.8-mile road circuit towing his Formula Junior Cooper on a trailer behind his Mk 1 Ford Zodiac, pointing out the salient points of the triangular course, which ran as a long straight along the Adriatic sea front and then wriggled up into the mountains. Racing started there in 1924 when no less a conductor than Enzo Ferrari won in an Alfa Romeo. The last Grand Prix to be held there was in 1957, when Stirling Moss won in a Vanwall and set the lap record at 97.87 mph (157.507 kph). It was very apparent that warm afternoon in 1961 that Denny was quietly proud of his performance on that demanding road circuit.

An entry of 55 cars had been received by the Pescara organisers, the competitors being divided between two three-lap heats, the 32 fastest survivors going forward to the seven-lap final. Practice was a problem on this circuit and several drivers who wanted to conserve their cars put in many laps in private cars in an effort to learn some of the trickier sections. John Love went straight into the lead with the Tyrrell Cooper in the first heat, but he was soon swallowed by the OSCAs of Colin Davis and Ludovico Scarfiotti. The second heat was won by Lorenzo Bandini, with Denny in second place.

The final developed into an exciting battle between Davis (son of the famous S.C.H. 'Sammy' Davis, who had won the 1927 Le Mans race for Bentley and was by this time a respected motoring journalist) and Hulme. At one stage Davis, who did most of the pace-making, extended his lead to over 10 seconds, but Hulme fought back, lapping faster and faster as the race progressed until in the closing stages he was only a few car lengths behind. Then, on the very last lap, when it looked as though Davis was set for a win, he spun off the course and Denny went on to win by 10 seconds from Bordeau in a Stanguellini. Hulme had set a new lap record at 11:10.4 and his win brought him up to second place in the World Trophy contest, with 38 points to Davis' 50.

In *Autosport* they carried the headline 'Hulme Wins The Grand Prix de Pescara' and started the report, 'George Hulme (Cooper Junior) won the Grand Prix de Pescara from Juan Manuel Bordeau (Stanguellini) and John Love (Cooper Junior) . . . '. *George* Hulme.

In an *Autosport* profile on Denny written in 1964, Bill Gavin wrote: 'I accompanied Denny when he campaigned with the FJ Cooper-BMC in Italy. In four races he scored one win, two seconds and a third, for at that stage of development the BMC engine was no match for the Maserati brothers' Fiat engine in Colin Davis' works OSCA. Denny's BMC engine was twice measured, after Monza and again after his splendid victory at Pescara, and both times the Italian scrutineers measured the capacity at 948 cc. So honest is Denny himself that he was convinced the Italians were miscalculating — the more likely explanation being that the engine had been sold as a FJ unit and had the standard bore and stroke of a Healey Sprite never occurred to him. Denny is still blessed with this naïve honesty which inspires the smarter folk in racing to take advantage of him, yet he is no doubt confident that his ability is sufficient to get him to the top without resort to the intrigues which pollute a sport so professional as motor racing is today. Slow of speech, and invariably noncommittal to the point of exasperation, his rugged exterior conceals most effectively a keen intelligence. Likewise he is physically slow moving, but nevertheless extremely industrious; long periods of idleness, such as the enforced long spells at the dinner table on the continent, infuriate him.'

In the rain at Crystal Palace, Denny spun and finished fourth. George was second behind Trevor Taylor's Lotus. Early in August at Snetterton, George jumped the start and although he led in the early stages of the race he was penalised a minute for his indiscretion and dropped to seventh in the overall result. Denny was a non-starter. The Kentish '100' at Brands Hatch on 28 August will be remembered for Jim Clark's first notable victory in a Lotus — and for world motorcycle champions John Surtees and Geoff Duke colliding and retiring with mutual damage! George finished fourth and Denny was a retirement after clashing with Mike McKee's similar Cooper.

The first Danish Grand Prix on the unusual little Roskildering on 11 September was tragic for the New Zealand team. The track was just under three-quarters of a mile in length with two slightly banked hairpins. George had rolled his Cooper during practice but he was unhurt and they were able to repair the car in time for the race on Sunday. Sadly, on the seventh lap, George crashed again in the race and was thrown out of the somersaulting car, which then fell on him. Denny stopped and was first to the aid of his friend, but he was already dead.

It was a cruel termination of a career that was about to take off. He had agreed a deal to race for the Yeoman Credit team in Formula 1 and was to have driven for the team in the New Zealand series in 1961.

Anita first learned of George's accident in a London newspaper. 'There was a front-page photo of George flying through the air. It was really gross.' She took over in London, went to their flat, laundered George's clothes, packed his belongings and drove his Mini to the docks.

Afterwards there would be unpleasantness back in New Zealand over the fate of the crashed Cooper, but it was eventually sorted out financially by Clive Hulme.

Bill Gavin wrote in *Autosport*: 'There was never much to pick between Denny and George in European F2 races but by the season's end George had been offered a ride in one of Ken Gregory's Yeoman Credit Coopers for a Formula 1 race at Snetterton.' George's death resulted in the drive being offered to Denny. It was his debut in Formula 1, although the importance of this was probably not appreciated at the time. Gavin: 'Much shaken by seeing his friend killed outright in front of him seven days earlier, Denny was not on the greatest form but nevertheless did a good job to finish fifth behind Ireland, Clark, Bonnier and Salvadori. It was only the twenty-ninth race of his career . . .'

Feo Stanton had arranged the lease of a 2.5-litre Cooper Type 51 for Denny to race in the New Zealand series in January 1961, perhaps the car originally destined to be raced by George. This had a distinctive air scoop mounted on the nose and vented back to the engine.

The Grand Prix on the Ardmore airfield circuit was to be run as two short heats and a 75-lap final. Denny finished fourth in his heat behind Brabham (Cooper), Innes Ireland (Lotus) and Dan Gurney (BRM). In the race he motored unspectacularly to fifth place, two laps down on Brabham and McLaren, who had raced hard to the finish in their Coopers. Denny received the Leonard Lord Trophy for the first New Zealand driver to finish, Bruce by now being regarded as an overseas driver.

On the night of the Grand Prix prize-giving at the Sorrento club on One Tree Hill, Denny and Greeta became engaged. Greeta still had six months of her nurse's training to complete, and as a special engagement present Denny's parents told Greeta they would pay her air fare to London if she stayed and completed her course. She would eventually arrive in August as a fully qualified State Registered Nurse.

On the tight Levin track the following weekend Denny finished third behind Jo Bonnier (Cooper) and Jim Clark (Lotus). Bonnier had just learned of his father's death and he would fly home to Sweden for the funeral and be back the following weekend for the race at Wigram.

The race on the fast, open airfield course was run in teeming, drenching rain that saw all the famous visitors survive huge spins. Denny was fifth again. Brabham was the winner from Stirling Moss, Angus Hyslop (Cooper) and McLaren.

There were no international drivers for the Dunedin street race and Denny came into his own, taking pole position in the Cooper and setting fastest lap on the way to a fine win. Pat Hoare was second in his Ferrari and Hyslop third in his Cooper. Later in the season Hulme and Hyslop would drive together in a works Abarth at Le Mans and trail their Formula Junior cars to European events. Bonnier won again at Teretonga, as he had at Levin, Roy Salvadori was second and Denny was a safe third ahead of Hoare's Ferrari.

There had been some discussion as to whether Denny should be classified as an overseas driver as Bruce McLaren had been when he came back to race in 1959, but the rules had apparently been relaxed and Denny won the New Zealand Gold Star with 47 points from Hoare (31) and Hyslop (25).

4 The summer of '61

At the Cooper factory in Surbiton, Denny built his own Formula Junior Cooper T56 for the 1961 season. At that time the Cooper headquarters was the centre of the motor-racing world, their cars having won the World Championship in 1959 and 1960, but that would be their zenith. Ferrari hit form in the summer of 1961. In his first three Formula Junior races at Silverstone, Crystal Palace and Roskilde in May, Denny finished seventh each time!

I would travel thousands of miles with Denny in later seasons when the CanAm series was in full swing, but my first taste of travel with the Hulme équipe kicked off on 24 May 1961, according to my diary. He was towing the black and silver Cooper-Ford on an open trailer behind an 80,000-mile Mk 1 Ford Zodiac that he had bought for £300. For some reason it was fitted with a police-style siren, which was useful for clearing race traffic on occasion, but also nearly set the car on fire. Smoke poured out from under the bonnet and Denny leapt out, shouting that it was a problem with the 'fuses'. The problem was actually that the siren had overloaded the Ford electrics and the 'fuses' were a drill bit and a screwdriver blade!

The old Zodiac was very much a two-seater. The back seat had been removed and the space filled with tools, spares and fuel cans. The fuel contract for the racing car stipulated that the free supply was as much as required at the track. This was obviously written to cover the amount of fuel used in the race, but all the drivers on the series would fill the race car, the tow car and as many cans as they could carry in the tow car and on

∧
Denny and Anita with their parents at home in Motueka.

PHOTO: NELSON PROVINCIAL MUSEUM, COURTESY HULME FAMILY COLLECTION

∧
Toddler Denny in his first racing car.

COURTESY HULME FAMILY COLLECTION

∧
Denny hill-climbing with his MG TF.

<
In his 2-litre Cooper
in 1959.
PHOTO: *MOTOR*, COURTESY HULME
FAMILY COLLECTION

<
Team manager Feo
Stanton (left) helping
Denny load the 2-litre
Cooper in 1960.
PHOTO: *NEW ZEALAND HERALD*,
COURTESY HULME FAMILY
COLLECTION

∧
Denny with his Formula Junior Cooper in the sunshine on the Messina grid in Italy in 1961.

∧
Greeta as pit crew signalling Denny at Rouen in France.

Denny and Greeta together at the track for one of Denny's early races in Britain.

∧
Kiwi trio at Silverstone, mid-sixties: Denny, Chris Amon and Bruce McLaren.

∧
Phil Kerr and Jack Brabham confer with Denny on the grid in 1963.

∧
Denny leads a Formula 3 train at Oulton Park in 1964.

∧
Stalled in the Brabham, on the start at the 1964 Tasman Series race on Sydney's Warwick
Farm circuit.

∧
Denny was a regular winner in Sid Taylor's 5.5-litre Lola.

the trailer, to get them to the next race, which could be at the other end of Europe the following weekend.

Our problems started early. On the way to Dover, Denny had been hurrying to make the ferry and he lost top gear. Rather than battle with the language as well as the gearbox across the Channel in France, Denny opted to stop and have the gearbox repaired in Dover. We caught a later ferry and drove all night through Germany to meet the Hyslop équipe at the Grossenbrode ferry for the crossing to Denmark.

Angus Hyslop had driven well in a 2.5-litre Cooper-Climax in New Zealand and would have been a certainty for the Driver to Europe scholarship, but it was not awarded. He bought a Lotus 20 Formula Junior car and a Hillman Husky and set out to do the same races as Denny in Europe, benefiting from the Hulme experience the previous summer.

It was my first time in France and it seemed important that we had a French roadside picnic for lunch. This was not at all part of the Hulme travel plan. The Hulme travel plan had one goal — getting there — and stops would only be made for fuel, perhaps grabbing a sandwich or an apple to eat on the move. It was my first experience of travelling with Denny and I persuaded him to stop in a village to buy a stick of French bread, some cheese and tomatoes — and a bottle of wine — to construct a French picnic at a roadside stop. We finally stopped, Denny grudgingly allowing valuable time for what he undoubtedly regarded as a poncey picnic. We didn't have a corkscrew. It appeared that lunch would require at least two more stops and the Hulme patience was eroding fast. We screeched to a halt outside a hardware shop and I mimed a corkscrew, thus learning my first and probably most important expression in French. 'Ah, m'seiu . . . un tire bouchon!' So we stopped yet again, I threw the picnic together, slugged back some of the rough red, and we were back on the road. I think that may have been the first — and the last — picnic stop that we made all summer.

A few miles from Grossenbrode there was a loud bang and the car lurched down with a broken main leaf in the rear spring. We crawled to the dock and on to the ferry for the four-hour crossing; on the other side, Denny bound the spring with wire.

The Roskildering held sad memories for Denny as it was the track where George had been killed the year before — the marks were still on the track where the car had skidded for 80 yards and then overturned.

Angus won both heats of the Formula Junior race and Denny struggled with engine problems. The next race was at Rouen and we headed south in convoy. David Piper was staying at our hotel and he took us around Les Essarts circuit, which was made up of French public roads a short distance from the town. He showed us one bend where he had stopped during a race the year before and Innes Ireland had crashed a few laps later, going right over the top of Piper's car and over the bank, landing high in some trees. There was always some 'old hand' anxious to show a new driver the circuit and point out where others had crashed in the past. Piper had raced a front-engined 2.5-litre Lotus 16 in the New Zealand series in 1960, with second-place finishes at Wigram and Teretonga. He was a veteran of the European series, spending much of each summer on the continental circuit.

Angus was third fastest in first practice at Rouen and Denny was sixth. The following day Denny moved up to third on the grid behind John Love and Henri Grandsire, with Angus fourth. Both Kiwis retired from the race with engine problems.

The next race for Hulme and Hyslop was the 24-hour race at Le Mans. BP had arranged for them to share a works Abarth, but it was made apparent from the moment the two New Zealanders arrived that it was very much an arrangement that had been wished upon the reluctant team by their sponsoring oil company. They were given an 850 cc GT, but the works effort was behind several 750 cc cars, which had the best chance of wresting the coveted Index of Performance from the French.

The complicated Index had been carefully worked out to favour the smaller French cars, which were never in with a chance of outright victory in 'their' major international event. The 750 cc Italian Abarths looked likely to mount a strong challenge. The 850 cc Abarth was essentially an unloved orphan.

The Abarth GT had not been fitted with a safety harness, so Denny asked for one to be installed. Angus said the car had very positive steering like his Formula Junior and had nearly as much performance, but it was much noisier than the single-seater because they were sitting in a closed sound-shell, and this would be a consideration in a race that ran twice round the clock.

Angus did the first stint in the race and after two hours Denny took over with the car running thirty-fifth in a field of 53 and eighth on the Index. At midnight the drivers were complaining of a clutch problem. By dawn on Saturday morning the clutch had failed altogether, and starting after a refuelling pit stop was a major problem. Denny had been cautioned after grinding away on the starter, so he and Angus worked out a way of starting the engine, then crashing in a gear to get under way. The final hours of the long race were a fingers-crossed drone to the finish, with most drivers cruising and Phil Hill and Olivier Gendebien way out in front and winning for Ferrari, covering 4477 kilometres. Phil Hill would also win the Grand Prix world championship for Ferrari that summer. The Hulme/ Hyslop Abarth finished fourteenth, covered 3531 kilometres, and was the only one of the army of Abarths that started to finish the race. In fact, it was the first time an Abarth had *ever* finished in the 24-hour classic. During the closing laps, the atmosphere in the pit became warmer, and by the finish Carlo Abarth was a close friend of the two New Zealanders.

Denny's next race was at Caserta, near Sorrento in Italy. We headed over the Mont Cenis Pass and down to Turin to visit the Abarth factory and collect the Le Mans money, and then down through Milan and Florence. Approaching Turin we were wondering how we would find the Abarth factory when a Fiat 600 dived inside us, carving up our trailer-towing entourage going into a roundabout. Denny was busy delivering Hulme-style invective at the top of his voice and shaking his fist out the window when he realised that the little Fiat had an Abarth scorpion badge on its door and that the driver was his old buddy Carlo Abarth himself. We shouted and I banged on the door, and Abarth swung round looking suitably indignant until he realised that it was his favourite New Zealand racing driver. Then he was all smiles and we followed him to the factory headquarters, Denny was paid the Le Mans prize money and we were soon on the road again, meeting up with David Piper as we were struggling to find the Autostrada on the way out of Milan. He told us that the Caserta race was the next weekend and practice was starting at 4.30 the following afternoon. We were under the impression that it was a fortnight away. I was to find that Denny's diary was not his most reliable asset.

We left Milan at noon, went through Florence at 5.30 p.m., Rome at just past midnight and arrived at Caserta at 3.30 a.m., parking up in what we thought was a park in the darkness. We slept like logs until dawn, then discovered that we had inadvertently parked in the grounds of a former royal palace . . .

David Young, who had raced a C-Type Jaguar in New Zealand and now had a new Formula Junior Cooper, was sharing a huge five-bedded room with Tyrrell Cooper driver John Love and team mechanic Neil Davis. David had already raced at Teramo in Italy but had suffered engine and clutch problems and then crashed. Angus's friend and engineer Bill Hannah had trailed the Hyslop Lotus on a trip through Switzerland and planned to meet Angus at Caserta, but while Angus may have learned that the race was in fact a week earlier than we had thought, there was no way of finding his racing car and mechanic in Switzerland.

By some international family quirk, Denny had an Italian full cousin, Giovanni, who was a lawyer in Sorrento and couldn't speak a word of English; we visited him for lunch on the day before practice.

There was a delay during scrutineering when the doctors would not clear Denny because his heart was beating too fast. I noted this in my diary then and realised much later that this was an early indication of his heart condition; there were suggestions before his death in Australia all those years later that he had still been having heart-related problems. With his medical certificate finally ticked, he qualified fastest in the heat for pole position in the final, while David, having been quick in practice, tangled with an Italian who spun in front of him on the opening lap and was put out for the weekend. In the final, Denny bent a gear selector and finished third behind John Love and Jo Siffert.

The next race, according to the Hulme schedule, was Monza, so he decided to check the engine bearings and change gear ratios before we left Sorrento. He told me how to take the gearbox off, showed which ratios he wanted changed, and let me get on with it. I thought I had done quite well to get it all back together and bolted up . . . and so did Denny when I told him I was finished. But when I told him that I had a few bits left over that he might like to put in his spares kit, I thought our friendship had come to an abrupt end. He was *furious!* I couldn't understand. I had done exactly what he had told me and saved a few parts, and he didn't seem best pleased about it. He called into question my abilities as a mechanic and I pointed out that I had never done any mechanical work in my life. So why had I told him I was a mechanic when he asked me to come on the trip with him? I said I'd told him nothing of the sort — if he cared to think back, he had asked me if I wanted to come with him and I'd said yes. No mention of being a mechanic. It then went all quiet for about half an hour as he set about taking the gearbox off again and making good my best efforts.

It was an event that became part of my personal folklore and has stood me in excellent stead, as I have never been asked to offer mechanical aid to anyone ever since . . .

As it was my first trip to Europe this chapter is a detailed record from my diary. Like most first-timers, I kept a careful diary of my year 'abroad' . . . and never kept a diary since.

We took time off to visit the nearby ruins of Pompei, buried in lava when Mount Vesuvius had erupted centuries before. We were badgered by would-be guides, but Denny had been there the year before and he knew the dodges. His main interest seemed to be to visit the buried brothels and bath houses. Most of the buildings of interest were locked and only the guides had keys, but my 'guide' solved this problem on an unofficial basis by climbing over the walls. The next tourist target we saw was the Colosseum in Rome, but this was by sheer chance, passing it when we were lost, endeavouring to find our way out of the city.

We arrived at Monza and unloaded the car in the historic paved paddock only for Denny to discover another error in his season-planner. We were in the wrong country. He had entered for the Formula Junior race supporting the Grand Prix at Reims in France, not Monza in Italy. We loaded the trailer again and set off for another overnight drive.

By 8 p.m. we were at 6500 feet, crossing the Simplon Pass. I was driving while Denny slept. I was aware that the road was climbing more steeply and becoming narrower than I had imagined a national through route might be, but I didn't risk waking Denny until the trailer mudguards were brushing both verges. My problem was to explain that (a) we were lost, (b) there was no place to turn round, and (c) I didn't know how to reverse a trailer. Denny could, and had to . . . for two miles downhill!

We crossed into France before dawn in thick fog and running low on fuel. Because the border banks had yet to open for the day we only had Italian currency, but we found a small petrol station that opened early and Denny scrabbled around in a shoebox of mixed coinage gathered during his two seasons of European travelling, getting together sufficient francs for enough fuel to get us to Reims by 8.15 a.m. We managed to get a fifth-floor room at the Hotel Cecyl — the last hotel room in town — paying the equivalent of £5 for the five-day race weekend.

We were now in the centre of champagne country and the circuit was a flat-out sprawling triangle made up of Routes Nationale and country roads closed for the weekend. It held the distinction of being the only race circuit ever to have a curtain to keep the sun from the drivers' eyes. Journalist Denis Jenkinson explained that as the cars came down the hill to the Thillois hairpin leading out on to the pit straight, at sunrise the sun was dead centre in line with the road, so beyond the hairpin a bridge was built and vast velvet curtains were hung from it, which blotted out the sun-strike until the sun had risen quite high!

During practice Angus towed Denny up to third place behind the Lotuses of Trevor Taylor and Alan Rees, but the social side of the French Grand Prix seemed to be the major attraction of the weekend. Denny took me to the famous Brigitte's Bar, where we found Jack Brabham, Bruce McLaren, Trevor Taylor and John Whitmore. There was a commotion at one point in the evening when John Cooper climbed in through the window. It seemed that if the *gendarmerie* was not called at some point in the evening, it was regarded as a quiet night.

The following morning we went to the Reims municipal swimming pool to find Stirling Moss, Jack Brabham, Bruce McLaren, Jim Clark, Trevor Taylor, Innes Ireland, Colin Chapman and John Cooper already taking the sun. That afternoon Denny and I were in the Cooper pit watching Phil Hill in the Ferrari take pole position, then go out again to tow fellow

Californian Dan Gurney in the works Porsche higher up the grid than he had been!

On race morning Denny and I were leaving our room when a driver in blue Dunlop overalls came out of the room next door, nodding to us as he locked the door. I asked Denny who it was. He had no idea. Never seen him before. That afternoon the driver we didn't know drove his way into the record books when he won his first World Championship Grand Prix for Ferrari. It was Giancarlo Baghetti. Denny finished sixth overall in the Formula Junior race.

We returned to Surrey for 10 days and then we were on the road again, this time down the length of Italy to Messina in Sicily. Forty hours later we were in Rimini to pause for the night, then on to Pescara where Denny had won the year before after a race-long battle with Colin Davis.

In those pre-transporter days there were always terrifying tales of the trips, which made towing to the race sound more dangerous than the race itself. On the ferry to Reggio Calabria was an American named Peterson, who had put his tow-car, trailer and new Cooper-DKW over a bank when he went to sleep while driving. David Piper's mechanic was towing his Lotus when the lashing ropes broke. The car slid off the trailer and the mechanic had to backtrack 10 miles, where he found the Lotus Formula Junior in a ditch and only slightly damaged. Bob Anderson, the racing motorcyclist who had switched to four wheels, towed his Lotus on a trailer behind his van with two camp beds bolted to the floor in the back. Bill McGowan, racing a Lola for the Fitzwilliam team, travelled in the AC-Bristol he had raced the previous season. The Fitzwilliam mechanics carried their cars in a converted bus that had a top speed of 38 mph, its advantage being that the mechanics not driving could sunbathe on the roof!

Colin Davis led the early stages of the race at Messina in a De Sanctis, but he went out with a broken con rod on the ninth lap, leaving Bob Anderson in his Lotus 20 leading from Hyslop's similar car. Then Anderson's engine blew, letting Angus into the lead with Denny in second place and they ran that way to the chequered flag. We were delighted — New Zealand drivers first and second in Italy. The Italians weren't quite sure what to make of it, asking each other where *is* this country?

Denny's next foreign foray was to Karlskoga in Sweden followed by another race at Roskilde in Denmark in August. He was fourth in Sweden and fourth again on aggregate of race heat results in Denmark.

One day in August 1961 Greeta arrived at Heathrow at 6 a.m., but Denny didn't. His new fiancée was sitting on her suitcase in the arrivals hall wondering whether she had done the right thing when Denny eventually arrived. 'He had slept in! He was living at the Lamb Hotel in Kingston-on-Thames with Angus Hyslop and Bill Hannah and he collected me in the Zodiac tow car. He took me to Patty's little flat just outside Kingston, a bed-sitter with a shared bathroom, and when my nursing papers came through I moved into the Nurses' Home at Surbiton Cottage Hospital, not far from the Cooper factory.'

The season was all but over for Denny and the prospects were not rosy. Phil Kerr was running Jack Brabham's commercial garage business and he offered Denny a job as a mechanic working on customer road cars. It was a matter of making ends meet until the start of the 1962 season.

5 The down years

The apparent rejection of Hulme by motor racing in 1962 became a huge part of Denny's make-up, perhaps a sliver of the reason for his gruffness, his 'bear' reputation in later years. As compensation, Phil Kerr offered him a 9-to-5 job working for Jack Brabham Motors in the department that fitted Coventry Climax engines into Triumph Heralds and other such specialised conversions. Greeta had arrived from New Zealand the previous August and took up nursing local to their flat in Surbiton, so they became something of a surburban couple during the winter off-season while the rest of Denny's mates enjoyed themselves in New Zealand and Australia.

Denny converted his 1961 Cooper suspension to 1962 Formula Junior specifications and would enjoy suitable results that included dead-heating with John Fenning's new Lotus 20, and setting a new lap record at Silverstone.

In an *Autosport* profile on Denny late in 1964, Bill Gavin wrote of that 1962 summer: 'It was as obvious as ever that Denny had lots of ability; when the car finished it was always close to the works or semi-works FJ cars and certainly the highest finishing of the '61 models. Denny deserved a better drive and I approached Colin Chapman and Mike Costin about giving him a tryout for Team Lotus.'

This was a well-meaning move by Gavin, but Denny had a turn of mind that led him to believe that his ability would open doors and that he was capable of doing his own negotiating for drives. This was not Hulme ungratefulness, just the way he was made. A measure of stubborn country Kiwi, perhaps.

'They agreed he could try a car the next time they went testing. But Denny has some sort of fierce independence and probably resented this intrusion — certainly he never availed himself of the offer. Tony Maggs's F1 commitments (with Cooper) sometimes left a gap in the Tyrrell team and Denny drove Ken's Coopers with John Love at Roskilde where he came second, at Reims and Rouen, then at Albi where he was placed third — the BMC engines were outclassed by the Ford units and only when the British works teams abstained were the Tyrrell cars likely to gain a victory.'

Another milestone in the Hulme career happened almost by accident. In fact, it *did* happen by accident, the accident to Gavin Youl, who overturned the prototype Brabham Formula Junior (FJ) at Brands Hatch and broke his collarbone.

Bill Gavin: '[Denny's] first race in a Brabham had come in June when he raced a Ford-engined Junior at Crystal Palace. He was fastest in practice but got a bit involved in the race and finished fourth. All season he had continued to work at Brabham Motors, taking time off for racing. At the end of the season he spent some time down at the racing department, building up a Brabham FJ for the Boxing Day meeting at Brands Hatch. Here he lapped at 53.6 seconds during practice and set a new outright lap record of 54.4 seconds on his way to winning the FJ event. It was then agreed that he would drive the works Brabham for all of the 1963 season.'

Phil Kerr had been in the background of Denny's opportunity with the Formula Junior team, making sure that he was in the right place at the right time should a vacancy emerge. 'I took him on and gave him a job working at Brabham and he worked in the workshop there for quite a while. It was to help him so that he could derive some income other than what little he might earn from racing Formula Juniors. He subsequently ended up working on building the production Brabham cars as well and then eventually, after many discussions with Jack, I managed to persuade him to let Denny have a works drive in 1963 and on into 1964. He had to do it the hard way, that's for sure. It was tough for him, but he was so determined that nobody was going to stop him.

'He was mechanically very sensitive because he was a very good mechanical engineer and very much in tune with cars and anything mechanical. He had a very good intuition for that sort of equipment.'

Howden Ganley, the Kiwi McLaren mechanic who would follow in Hulme's Formula 1 footsteps with drives for Williams and BRM, recalled Hulme's reputation of having an eagle-eye for detail. 'There is the legend of how he came in and told the mechanics that there was a 1.5-inch pip pin lying on the track at some very fast corner, but had decided that it was probably not the size they were using. The amazement was that he could see it *at all*, never mind what size it was . . .'

Kerr: 'He was hard on a car in that he would extract whatever was needed out of a race car in order to win, but he wasn't brutal with a race car. He was very hard on brakes, but that was because he was a pretty strong character and he could see that the braking area was for overtaking and he was as good as any of the late-brakers, that's for sure, but his general driving style was remarkably smooth.'

Kerr had campaigned for Hulme to have a Brabham drive at the end of the 1962 season and it would be Kerr who engineered the move to the McLaren team in 1968 after 'his man' had won the World Championship for Brabham in 1967.

'Jack sort of didn't believe in Denny at first,' recalls Kerr. 'Believe it or not, Denny *still* worked in the workshop in bare feet. That was until the day he dropped a crankshaft on his foot and did severe damage to his big toe, which took some time to come right and nurse/wife Greeta helped him to repair the damage. It was then that I had to suggest that it was time we quit the bare-foot thing, apart from the fact that I couldn't deal with the oily footprints round the workshops and through the car showroom . . .'

Greeta has graphic recall of Denny's battered big toe: 'He had this big blood blister under the nail and he came home in absolute agony, so I heated up a paperclip on the stove, got him to sit down and sizzled a hole in the nail and released the pressure. He kicked like a mule but the pain was gone instantly. There was blood all over the place!'

It was generally reckoned that the last season of Formula Junior in 1963 was the best since the formula began in 1959. In his *Autosport* season review, Michael Kettlewell wrote: 'Although there were fewer races, fewer manufacturers and fewer drivers, 1963 produced many entertaining races (as opposed to processions) and, in the most important of these, honours were divided equally between the marques Lotus and Brabham and their drivers Peter Arundell and Denis Hulme.

'Lotus, Cooper, Lola, Brabham, Alexis, Gemini and Merlyn offered cars for sale; yet, of these seven manufacturers, only one directly entered a works car regularly: Brabham Racing Developments with a lone Repco-Brabham for Denis Hulme to drive.' Other Brabhams that season were private entries.

First win went to Arundell and Lotus at Oulton Park in early April. Hulme's Brabham had carburetion problems and never featured. Easter Monday at Goodwood went to Ian Walker's private Brabham driven by laconic Australian Frank Gardner, with Hulme second. In the rain at Aintree the British teams were together again and it was Hulme who won from Gardner. At Silverstone in May, Hulme won the 73-mile race from David Hobbs in a Lola.

The Formula Junior curtainraiser at Monaco was the star race of the season for the small cars, but Denis was concentrating on UK events and he chose to race and win at Aintree again. A month later he won at Crystal Palace, once more ahead of Gardner in second place. Denny had won his heat and the final, underlining his form and, he hoped, gathering Jack Brabham's attention.

The Formula Junior circus moved to France in June, and at Rouen in the first heat Denis and Peter Arundell in the works Lotus had a torrid race for the lead until the last lap when Arundell overdid it and eventually finished sixth. Hulme won, then led the final until his transmission failed. Gardner took over in the Walker Brabham until his engine quit five laps from the finish and it was fellow-Australian Paul Hawkins who inherited the win in another Brabham.

Kettlewell: 'Now to Reims for another Denis Hulme benefit match. Driving the Cosworth-Ford-engined works Brabham (a very potent Holbay unit tried in practice blew up), Denis "did a Jim Clark" and shook off everyone, but the desperate struggle for second position kept the race very much alive. Hobbs (Lola), Attwood (Lola), Fenning (Lotus), Arundell (Lotus), Schlesser (Brabham), Spence (Lotus) and Prophet (Brabham) were all slipstreaming each other, while, farther back, there were many retirements. Eventually Arundell secured second position, leading Attwood and Spence across the line by a whisker.'

Greeta remembers those days on the road, taking time off from her nursing in Surrey to travel with Denny. 'When we used to drive round the races in Europe I was the chief cook and bottle washer and he was his own mechanic. I'd get everything ready and I'd stand there with my stopwatch and the signal board, all organised. I'd watch him going through the car and I'd say something like "Have you topped up the brake fluid?" and, oooh, a withering look . . . or I'd say "Lunch is ready, I've got it all organised" and oooh, another withering look. So in the end I'd just tell him lunch was in the boot of the car if he wanted it . . .' She laughs now. 'Shivers . . . I learned my place real quick and I learned to butt out.

'We used to travel with Paul Hawkins, Frank Gardner, Richard Attwood, David Hobbs, all those guys. It was just like a circus from one track to another. There was so much camaraderie. If you didn't have something, someone else would loan it to you. Then there was the starting money special. If you didn't have wet weather tyres in the rain, you'd tippy-toe round for a few laps and then come in with an excuse something was wrong with the car, and then you'd have enough money to afford to go to the next race meeting. It was really, really good fun . . .'

The British Grand Prix meeting at Silverstone in July saw all the 'usual suspects' in a furious battle for the lead, well aware that all the Formula 1 team managers would be watching.

Hulme and Arundell were out front in a torrid dispute for the lead that went down to the very last lap when Hulme, trying to get to grips with Arundell into Club corner, lost control and hit the barrier, badly damaging the Brabham. Arundell sailed on to win the prestigious race leaving Denny to lick his wounds and wonder at what could have been, dwelling perhaps on the exception proving the rule.

The following weekend Denny was out of context in his terms, sharing a Jaguar 3.8-litre saloon entered by Tommy Atkins with Roy Salvadori in the Six-Hour Saloon Car Race at Brands Hatch sponsored by *The Motor*. In practice the Salvadori/Hulme car was second fastest to the 7.6-litre drum-braked Ford Galaxie shared by Jack Brabham and Dan Gurney. The Galaxie would be defeated by the downpour conditions during the long race. The Atkins Jaguar had its problems when it lost a wheel in pre-race testing and then cracked its sump during official practice. Not that it affected their grid placing, because positions were selected by the arcane arrangement of placing all cars in order of capacity, starting with the largest capacity at the front, and then drawing lots. Thus, the slowest Galaxie, driven by Sprinzel and Lucia, found itself on pole position. It echoed the grid arrangement for the first Indianapolis 500 run in 1911, when pole position was decided on the first entry received by the race organiser . . .

Autosport reporter Kettlewell wrote that track conditions at the start were more akin to the Henley Regatta than a serious motor race. The field was allowed three exploratory laps and immediately Gurney was in trouble with the fastest big Ford, complaining that it failed to answer the helm. In desperation the front Goodyears were changed to Firestones, but there was no time for a full wheel change.

The Jaguars were better suited to the swimming track and were soon in complete charge, with Mike Salmon leading from Salvadori and Peter Lindner. By lap 37 only the Salmon and Salvadori Jaguars were on the lead lap and they would run away with the long, wet race in that order, apart from brief shuffles during scheduled pit stops. Just before half distance, Savadori, still driving, passed Peter Sutcliffe, who was at the wheel of the Jaguar he was sharing with Salmon, for the lead and the more experienced Salvadori drew away.

Salvadori held the lead until lap 96 (of 165) and then pitted for fuel, oil and tyres. A lengthy brake pad change meant that when Denny finally took the circuit for the first time, he was two laps down on the Salmon/Sutcliffe Jaguar, which had thus far made only one routine stop. They caught a lap by the time Salmon took over from Sutcliffe on lap 114, but they were still a lap down with two hours left. When Hulme became accustomed to the wet circuit he unlapped himself on the lead car, setting fastest lap of the race on the 130th, at 2:04 (76.93 mph). With 20 minutes left Denny made a pit stop to check his tyres and Salmon regathered the lap lead.

Second place must have felt like a win to the embattled pair in the Atkins Jaguar, but the post-race scrutineering of the winning Salmon/Sutcliffe Jaguar resulted in it being disqualified because the inlet valves were found to be oversized, and Roy and Denny were announced the victors!

Denny had slaved for three days to build a brand new Holbay-engined FJ Brabham for the race at Solitude in Germany, but it was Peter Arundell in the Ron Harris Lotus who motored away to win from Denny by 12.5 seconds. At Goodwood Arundell won again and Denny was third with grabbing brakes, behind Attwood's Lola. Arundell and Hulme were 1-2 and just 1.8 seconds apart at Albi in France, after both had won their heats. At Brands Hatch in September, Formula Junior officially came to an end, Arundell and Hulme were once again 1-2 and Arundell was announced winner of the *Express & Star* Formula Junior championship by just 1 point from Denny, after a long and hectic season of racing. The British championship might have been decided, but there were further races before the season ended and Denny won his last Formula Junior race at Snetterton from Hobbs and Rees in Lolas.

Summing up the important feeder series, Kettlewell wrote in his *Autosport* review: 'During its life span, Formula Junior produced a crop of racing drivers now established in Formula 1 racing. Do not forget that Jim Clark had his first single-seater drive in a Gemini, while John Surtees had his baptism on four wheels in a Cooper. Giancarlo Baghetti, Lorenzo Bandini, Joseph Siffert, Tony Maggs, Trevor Taylor, Peter Arundell, Denis Hulme and others have really made a name for themselves in Formula Junior racing, all having had Formula 1 drives as a result.

'Formula Junior died on 31st December, 1963, but on 1st January (1964) both Formula 2 and Formula 3 were born and took its place. Formula 2 is the successor to Formula Junior as far as big races and works teams go, but Formula 3 should provide a lot of amusement for private entrants, with possible participation of the works teams in the more important races.

'Formula 2 allows single-seaters with four-cylinder engines of 1000 cc and a minimum weight limit of 420 kg is imposed. Formula 3 cars have to employ homologated series-production engines having one carburettor and cars must not have more than four speeds or weigh less than 400 kg.'

The Hulme pace was branded on the series with Formula Junior lap records in perpetuity at the long and short Brands Hatch circuits, Snetterton, Crystal Palace and Rouen.

Lap records and race wins in France brought champagne, and Greeta had earmarked this for their wedding in New Zealand on 7 December 1963. 'We had saved six bottles of pink champagne for the top table at our wedding and another two dozen bottles of vintage champagne.

'We shipped the champagne to New Zealand and Denis's dad went to collect it but Customs wanted duty paid on it. We argued that it was a trophy so they asked for a newspaper cutting to prove it. We supplied this and got all the champagne through for our wedding. In those days at a wedding in New Zealand you had a bottle of beer, soft drinks and a bottle of champagne in the middle of each long table. My mother had gone absolutely berserk. I'd arranged my wedding dress in England and sent back all the cake decorations. You name it, I'd done it . . .

'My mother had made a *five-tier* wedding cake and she took all these fruit cakes down town to get them iced and fitted out with all the decorations I'd sent over. Problem was they never put any plates in for support and it ended up looking like the Leaning Tower of Pisa, but nobody seemed to notice because they had one glass of the French champagne and they were on their ear! Nobody remembers our wedding . . .

'One of my cousin's husbands staggered out on to the footpath after the reception and they were all chattering away when one of them said "Archie — isn't that your car?" Someone had stolen his car and driven off while he was standing there!'

Denny was no party animal. He enjoyed being with his mates but he was no drinker, as Greeta recalls: 'We went to a party and Paul Hawkins had imported all this Fosters beer from Australia and they plied Denis with this stuff. He ended up literally under the table in the kitchen and I'm trying to get him home but he won't come. He's hanging on to the legs of the table because he's *drunk* as anything. So we pour him into the car and I'm driving and we're coming through Esher and he shouts at me to stop. He falls out of the car and he's sick as a dog. He's promising me that he's never ever going to drink again and he's telling me that I'm driving too fast and I was just *creeping* along. And he never got drunk again after that. No way . . .'

6 The Hulme star starts to shine

The glorious Tasman Series summer races in New Zealand and Australia — named after the Tasman Sea, 'the ditch', separating Australia and New Zealand — started in 1964, with four races in both countries. In New Zealand there were to be races at Levin, Pukekohe (Auckland), Wigram airfield (Christchurch) and Teretonga (Invercargill). The Australian races were to be at Warwick Farm (Sydney), Lakeside (Brisbane), Longford (Tasmania) and Sandown Park (Melbourne).

The Down Under races had always been Formula Libre, an open series where entrants could bring whatever might be competitive away from the stricter European or American races. From 1964 the Tasman capacity ceiling was 2.5 litres, normally aspirated and on pump fuel. Of course, there were complaints that the Formula 1 regulations called for a 1.5-litre formula and this had already been scheduled to change to 3 litres in 1966, so surely the Tasman series would be an instant orphan. The feeling was that the 2.5-litre 4-cylinder Coventry Climax engine from the previous Formula 1 that changed in 1961 would be readily available and reasonably reliable. Bruce McLaren and Jack Brabham had been investing in the 'Indy' versions of the Climax 4, enlarged to 2.7 litres, but these were costly and not necessarily reliable. In fact, Lotus and BRM would move to enlarged versions of their 1.5-litre Coventry Climax or BRM V8 engines as the series progressed, but Brabham and McLaren used their 2.7-litre Climax 4s reduced to 2.5 litres for the new formula. For 1964 the front-runners used the 2.5-litre Climax 4. There were the annual rumours that Ferrari, Lotus, BRM and Cooper would be fielding works entries, but reality turned out to be works Brabhams for Jack and Denny, while McLaren entered Coopers for Bruce and the young American, Timmy Mayer, who was slated to drive in the works GP team later in the year. Chris Amon was in a Parnell team Lola-Climax. Denny was driving a Brabham-Climax BT7A works car in a two-car team with Jack, but he was on his own for the season-opener at Levin and in sparkling form, taking pole on the tight circuit inside the country horse racecourse at 50.7 seconds from the Coopers of McLaren (51.4 seconds), Mayer (51.7 seconds) and John Youl's Tasmanian Cooper (52 seconds). John Youl was the older brother of Gavin, whose broken shoulder blade suffered in a Brands Hatch crash had given Hulme the opportunity to drive the prototype Brabham Formula Junior.

In the first heat McLaren led but Hulme caught and passed to win, setting a lap record at 50.3 seconds. Denny was in flying form, fresh from his Formula Junior series overseas and he won the final after an initial tussle with Timmy Mayer. It was a good start to the series for the local boy in front of his home crowd.

Qualifying for the Grand Prix at Pukekohe, another circuit within a horse racecourse, was a struggle for Denny, who couldn't better sixth on the grid. McLaren and Jack Brabham had disputed pole, with Bruce grabbing the advantage. McLaren won his heat from Youl and Hulme, but Denny was now finding his pace and improved his lap time.

Mayer snatched the lead, jumping from the second row and leading Brabham and Hulme, but within a couple of laps the race order had settled down with Brabham in front leading his old Formula 1 team-mate McLaren. Behind them the Australian Frank Matich was giving Hulme a hard time. Denny spun on lap 16, losing touch with Matich and Mayer, but they would take care of each other 10 laps later when Matich's motor blew in a big way and Mayer slid off the circuit, recovering just as Hulme went by. Then it was Brabham's turn to make a lurid exit when he miscalculated a pass on New Zealander Tony Shelly's Lotus and crashed heavily. This left McLaren in the lead and easing to protect his position, with Hulme closing in the final laps for a Kiwi 1-2 in their home Grand Prix.

On the fast, open Wigram airfield circuit Hulme was quickest in open practice and he went on to win his heat after Mayer had to cope with two 'offs' caused by throttle slides sticking on his Cooper-Climax. Brabham and McLaren dominated their race heat, keeping each other honest — and fast — and Brabham started from pole with McLaren, Hulme and Youl across the front row. There was the usual hectic first-lap action, but it settled to Brabham-Hulme-McLaren-Youl. It was then McLaren's Climax engine that gummed its throttle slides with dust from a new section of the course and he lost over 20 seconds regaining his composure. Mayer spun with the same problem — again! — and had a long pit stop, but McLaren was flying and closing on Brabham amd Hulme. With five laps left McLaren seized his chance as he and Jack lapped either side of a slower car. They finished 1-2, with Brabham following his former protégé over the line, Hulme a slowing third with engine-bearing failure.

Brabham headed home to Britain for the Racing Car Show after the Wigram race, so Denny was the sole Brabham works driver at Teretonga. After his Wigram engine failure, he had fitted Brabham's Repco-built Climax 4 and he was also using a wide experimental set of Goodyear tyres, seen for the first time on the Tasman series. These were good for a 2-second advantage over McLaren's Cooper at the end of practice.

Grid positions came from race heat positions and McLaren had found pace to head Hulme on his new tyres, so would start on pole, with Hulme, Mayer and Amon across the front row of the grid. From the start Denny regained his form and pulled comfortably away from the field, using his new wide American tyres to maximum advantage and setting a new lap record on lap 6. Two laps later he was missing, having spun coming out of the long loop and smashed into a fence post. McLaren and Mayer finished 1-2 in their team Coopers.

The Australian half of the 1964 series brought no joy to Denny. Jack won at Sandown Park, Warwick Farm and Lakeside, and Denny took fifths at Sandown and Warwick Farm, retiring from the Lakeside race and giving the final at Longford a miss.

Denny: 'In 1964 I had a 1000 cc Formula 2 Brabham and my most memorable race in that car was at Clermont-Ferrand. I liked the circuit. It was five miles to the lap, 1500 foot above the historic old town. It was a bit like a miniature Nürburgring, around the top of a mountain. It probably rises and falls more than any other circuit in Europe and the pits are situated at one of the highest points. From the first hairpin you actually look out over the town over a thousand feet below. You can see the cathedral and the church steeples sticking up quite high, which makes it doubly impressive.

'I had pole position for the Formula 2 race in 1964 and they asked me which side of the track I would like to start from. I picked the outside, because it would give me a better run at the first corner and this really helped me. It was all foggy at the top of the hill, but being first away I didn't have to worry about anybody being in front of me and I just disappeared into the fog. Towards the end of the race one of the spokes in my steering wheel broke, and it was really difficult to control the car when braking, but I just managed to stay ahead of Jackie Stewart's Lotus.'

Jack and Denny were running BT120 Brabhams in the Formula 2 series and Jack scored four wins and took the Grands Prix de France Championship. There was no official Formula 2 championship in 1964, but the Brabham cars were dominant at all the races.

Even Honda tends to forget that the first racing success for a Honda road car in Europe was in the International 500-kilometre event on the

14.2-mile Nürburgring on 6 September 1964, just five weeks after the first Honda Formula 1 car had debuted on the same daunting circuit in the German Grand Prix. The S600 Honda sports car was entered by the Brabham Racing Organisation and driven by Denny Hulme. It was the first time Denny had laid eyes on the Nürburgring, a long and complicated mountain track that he regarded as a challenge to be conquered. He won the 1000 cc GT class in the little Honda, averaging 60.5 mph, a lap ahead of Geise in a Fiat-Abarth and Sutton's Marcos. Three years later Hulme would win the Grand Prix there and go on to win the World Championship.

Abarths dominated the entry, with eight cars, and Hans Hermann duly headed a 1-2-3 overall victory for the 1300 cc Abarth-Simca prototypes, averaging 72.08 mph. Ernst Furtmayr was second and Kurt Ahrens was third. Andrew Hedges was fourth in one of Dick Jacobs' MG Midgets and Keith Greene/Alan Foster shared the sixth placed MG.

Jack Brabham had tried the little sports car on the Suzuka test track in Japan early in 1964. He tried two versions of the S600s over a hundred laps. 'The car is quite fabulous,' Jack wrote at the time. 'It has a gem of an engine with twin overhead camshafts and an output of roughly 60 horsepower. It sings along very happily with 10,000 rpm showing on the clock. It's like a little sewing machine to drive, with a nice steady push from the engine right through the range. The 5-speed gearbox is very pleasant to use and the brakes — drums all round — are really excellent. It handles extremely well for a production motor car, is well finished and a good looker.'

Interesting that Jack took one of Honda's experimental staff round in the car with him. 'His name was Nakamura and he was very interested in the way the car handled.' Nakamura would be vital to the success of Honda's international racing programme in Formula 1 and eventually head the entire company.

Denny was the junior member of the Brabham team — Jack was number one and Dan Gurney was number two. He tested with the little Honda at

Goodwood and then went to Germany, where he spent time learning the 'Ring in his Mk 2 Ford Zephyr while waiting for the Japanese to arrive. There was a field of 140 entered in the 500-kilometre race, which had a top limit of 1.5 litres; Denny would be racing against Alfa Romeos, Abarths and Healey Sprites in the sub-litre class.

'No one was taking the little Honda too seriously,' Denny recalled. 'My most vivid recollection was the lack of brakes. It just didn't have *any* by the time the car had done about 5 kilometres. To overcome this, the Japanese adjusted them up so tight that three people could only just push the car. No disc brakes then, of course.

'The 630 cc engine had twin cams and a Keihin carburettor for each of the four cylinders. These were like SUs in function and construction. Our motor developed 74 bhp, outstanding for the early sixties, but none of our competitors knew how much power we had. I think they thought it was a bit of a joke, but it revved out to 12,500 rpm!'

Denny was fascinated by the technical specifications of the little Honda sports car. 'It had a normal cutch, a 5-speed gearbox and then a differential immediately on the back of the gearbox with sprockets and chains in swing arms back to the rear wheels. Chain drive? Even I was beginning to think they couldn't be serious. Front suspension was by wishbones, with vertical piston dampers and torsion bars and the rear suspension was by trailing arms formed by the chain cases and coil-spring damper units mounted forwards on to a pair of high-mounted arms at the rear of the chassis.

'True to all Honda engines, this one had roller bearings so that there was no need to worry about an oil pressure gauge or warning light. Good lubrication was ensured without high oil pressure and this engine ran at only about 2 psi oil pressure.

'The canvas hood flapped at speed and was a bit annoying and the fuel tank only held 60 litres, so I would need a stop for fuel. Late in practice the S600 broke a rear half-shaft out on the circuit and by the time the session ended and we got the car back to the pits, a Japanese mechanic had to set off for Brussels, 200 kilometres away, to get a replacement.

'When we got to the track the next morning, we were unaware of any dramas, but found my race mechanic asleep in the car. The mechanic returning from Brussels with the new half-shaft had crashed his car and was on his way back to the 'Ring in a Belgian taxi! He arrived at 10 a.m. on race morning and we only just made it to the start. Heaven knows how he sorted out the hire car accident and persuaded the taxi driver to take him to the Nürburgring. They didn't speak English and it was always communication by hand signals or lots of drawings on the concrete floor of the pits, sorting out spring rates, lap times and horsepower figures . . .

'I qualified well down in the field, probably about fortieth, but we knew we were lucky to be able to make the start at all. It got worse. It was a Le Mans start and everyone got away except one car. My little Honda. When I turned the key, it merely wound up the wiring loom, which had come loose in the dash. My mechanic arrived, grabbed at the loom under the dashboard and turned the key. I was last away but I passed 45 cars on that first lap and there were 17 more laps to go.

'The brakes held up well, much to my surprise, and on some of the downhill stretches we were showing 118 mph, which was just amazing for the size of the engine in 1964 and when you consider what other road cars in its class could do. Most other cars were running out of revs with their 4-speed gearboxes, but with our 5-speeder and big rev range, we were making up heaps of ground.

'I stopped for fuel and a litre of oil at half-distance, filling up with a drum and a funnel, and we won our class for cars up to 1000 cc. Most of the others had to make two stops. I was told that on the final lap, the Japanese mechanics were in the back of the pits praying. When the race ended my exhausted mechanics were overjoyed and carried me shoulder-high to the victory dais. I suppose, looking back, in a lot of ways this was one of my more memorable races. It was the first international car race victory for Honda, and at the prize-giving the Germans made a big thing of the Honda winning and kept inventing new prizes, most of them in the form of cases of German wine!'

Phil Kerr, the New Zealander who was Brabham's manager and who would switch to the McLaren team with Hulme four years later, went to the Nürburgring with Denny and his wife for the S600 race. 'Denny said he was flat everywhere. When he made the pit stop he didn't dare switch off in case the ignition didn't work again. He finally got back to the lead in his class and the Japanese were all huddled in the back of the pit, nervous as anything, fingers crossed, praying. One of them produced a bottle of whiskey and they were getting into that to settle their nerves. All they wanted was to win their class. The *elation* among those guys was unbelievable. This was Honda's first success in international motor racing, as opposed to motorcycle racing. It was the start of something enormous in anyone's terms.'

The S600 sports car win for Hulme, the Brabham team and Honda was just the beginning. Jack had done a deal with Honda for the use of their engines in Formula 2, with no charge for use or maintenance.

It was more than a change of country, base and type of racing for the Japanese mechanics on the Formula 2 project. It was a complete change of lifestyle. 'They turned up at the Brabham factory in Weybridge with various people to look after the engines and worry about the installation,' Phil Kerr recalls. 'None of them spoke English and we didn't speak Japanese, but that was overcome with a piece of chalk and pictures drawn on the concrete floor. They were absolutely brilliant at depicting what they were trying to do or say with drawings. They had a bit of English, but not a heck of a lot.

'We had never worked with Japanese before and we realised that they were all too short to reach the normal work height of benches, and our guys had to make up duckboards six inches high so that the Japanese mechanics could work at the benches. They adapted quite well. They ate sandwiches from lunch-bars, because there were no sushi bars in Surrey in those days. The first week or so was interesting, because the English mechanics worked all the hours God gave them. They would stay all night, seven days a week if necessary. The programme was fairly rushed, getting the cars built and the engines in, and for the Japanese it was a point of honour that they couldn't go back to their hotel until their English counterparts did. After a couple of days of those hours, they didn't appear. They arrived late, apologetic, having slept in. They couldn't believe how late the English mechanics worked . . . They were meticulous workers and did their best to fit in, looking and following. They all had cameras and took pictures of everything. After a while their English improved and communications got better. They were very Honda-oriented. With their own personal pride plus the company's, they *had* to succeed. They didn't dare fail. That explains why they were so tense during that last lap at the Nürburgring.'

While I was writing this book in New Zealand in 2006 I received an email from my erstwhile travelling mate Laurence Edscer in the UK, reminding me of the incident with Denny at the Nürburgring when he returned to drive a Honda S600 owned by a German friend, in the 1991 'Oldtimer' classic races. Remember, this is Denny Hulme Grand Prix driver (retired), who had won the German Grand Prix and the world championship in 1967. 'Denny said the S600 was the only race car he ever had to change down in on the long uphill straight on the old circuit. You and I were there in our official capacity as chauffeur and designated drinker and had every wristband and pass available for free booze and food over the weekend. We decided to go with Denny for a snack and drink in the sponsoring Steigenberger marquee at lunchtime. You and I were allowed in with the correct wristband, but the goon on the entry stopped Denny because all he had was the race suit he was wearing. It had his name embroidered, but despite protests the guy wasn't about to let Denny in without a wristband. You went berserk and tried single-handedly to start World War 3. It didn't have any effect, but you said to us "Wait here. Don't move. I'll be back." A few minutes later you returned and said, "Follow me." We dutifully did and were ushered into the reception area of the British Aerospace hospitality marquee, handed a glass of champagne each and shown to our table. We spent the next few hours there and I think you wrote about the dramas in your *Autocar* column.'

Long before all that happened, though, Denny was still making his mark on the world of motor sport. As Phil Kerr recalls: 'For 1965 Jack was starting to think ahead and agreed to ease Denny into a number of Formula 1 drives. Jack stood down for a couple of races and Denny opened the year in the International Trophy at Silverstone, followed by the Monaco Grand Prix. It was the first time he had raced on the streets of the principality and he qualified on the fourth row beside fellow Kiwi Bruce McLaren in the Cooper. Jack started from the front row, led briefly, but then retired with engine failure. Denny finished a creditable eighth.'

His next Grand Prix was the French at Clermont-Ferrand and Denny surprised by being fastest on the first day of practice in what was only his second-ever Grand Prix, benefiting from his Formula 2 experience the year before. He went on to start from the third row and finish fourth.

Phil: 'This was the last year of the 1.5-litre Formula 1, before the formula doubled in capacity to 3 litres in 1966, and it was valuable experience. Dan Gurney had joined the team in 1963 and I think Jack planned to ease himself out of Formula 1 and have Dan and Denny as the Brabham works team. Then Dan surprised us all by leaving, not only leaving but building his own All American Racers Eagle cars. But it was understandable why Dan had done this and Jack couldn't really say too much because he had done the same thing when he left the Cooper team. I know Jack was thinking of retirement, but he didn't say when, so the Dan and Denny plans came to nothing and Jack carried on racing. For 1966 Denny was a full works Grand Prix driver. He'd made it.

'Even back in 1963 and 1964 Denny wasn't a full-time professional. He had a car provided by the works, but he had to transport it and maintain it. He didn't have a permanent mechanic but every now and then one of the guys from the workshop would be allowed to go along with him and give him a hand. But it wasn't a full works car in the strict sense of the word, where Denny just turned up and drove it. In 1963 he was spending some of his time working on the production cars at Motor Racing Developments, for which he would be paid, but the time he spent preparing his racing car was down to him. That was the deal. It was a pretty tough deal and Denny would say so, but I'd have to tell him, "Hang on, Denny — no one said this was going to be easy to get anywhere in motor racing. That's the way it is and I can't change it." All I could do was keep pushing to get him into the confidence of Jack and designer partner Ron Tauranac.

'We were always understaffed at Brabhams, always had fewer mechanics than we should have had, because Jack either didn't want to spend the money or didn't have it to spend. His approach was that if we could get by with four, why did we need five? But Denny was able to pay his way. He had enough income and he had his Formula 1 contract so that if he did well he would be paid as a driver.'

In the British Grand Prix at Silverstone Denny qualified on the fourth row of the 4-3-4 grid in good company, with team boss Brabham, Lorenzo Bandini's Ferrari and Bruce McLaren's Cooper. In the race he retired with a broken alternator belt. The next Grand Prix was the Dutch at Zandvoort, where he started on the third row and worked his way past Surtees' Ferrari for sixth place before an exhaust pipe came loose and a pit stop for repairs lost him a lap. He still finished fifth behind Clark (Lotus), Stewart (BRM),

Gurney (Brabham) and Hill (BRM). He had two more Grands Prix that summer, the German and the Italian.

At the Nürburgring Denny qualified on the fourth row of the grid, beside Brabham and 2.6 seconds faster than the boss, but that was nothing considering the length of the circuit. At least it showed Denny was on the pace in Formula 1, but he was out of the race with a split fuel tank on the sixth lap. At Monza for the first time Denny was in the middle of the fifth row, once again beside Bruce in the Cooper, but the race was not a success as he was sidelined with front suspension failure.

7 Grand Prix starts here

The 1966 season saw Denny step up to a permanent place in Formula 1 as number two to Jack in the Brabham works team, using the new 3-litre Repco V8 engine for the first time. The formula doubled in size from 1500 cc to 3 litres for the 1966 season and Jack had anticipated the change with a special engine built up at Repco in Australia and based on the old F85 aluminium-block Oldsmobile V8. Ironically, Bruce McLaren had used this Olds engine with success in CanAm sports car racing, but opted to abandon it in favour of an expensive and complicated conversion of the 4-cam Indianapolis Ford V8 that proved disastrous . . . while Jack went on to win the World Championship with an engine reckoned to be underpowered in the face of the Italian V12 opposition and the British H16 BRM!

Denny started the season with the 2.5-litre 4-cylinder Coventry Climax, graduating to the Repco V8 for the mid-season French Grand Prix at Reims.

The season started at Monaco and it was soon apparent that the competitive cars were using enlarged 2-litre versions of the 1.5-litre Coventry Climax and BRM V8 engines. Denny started from the third row of the grid beside Bandini's Ferrari — and three rows ahead of Jack! He was a retirement after 16 laps, with a broken drive shaft coupling. Jack was out two laps later with gearbox failure.

The Belgian Grand Prix at Spa was ruined by a rainstorm that lashed the circuit part-way round the opening lap and sent cars spinning in all directions. It was Denny's first race on the fast Spa course and he was well back on the grid. Only seven cars completed the opening lap. Denny had spun into a bank on the streaming track and jumped out of his car to climb the bank out of harm's way, leaving the docile Coventry Climax ticking over. It took him a couple of laps to get back to the pits, where he retired with cock-eyed front wheels. Jack survived to finish fourth.

Reims was run in baking heat and Denny put his new 3-litre Repco-Brabham on to the fourth row. By half-distance he was one of only four on the same lap as the leader — Bandini's Ferrari heading off Brabham, Mike Parkes' Ferrari and Denny. Jack would win, becoming the first driver ever to win a Grande Épreuve in a car bearing his own name.

Denny felt more at home in the British Grand Prix at Brands Hatch, topping the practice sheets on two of the three sessions to start the race from the centre of the front row, with Dan Gurney's Eagle on pole and Jack on the outside. Denny made a poor start and at one stage was down as far as ninth, but he battled back up through the field and by lap 40 he had passed Clark's Lotus and Hill's BRM to take second place, and Jack and he finished 1-2, 9.6 seconds apart. Jack was leading the world championship now and Denny, in his first full season, was third equal with Bandini.

Jack made it three in a row at Zandvoort and the Brabhams underlined their superiority by qualifying 1-2 on the grid, but it was not without excitement. With half an hour left in the last session Jack had just annexed pole when Denny's engine let go in a big way passing the pits. *Autocourse*: 'Inspection of Hulme's engine revealed that a big end bolt had broken and two bearing caps had departed through the side of the block; so much for using production parts (Daimler, in this instance) in racing engines.'

As luck would have it, Denny managed to organise an unofficial running-in practice session on Sunday morning . . . and reverse gear came out the side of the gearbox, but it was repaired for the race! This Dutch Grand Prix was the race where Brabham donned a false beard and hobbled to his car on the grid with a walking stick, poking fun at those who had suggested that, at 40, he was too old to be racing . . . and had no sense of humour. Jack and Jim Clark raced off into the lead, but Denny, who was supposed to be running in a new engine and nursing a suspect gearbox, equalled the lap record on the second lap and passed Clark's Lotus after three laps to tuck in behind his boss. This lasted until lap 17, when Denny headed down the pit lane with what turned out to be a faulty distributor. He had it changed, but the problems stayed and he was out after 37 laps.

Jack went on to his score his fourth successive Grand Prix win at the Nürburgring and move further ahead in the title race. Denny had a bad time in practice, unable to cure the quirky handling of his car; at one stage Jack took Denny's car out to try to diagnose the problem. It turned out to be a solid differential and Denny couldn't better a place on the fifth row of the 4-3-4 grid, beside Jacky Ickx in the fastest Formula 2 Matra. He was out after nine laps with ignition problems. It was a race he would have preferred to forget.

For Monza and the Italian Grand Prix, Jack was on the third row, Denny on the fourth and the crowd were shouting for the Ferraris, two of which — Parkes and Scarfiotti — were fastest on the front row. In the race, Denny found himself in a slipstreaming dice with Parkes, which was dragging him towards the top end of the race. *Autocourse*: 'Behind [race leader] Scarfiotti, Parkes and Hulme carried on their battle for second place in such a manner that the commentator ran out of superlatives; Hulme was more than making up on the corners what he was losing on the straights, and he was quite happy to go round the Ferrari on the outside if there was no room on the inside.' Parkes came in second, with Denny just three-tenths behind, for his best race of that first full Formula 1 season, an indication of the form that would take him to the title a year later.

The American Grand Prix at Watkins Glen produced a freak finish when an H16 BRM powered the winner, but the winner was Jim Clark in a Lotus. Brabham had a strong lead at half-distance after a battle with Bandini's Ferrari, but then Jack was also sidelined with a broken tappet.

Denny had been spooked by the wind in the first practice session, saying that he hadn't had a problem like this at the Glen in Sid Taylor's Lola sports car. Others also complained and settled to wait for the next day's session. Denny started on the fourth row, ironically with Richie Ginther in the Honda, who had also been bothered by the wind on that first day. Denny was running seventh when the oil pressure went south after 18 laps.

Mexico brought another freak result when John Surtees dominated in the V12 Cooper-Maserati, perhaps least confused at the high altitude. Denny had lost time with a broken gear selector, but started from the third row beside Jochen Rindt in the other Cooper-Maserati. Jack was on the second row. Denny had been running behind the leading bunch, but then he lost his clutch — not a terminal fault in itself — spun and stalled at the hairpin. *Autocourse*: 'The lack of a clutch also made it very difficult for him to get away again, but after several attempts he stuttered off in fourth gear — and in eleventh place. Aided somewhat by retirements he soon got back up to sixth, and then took over fifth from Gurney, who was having trouble with a deranged throttle linkage. The retirement of Pedro Rodriguez took him back to fourth and just two laps from the end he caught and passed Ginther, who had slowed earlier because of low oil pressure but then speeded up and recorded the fastest lap of the race in an attempt to regain third place.'

So Jack won his third world title with 42 points and Denny, the newest works Brabham driver, was fourth with 18 points obtained from a second and three third places. David Phipps, editor of *Autocourse*, indulged himself with his Top Ten rating of Formula 1 drivers, placing the new world champion down in sixth place, commenting: 'One of the oldest adages of motor racing concerns the expediency of winning at the least possible speed. One of the most difficult facets of motor racing is to slow down without losing concentration. Jack Brabham is a master in both respects. At Reims he built up a lead of over 40 seconds but let it dwindle to 9.5 seconds. At Brands Hatch his winning margin was 9.6 seconds, and at many Formula Two races it was even less. The same foresight encouraged him to go Grand Prix racing with a car which many people considered hopelessly outclassed. He may not have much to say for himself, but he is usually up on the rostrum, grinning mischievously, when the prizes are handed out.'

Jim Clark topped Phipps' rating, followed by Surtees, Rindt, Stewart and Gurney before the Aussie who won the title. Of special interest to this tome is that, after his first full season, Phipps placed Denny seventh on his Grand Prix scale, one behind Jack, writing that Denny should really be higher than number seven but he could hardly put him ahead of Jack as team owner and leader. 'He has worked his way up slowly, and until 1966 he was generally underestimated, but he showed his ability with a series of sports car victories and followed up a successful Formula 1 season by leading the 1967 South African Grand Prix until his brakes failed. Give Denny the tools and he will undoubtedly finish the job.' Quite what the first Grand Prix of the next season had to do with the 1966 scale of driving scoring is not immediately clear 40 years on, but Denny would prove Phipps' forecasting to be correct.

8 Drama at Le Mans

The Le Mans 24-hour race has all the international importance of a world championship run over a single weekend. In 1966 the Ford Motor Company attacked the French race as though it were a major military exercise. There was a total of 12 Fords in the entry list, with three major teams within the marque line-up. Shelby American, run by the rangy Texan, Carroll Shelby, who had won Le Mans with Roy Salvadori in an Aston Martin in 1959, entered three 7-litre Mk 2 Fords for Ken Miles/Denny Hulme (car No. 1), Bruce McLaren/Chris Amon (No. 2) and Dan Gurney/Jerry Grant (No. 3). Ken Miles was a British ex-pat racing driver and engineer working with Shelby in California. He was 48, Denny was 30. Miles was an established West Coast sports car racer who had made his name with MG specials and Porsches before switching to Fords with Shelby. He was a prickly character, as described by his biographer Art Evans: 'I am fully aware that all who came into contact with Ken Miles didn't have smooth sailing. Even though he lacked much formal education, he was highly intelligent and didn't suffer fools. One of his failings, I think, in personal relationships, was that he would often let the fool know about his foolishness . . .'

That summer Miles had shared the winning Ford in the 24-hour race at Daytona and the 12-hour race at Sebring with the enigmatic Indy driver Lloyd Ruby. Ruby captured my imagination when I discovered that his breakfast was washed down with a mix of Schlitz beer and tomato juice. A win at Le Mans would mean a golden hat-trick for Miles, but his tendency to race his own way and buck corporate race-strategy suggestions did not necessarily stand him in good stead with the Ford hierarchy, who were understandably more anxious for a Ford car to win than any particular driver.

There were a hundred people in the Ford army, with six cars flown to Paris. A 40-foot tractor-trailer outfitted as a machine shop on wheels was shipped from New York to Le Havre. These logistics look unimpressive compared with the modern set-up of the most modest Formula 1 team at any Grand Prix, but in 1966 they were totally awe-inspiring.

Denny had raced at Le Mans in 1961, but things had moved on in the five years since. He was coming back as a front-runner, having gathered big-car experience winning three major races in Britain in Sid Taylor's 6-litre Lola T70 earlier that summer. In *Ford: The Dust and the Glory*, historian Leo Levine describes Miles' team-mate as 'Denis Hulme of New Zealand, at the time the back-up driver on the Brabham team for single-seater events.' In fact, he had driven a 250LM Ferrari at Daytona, but while Miles was winning the race, after 53 laps Denny's Ferrari was the first retirement with transmission failure. They made an odd pairing of talent for Le Mans.

It was a major face-off, with 12 Fords against 13 Ferraris, which ranged from factory cars to private entries. Their challenge was slightly blunted on the second day of practice when John Surtees had an argument with the Ferrari team management, packed his bag and left. Shelby cheekily offered the angry Surtees a Ford drive, but he was rebuffed.

Gurney had been fastest in practice in Ford chassis 1047, from Miles/Hulme (chassis 1015) and Whitmore/Gardner (chassis 1032). The McLaren /Amon Ford (chassis 1046) was fourth in the angled line-up, with starting drivers in circles across the track. They ran, climbed into their cars, and stormed off into the race. Or not, as the case may be. Sir John Whitmore was fast to his car and leapt away but stalled, directly across the nose of Ken Miles' Ford. Miles accelerated away, whacking the side of the stalled car as he took off. He was in at the end of the first lap to fix a door that wouldn't shut properly. It was a brief stop and Miles was back in the race, hammering the lap record as he made up for time lost.

After the first scheduled pit stops the order was Gurney(Ford)-Miles (Ford)-Rodriguez(Ferrari)-Bucknum(Ford)-Hill(Ford)-Parkes(Ferrari)-McLaren(Ford). The McLaren Ford was losing ground through pit stops to change chunking tyres. Such was Bruce McLaren's standing in the racing community that Ford and Shelby were willing to accommodate the black McLaren/Amon Ford on Firestone tyres (to which the two New Zealand drivers were contracted) despite Shelby's team being contracted to Goodyear. In the early stages of the race, McLaren realised their tyre problems could be terminal and agreed a switch to Goodyear, immediately gathering pace and climbing back through the field. These dramas were either unknown or ignored in Levine's official Ford racing history.

The result of the race was not obvious from the standings at 10 p.m., six hours after the start, when Rodriguez and Scarfiotti were running first and second in Ferraris. Three of the mainstream Fords were out of the race. An hour later and the face of the race had changed again, with the Miles/Hulme Ford now leading from Gurney's Ford. There had been problems with brake discs as the torrid early race pace told. There were rain showers during the night, but by dawn the race had settled and the Fords looked comfortable. Gurney, Miles and McLaren were running close, leading the field. By 8 a.m. on Sunday morning the fastest Ferrari was back in eleventh place. An hour later and Gurney's car was crippled with a water leak.

The Fords had eased back, adding half a minute to their lap times, with the race seemingly sown up, depending on fate. And there would be plenty of fate in the next six hours, mainly man-made and manipulated.

Levine records the situation, as it seemed that Ford management could decide the winner: 'Miles smiled when someone asked him about it. It was a typical Miles answer. "I work for the Ford Motor Company," he said, "and they pay me so much a month to do what they want. If they want me to win the race, why I'll do it . . . and if they want me to jump in the lake, why I guess I'll have to do that too." Then he laughed again. Miles and Hulme were in the lead at this stage, a lap ahead of McLaren and Amon, and the lean Englishman assumed he would stay there. A short time later he was told otherwise.' There wouldn't be a lot for Miles to laugh about for the rest of his life.

With two hours left the Ford directors and team management met to discuss the finish. The Miles/Hulme Ford had been well ahead of the McLaren/Amon car, but now they were running together and the management seemingly had the options of (a) letting the two cars race for the finish with the obvious chance of taking each other out, or (b) deciding which drivers would win, inevitably incensing the other pairing. Then there was a (c) option in the offing, too — someone suggested orchestrating a dead heat. There are a variety of fathers of this suggestion. One version has Bruce McLaren having a quiet word with Henry Ford II to suggest a dead heat that would re-arrange the running order, and have the Miles/Hulme pairing warned against a late-race disappearance into the distance.

Before Miles and McLaren took off for their final stint to the finish, they were told that there would be a dead heat. They would cross the line side by side, followed by the Bucknum/Hutcherson Ford several laps back in third place, which would still be OK for a group photograph.

Levine wrote that neither driver liked the dead-heat decision: 'Both wanted to race, but Beebe [Ford Director, Leo Beebe] would have none of that. With a multimillion-dollar programme on the brink of success, he would not take a chance on one of them going off the road in the rain, or on one of them blowing an already tired engine. They were given the procedure. They got in the cars and took off.'

Then word came from the control tower that race officials had realised it was not possible to arrange a dead heat if the cars had been staggered at the start on the unique 'Le Mans start' principle, since abandoned for safety reasons. The McLaren/Amon Ford had been 20 yards beyond the Miles/Hulme car, which had been faster in qualifying, so a 'dead heat' with the cars crossing the line side by side at 4 p.m. would in fact mean that the McLaren/Amon car would officially be the winner on a distance count back.

Chris Amon, the only survivor of the finishing fracas, thinks that his team-mate had engineered a political situation that would see their car winning. In *Forza Amon!* Chris recalled: 'It was pouring with rain and there was a genuine desire among the Ford hierarchy not to take any chances. Then somebody had the bright idea that it might be nice to have a dead heat, but I think the organisers got wind of it and decided it wasn't going to be a dead heat. It didn't really detract from anything as far as I was concerned, because we'd been way behind, we'd caught up, and Bruce was driving the last stint. I had a feeling that Bruce had made up his mind that we were going to win anyway, despite any arrangements the team was trying to make about crossing the line in a photo finish.'

There were further factors to consider now. They could let the drivers continue to the unravelling 'dead heat' and argue the toss later, or they could decide on one driver or another to win, but which driver would that be?

Leo Levine reveals in *Ford: The Dust and the Glory* that all was not what it might have seemed behind the scenes at the Sarthe circuit: 'During the night Beebe had censured both Miles and Gurney for racing for the lead after all the Ferraris had dropped out. They also had trouble of this type with Miles at Sebring and now, at Le Mans, Beebe had threatened to pull him out of the car if the intramural dicing continued. With one team or the other to be favoured, these actions were to weigh against Miles and Hulme, as both McLaren and Amon had run to team orders. Beebe's description of his thought process:

"We could let them go as instructed or we could call them back and reinstruct them. If we did this, we could tell them to go ahead and race — obviously not a good choice — to let Miles win or to let McLaren win. If you let Miles win, you were giving it to a guy who had given you a hard time. If you let McLaren win, you would take it away from a guy who had earned it over the years. From a public relations standpoint, if McLaren won it might look like we didn't know what we were doing. Someone might construe we had an anti-Miles attitude. On the other hand, if we let Miles win we might be thought of, by the foreign press, as being predisposed toward having an American driver up front. Anyone can question the judgement, but no one can say it was not a consciously arrived-at decision — and on the grounds we considered valid and just. To have Ken win would have been more expedient and more popular. But the extent to which McLaren and Amon had played exactly according to our rules militated against Miles. The result was not necessarily popular, even with me . . ." '

This exploration of the background tends to dedicate itself to Ken Miles, leaving Denny in a support role, which in fact he was. But in a situation where neither of the two drivers on the track knew of the dead-heat foul-up, Denny was being judged, by Leo Beebe at least, inevitably as a partner with Miles in his indiscretions and therefore having to accept a situation not of his making.

I have always understood from those watching on the pit counter in the rain as the two Fords rolled up to the finishing flag, side by side, that McLaren accelerated at the last minute to guarantee the win. But now contemporary views suggest that it was actually Miles backing off in a blank gesture of frustration at team instructions.

Ford had finally won and dominated the Le Mans 24-hour race. They would win again, but the first taste of victory is always the best. Their cars finished 1-2-3 and in a strange twist of racing fate, there were three New Zealand drivers in the first two cars — Bruce McLaren, Chris Amon and Denis Hulme. The winning car had been painted black with a silver stripe as a gesture to the New Zealand international sporting colours made famous by the rugby All Blacks.

There were a variety of views on the result. In his *Road & Track* report, Henry Manney wrote: 'It doesn't matter that there was a lot of curious comment in the French papers afterward about Miles and Hulme being almost dragged up on to the winner's podium first and then suddenly being shoved aside for the New Zealanders McLaren and Amon. It doesn't matter about Miles being a bit choked, as why shouldn't he be, having driven a lot of the race out in front and done a lot of the development work. It doesn't matter although it is puzzling. It doesn't matter that an English pilot was heard to remark in jest (not Miles) that those flymin' Antipodeans shouldn't have been transported and why after all that trouble for an American win, Ford didn't have an American driver.'

Miles was furious at the turn of events, in tears of rage at what he regarded as something of a team betrayal. Denny was more pragmatic. He shrugged his shoulders and kicked his heel when asked about his feelings. To him it was just another race and second place wasn't all bad.

Denny would provide his own view to Al Bochroch, author of *Americans at Le Mans*: 'There isn't any question about it. The starting position hassle was academic as Bruce speeded up at the very end and was a car length ahead of Ken at the finish. Ken was very upset. We had led most of the race and we had to slow way down to let Chris and Bruce catch up. Ken just couldn't get over it . . .'

In November 2003, Shelby told Art Evans: 'What we decided was that all three of them [Miles, McLaren and Bucknum], would go over the finish line at the same time. That was a decision made by Leo Beebe and myself. It was passed by Mr Ford [Henry II]. There was never any thought that we didn't want Ken Miles to win. We slowed Ken to let the others catch up. Ken was not asked to let McLaren win. We decided to have all three cars cross the finish line at the same time. The Le Mans officials made up a rule that said that the car that had travelled the farthest by 10 feet would win. It was a rule that wasn't in the book. This is what cost Ken the race. I felt very bad about it. I felt very guilty because Ken did deserve to win. I felt worse about it after he was killed . . .'

Shelby would add that he didn't believe Miles had backed off to let McLaren get ahead.

In 2004, Art Evans wrote in his biography of Miles (*Ken Miles*): 'As the cars approached the finish line on their final lap, Ken purposely slowed down and allowed Bruce to cross ahead. He was angry with the Ford gurus and became rather disconsolate. Winning the world's most prestigious sports car race would have been a real crown to his career.'

Less than a month later — 28 days to be exact — Miles was killed in an unexplained crash while testing a Ford J-car prototype at Riverside in California.

Denny had his first taste of sports car racing in North America that was the basis of the CanAm series in 1966, driving a Lola-Chev entered by the colourful Irishman Sid Taylor. 'Although the Lola failed to finish in all four events we started — Mosport, Laguna Seca, Riverside and Las Vegas — it was a terrific experience. Why did the Lola fail? I suppose the basic reason was that it was getting to be a tired old beast. We had a stub axle break at Mosport, a gearbox input shaft went at Laguna, the crankshaft broke at Riverside and the gearbox split at Las Vegas. But there was very good racing over there and when I could stay up with the boys, or reasonably close to them, I was always quite satisfied. Matter of fact, I thought I would be left behind, because I had no knowledge of any of the circuits. The interesting thing was the way the American drivers seemed to improve as we went along. I thought there were some terrible examples of driving at Mosport, with the notable exception of Mark Donohue, who was young and really good. He has seen some European racing and I think this showed in the way he drove. The big problem at the start of the series was when we came up to lap back markers and they simply didn't look in their mirrors. I saw at least two accidents sparked by this inattention. But as the series progressed, most of the drivers got the message and things improved.'

9 Indy rookie 1967

In May 1967 Denny went to Indianapolis for his first look at the Speedway, testing the Eagle that Lloyd Ruby had driven in the 1966 Indy 500. Ruby would team with Denny in the Ford team for the long-distance races. Denny: 'Jochen Rindt was also at Indy for tests laid on by Goodyear and before we were allowed out we had a great lecture on going slowly while we learned our way round and making sure we didn't lap over 135 mph. Jochen went out in another Eagle and on his third lap he was timed at 149 mph! That caused some consternation and he was called in for an even bigger lecture, while they told me that if I did that I might as well catch the next plane home. So I did my best to be a good boy and eventually turned a lap at 125 mph.

'Indy is definitely different. Going down the straights is no problem at all. The car was really beautiful; there was no wind and no buffeting. Even when I was lapping at 150 mph and the car must have been getting up to 190 mph at the end of the two longer straights, there was surprisingly little noise. It was more like driving a big American sedan. The car didn't appear to change attitude in a corner and at the speed I was doing I only once had understeer in one of the four turns.

'I did around 30 laps during the two days and was beginning to get the hang of things. When you know the circuit better you can begin to judge how much the car is going to slide sideways in a turn, but I would need more experience before I could feel confident about going as close to the protective wall as Mario Andretti does. It would help if there was a grass verge round the outside of the circuit to make me feel at home, I suppose, but Indianapolis isn't made that way and you've just got to learn to drive it the way it's been built.

'One of the things that was initially confusing was the left-foot brake on the Eagle I drove. Most of the Indy cars have this sort of pedal set-up, with the clutch in the centre over the top of the steering column. This takes a little getting used to, but fortunately I'd had experience left-foot braking in my automatic Ford Zodiac in England. But I did get caught out when I first came into the pits, because I trod on the "clutch" and the car pulled up with the devil of a jerk! What you have to remember to do when you're making for the pits is to give the brakes a touch, contort your left foot up to give the clutch a dab while you throw the thing out of gear and then dive back for the brake pedal. The throttle pedal had a hook-over piece, rather like the pedals on a racing bicycle, so that you could heave it back in case of the throttle system jamming. It's important to remember not to let the revs drop too low when you're on dope fuel, because it then takes a little while to pick up the revs again and the whole lot explodes round you in sheets of flame! Very exciting . . .

'One thing I did like with the Eagle was the ignition switch on the steering wheel, but I didn't like the steering wheel itself because it was, in effect, only two side segments of a wheel. Since the steering was so low-geared, I tended to find myself grabbing at nothing when I was turning into the pit lane! The Ford engine in the Eagle was pleasant and reminded me of the engine in our Le Mans Ford. Problem is that the Ford Indy engines don't have as much torque as the Offys, which are definitely quicker out of the corners and with their turbochargers the Offys really go honking on.'

Denny's view of his first appearance in the 1967 Indianapolis 500 is somewhat different from that of the American who ran his car. The Eagle was run by the legendary Smokey Yunick, a race engineer who worked in NASCAR and at Indianapolis, and whose talent saw him linked with the top men at Ford, Chevrolet and Pontiac. Yunick was his real name. It might be pronounced the same as 'eunuch', but that was where the similarity ended. Smokey most definitely had balls and he was a law unto himself. His motto and trademark was 'The Best Damn Garage in Town'. He wrote his autobiography with instructions that it only be published after his death and he set up his own publishing company so that not a word of the book would be changed. It probably suffered from not being edited, but it is certainly Smokey in the first person. It was initially put out as a three-volume set in hardback and later as a thick 650-page paperback, and is well worth finding.

Goodyear wanted to put several Formula 1 drivers into the 1967 Indianapolis 500, including Mike Spence, Jochen Rindt and Denny Hulme. All were rookies. Yunick drove a hard bargain with Goodyear boss, Larry Truesdale. They agreed that Smokey would own the car and the driver would get 50 per cent of the purse. Smokey's contract said he had the right to fire the driver if he didn't qualify on the first day. Goodyear would pay for team mechanics and special tools and all travel expenses. And $40,000 up front . . .

The Indianapolis 500 was also a law unto itself. The track was a 2.5-mile rectangle with four banked turns. It was known as The Brickyard because the track was originally paved with bricks. The shape of the track layout skirted the fields on the outskirts of town that entrepreneur Carl Fisher had bought. Five hundred miles was the furthest distance that could be covered in daylight when the race was first run in 1911.

The event traditionally covered the whole month of May, with the track open for practice until the first weekend of qualifying. Each driver had four laps to set a qualifying time and if they did their run on the first day, those times counted for the front rows of the grid. Times set on the second weekend filled the back half of the grid regardless of whether faster times were set before. So it was important to be fast on the first weekend.

To put the Indy 500 in perspective, it pulled crowds of around 300,000 for the race, making it the biggest sporting event in the world. The first day of qualifying for the Indy 500 was the second biggest sporting crowd in the world. Today, the race is a shadow of its former self, with the traditional 'name' drivers — Foyt, Andretti, Jones, Unser — long retired. Even their sons have raced, won and retired, and now Mario Andretti's grandson, Marco, is racing.

In the sixties, Indianapolis was still a race that drivers like Jim Clark and Jack Brabham regarded as important enough to jet back and forth between Indy qualifying and the Monaco Grand Prix, jeopardising their Grand Prix chances because the Indianapolis purse was so huge.

Denny was Smokey's third choice of the three Formula 1 men offered. It was probably fair to say that Smokey had never heard of Denny and Denny had never heard of Smokey. The car would be a new Eagle from Dan Gurney's workshop in California and it would be powered by a normally aspirated 4-cam 4.2-litre Ford V8. Smokey had never seen one before he opened the crate in Daytona. 'I put the engine on the dyno. I'm disappointed. I decided to clean up the race car body, fair-in the engine, run inner and outer wheel discs and backing-plate fairings to reduce wheel drag and use elliptical metal for suspension components. For the engine, I get more aggressive cams made, and open up the cylinder head ports; in short, I run it 500 rpm more and pick up 40 horsepower.'

Smokey's crew for Indy consisted of himself, T.A. Toomes and his 19-year-old son, Smokey Jr. 'We arrive at Indy last day of April half dead with a bad motel deal. We're in a real-life whorehouse catering mostly to black patrons, but that's not the problem. It's too damn far from the racetrack.'

He describes Denny on first meeting as 'a New Zealander 'bout five foot nine, a little on the porky side, ruddy face. This don't turn out to be love at first sight.'

Jack Brabham and his designer Ron Tauranac were also with Denny.

∧
Finishing a famous second in the 'photo finish' at Le Mans in 1966, sharing the big Ford Mk 2 with Ken Miles. COURTESY HULME FAMILY COLLECTION

∧
In 1967 Denny shared this works Ford with Indy driver Lloyd Ruby. COURTESY HULME FAMILY COLLECTION

^
Denny raises dust ahead of Jackie Stewart's BRM on his way to winning the
1967 Monaco Grand Prix.

^
Taking the chequer to win the 1967 Monaco Grand Prix for Brabham.

^
Denny flying on his way to win the 1967 German Grand Prix at the Nürburgring.

∧
After the Mexican Grand Prix in 1967 Denny was World Champion; he chats with Jim Clark, who had won the race for Lotus.

∧
A concussed Denny being helped away from the wreck of his Brabham after the crash at Pukekohe in 1968.

∧
Indianapolis with the 1968 Eagle.

∧
Jackie Stewart (left) and Denny with Indianapolis drivers Mario Andretti and Bobby Unser at Monza in 1968.

>
Denny shows his bandaged hands at Indianapolis after he received bad burns in an accident during testing in May 1970.

∧
After a CanAm win at Ste-Jovite, Canada in 1969, Denny with Stirling Moss, Bruce McLaren and Lothar Motschenbacher. Bruce came second and Lothar fourth — six of the first seven cars home were McLarens.

PHOTO: J-WAX/CAN-AM NEWS BUREAU, COURTESY EOIN YOUNG

∧
Denny in 1973 with his young South African protégé, Jody Scheckter, nicknamed 'Baby Bear'.
He would win the World Championship for Ferrari in 1979.

PHOTO: BERNARD CAHIER, COURTESY HULME FAMILY COLLECTION

∧
With the Grand Prix 'Golden Oldies' at the 1974 French Grand Prix. From left: Johnny Lurani,
Tony Brooks, Phil Hill, Emerson Fittipaldi, Gi-Gi Villoresi, (unknown in cap), Hans Hermann,
Toulo de Graffenried, Graham Hill, John Surtees and Louis Chiron.

PHOTO: LAT PHOTOGRAPHS, COURTESY HULME FAMILY COLLECTION

In his book, Smokey confesses he can't remember Ron's name and spells Denis 'Dennis'. He knows and likes Jack, who offers to engineer the Eagle chassis if Smokey does the engine. 'How can I get pissed? I got two of the world's best chassis men for free. Jack calls the shots and we do the work.'

The first week was the driver's test and then they had to work up to speed. 'We run a week. He's four miles per hour short and bitching.' Smokey's son quits. He next saw him *four years* later. Jack and Ron worked on the car set-up for 10 days and then went back to Byfleet. Denny tells Smokey he's going back to Surrey too. He will miss the first qualifying weekend and come back to put more miles in the car, get more experience to qualify on the second weekend. This is not what Smokey wants to hear and they get down to arguing over contract details and driver replacement. Then they discuss the car.

Smokey asks, 'Does the car dart on the straights and sometimes jump two lanes either way?' Denny says it does. Smokey asks, 'In the corners does it feel like it's on ice and you are on the edge of push, or loose all the way through the corners in the "on the throttle" parts? If you get a good shot at four and two do you get a little wheel-spin? And does the car get twitchy?' Denny says it's *exactly* like that. It's like Smokey's been riding with him out there.

Smokey says, 'Denny, you need to make up your mind whether you want to risk your fat ass or get behind the concrete wall with me. Every fuckin' car out there that's in the running does all that bad shit and more. If you ain't willin' to extend yourself, go back to Europe. I'm gonna give you 'bout 25 more horsepower for tomorrow. I'm gonna bump steer all four wheels to damn zero. By 9 a.m. tomorrow morning this car will be as ready as it ever will be to qualify. Either go to the driver's meeting and draw a qualifying number or I will. I'm gonna get qualified tomorrow with or without you.' Yunick told Denny that he would sign Rindt in his place, but in fact he had never even spoken to Rindt.

Denny says if he stays and kills himself the next day it will be on Smokey's conscience forever. Smokey retorts, 'If you believe that shit, go home. I've never had anybody hurt bad, let alone dead.'

When Denny is getting into the Eagle the next morning, Yunick says, 'I told him the car and tyres are as good as it gets. Drive it like I tell you, stay off the brakes and when you get back in it, stay in it. Man, he is pissed. I get the bullshit about "If I get killed" again. Three warm-up laps and then the dumb shit wastes his best lap forgetting to put his hand up [the signal to timekeepers that he is starting his run], but fifth, sixth and seventh laps are fast enough to sit outside front row. I bring him in. Goodyear is going ape-shit. Denny is grinning like a hog in a mud hole. First time he calls me "mate". He says, "It's easier going fast than going slower." I say, "No shit . . ."'

By the end of qualifying they have been pushed back to the fourth row of the three-car grid line-up, but they're still well satisfied. The race is on-off for two days, the start delayed by rain. 'We sit under the tarps, lined up on track waiting for the rain to quit, asking and answering the same dumb questions a thousand times. We are about as spooky as 100 cats in a room with 100 rocking chairs.

'When the race finally happens, Denny shows he is a racer and despite all the distractions he ends up fourth. I don't go to the dinner to get the money. Denny gets the check and we split it by mail. He is gone from my life as though we had never met . . .'

Denny found himself one of the Formula 1 Indy commuters after Monaco in 1967. 'There wasn't much time to think about Monaco, though, because the morning after I was flying back to London and then straight on to Indianapolis. And this was an entirely different sort of business. I had done some laps at Indy previously, but I was very raw and inexperienced when I got there this May to drive an Eagle-Ford entered by a very clued-up chap, Smokey Yunick. The car was called "City of Daytona" and I don't think I have ever driven a more thoroughly prepared machine. Smokey really knows his Indy, and I was full of admiration for the way he and his boys went about their business.'

In hindsight Denny obviously had a rosier view of the situation than Smokey did . . .

Donald Davidson, an English ex-pat who worked on the statistics side of the United States Auto Club as a race historian, first met up with Denny when he had arrived back from his win in the 1967 Monaco Grand Prix and was ready for his debut race at Indy. 'I was with *Autoweek* editor Leon Mandel, and Leon asked Denny what he had thought of the American ABC television coverage of Lorenzo Bandini's blazing crash at Monaco. I remember Denny shrugging and saying, "Well . . . it happened . . ." I thought that was typical of Denny. I told him I was amazed that he was going to drive for Smokey Yunick. I said, "You two guys are from such different worlds that I can't believe you'd ever have *heard* of each other . . . how did you two get together?" He said, "Well, as a matter of fact I had *not* heard of him. I first learned about the drive when I read it in Pit & Paddock in *Autosport!* A day or two later I got a telegram from Goodyear telling me to report to garage so-and-so at Indianapolis and I'd be driving for Smokey Yunick. I honestly had no idea who he was! So I showed up in the garage area, went into the garage and asked if there was a guy called Smokey Yunick in here? They pointed to a guy in a cowboy hat and I said, 'I'm Denis Hulme . . . I'm your driver.' " And that's how the two of them met, after the car assignment had been made! That was kind of alarming in some ways, because the days of the driver being hired by the car owner upon reputation had obviously changed quite a bit . . .'

Denny takes up the story in his *Motor Racing* column: 'Of course, I had to take my rookie test, since I hadn't raced there before. And before that I had to take the most thorough medical I've ever known. At least I came away satisfied that I was fairly healthy! The rookie tests were quite a challenge, and the first of them — 10 laps at 130 mph — was the toughest. You can't count any lap slower than 129 miles an hour, or quicker than 134 miles an hour. And believe me it's not easy to gauge your speed accurately, because the rev counter fluctuates and is no real guide.

'Anyway, I got through the first three stages of the test, moving up from 130 mph to 135 mph and then to 140 mph, and then took the final 145 mph test the next morning. You have to wait at least half an hour between each of the first three tests, and since there are other cars on the circuit at the same time you can be messed about through the yellow caution light going on. The first three stages took up a whole day, and I was very relieved when they were over.

'After passing my final test I went out again to try to build up some reasonable speeds, and the same afternoon got round at 157 mph. I had the feeling it was going to be fairly straightforward, but then I got stuck and it took me another two weeks to break into the 161–162 mph bracket. It was very worrying not to be able to get over the 160 mph barrier, and we thought we had a handling problem. It was a problem I just couldn't work out, because though I could drive the car round the corners to a point where it would understeer or hang the tail out, I was not sure what would happen if I tried to do it a little quicker.

'The only thing to do was to get some good advice, and so Smokey asked Gordon Johncock — he qualified third fastest — to take out the car and give his opinion. He took it up to 155 mph and came in to say very firmly that he didn't like it, though he couldn't tell us exactly what was wrong with it. It was a big help knowing that a good Indy driver thought the car was wrong, because it confirmed my opinion and assured Smokey that I was correct in my assessment.

'The result was a terrific overnight session on the car, during which everything was checked and the suspension was put back more or less symmetrical, instead of having an extra 30 lb loading on the left rear wheel.

This did the trick, and the car immediately felt greatly improved. I went out the next morning and with 10 per cent nitro in the fuel got up to 163 mph. Quite a few people qualified and I went out for two laps more, just to get the feel of the car on 20 per cent nitro.

'They wheeled me out around 3 o'clock in the afternoon, which is not regarded as a good time (the most favoured period is between 5 and 6 o'clock, when the atmosphere is said to be better for high speeds) and I got myself into the right frame of mind for qualifying. You are allowed a maximum of three laps before taking the green flag for the qualifying effort of four laps. In fact, my second lap was my quickest — almost 165 mph — but I hadn't been expecting this, and I didn't indicate I wanted to be officially timed until the third lap. I found it very difficult to judge the sort of speed I was getting.' This sparked Smokey's 'dumb shit' comment . . .

'I knew that I had to qualify at over 163 mph, and it was arranged that I would stop if I dropped under that speed. To my surprise, I got over 164 mph on the first lap, and was just under 164 mph on the next two. But, on the third lap I got it all sideways on one corner, and that sobered me up for the last lap, which was just under 162 mph. My average was 163.376 mph, and this was enough to get me on to the grid without any danger of being 'bumped' off. I was very relieved, I can tell you, because this qualification is a very nerve-wracking business.

'The boys immediately got to work on the car, and about three hours later it was nothing but a shell. The whole machine was stripped and everything was crack-tested. Everything that had a bearing was replaced, and the mechanics found two cracked parts — one in the transmission and one a half-shaft — either of which could have put me out of the race. They slipped in another Ford V8 engine, fitted an extra oil cooler, gave me about 15 laps on the Friday before the race for carburetion tests, and then made the final preparations.

'The race engine was the fourth one we had used. Only one of them had broken — a bolt came out of the timing case and went through the top of the cam cover — and the race engine came straight off the production line. I have no idea at all what power it was giving, but it was a really sweet one.

'During those two weeks I spent at Indy before the race the driver who really impressed me was Mario Andretti. It was almost worrying to watch the nonchalant way he would get into his car and warm up at 163 mph while I was still struggling to reach that speed. His driving at Indy was the best confirmation that experience there really does pay off.

'The turbine car was very interesting, but I think that Indianapolis will lose its flavour if such things are allowed. It had no noise — just a whisper along the straight, so quiet you hardly knew it had gone past — and it had no glamour for the crowds. But it looked like being a sure winner. Everyone agreed that though the brakes and transmission might fail, the turbine engine would never break. And sure enough it was the transmission that went.

'When we started the race on the first day I was on the eighth row of the grid, and was taking it easy, playing myself in, when the rain came down and the race was postponed to the next day. I was very pleased that it did rain, because I was already out of brakes! We'd got the wheels faired-in with ally plates, and these were preventing air from getting to the brakes. These were cut off before the race began again the next day, otherwise I would never have finished fourth.

'Everyone was allowed to do any work on the cars when the race was stopped, so long as it was carried out on the road in front of the pits. Andretti, for example, changed his clutch, and I suppose an engine could have been changed providing it was done in the pit road. Everyone took advantage of this prolonged pit stop to top up with fuel, which was a relief to many drivers. [The cars use about a gallon for each 2.5-mile lap!]

'When we restarted again next morning, in line astern in the positions we were holding when the race was postponed the day before, I picked up about four places and then settled down in around fifteenth position. By halfway I had moved up to seventh, but when various fuel stops had been made and things were stabilised I was back to tenth. Then I suddenly found myself seventh again. You don't really know who you are passing, or who is passing you. You just keep going and hope you are doing well.

'I saw Jackie Stewart walking back to his pits and learned that I was fifth. Then I saw the turbine car in trouble and knew I had moved up another place. Although the race average was quicker than ever, the yellow light was on for a total of an hour and a quarter, which meant that the pace was really hot on the green. I was averaging around 160 mph for a long time.

'On the second to last lap we had been on the amber light, and I was hoping it would stay on until the chequered flag, to make sure of my fourth place. But the light went green again out of turn 4, and I accelerated behind Al Unser — who was in second place — as he pulled out to pass a bunch of cars. The next thing I knew was that the yellow light was on again and four cars behind me had all disappeared! I knew there had been some sort of accident, and so the next lap round I went carefully, and sure enough found the track completely blocked — or so it seemed. I knocked the car out of gear and let the engine tick over as I picked my way through the wreckage, and then I saw Smokey waving at me to cross the finish line.

'It was over, and I was really tired. They asked me if I wanted lifting out of the cockpit, and I said, "Yes, you might as well", because I had developed cramp in my right leg during the race. I had been strapped in very tight, and the wind buffeting was tiring. Before the race I had had the cockpit sides built up to cure the buffeting, but it is always a problem at these high speeds.

'The biggest problem driving at Indianapolis is to keep out of trouble. But I don't think there is any excuse for people having accidents on the yellow light (when everyone is supposed to keep the same position). These

Indy cars are interesting to drive, and they take a lot of stopping — you probably don't realise how quick you are going at the end of the straights.

'One interesting feature is that you can switch your fuel supply from either tank, and by operating the fuel tap you can drain a tank depending on whether you want understeer or oversteer. The car tended to oversteer on full tanks, and so I drained the outside tank first to get this under control. Between each fuel stop I changed the fuel flow a couple of times, to try to keep the car neutral. You can tell you are carrying a lot of fuel, because when you brake hard all the fuel goes rushing to the front, and the fuel bags squeeze in on your legs. Our boys did a great job at the fuel stops, and each of them only cost 25 seconds. We used the same tyres throughout.

'I had started the race determined to play it cool. There were to be no heroics from me and I made up my mind not to take any chances. These tactics paid off, and I left Indianapolis feeling I had a lot more to learn if I wanted to go back there again next year. If I do drive at Indy again I would want to spend more time there before the race, because this year I hadn't enough time to do everything properly. But there was a lot of satisfaction in coming fourth, and I can only say "thank you" to Smokey and his boys for giving me such a good car and such wonderful service.'

10 World Champion!

Denny started the season that would see him become champion of the world by embarking on a do-it-himself project fitting the Hulme Surbiton flat with central heating. The fact that it was winter in Surrey prompted the exercise and, as he observed, it was rather different to putting tubes together to make a space frame racing car chassis . . .

'It will be pleasant to go back to New Zealand because I haven't been there since the 1964 Tasman Series. I'm naturally looking forward to seeing my parents again, but it will be fairly rushed. There are nine races in the series — four in New Zealand and five in Australia — and the car I'll be driving left Liverpool at the end of November and is due in Auckland around Christmas Day.

'It's the car I used in the earlier Grands Prix in 1966 when it was fitted with a 2.5-litre 4-cylinder Climax and I reckon it's a good chassis. It handled very well and I've got special memories of it in practice at Monaco. With a 2.5-litre Repco V8 it should suit the tight and twisty New Zealand tracks.'

The 1967 season would be Denny's busiest yet. Busiest ever. The Tasman Series, the Formula 1 championship Grands Prix, Daytona and Le Mans with the big Fords, the Indianapolis 500, and the CanAm series.

At Kyalami for the first Grand Prix of the season, Denny had the same Brabham he had raced at Mexico, with the same Repco V8, which had been pulled down and rebuilt over the winter. Jack had a new type of cam follower in his engine and the cam follower guides came loose on the first day of practice, coming out and hitting the camshaft, doing a lot of damage to the head. Fortunately it could be repaired overnight.

'Jack was fastest on the first day of practice before his engine lunched itself, and I was fourth, but I made up for it the next day and we had both Brabhams on the front row. Jack had raced at Kyalami before but it was my first time there and I found the circuit very interesting. At first I thought it was a bit narrow, but after driving around it I decided that widening it wouldn't be the answer to the overtaking problem. You still wouldn't get round some of the fast curves even if they were made wider. There were some interesting uphill and downhill sections, a couple of tight corners and one or two very fast ones. It was the nicest track I'd been on for a long time.

'Everybody had overheating problems in practice and during the heat of the second day, which was probably the hottest of the four days we were at the track, the tarmac temperature was 136°F! We had a problem with fuel vaporisation and we made up some special air ducting to cool the fuel injection pump. We also used dry ice to cool the petrol before the start and had a special arrangement to cool the Lucas injection "Bomb", which we didn't show until race morning.

'We had half an hour of practice time on race day but I didn't go out, preferring to save my tyres. When the race started I got away to a flier and was leading comfortably. I remember feeling that this was very pleasing and when Jack spun off on the third lap, I was left with a 5-second lead and nobody in my mirrors. From then on I found it possible to extend my lead all the way. The car was running beautifully, the temperatures were reading normally, and at half-distance, when I had a minute's lead, I was reckoning the race was in the bag. I told myself that all I had to do was to start easing up and taking it steady. I'd set a new lap record on my third lap and this was with almost full tanks. I was keeping a close watch on the tyre wear in my mirrors because we had an idea we might have a problem, but fortunately there was a lot of oil going down and this helped to preserve the rubber. There was also a lot of cement dust and this actually jammed the throttle slides on my car for a few laps. I was getting angry at the marshals, but then I realised that when I'd gone through the dust, the others had vision problems behind me.

'On the sixtieth lap — with 20 to go — I had to pump the brake pedal, first once and then on the next lap I'd have to pump the pedal twice . . . then the brakes completely disappeared! I couldn't believe it — I'd been out front cruising and now I was heading down the pit lane, shouting for the mechanics to get some brake fluid, and going out again because I knew they wouldn't have been expecting me in the pits, let alone for brake fluid. I stopped again next time round — *just* — and they topped up the master cylinders. The pause and the stop had cost me 90 seconds and I went out again to discover that I couldn't get any more pressure than I'd had before. I came in again after three laps and asked them to bleed the brakes, but they discovered that this was impossible because the bleed nipple was tucked in behind the wheel, so I went out again and eventually finished fourth. So near and yet so far. If I'd realised what the problem was I probably wouldn't have stopped, just kept soldiering on because, even with my pedal problem, I could still stay ahead of Pedro Rodriguez who eventually won in the Cooper-Maserati.

'Without anchors it was quite impossible. It was a terrible sensation, driving without any brakes at all. I was using the gearbox as much as I could, but that was nowhere near enough to maintain any sort of lap time. After hurtling down that long swooping straight at over 160 mph it takes quite a bit of stopping . . . without brakes.

'One minute I thought I had 9 points in the bag and eventually I only got 3, which was rather disappointing. It was going to be my first Grand Prix win and it was all so easy . . . too easy to be true. I couldn't imagine where the rest of the field had got to! But there was no time to moan about the South African result because we had to catch a plane straight after the race on our way to New Zealand. Unfortunately our plane was late into Sydney and we missed the connection to Auckland. This meant that we only had one day of practice.

'Jack's car was late arriving by boat and it was in terrible shape when it arrived, having been left out in the weather at Liverpool before being loaded. It was fitted with the new 2.5-litre Repco V8 and it looked really beautiful, just like the genuine racing engine that it is. The heads sit lower on to the block, it had a different cam, different timing gear and different cam covers and exhaust system. There was a slight oiling problem — the cam cover gaskets weren't fitting properly — but after a night's work by the mechanics, who had to get it into the chassis for the first time, it did a very good lap in the short time Jack had for practice.

'This particular engine had 255 bhp when it was run up for the first time, but the previous 2.5 only had 230 bhp, so we were pleased with the outcome.

'My car was ready and looking good and I was looking forward to racing in my own country again. The organisers let Jack and me have a drive on the Friday, but it was not an official practice session so we had to start from the back row. My car was the car Jack had driven in 1964 when he had his accident at Pukekohe. The Climax engine was actually the unit that powered Bruce McLaren's Cooper when he won the 1960 Argentine Grand Prix, so it was an oldie but a goodie.

'We changed the gear ratios overnight and gave the car a thorough check-over. We had a bunch of amateur mechanics who hadn't worked on racing cars before, but we gave them a list of things to do. They worked all through the night and were quite pleased to, because they were thrilled at the way the car had been performing.

'We started the 12-lap preliminary from the back of the grid and Jack was having his problems with several of the back markers, eventually overdoing it and going off the track. The damage was not too bad but it had to be taken 20 miles to a garage to have new radius arms and the suspension straightened. All this was done in an hour and a half, which was a good effort!

'I finished fourth in that race to put me on the second row of the grid for the Grand Prix. We were full to the top on fuel but the car didn't have its original tanks and we hoped 15 gallons would last the race. When the flag dropped Jackie Stewart (BRM), Jim Clark (Lotus) and Richard Attwood (BRM) were ahead of me and while Jackie and Jimmy pulled away, I found I could stay with Richard until he spun trying to avoid a back marker. Close to the finish, Jimmy was carved up by a back marker, lost his nose and drove the last laps hanging on to his helmet, keeping Jackie's BRM in sight and finishing second. I watched it all happen from the pit lane. My race finished with seven laps left. The car was running perfectly and was 18 seconds ahead of Richard's BRM when a stub axle broke. Nothing dramatic happened. The wheel didn't come off because the disc brake held it jammed between the callipers, so we didn't come to any harm and I received quite an ovation — which I thought was quite unusual for a New Zealand crowd! Jack retired with a broken half-shaft. Jackie won for BRM, with the battered Jimmy second in the Lotus and Richard third in his BRM.

'The next weekend we were at Levin but the less said about that race the better. I didn't finish but the race didn't count for Tasman points. At Wigram I finished fifth in the preliminary with a mysterious misfire, so we changed the shims on the injection metering unit and also changed spring rates, because on the long, fast back straight the car was picking up the inside rear wheel. This was at around 120 mph and there was smoke coming off the tyre, which was a bit disconcerting for the tyre guys. In the final, my car got worse and worse but I still managed a third place finish. Down at Teretonga outside Invercargill things hadn't improved, although the fuel injection had been checked and the electrics were changed, but we kept richening the metering unit and eventually it started running a lot better.

'Jim beat me for pole by 0.1 seconds. I had very close ratios in the gearbox, with a very long top gear because it has one long straight and the rest is very twisty and tight. I won the first eight-lap heat from Jimmy, but we were worried at the fuel mileage. I started the main race from pole with Jim Clark, Richard Attwood and Piers Courage, who was having his first Tasman race for BRM. At least I *should* have started, but when I let the clutch in, the car just stood still on the grid, with bottom gear stripped. We quickly stripped the box, picked all the lumps out of it, put a new low gear in and I set off again to check the car on full tanks, but after a few laps fourth gear stripped and we called it a day.'

At Lakeside near Brisbane, Denny was battling Repco oil leaks with Araldite after practice when the two Scots annexed the front row, Clark on pole with the Lotus and Stewart beside him in the BRM. Jack and Denny were on the second row with the Brabhams. Denny was running fourth in the race, though he had to make a pit stop to tighten nuts on the left front wheel. He finished fourth with near-bald Goodyears, behind Clark, Brabham and Gardner.

Down to Sydney's Warwick Farm circuit and Denny was entertaining the reporter from *Sports Car World*: 'Hulme was going through the Esses in a series of full-bore crossed arm slides with smoke pouring off both rear tyres, practically yawning with the sheer boredom of it all as the flaggies took to their heels at his approach . . . ' There were problems with the metering unit later and Denny was back on the third row with sixth fastest time. He battled down in fifth and sixth and was probably relieved when the radiator hose blew on lap 41 and he stopped out at Creek Corner. Next race on the Tasman schedule was at Sandown Park outside Melbourne.

'Sandown is a really nice circuit on a horse race track as at Pukekohe,

Levin and Warwick Farm. It's got a fantastic grandstand and the motor circuit goes even closer to the grandstand than the horses do, which gives the spectators really good value and view. It's a circuit I like to race on, with two reasonably long straights, a few twists and Esses. We spent a few days testing, trying different oil breathers and wheel sizes, but our main problem was the heat. For the three days we were there, we were working in temperatures around 104° — there were times when I wished we could be back in England to cool down a bit! For all the testing, we had engine problems on the first day of practice, so I only did one day of qualifying which got me on the front row with Jack and Jackie. In the first 10-lap race Jack won, but he coasted over the line with a dead engine, just pipping Jackie's BRM and I was third. Fortunately we had a spare block with us, with the heads polished and the valves in and this was used to build up a spare engine in a hurry. The big rumour round the paddock was that Jack had taken out this 2.5-litre V8 in order to put in a 3-litre for the final!

'Jack led from the start and I got past Jim Clark's Lotus on the first straight and then went with Jackie. Things were looking better for us . . . until a wire came adrift in Jack's ignition, which put him out of the race. Jackie was now leading, but not for long — he was out with a broken transmission. Now I was leading and it felt comfortable, but it was only to last another few laps and my engine started misfiring, as it had done in earlier races. Jim was now up with me and we swapped the lead lap after lap until we arrived at the Esses and my gearbox felt queer. It had broken the third gear selector, but I didn't realise it at the time. After pulling into the pits I fiddled with the gear lever, got two gears at once and that was the end of my race. Jim went on to another series win and our only consolation was Jack's new lap record.

'The final race of the series was at Longford in Tasmania. In the first practice, Jackie went out and really trampled the lap record. It was a very fast circuit with lots of interest, including a couple of bridges and a railway viaduct. There was also a level crossing where the cars were airborne. On the fastest stretch there was a timed one-eighth of a mile where we were recorded at 173 mph, which was 9100 rpm in my car, without a tow. At the end of this long straight you had to stand on the brakes because the corner was sharper than Thillois at Reims. Longford was a track where horsepower paid off and it became apparent that Jackie's BRM had as many horses as we did from our Repcos. At the end of practice Jackie and Jack shared fastest lap — and the hundred bottles of champagne. I was third fastest, with Jim just behind me. There were two heats on the Saturday and the final was on the Monday. In the first heat Jackie broke his transmission on the line and Jack and I romped away, leaving Jim in our wake. In the second heat Jackie was in Chris Irwin's BRM and finished second to Jack, while I retired with a burned-out ignition box. We fitted a new one for the final, but it lasted only four laps again . . . so at least I was consistent. Jack won from Jackie, now back in his own BRM, and Jack must have been relieved to see the chequered flag because he'd had a broken exhaust pipe and he had flames pouring out of the pipe directly on to the metering unit and we worried that the whole car would go up! So Jack's win was good news for our team and I had further good news on the morning of the race when I learned that I'd become the father of a big bouncing boy we would call Martin.

'After Longford I took time off to visit Greeta and our new arrival in New Zealand and got back to England on the Friday night before the Race of Champions at Brands Hatch. The car I had was the one Jack had won with at Silverstone the previous season, and during the short practice session on the Saturday we found that our cars weren't as quick as they'd been for the British Grand Prix at Brands the year before. So much for progress. The first heat was dismal and the mechanics changed roll bars and altered braking ratios, but then the timing chain broke . . .

'Easter was a busy weekend and I was racing Sid Taylor's GT40 at Snetterton, but the brakes faded and I finished second to Aussie Paul Hawkins in another GT40. In the Formula 2 race I could only manage fourth and Jack was sixth. The interesting thing about these new Formula 2 cars is that they don't give the impression that they're going as fast as the stopwatches show!'

At Silverstone on Easter Monday Denny won in the GT40, with Hawkins second. 'We had more cooling ducts for the brakes. Paul had led initially until he had a really monumental spin at Becketts on the second lap. Paul had passed me when I selected a bunch of wrong gears twice on the first lap. The ZF gearbox in the GT40 has a nice change . . . providing you know which gear you're going to select. It's rather embarrassing when you get the wrong ratio at 150 mph! I think the problem is that there is no feel in the change. Frankly, I would prefer a crash box . . .'

May 1967 was Denny's month, perhaps the most important month of his career. He had been disappointed in the opening Grand Prix of the season in South Africa, when he looked like winning and then his brakes had failed. 'I suppose it could have happened again at Monaco, but somehow everything seemed to click on the day. Believe me, it was a wonderful feeling to cross the line with Louis Chiron waving the chequered flag and knowing that at last I had achieved my ambition of winning a classic Grand Prix.'

Chiron was a Monegasque born in 1900 and had won the Monaco Grand Prix driving a Bugatti in 1931. He was a character from racing history and was not quite up with the modern generation. As he led Denny to the royal box to meet Prince Rainier and Grace Kelly he leaned across and said, 'Excuse me, monsieur, but what is your name?'

'Things went quite well during practice, although I was still well back on the grid with only a short time to go in the last session. I couldn't get the car to handle as I wanted at the two hairpins at the Gasometer and the Station. I felt I was probably as quick as anybody else on the rest of the circuit, but I wanted to save time on these two vital points. At Monaco in 1966 with the 2.5-litre Climax-engined car, I had found that the quick way round these corners was to brake very late and slide into them. This year with the 3-litre, I couldn't get this to happen absolutely right in practice until we put more braking on the rear wheels. It then became possible to lock up the rear wheels and make the car nearly — but not quite — spin. When I got that sorted I made a time I considered to be satisfactory for equal fourth.

'Almost as soon as the race had started I heard Jack's engine going on to seven cylinders going up the hill to the Casino. At the time I thought he must have fouled a plug, but then he spun at Mirabeau, which certainly suggested something more serious than a plug! I was right behind Jack when it happened and Jackie Stewart was right behind me, but to our surprise we got through quite easily. Behind us, the incident had sparked off a tricky situation, because Jack's car and also Jo Siffert's (which had nudged the back of Bruce's McLaren when they braked) dropped a lot of oil all the way along the waterfront to the Gasometer hairpin. The oil was the full width of the road and it gave me something of an advantage, because my car felt good on the oil. But I certainly didn't take any risks at the chicane after getting all crossed-up the first time through. This was where Jackie Stewart was so quick when the oil was down . . . in fact, it was the only point on the circuit where he was gaining on me.

'Jackie got by me at the Gasometer hairpin, slipping through on the inside, and after that he began to pull away. He was driving very well indeed, but then his crown wheel and pinion broke as it had done on the Tasman series, leaving me with quite a useful lead, but it wasn't going to be a cakewalk. Jim Clark — the one I was most concerned about — and some of the others started catching up and there seemed to be little I could do about it. Lorenzo Bandini was flying, too, and was catching me at about half a second a lap. When you're going really fast at Monaco the chicane seems to get narrower, and when you were powering through there I don't suppose there was more than an inch gap on either side of the car. During the race I got a bit tweaked on one occasion coming out of the chicane and brushed some of those straw bales on the quay, but fortunately the car got itself straight again. I also made contact with the guardrails at the Tabac corner and ran over the pavement at the Hôtel de Paris, but the car seemed to be able to stand the punishment. The engine took a good hammering too, because I decided to use first gear from the Station hairpin down to the waterfront, instead of going up to second gear as I had done in practice. This meant I was running up to 8000–8200 rpm on every lap, but the Repco stood up well.'

Denny skirted the fatal Bandini crash in his *Motor Racing* diary. Denny had taken the lead from Bandini's Ferrari coming out of the tunnel on the second lap. Jackie Stewart had been a brief irritant in the BRM, but on his retirement Denny was left in the lead with an 8-second margin over Bandini and was able to build this to 20 seconds on lap 82, when Lorenzo clipped the bales at the exit of the chicane, finishing upside down in a blazing car that also set fire to the straw bales. The Italian driver died later in hospital. It was the twenty-fifth running of the Grand Prix on the streets of Monaco; there were only six finishers and Denny won his first Grand Prix by a clear lap from Graham Hill's BRM at an average of 75.9 mph.

Denny flew to Indianapolis for the 500 and when he came back to Europe for the Dutch Grand Prix at Zandvoort his Monaco-winning car felt strangely small and light compared with the car he had driven on the Speedway. 'It was a change, but a pleasant change and I was soon tossing the car around and doing anything I liked with it.' Denny qualified sixth on full tanks, but his start was compromised by a man standing in front of him on the grid! 'I remember thinking to myself: suppose I run him down, it will make a hell of a mess and probably put me out of the race. The starter with the flag should have seen the chap standing in the middle of the cars, should have waited, but he didn't and I was delayed. I didn't want the leaders to get too far ahead. I caught Jack with the new Repco in his car and it was clear that it was giving more power. It accelerated better than mine, but there were big sheets of flames coming from his exhausts on the over-run, which made it rather alarming if you got too close. Then I had a fine old dice with Chris Amon's Ferrari. I had passed him early on and then got ahead of Jochen Rindt, leaving Chris stuck behind the Cooper, but he was soon through and cut down the gap. He could out-brake me into the hairpin, but I could pull away on the back section of the circuit. This meant that when we came on to the main straight he was not close enough to slipstream me and overtake.' Denny finished third.

For Le Mans, Ford had paired Denny with American Indy driver Lloyd Ruby in the big Mk 4 GT. 'Lloyd had never driven at Le Mans before and he wasn't particularly keen on trying to set up the car, so he left that part of it to me. We were fourth fastest in practice and I took the first stint in the race, but early on I had to make a pit stop to deal with a sticking throttle that had put me off the road at Tertre Rouge and again at Arnage. The stop for repairs cost us time within a few minutes of the start, so when I went out again I tried to catch up what had been lost and without overstraining the car. This wasn't particularly easy because there were a lot of cars in the race and it was like London in the rush hour going down the Mulsanne straight.

'I pressed on and slowly picked up places, not taking too much notice of the set times that had been suggested, and managed to break the lap record. Two laps later I broke it again! I caught up with Frank Gardner in a Ford Mk 2 and we started to circulate together, helping him with a tow. We weren't swapping places in the slipstream because these Fords go too fast for that and the circuit isn't wide enough for you-tow-me-and-I'll-tow-you with the speeds these Fords can reach. You can feel another Ford coming up behind down Mulsanne and the air pressure from the nose of that car turns the back of yours, so if there is a Ford behind that is determined to pass, the safest thing to do is lift off and let him through, otherwise you could *both* be off the road.

'Frank and I got faster and faster and I eventually topped my own lap record, and all done without caning the car unduly. We were doing close to 220 mph and at that speed it was necessary to watch things closely, especially towards the end of the straight where there was a gap in the trees with a cross-wind that sent the car from one side of the road to the other without turning the wheel! With the extra speed of the Mk 4, we couldn't take the kink on the straight flat this year.

'The car seemed good and we were hauling back some of the lost time when my mate Lloyd put it into the sand sideways, damaging the front. This took half an hour to repair, but a few hours later the car was back in the sand at Tertre Rouge and we were out of the race. I set off for home Sunday morning and was back in time to listen to the finish on the radio at 4 p.m. that afternoon. It was good to see Dan Gurney winning for Ford. When the team had a triple shunt during the night they must have had their fingers crossed. I thought A.J. Foyt proved a very capable partner for Dan. It was his first time at Le Mans, but he didn't do anything silly at any time. Frankly, though, I did feel that the Americans doing Le Mans for the first time found it a bit daunting.'

For the Belgian Grand Prix at Spa, Jack had a new lightweight car and Denny had his cast-off fitted with one of the new engines, but he was having problems making the car handle. 'The moment I lifted off and touched the brakes, it wanted to sort of jack-knife and at the kind of speeds you get up to at Spa this was a bit off-putting . . .' He qualified fourteenth and was out with engine problems but happy for Gurney to win again. 'It's always good to see a new marque getting its first Grand Prix win and I'll bet Dan felt better about Spa than he did about Le Mans. To have these two wins on successive weekends must have put his tail right up!'

The old Spa course over public roads was all about raw speed and Denny was bothered by the siting of some of the guardrails. 'There are guardrails on the Masta Kink that appear to have been so placed that if you get into trouble, you are bound to be deflected straight into a house!'

Denny Hulme was definitely the hot ticket during the European summer of '67. At Reims the weekend after Spa he was signed to drive a Brabham in the Formula 2 race and shared Sid Taylor's brand new Lola-Chev T70 GT in the 12-hour race with Frank Gardner. 'It hadn't turned a wheel until we took it out for practice and on the second lap it nearly became a very second-hand piece of machinery. A radius arm had pulled out of a top wishbone and it was fortunate that we were still running the car in and I wasn't going much more than 100 mph, because the front upright fell off. I ran out on to the grass and pulled up safely, but it certainly gathered my total attention . . .'

The new Lolas were fast, but they were also fragile. 'We were running a lap behind the 6-litre Lola-Chevs of John Surtees and Paul Hawkins, and they both went out within 10 minutes of each other. I think they tried to turn the race into a sprint and I'm doubtful whether reasonably highly tuned Chev units are quite the thing for a 12-hour race. When they retired we were left with a lead of about three laps and after another hour we were four laps in the lead. It looked as though we had it made, but at 6.30 a.m. the fan pulley broke on the crankshaft and it took 20 minutes to repair. I took over the wheel and decided to press on as hard as I was able and we pulled back from fifteenth to fifth, and then the water temperature started to climb and it started to boil and by 8 a.m. it was on seven cylinders and out of the race.'

It was not unusual then to drive in several different races over a weekend and Denny slipped back to his hotel for some sleep before the start of his Formula 2 race for Brabham. 'The Formula 2 affair was a real slipstream special, the sort you expect at Reims, and I realised halfway through that fifth would be the best I could manage. The brakes on my car were most impressive, but I was always the last of the leading five at the end of the long Thillois straight. Whatever I did, I could never manage to lead the pack because my engine just didn't have enough horses, and Jochen Rindt went through to win. This Reims slipstreaming looks dangerous and on a number of occasions it has been, with the odd near-miss now and then, but at least it provides more of a spectacle than the boring Bugatti circuit at Le Mans, where we went the next weekend.

'The Bugatti circuit twists through the car park of the long 24-hour course and is definitely *not* a Grand Prix track, even though it would suit our Brabhams. Le Mans gets its fair share of racing with the 24-hours and I don't see why they should have a Grand Prix three weeks later.'

Denny didn't like the place. He preferred life to be smooth and casual and at his relaxed pace, and he was fed up with the problems over passes and facilities and access during the 24-hour race. To have to go through it all again so soon in the same place was too much of a challenge to his patience. He had a new BT24, a lighter version of the car Jack was racing. 'I liked my new car the first time I drove it. The brakes were very impressive, but the surprising feature was that it didn't give the impression of being a 3-litre machine. There wasn't a tremendous feeling of acceleration when I put my foot down, but it was getting away from corners very quickly and of course the combination of light weight and a useful torque band was nicely matched to the circuit. I couldn't help feeling that this BT24 would have been really great at Monaco earlier in the season!'

Denny's major race problem was in the cockpit. 'My car was modified slightly during the race because after three laps I lost the gear lever knob. The thread stripped on the lever and so the next time I came round I threw the knob into the pits, so that they'd know what was wrong if they heard me miss a change! Unfortunately, the lever itself was very short and didn't give much leverage, besides which it was a pretty hard piece of metal when the knob had disappeared. Since I was making about 19 changes every lap it wasn't surprising that my right palm was decorated with a few blisters and bruised by the end of the race. Apart from that, my car ran perfectly, with temperatures and pressures all according to the book, and Jack's car was the same. I had a pleasant tussle with Chris Amon's Ferrari during the race but eventually pulled away from him. Both the Lotuses broke and Jack and I finished first and second, which increased my lead in the world championship and brought Jack up to second place. I don't know whether this is enough of an advantage to see us through — probably not, but at least for the moment we are keeping it in the "family".'

At Silverstone for the British Grand Prix, Denny was fourth fastest in qualifying, giving an outside spot on the front row of the grid. Jim Clark was on pole with the Lotus and Denny was impressed with his performance. 'The way he drives that Lotus suggests that he could well have pole position for the rest of the season . . .

'When the flag dropped I attempted a really good start, but something got all fouled up and half the field just bored on by. I made a quick check of the rev counter to see if things were working all right, but though every- thing suggested it was pulling, it just wasn't. This rather annoyed me and I started a big old tweak-up to catch the leaders. I seemed to overtake someone on almost every lap before I got up to fourth, behind Jack. I think it took me two laps to get past Dan Gurney, one to overtake John Surtees, one for Jackie Stewart and one for Chris Amon. On each occasion I did them going into Woodcote.

'After getting up behind Jack it was quite a few laps before I could pick him off. I didn't realise at the time that he was without his mirrors, but I finally managed to squeeze through going into Stowe.'

Jim Clark and Graham Hill were running 1-2 in the Lotuses and Denny, now third, was pressing Graham; when Graham retired, Denny inherited second place. Chris Amon had been having huge problems getting his Ferrari past Jack's mirrorless Brabham and this may have saved Denny's second spot.

'When Chris got past Jack I could see the red Ferrari in my mirrors at several different points around the circuit. If he had been able to pass Jack 10 laps earlier, he might have made things more difficult for me. During the last three laps something started to vibrate on my car and I decided to take things a little easier, and Chris was now making ground. We never found out what was causing the vibration. I thought it might have been the crown wheel and pinion, but later investigation showed it was perfect.'

Denny was happy with his second place and the extra title points, but he was not totally confident about his chances on the 14.2-mile Nürburgring.

Henry N. Manney, who reported European racing for *Road & Track*, was a good friend of Denny's and Denny enjoyed the American's sense of humour. He captured the spirit of the 1967 German Grand Prix in the opening paragraph of his report: 'After the flat and undemanding spaces of Silverstone, it was a distinct relief to trundle off to the Nürburgring. Despite brooding pines, a fair chance of inclement weather, a really good chance of getting messed about by the inefficient press office, and one of the biggest collection of drunken yobboes in the world, the Nürburgring remains a man's circuit and not just a high-speed balancing act. I think that the 'Ring draws more enthusiastic spectators (reportedly 260,000 on race day) at one fell swoop than any other sporting event in Europe because there is lots of room around its 14-mile-plus length to set up tents, hang over the fence well out of the way of the cars, and see just who has got everything taped. With all the blind brows, odd cambers and successions of twiddly bits, it takes a good man to make a fast time and as Sophie Tucker was wont to say, a good man is hard to find.'

Denny, that Sunday, was a *very* good man . . .

'I remember trying to memorise the whole of the circuit while we were flying over in Jack's plane, but that only served to remind me just how many difficult corners there were! Two days earlier we had taken the car to Goodwood to scrub tyres to save the time and trouble of doing it at the 'Ring.'

They experimented with different-size tyres and fuel loads and Denny was down to 8:13.5, which stood as the fastest time in first practice and would stay as second fastest for the grid. It was as well that Denny's car was race ready. 'The mechanics had their hands full during the night after the first day's practice, getting Jack's car repaired after his alarming accident when a bolt sheared in the rear suspension. Because of Jack's shunt the bolts were changed on my car too, and everything was crack-tested — even the shock absorbers! On a circuit as tough as the 'Ring it's important to make sure nothing is going to break . . .

'I knew I had to make a better start than I had at Silverstone and keep up with the leading bunch. Going round the South Curve for the first time I noticed a lot of smoke in the air and knew someone had made a nonsense, but I didn't realise it had been Graham Hill in the Lotus. What really surprised me on that first lap was that the three of us — Jim Clark, Dan Gurney and myself — quickly lost the others and that Jim hadn't set off like a rocket as I had expected. I tucked in behind the Lotus and got a fantastic tow. The rev counter soared up to 8000 rpm in Jim's slipstream, which was a few hundred more than I wanted, but I was prepared to keep my foot down and determined not to lose contact. That tow lasted for three laps and continued for a while later when Dan slipped by.

'On lap 4, Jim was in trouble. I knew he was having problems because he was looking over his shoulder to see if anything was wrong with his car. I was close on his tail but there didn't seem to be anything obviously wrong. Both Dan and I overtook him shortly after going into the country after the pits and then I did all I could to get away from the Eagle, but at Adenau he was still right on my tail and I knew he was beginning to get serious about it all! Then we came up to the big jump on the far side of the circuit and I landed all crossed up. I should have changed gear, because in recovering from that effort I had slowed down and while I was gathering speed, Dan came past. Then I *knew* he was serious, because on certain parts of the track he was really trying and going *very* quickly. I hung on to my tow for a lap, but after that Dan broke away and started to extend his lead. He really had that Eagle sorted out and it didn't seem to be leaving the ground as often as my car. This was important, because I'm sure that most people found more bumps at the 'Ring through travelling so much quicker. There is, for example, a very nasty bump coming back up on the home straight — which I'm sure no one had realised was a bump until this year!

'Dan pulled out a very useful lead of 45 seconds, but then he had the misfortune to break down on the circuit, surrounded by a pool of oil. That gave *me* a lead of 45 seconds over Jack with three laps to go, which was a very comforting situation, I can tell you! I kept going as quickly as I could, but without using all the revs. I changed up earlier and concentrated on saving the car. The engine never missed a beat all the way to the finish and the brakes stood up to the job wonderfully.

'The car had suffered no damage at all during the race, but when I stepped out of the cockpit I broke the windscreen! But with a first and second place, Ron Tauranac didn't worry too much . . .'

It was the first time Denny had finished the German Grand Prix. His total number of laps on the two previous occasions had been nine. Denis Jenkinson noted in *Motor Sport*: 'Although Hulme was not at the limit he set up a new race average record of over 101 mph for the 15 laps.' And this on the ultimate challenging mountain circuit on the Grand Prix trail!

Denny and Jack were driving the Sid Taylor Lola in the BOAC International 500 at Brands Hatch and they qualified well. They had expected the Chaparral to be quicker than it was and reckoned they had the legs on the Ferraris and Porsches.

'The first stint was mine and I'm afraid I didn't make a very bright start, but I kept up with the leaders and then got in front without trying too hard. The engine sounded really smooth and quiet and the car seemed comfortable for six hours. We reckoned we could get through on one set of Goodyears and thought we wouldn't have to change brake pads, either. I started to build up something of a lead, hoping to hand over to Jack after 70 laps with a useful margin, but the engine suddenly went horrible and I came in to have a broken rocker replaced. That cost valuable time, but then the clutch suddenly gave up and Jack never got to drive at all.'

The Canadian Grand Prix at Mosport was an up-and-down race with changing fortunes. 'I think that Bruce should have won but for the lack of an alternator. He took it off to save weight, but the calculations weren't quite right and the electrics took more out of the battery than he expected. He had to stop to replace it and this put paid to his hopes of winning first time out with his new car with the BRM V12 engine. If it hadn't rained for a second time, Jim Clark would have won. He was going very well when the track was drier, but the second lot of rain got into his electrics and stopped him.

'Then I suppose I might have won, but for having to make two pit stops to change my goggles. The curious thing was that I didn't have any trouble for the first 20 or 30 laps, but after that they started to fog up inside. I changed them for another pair but they were soon misted up as well, so I made another stop to change them for a Bell "bubble" visor. This was great and I wished I had known about it earlier.'

Denny had been to Mosport for the CanAm race, so he knew the circuit and was able to choose the right gear ratios for the first practice.

'Jim Clark and Graham Hill were fastest in practice, but I managed third spot in the closing minutes of the final session. Jack wasn't as high up the grid as he wanted to be because of problems with an oil breather. The new V12 McLaren-BRM was very impressive. It started to rain while we were warming up. When the flag fell I got away well and beat Graham into the first corner, but I couldn't quite get past Jim. I followed his Lotus for two or three laps and discovered that by using the extreme outside of the track — the part which had been little used and which didn't have much rubber on it — I could get better grip. Of course, there were occasions when you had to cross the rubber-coated patches and this was *really* slippery, but by using the outside of the track I was able to go quicker and got past Jim on about lap 4. The drizzle eventually stopped, but it took a while for the track to dry. I managed to lap Dan Gurney and when the track dried we had a splendid dice. Dan was quite a help, giving me a tow, but then he had trouble with his fuel system and dropped back.

'On the drying circuit Jim was pulling back a second a lap on me and I got baulked in traffic, which meant another 2 or 3 seconds. If I hadn't been baulked, I don't think Jim could have caught me before the second shower of rain and this could have had a real effect on the outcome of the race. The moment Jim got past, it started to pour with rain and I was caught in the very heavy spray from his wheels. It was probably this heavy spray that affected my goggles. I tried to press on for a couple of laps and once I tried driving without the goggles, but this was impossible. Eventually I had the visor and then I had a spin. I've really no idea why this happened, because it occurred at a point where I'd had no previous trouble and I wasn't going any quicker when things went wrong. I left the course and the engine stopped, but fortunately it restarted immediately and I was able to get away again. After that I motored home fairly gently, relieved to be second behind Jack again.'

In his *Motor Racing* diaries Denny was now being very complimentary to Bruce, his new car and his driving, presumably building the platform for his total team switch at the end of the season. In the meantime, he was driving for McLaren in the CanAm series and the next race was the season opener at Elkhart Lake.

With the world championship gathering pace and Denny in the lead with three races left, we will stay on the Grand Prix trail and devote the next chapter to the start of the Hulme–McLaren relationship.

The Italian Grand Prix at Monza was always a search for ultimate speed on the long straights — Jack went to the lengths of fitting a streamlined cockpit bubble and one was made ready for Denny's car. 'There was a small gain on top speed, but there was also a slight disadvantage with visibility, so I didn't use mine and Jack also decided against using his in the race.'

A blown head gasket stopped Denny's practice on the first day and a heavy downpour of rain on the second day meant Denny's track time had been severely restricted and he also missed the chance of getting a slipstreaming 'tow'. 'A good tow could make a big difference to Monza lap times. While the track was wet I tried to play around with Dan Gurney's Eagle, just to compare our two cars . . . and I came to the conclusion that his car was very quick on some parts of the course!'

Denny was back on the third row of the grid and was anxious to make a good start and not get left behind by the leaders. 'I've rarely known a more ridiculous start. The 30-second board went up and after half a minute someone dropped a green flag while we were still on the dummy grid. Some drivers took this as the starting signal and took off, while others hesitated, thinking they had to crawl up to the proper grid. It was a real shambles! My reaction was that the signal was the real thing, but then I realised that Jim Clark — ahead of me on the front row — hadn't moved and his slow getaway held me up while the others were screaming away ahead of us.

'I had expected the field to go a lot faster than they did in the early stages. I saw Dan Gurney away up front and decided to have a go and catch as many cars as I could. This I did. When I caught up with Jim Clark I spotted that one of his tyres was going flat. It's amazing how that tyre stood up on the faster parts of the circuit, because it was dished in the middle and when he started to go round a corner, it got all twitchy. I tried to get alongside to point it out to him, but when I did go by, I overtook so quickly that I couldn't do it and it was Jack who pointed out his problem.

'That just left Graham Hill, Jack and myself slipstreaming for the lead. When I was behind Graham I was pulling 600 more revs than I could on my own, and provided I could leave the corners close to the Lotus, he couldn't get away. Then I lost a lot of ground when Graham dived inside a tail-ender, I lost my tow and I discovered that the water temperature was climbing. So I went into the pits . . . and stayed there.

'For me it was a boring sort of race, and of course disappointing, but the spectators certainly had their fill. Jim drove a stupendous race, gathering up a lost lap after his puncture and was terribly unlucky to suffer a fuel blockage right at the end.'

There were CanAm races at Bridgehampton and Mosport and Denny would win both, leading up to the US Grand Prix at Watkins Glen, where he would be back in his Brabham uniform. It must have made for a delicate family atmosphere, as if Denny was effectively living at home and having an affair that everyone knew about. There was also the situation where Denny was looking as though he would wrest the world title from Jack, the man with his name on the nose of the green and gold cars. Denny was driving the same car he had raced at Monza and the reason for his retirement there was still a mystery. It had been thought that it was a head gasket problem, but now this was being rejected in favour of a radiator cap that was letting off at too low a pressure.

'The first day of practice was very foggy and wet and I decided that unless it cleared up I would miss the session completely, because I didn't feel that I needed to learn the circuit. If it rained the next day, at least there would be plenty of opportunity for wet weather practice!'

The weather cleared and it was track business as usual, testing tyres and wheel sizes. 'After that first day I felt my car was running pretty well, but Jack only managed a couple of laps before his engine was history after something went wrong with the valve gear. At the time we only had one spare engine, so Jack had to have it, but another engine was flown out from England on Saturday and this was put into Jack's car during the night before the race.'

Denny qualified on the third row of the 2-2-2 grid. The start was slow and Denny realised he was losing ground to the leaders. 'This started around lap 20, when the engine began to lose some of its edge and it became really noticeable after Chris Amon got past me in his Ferrari. This was a worry, because I had this feeling that something might be about to break or that a valve had got bent, but it picked up again. It could have been a bent valve that had got hit back into shape. I'd known that happen before. Jack lost three laps with a puncture and it was his misfortune that helped me to the finish. The pit crew were worried about tyre wear and they slowed me down. As it turned out, I ran out of fuel coming down the back straight on the last lap — it had coughed ominously at the hairpin with one lap to go — and I only just managed to coast home with a dead engine. If I hadn't been slowed down I would have run out of fuel much earlier and wouldn't have made third place . . .'

Jim Clark and Graham Hill were first and second in their Lotus-Fords and were able to out-pace the Brabhams. 'I couldn't keep up without a tow late in the race.'

There was now one race left — the Mexican Grand Prix — and the world title was up for grabs. To win the title for the second year running Jack had to win in Mexico, with Denny finishing no higher than fourth. If Denny finished higher, he would become champion. It would be a race of care and calculations rather than outright pace as far as the Brabham team drivers were concerned.

'I decided to play it very calm and quiet. I was well aware of what I had to do in order to win the title — which was to keep an eye on Jack! It worked out exactly as I had figured it. From the way he was going it was obvious that nobody but Jim Clark could win the race, providing his car stayed healthy. I certainly wasn't going to burst my engine trying to get in front of him, but of course I had to watch Jack and see that he didn't get too many places in front, just in case he won. So this was something of a gentle effort for me. I only used 7500 rpm in the race instead of the possible 8300–8400 rpm, and it never gave me a single moment of anxiety.

'The engine I used in Mexico was the same one I had for Monza, Mosport and Watkins Glen. It had been rebuilt after the Glen and they discovered why the engine had gone off-colour there. Two of the valves were chipped — there were two complete "Vs" out of them — and that was the explanation. As I suspected, one of the valves had been bent and this was because the chipped-off piece had got underneath it.

'The race in Mexico was one that I knew a lot about! I made sure that I got signals telling me where everybody who mattered was lying during the whole of the race. I was probably better informed of the race situation than I had ever been. Jack had all sorts of problems with oil temperatures and he did very well to finish in second place. My car went perfectly, both in practice and during the race. I was just a little surprised to see how fast Chris Amon was in the Ferrari and he was very unlucky to run short of fuel. Jim Clark gave his car to local driver Solana for the race, and once again he chose well, because both Solana and Graham Hill had things break. You might say that was luck, but don't forget that Jim has had his fair share of bad luck — Monza for example.

'After about 10 laps I knew I was sitting comfortable for the championship as long as the car kept running and I knew that even if Jack had won the race, I was OK, since I was only one place behind him. Towards the end of the race, when things looked as certain as they could be in racing, I remember thinking about all those speeches I looked like having to make.

These things worried me far more than driving a hard race. I also thought of all the people who would be happy back in New Zealand and I was delighted to learn later than I'd been chosen as Sportsman of the Year.'

The final race order was Clark from Brabham, with Denny happy a lap down in third place, clinching the world title with 51 points ahead of Jack on 46 points and Jim Clark with 41. There is a famous photograph of Jim and Denny, both in the same laurel wreath — Jim as race winner, and Denny as champion.

Autocar captured the scene in Mexico as Denny became World Champion: 'Jim Clark is surrounded by photographers and receives his trophy from a local beauty queen, but Hulme wanders off along the back of the pits and seems totally unconcerned about his World Championship. The crowd begins to drift away and the drivers pile into their borrowed Renaults and head for the prize-giving, somewhat daunted by the fact that it is being held in a bull ring and they have been told they will have to fight for their prizes.

'However, the bulls turn out to be very small and with a bit of persuasion most of the drivers go into the ring. The danger of it all is shown by a local photographer, who stands in the middle of the ring and shoos the bulls away with a wave of his hand. Clark insists on wearing his crash hat, but Graham Hill and Jo Bonnier wear more traditional headgear and a good time is had by all — even the bulls. Guy Ligier, riding a donkey, puts up a good performance as a picador and Lotus mechanic Allan McCall becomes the star of the evening by riding a bull! 'They gave me a proper matador's cape,' Hulme says. 'I wasn't frightened, oh no. They weren't really bulls, they were calves. It was quite an evening . . ."'

Denny was philosophical about his situation. 'Everybody who goes motor racing must nurse the ambition to be World Champion because, like Mount Everest, it's the highest peak. Now having won the title in Mexico, frankly I don't feel that much different. I feel very honoured to have the title and I know it will mean I'll have more responsibilities towards the public. In fact, it will be something of a burden, but I hope I will carry it with the right sort of dignity!

'I've had the ambition to be World Champion for years now, but in fact I've achieved it a little sooner than I thought possible — perhaps four years earlier than I'd anticipated. To get the title in what was only my second full year of Grand Prix racing doesn't necessarily mean I am the best driver in the world, not by any means. What it does mean is that I have managed to be consistently quick, to pick up a lot of placings and win a couple of Grands Prix with a reliable car.

'Reliable? When you consider there were 11 world championship Grands Prix this season, and Jack and I were able to pick up points in nine of them, with four wins between us, that's a real tribute to the cars and the way the boys prepared them. I must say that Jack gave me a very useful car for the season. Maybe I didn't always have the latest equipment on my car, but it was possibly more reliable than his because of this. There were occasions when Jack carried out some experiments with his car that didn't come off — like trying a big-valve engine which didn't prove successful. Mind you, if the experiments had worked, he might have won, so I was perhaps in the happier position of not having to drive a "guinea pig" car.

'The first inkling that I might have a good season came in South Africa in January, when I found myself leading the field for the first time, and doing so comfortably. Then the brakes failed completely and after a couple of pit stops I only managed to finish fourth. In retrospect I made an error in deciding to call at the pits, because if I'd gone on I might have finished a couple of places higher. Of course, Monaco was the turning point. This was the win I really needed to set me up and I think it was partly because of the oil on the circuit in the early part of the race. The car was handling superbly that day and on the slippery circuit it didn't seem to lose anything on lap times compared with my rivals. I don't know why this was so. It was just that the characteristics of the car were terrific that day . . . you could have talked to it and it would have gone round the corners on May 7!

'Monaco gave me a morale boost for the rest of the season. After that, I knew I was competitive and it was just a matter of staying there. The Monaco win also helped me at Indianapolis, which came soon after and everyone was extremely good to me there. And when I got fourth at Indy, I came back to Europe feeling even better . . .'

Back home, things would be relegated to perspective in *A Short, Short History of New Zealand*, published by Penguin Books in 2005. Under 1967, the entry was:

Decimal currency is introduced.

After 50 years of 6 o'clock closing, hotel (pub bar) hours
    are extended until 10 o'clock.

Denis Hulme becomes World Champion.

. . . in that order! The end of the infamous 'six o'clock swill' had precedence over Denny's world title in the national scheme of things. He'd probably have agreed . . .

11 Denny joins McLaren for CanAm

It simply couldn't happen today. Denny was to drive a second McLaren alongside Bruce in the CanAm series of sports car races in North America during 1967, the same summer when he would be racing *against* Bruce in Formula 1 every other Sunday. Today your modern Grand Prix driver wouldn't consider taking part in anything other than his chosen series, let alone be allowed to by contract. Denny had grown to like sports car racing, driving for Sid Taylor's team in the Brabham BT8, a GT40 Ford and then the Lola-Chevrolets. A no-limits, few-holds-barred series like CanAm appealed to Denny's way of doing things.

'The McLaren M6A was specially tailored for me and I was appreciative of that because it meant quite a lot of extra work to give me about three inches more in the cockpit, compared with Bruce's car, and two inches in the wheelbase. That meant different jigs and different body panels. While it was being built I went over from time to time to check it out, to make sure that the steering wheel, pedals and gear lever were exactly where I wanted them. I had a "personal fitting" several times before the car was completed.'

The first test runs were at Silverstone and Bruce eventually got down to 1:28 after getting the car set up and settled down. 'After quite a few laps I got down below my own Lola record and we felt we were really getting somewhere.'

The car was then stripped, checked and rebuilt, and taken down to Goodwood for Denny to press on with tests. 'After a couple of days I was down to 1:13.4 and from all accounts this was easily the fastest lap at Goodwood and we felt that all the hard work was paying off. I liked the basic simplicity of the M6A and also the way it was possible to drive it quickly without appearing to be quick. It seems to go round corners like a slot-racing car and the engines we are using are very sweet with little vibration. We were going to the season-opener at Elkhart Lake in Wisconsin a little apprehensive, wondering what the opposition would produce, though confident our cars would be quick. We knew that if anyone was quicker they really would be flying!

'Elkhart Lake was a fine circuit in beautiful scenery and a good surface, with the lap record standing at 2:21. After seven laps on the first practice session I was 7 seconds inside the record, so that gave the opposition something to think about. I finally got down to 2:12.7 — and Bruce was on pole position a tenth faster than me!

'There was a rolling start with Stirling Moss driving the pace car. That was quite a sight, as Stirling went through the timed section at 105 mph with three journalists in the back of his car taking photographs, while we were in second gear and not quite on the cam.'

Denny won his first CanAm race for McLaren with some ease, leading from start to finish, but what might have been a 1-2 for the orange cars faded when Bruce retired with a broken oil line. The Lolas of Donohue and Surtees were second and third.

The debut win must have felt and looked good, but in fact there had been problems behind the scenes that the team worked to cure while Bruce and Denny were at the Italian Grand Prix, before the next CanAm round at Bridgehampton.

'The first problem was excessive brake pad wear and the second was twisting drive shafts. We fixed the drive shafts easily by fitting stronger ones, having new parts made in England and rushed over to the States, but the brake problem wasn't the work of a moment. It involved quite a lot of tricky adaptation and we ended up with an entirely new set-up with large ventilated discs front and rear, twin-pot callipers on the front and special horseshoe-type strengthening pieces at the rear, where the callipers had to be machined down to allow the discs to go through. The new drive shafts saved us about 6 lb in weight each side so we felt we could be even more competitive at Bridgehampton than we had been at Elkhart Lake.'

The Bridgehampton circuit lay in rough, rugged country close to the end of Long Island, NY, about 120 miles from New York City.

'It was kidney-shaped, like an oversized Brands Hatch built among the sand hills, so there was usually plenty of sand on the track to make it slippery. The surface was fairly rough, so we used stiffer shock absorbers to jack the suspension up higher.

'Our first job in practice was to check the new brakes and Bruce was out bedding his in very carefully, but after four or five laps I got impatient, went too quickly too soon and paid the penalty with discs that started to "blue up" and developed a couple of hot spots. Though they took time to bed in, the new brakes were a big bonus over the old — they ran extremely cool and felt really good and within a few laps I was 2 seconds under the record, with Bruce close behind.

'Then the drama started. My engine broke a cylinder head stud and one went in Bruce's engine too. This meant a complete change of studs and although mine came out easily, three of Bruce's broke and this caused a panic. Special drills had to be found to remove the offending studs and, of course, all the taps were damaged in the process, so Bruce had to sit out the second day of practice.

'There was an hour of unofficial practice on race morning and I reckon this won me the race. During practice there had been a hurricane in the vicinity and this had resulted in a fairly consistent 25–30 mph tail wind down the straight, but race day dawned foggy and when the wind arrived to give us a beautiful clear day, it turned out to be a head wind. Bruce had done just the right thing and I decided that I would also switch to a lower third gear to help me on the uphill section with a full fuel load, and a lower fifth for the straight.'

They had also discovered a serious oil leak on Denny's engine and sealed it with Araldite. 'Before the race I also had the rear spoiler raised to its high position, as I reckoned this would be a big advantage going over the high-speed hump on the circuit, where I was having to touch the brakes. Our rapid ratio-change on race morning really had the opposition wondering — I don't think they'd ever seen such a thing before! — and I think we caused consternation all round.'

Denny was on pole, with Bruce beside him and Dan Gurney on the outside of the front row in his Lola, now with fuel injection on its Ford engine.

'As we approached the start line and the flag was waved, I floored the accelerator and out-dragged Bruce to the first corner, where I saw that the oil flags were already out! Someone had dropped a stream of oil on the warm-up lap and I could pick out the thin line nearly all the way round the course. I only hoped it wasn't from my car and just to check I went off line at one or two places on the second lap . . . and next time round I was very disturbed to find that the oil slick had too! But the following lap the oil was on a different line again, so I could relax.'

Denny found that he could lap almost as quickly 'off line' dodging the oil as he could on the proper line, and he put that down to the new M6A, feeling that they could change direction quickly and were far more manoeuvrable than their opposition. 'This meant that you could change your line in the middle of a corner, whereas I could never do that in last year's Lola. My only real incident came in a spin on a long uphill second-gear curve, when I had a lead of about half a minute. What I didn't know was that Surtees had spun at almost the same time, and when I recovered and looked in my mirrors, I found them full of Lola red! It had been impossible to read any of the pit signals because of the sun and I assumed that Surtees was up in second place — in fact, he was fourth and a lap behind! — so I shot off, and that's when I set the new lap record!'

Denny and Bruce finished first and second. It was Denny's second race win in the series and the next race was at Mosport in Canada the following weekend. He spent a few days having his first game of golf. 'It struck me as not a bad game hitting the ball, but I thought chasing it all over the countryside was a bit off . . .' As with life, Denny had his own special way of playing golf. He held the club cross-handed in a manner that defied description, yet he could smite the ball huge distances down the fairways.

'For some reason my gearbox ran very hot at Bridgehampton — everything was very black inside — but we never discovered why. The Mosport circuit seems traditionally to provide rain — sheets of it — for the first day of practice. It was just bucketing down and so after scrutineering we just loaded the cars on the trailers and headed for home. Friday was fortunately dry and by the end of the first of two sessions I had collected pole position.

'The Mosport result turned out to be a repeat of Bridgehampton, but not before we had real dramas both before the race and right at the end. About an hour before the start, one of Bruce's fuel bladders was found to be leaking and there was a terrific flap as everyone set to drain the system and fit a new rubber bag. Just try giving away 50 gallons of fuel in a hurry and you'll be amazed how few takers you can find! After every vehicle in sight had been topped up, the rest of it had to be poured down the drain! The team worked wonders to get the replacement bag installed just as the 5-minute signal went, but there was a big Bruce-sized gap beside me as the rest of us set off on our pace lap. Bruce had just failed to make it by less than a minute, and he rushed out, having filled his tanks, to try to cut down the gap before we completed our rolling-start lap, but he was still 45 seconds down when he took the flag.

'He then drove what was probably his best-ever race, cutting his way through the field from twenty-sixth to fourth place behind Gurney (Lola) and Mike Spence (McLaren) by half-distance — 40 laps. By lap 66 Bruce was up to second place. I'd had a slow spin on a tricky tightening-radius corner and took my time in re-starting so as not to damage the clutch, as I had plenty of time in hand. I'd been having trouble with a sticking throttle — after it twice stuck open in the early laps I never used full throttle again — and I was quite worried by what felt like loose steering. In fact, the clamps had worked loose, allowing the box to revolve in its mountings, but I didn't know that then.

'It didn't seem to get any worse and everything seemed set for a smooth run to the finish when, with one and a bit laps to go, the car just went straight on at a tricky right-hander and I charged nose-first up a steep bank. The Chev engine restarted immediately when I pressed the button and I reversed back down, steering on to the track. The radiator was clogged solid with dirt and the nearside front of the body was badly damaged. As I motored off there were clouds of smoke billowing up from the front and I watched the body gradually break up in front of me as more and more of it was pulled round by the left front wheel, until the wheel itself was jammed solid by the glass fibre and the shredded tyre. It would have been better if the wheel had come clean off, because the M6A's chassis is so stiff that it would run level on three wheels without even damaging the brake disc, but as it was I had a car that would go round left-handers but which had practically no right lock at all — and Mosport has about five right-handers! Somehow, by using loads of grass verge, I was able to tug it round for that final lap, which was apparently only about 20 seconds slower than normal, but I was mighty glad to see those crowds cheering in the grandstand as I came on to the finishing straight for the last time.

'I parked it just past the flag and afterwards we found that though the front sub-frame was bent — it had been designed "soft" for just such a purpose — the main monocoque was unharmed. Even the body damage didn't worry us, because we had planned to fit new bodies for the three West Coast CanAms and these were already on their way across. So we had another 1-2, with Mike Spence a good third in last year's McLaren and there were quite a few smiles in the McLaren camp that night!'

Before the Californian CanAms, Denny had been down Mexico way, winning the world championship, but at Laguna Seca near San Francisco his string of three wins in the big orange McLaren sports cars was about to come to a halt. A valve broke in the big Chev V8 and this knocked a hole in the bore and the block, and he was out of the race.

'It had hardly been a trouble-free race before that, because I lost third gear early on and then my water drinking bottle came loose and got jammed under the brake pedal. Since it was a plastic bottle I found it was possible to still use the brakes by pressing harder and squashing the bottle, but it wasn't pleasant driving like that. It took me about 20 laps to get that darned bottle out. I had to undo my safety harness, accelerate hard so that the bottle would roll back, and then struggle to pick it up. Problem was that there were no straights at Laguna Seca and I think it would have been better if I'd stopped to retrieve the bottle.

'Bruce gave the team its fourth victory on the trot, but he finished the race with terrible heat burns. The weather was very hot and the hot air from the radiator badly burned Bruce's tongue, nose and all of his face. The only relief he got was a bucket of cold water thrown over him at the hairpin. I'd organised that for myself before the race and this encouraged Bruce to plan the same operation. In fact, I didn't need the water because for some reason I didn't have the same heat problem. I had the engine problem instead.'

A fortnight later they were at Riverside outside Los Angeles and Denny had a new motor but was worried that it sounded harsh. 'We discovered that the magneto had advanced itself 125 degrees, which accounted for the harshness. The interesting thing with these big engines is that it's difficult to tell whether they've lost 30 or 40 horsepower. You would certainly know about that sort of loss in the old 1.5-litre Grand Prix cars.'

The McLaren CanAm cars totally dominated the races, but they were not without their problems . . . it was just that they had most of their problems before the races started. Bruce broke his engine and put in a fresh one for the race, and in the last half hour of practice Denny's engine threw a rod. On his home track Dan Gurney was very fast during practice in his Lola Ford and started from pole, with Bruce beside him on the 2-2-2 grid and Denny on the second row in third position.

'Neither Bruce or I could match Dan's pace, but his car soon gave up in the race. I had a very short outing. As on several American circuits, Riverside had a number of half tyres to indicate the perimeter of the course. On the first lap someone ahead of me hit one of these tyres and threw it into the air, hitting one of my front wings. I stopped at the pits to have the loose bodywork cut away, but I was disqualified because too much of the wheel was showing. There was nothing I could complain about because the officials were only carrying out the rules, but I didn't think much of those tyre markers . . .'

Bruce went on to win the race after a long battle with Jim Hall in the Chaparral and they went to the final race at Las Vegas hoping for a 'six hit' for the series.

'The usual amount of thorough preparation went into our cars at Las Vegas and both machines were very sound up to a short time before the race. That's when we discovered that water was getting into the oil on Bruce's engine and there wasn't time to change the engine, so he wasn't really banking on continuing for long — and he was right! My car seemed in good shape and I felt it was capable of winning the race providing it kept running. Of course, this was another occasion where I was battling with a team-mate for a championship, as I had done with Jack in Formula 1 that summer, so I had every incentive to keep battling. But on the very first lap there was a major tangle in which eight cars were involved, and I got a puncture on the next lap. I hadn't been able to avoid running over some of the debris from the huge shunt and this put a big slice in one of my tyres. It took about a minute and a half to change the wheel and I left the pits lying a whole lap down on the leaders.

'After that setback I felt I had nothing to lose and everything to gain by driving as hard as I could. In doing this I managed to pull back into fourth place and the way the car was performing I think I could have been third, which would have given me the CanAm title. But any such fond thoughts disappeared in a big BANG after 51 laps, when a piston came off its rod right in front of the pits. It was a spectacular exit, just at the point where everyone was watching. It's true to say that I'd been driving the engine hard — certainly harder than in any of the previous races with the title in sight — but I hadn't been over-revving it.

'In earlier races I'd been using 6400–6500 revs, driving inside the limit, and at Las Vegas I had been pressing on to 6800 rpm on occasions. This must have put an extra strain on the engine and brought about the blow-up. So my only consolation was another lap record and at least Bruce and I had made a clear sweep of records in the series. I had fastest lap in the first three races and the last and Bruce was record-setter at Laguna Seca and Riverside.'

Emphasising the domination of the orange cars, Bruce won the CanAm title with 30 points from Denny on 27 and John Surtees and Mark Donohue in Lolas, equal third on 16 points.

A postscript to Denny's amazingly successful summer of '67 was an event that never happened. Denny had been entered in the British RAC Rally in a works-entered Triumph 2000 fitted with a fuel-injected TR5 sports car engine. The rally was cancelled at the last minute because of a foot-and-mouth disease epidemic.

'It was such a shame after the great efforts which were made to provide me with a car that would give me a chance of learning the way the rally boys go about their business . . . and how they do go! I had expected it to be tough and fast, but frankly I was amazed the first time I was given a flat-out demonstration by Roger Clark. What surprised me was the speed he went over the really rough stuff. At first, I'd been tending to try to nurse the car, but after Roger showed me how he did it, I realised that I had to forget nursing and press on, whatever the state of the surface.

'What Roger showed me was that the cars will stand up to this tremendous punishment. After he had taken me round the Army training ground at Bagshot Heath, there was no doubt that I had a new outlook and was much quicker doing it his way. I think I was beginning to get the hang of it by the end of the day and I felt confident that I could handle most situations. I was beginning to weigh up the type of surface and estimate how much adhesion I could expect.

'Though I'd done some rallying in New Zealand and over some rough roads, we had never run at such speed as the boys in Europe have to go if they are to get into the money. Rallying like this is very far removed from CanAm or Grand Prix racing, though as Jim Clark demonstrated in the 1966 RAC Rally, the circuit drivers can catch on quickly to this different sort of challenge. I'd decided that I would try at all costs to finish the rally, even if it meant losing a few points here and there. Just as in Grand Prix racing, I wanted to be present when the chequered flag fell and I thought this was the best approach as a new boy to the game. All the same, I wonder how far I would have got round the rally route!'

12 Ups and downs — Down Under 1968

The new World Champion's first Grand Prix for the McLaren team in 1968 was in the M5A fitted with the BRM V12 engine, the same car that Bruce had raced at the end of the previous season, qualifying on the front row at Monza but retiring in all the races. Before Denny left the UK for Kyalami, Bruce had said, 'Somehow I think you'll probably manage to keep it going.' Denny did. There were problems, but he brought the car home in fifth place, two laps down, and Denny observed that these two championship points might come in handy by the end of the season.

'We started off with the car just as Bruce had raced it in the Mexican Grand Prix, but we had quite a few spares with us, including different-sized wheels and different rim widths for the rear. Eventually I ended up with 15-inch front wheels and the wide CanAm sports-car-type rear ones. This was the best handling combination and I was pleased with the way it handled eventually. In fact, I would say it was handling every bit as well as the Brabhams. One problem with it is that it weighs so much more than the Repco Brabhams — I should think about 200 pounds more! — and though this doesn't matter very much at a circuit like Monza, on a course like Kyalami, where you have a couple of reasonably sharp corners and acceleration plays a big part, this weight handicap is really noticeable. Coming out of Club House Corner and past the pits — around half a mile — I found I was losing a second on acceleration to Jim Clark's Lotus.

'What it amounts to is that with new Ford engines coming up for our cars we can look forward to being pretty competitive. My car handled very well during the race and I was quite pleased with it, but it took a while to get used to it. It was like Bruce's CanAm cars set up pretty much for him, but once I got a bit of the twitchiness out of it by putting the CanAm-type rear wheels on and the 15-inch fronts — Bruce had it on 13-inch wheels — I thought it was handling damn well.

'The main problem during the race was fuel starvation through vaporisation. During the latter part of the race when a lot of the fuel had been used, the tanks started to expand with the heating of the air inside and eventually shut off the breather pipe, which made the air expand even more, and this eliminated the fuel starvation problem because it started to pressurise the fuel system. Rather like getting back to the old days when the riding mechanic used to hand-pump pressure into the petrol tank!

'Jochen Rindt was driving my old Brabham and I felt quite envious of him rushing around there when he was coming up to lap me. The interesting thing is that in driving a different car you can see where the Brabhams pick up their time, and it was certainly on acceleration out of the corners compared with my BRM-powered McLaren. Jochen's top speed was a lot higher than mine, although they quote a lower power figure.

'I thought the BRM V12 was quite a smooth unit. It was certainly a change for me to drive a 12-cylinder. It took a lot of fiddling to get the metering unit for the fuel injection system working properly for the high altitude. We had all our problems of overheating fuel in practice and the cure was to shift the catch tanks and fuel lines away from the chassis and the engine, putting them in the air-stream as much as possible. Then we directed cool air through a heater hose aimed at the metering unit, which had been getting so hot you couldn't touch it.

'The BRM engine ran for the last 28 laps with zero oil pressure round most of the circuit. The only place I had pressure was down the long straight, which I suppose was the best place to have it because the engine would be loaded up a lot harder. I had to finish the race somehow in order to pick up a point or two. We used about four gallons of oil during the race, but I shouldn't think the lack of oil pressure did any harm to the engine. Apparently this engine just burns it and doesn't spill it out. In fact, it was quite an oil-free engine. The whole car ran quite cool in the race.'

There were several Tasman drivers eager to get to New Zealand, and Qantas delayed the flight from Johannesburg for several hours until the helicopters arrived from Kyalami. 'There weren't many passengers on the flight so there was plenty of sleep to be had. I got quite a reception when we arrived at Auckland — local boy makes good, and all that sort of thing — and I was presented with the Sportsman of the Year trophy at Pukekohe . . . and then I had all the nonsense of having a big shunt in the race.

'My car was the Brabham Jochen Rindt had driven in Formula 2 last season and it was going remarkably well, but I hadn't expected Chris Amon's Ferrari or Jim Clark's 2.5-litre Ford to go quite as well as they did. I couldn't match their speed down the straight. I could pick up a lot round the corners but it was on the long straights where the 1600 cc F2 was really suffering. It handled absolutely beautifully and I don't think they had even changed the roll bars from the last time Jochen had raced it. Nothing needed doing to it so we thought we were in for an easy series.

'In the early part of the Grand Prix at Pukekohe I was chasing Pedro Rodriguez in the BRM. Jimmy and Chris had cleared off in the lead and Frank Gardner in the 2.5-litre Alfa-engined Brabham was ahead of Pedro. Then Pedro got tangled up with a back marker and while this was going on, I slipped past. Passing the back markers was a big problem. I suppose it was because the local drivers are pretty enthusiastic and want to dice with the visitors. Nevertheless, the quicker cars and drivers were getting through and I was closing on Frank, whose engine started to run a little rough; he was still pulling away on the straights, though.

'There were only two laps to go when the accident happened. I can't remember anything about it. I was knocked unconscious for a short time and the temporary loss of memory was probably a good thing. There were no photographs and people were all confused about what happened.'

Apparently history of a different kind was made when Tim Bickerstaff, commentating on live national radio from the back straight, looked up to see the somersaulting and crashing cars, blurted 'Oh, fuck!' and became the first person ever to utter the four-letter word live into New Zealand homes. Ho-hum now, but stunning in 1968.

Denny may not have been able to recall what happened, but there were reams written after the incident and the new World Champion came in for criticism. Perhaps the new title had a part to play in what happened. Or tall-poppy trimming, a popular pastime in New Zealand. It was his first race in front of his home crowd after winning the championship and he was chasing Frank Gardner hard for what would have been second place. In his book, *The Golden Era of New Zealand Motor Racing*, Graham Vercoe wrote: 'As the race drew to a close Hulme began tackling Gardner in earnest though Gardner, despite a flattening battery, could still open a gap on the straights. On lap 56 [of 58] Hulme came up behind Brownlie through Castrol shaking his fist at the Southlander who was already two laps down on the World Champion.'

Laurence Brownlie was a young driver with a bright future, driving a Brabham fitted with a 1.5-litre Vegantune Ford twin cam. His ability was underlined by the fact that he had negotiated to drive one of the factory 2.2-litre BRM V8s on his home track at Teretonga at the end of the New Zealand series. This would not happen.

'Even the flag marshals can't have noticed [the situation] as no blue flags were being shown or waved until Railway corner,' wrote Vercoe. This corner was a right-hander opening out on to the back straight. 'Obviously frustrated, Hulme bumped Brownlie's rear wheel with his front. It was some way down the straight before Hulme got alongside Brownlie and the latter took to the grass to avoid coming together. Amazingly, Hulme also appeared to get onto the grass and the two cars touched. Both were catapulted onto either side of the track, both turning over and disintegrating. Brownlie had also hit a pole in the disaster.

'Brownlie was trapped inside his car with a broken leg and foot and underwent many hours of surgery. Hulme appeared unscathed though furious.

'There was an enormous amount of media attention given the incident, most of which was putting forward the World Champion's (and newly created Sportsman of the Year) unwavering viewpoint. Brownlie's explanation was simple and believable: he hadn't seen Hulme come up behind him; no flags had been waved (until Railway, half a lap after Hulme came up behind him). Once he was aware of Hulme he pulled to one side of the straight, then actually on to the grass.

'How contact occurred will always be subject of conjecture. Each blamed the other. The media believed Hulme but Brownlie was found blameless in an official statement from MANZ officials. Unfortunately, a lot was said and written in the heat of the moment which reflected badly on both drivers and the sport.'

Donald McDonald remembered the incident in an article he wrote for the New Zealand *Driver* magazine in June 2002. He said that Brownlie's Brabham BT21 was actually a 'special' — a direct copy of a BT21 built by Fred McLean while he was in the UK working for Charles Lucas Racing. It was powered by the hottest Ford twin-cam available at the time, prepared by Vegantune. 'In early runs with the car it showed immense promise and the Brownlie fires were well stoked for the upcoming season.

'What was the incident at Pukekohe in the 1968 NZIGP that effectively ended his career? It's something that people have shied away from talking about for decades.

'New Zealand was celebrating its first, and to date only, Formula One World Champion. Denis Hulme had taken the 1967 title driving a works Repco Brabham. Ironically, however, the Brabham team wasn't interested in fielding a 2.5-litre version of the F1 car for Hulme to contest his home international season in, as he had given notice that he was moving to the fledgling McLaren outfit. New Zealanders wanted to see their new World Champion so Denis bought a Winkelmann Racing F2 Brabham, BT23 with a 1.6-litre FVA engine.

'In practice for the Grand Prix, Hulme had been sensational, taking sixth fastest time ahead of many quicker cars, but so too had Brownlie making his first appearance in his "Brabham". Brownlie's twin-cam had about 160 bhp compared to the 220 bhp of Hulme's FVA. Brownlie was tenth on the grid, the first of all the National Formula cars and ahead of established local stars like Roly Levis, Graeme Lawrence, Ken Smith and David Oxton.

'The race developed into a battle between Amon's Ferrari and Clark's Lotus, with victory going to Amon after a sensational drive, while Clark retired. Hulme, showing why he was World Champion, had the little Brabham flying and after Clark's retirement had moved up to third place and was chasing hard after Frank Gardner's 2.5 Brabham-Alfa.

'Brownlie, meanwhile, was going great guns and was leading the 1.5-litre section of the race, pushing as hard as he could.'

McDonald's review mentions that the crash happened with six laps to go, when Brownlie was being lapped for the second time, although the Vercoe race history indicates the accident happened on lap 56 with two laps to go. 'The World Champ was catching Brownlie — the Kelso Kid — as they came over Rothmans and down over the start/finish line and around Castrol. Into Railway he was right on his tail and waving his fist for Brownlie to pull over and let him past.

'This didn't happen and as the cars accelerated out of Railway Hulme got so close to Brownlie that his left front wheel touched Brownlie's right rear — a racing nudge. Down the long back straight at Pukekohe, Hulme used the superior power of the 1.6-litre FVA to draw alongside and he went to pass. But then the two cars tangled, Brownlie speared off and went head first at very high speed into a lamp-post (incredible as that may sound today) while Hulme's car cartwheeled, dropping him out of it from some height (this was the pre-seatbelt era) and he landed on the track some distance from the car.

'Brownlie's car was totally destroyed and one of his ankles smashed when a tube of the space frame came into the foot area. Hulme was dazed but otherwise unhurt and his car was repaired in time for Levin the following week.' In fact, Hulme's car was totally wrecked and another car was flown out in time for the Wigram race the following weekend.

'Brownlie's car was taken to the tip. Then followed weeks of shilly-shallying and buck-passing over what had happened. At first the finger was clearly pointed at Brownlie by both the greater unwashed press and by a section of motor sport officials. He was the driver who had nearly killed OUR World Champion. No direct action was taken against Brownlie, but it was clear he was getting the blame — until he threatened legal action.

'Witnesses came forward to say that Hulme's car moved into the path of Brownlie's — not the other way round. Then an "enquiry" decided that what had happened was that Hulme's car was caught in a freak gust of wind that moved it into Brownlie's, resulting in the terrible accident.

'And that's where the matter has "officially" lain ever since.

'What happened was that Brownlie got "The Bear" treatment from the World Champ. Denny was always a tough, hard racer, a no-nonsense bloke who was built like the proverbial brick toilet and as tough as old boots. He had the red mist up — he obviously thought that Brownlie should have moved over immediately on that section of track between the start of Castrol and Railway and let him through. So, Hulme, being the hard racer that he was, gave Brownlie the nudge at Railway and then gave him a "flick" as he went past — only the "flick" turned out to be bigger than intended. In other words, Hulme simply got it wrong. It was a silly thing to do and unusual for Hulme, who normally exhibited fine judgement in such matters.

'Brownlie said later that he wasn't aware at first that Hulme was catching him so quickly as he was busy trying to win the 1.5-litre class, and when he did become aware of the car in his mirrors he was committed to the corner.

'There seems to be some question over whether or not the flag marshals understood what was happening and if they showed Brownlie a blue flag.

'The upshot of it all was that Brownlie not only lost his car, into which he had poured his every last cent, but he was also on the end of some pretty malicious reporting and comments. He got no support from officials or the media at large — he was almost treated as a leper. Many people knew what had happened, but nobody was really prepared to say it publicly, and nobody was prepared to finger the World Champion. It was a gutless, spineless display by officials.'

Brownlie felt moved to register his own comment following the revisited accident that effectively cost him his racing career, and he wrote a letter that was published in the September 2002 issue of *Driver*.

In part, he wrote: 'The Brabham [I] used in the 1968 NZGP was a BT18 clone, the chassis being built by Fred McLean and, on my instructions, fitted with F2 BT23C rear suspension, gearbox and brakes.

'My injuries were more than "a busted ankle". I had 150 mm removed from my outer lower leg bone and a shattered foot on the other leg. I thank Allan Dick and Donald McDonald for raising the injustices involved in the "gust of wind" story the officials of the day concocted.

'I am, to this day, bitter about what was taken from me that day — my Brabham race car and my European driving career. The late Clive Hulme,

VC, rang my parents to tell them that I was in no way to blame. He also told my future wife that when he came to the hospital.

'I told officials I tried to avoid contact with Denis Hulme when he was veering towards me at an angle and I decided to leave the track, but I was followed onto the grass. Hulme could not remember any part of the accident and the official report said he drifted towards me perhaps due to wind. If my car had been a helicopter that day, I could have avoided Hulme.

'The stewards, J.O. Trevor and I. Daikee, said in their report to [Clerk of Course] Les Rankin that Hulme was dazed, that I had cuts and that statements could be obtained from the drivers, but since Hulme was concussed and couldn't remember any of it, then Brownlie's statement, by itself, would not serve much purpose.

'I said that there was no wind at the corner that day. Any intelligent person would know that if there had been wind it would have affected both cars because they were identical makes and profiles.

'Much later, Hulme was to strike again, using the same tactics on Kent Baigent and almost killing him. Having said that, I cannot take away what the late Denis Hulme achieved through straight guts, skill and determination and through his drives in CanAm, Indycars and F1 has earned his place in our proud sporting history . . .'

Denny told readers of his *Motor Racing* column that he thought he had been amazingly lucky to have emerged from the accident with only a slightly bloodshot eye. 'To crash over paddocks while staying in the car and then get tossed out of it with no broken bones, nothing except a stiff shoulder and a bit of a stiff neck. Looking at the car afterwards made me realise what luck I had, because there was hardly anything left that was worth straightening.

'Some fantastic organisation in England got me another F2 Brabham in double-quick time. I had nothing to do with it, because I was still under doctor's orders, but I left it to Merv Mayo, who comes round New Zealand with me and also helps Jack Brabham when he's out here. He has an engineering shop out here and raced cars here several years ago, being short-listed for the inaugural Driver to Europe scholarship with Phil Kerr and Bruce McLaren, who won the award. The new car was out here in a matter of a few days, built up and flown on down to Christchurch. I hopped straight into it and it felt 100 per cent. We never had to change a thing.

'At Wigram, Frank Gardner had a bit of a misfortune with a blown cylinder head gasket and Jim Clark cleared off from the rest of the field. I didn't make a brilliant start but kept going fairly quickly and was in third place early in the race, but then my engine started to misfire. I pressed on and managed to keep Piers Courage's F2 McLaren behind me to finish third.' They kept that engine in for the next race at Teretonga, hoping to track the cause of the misfire, but after two days without success they switched to a new engine that was worth an extra 300 rpm on the straight.

'The weather was fine for practice but come race morning it was raining like you've never seen rain before and the track was flooded. Jim Clark and Jim Palmer had big wet-weather Firestones and Piers put on little Dunlop rain tyres. All we did on our big normal Goodyear was aquaplane everywhere. The track got even worse during the final 60-lapper. When the flag dropped I was motoring around in fifth or sixth and thought the handling was peculiar, especially through the long loop. I was blaming oil on the circuit, but as Jim Clark went past he was pointing at the back of my car. When I looked in the mirror I could see a wheel wobbling. A nut had come undone, the top link had come off and the wheel was doing all sorts of strange things. The pit stop dropped me well back before the rain came down again and all sorts of incidents started happening. Chris shot off the track in the Ferrari and then Frank Gardner arrived in the Mildren Brabham-Alfa. There were no yellow flags and when Frank saw a marshal on the circuit he put his car into a big spin. Not having starter motors, both of them had to wait for someone to push them — which was perfectly legal in New Zealand provided the pushers were marshals.

'Meanwhile Jim was pressing on merrily in the Lotus, over 90 seconds ahead of the field. There was the concrete section with a bit of a bump in it across the start–finish line and Jim hit this at about 140 mph and went off in the biggest way. Fortunately the car went off to the left into a paddock. If he had gone off on the right he would have gone down into a big ditch, up a spectator protection bank and might well have launched himself. As it was, the Lotus got quite airborne, knocked down a post and went through a fence. Luckily the post was rotten, but I imagine the wires in the fence went off like banjo strings. After all this excitement, Jim got out, checked the damage, got back in, pressed his starter and motored off again. His mechanics wanted to take the broken bodywork off but Jim felt it was OK . . . until he got up to high speed and the body started to do queer things, so he had to make a pit stop and get the body ripped off.

'From then on it was all confusion and to this day I don't think they quite know who finished second and third, although I'm certain they got Bruce's win right. His win was quite amazing, considering that during the first heat his throttle stuck open and he slammed into a bank. He thought there was no way of getting the car back together again and he was all for telling the mechanics to forget it, but they worked hard, fitted new radiators, wishbones, radius arms, rear uprights . . . and he went out and won! That was the fifth time he had won at Teretonga in six years. I was sixth.

'Greeta and I went to Australia for the rest of the series, leaving baby Martin with his grandparents. I hadn't raced at Surfers Paradise and I had trouble in my heat, spinning off on oil and damaging the rear suspension. We had to make some parts to get the car on the grid for the main race. Fortunately there was a garage near the track, which looked after local speedboats, and we managed to weld up the suspension while the organisers held the start for a few minutes so we could get to the grid. Of course, I'd had no time to set the car up again and as a result it was nowhere near competitive. Then the roll bar disconnected and I was getting the most amazing understeer. So it was sixth place and a not very interesting outing.

'We got the car all squared up for Warwick Farm and I qualified fifth behind Clark, Hill, Amon and Courage, but in the race I had a handling problem and fifth was as good as I could expect. More bad luck at Sandown Park when I came to a stop when a spark plug dropped out. I thought a rod might have come through the side, but a quick check showed that the damage was far less expensive, thank goodness. But by the time I'd got back into the car and driven back to the pits for another plug, I'd lost three or four laps and I eventually came home eighth. The gremlins got at me again at Longford, the fast road course in Tasmania. I was fifth in the first race on the Saturday, but on the Monday the heavens opened and the race had to be deferred. I had to catch a plane immediately after the race to make the turbine tests at Phoenix, so I was forced to pull out of the race. Not that I was too worried, because I didn't have any rain tyres!'

After the turbine Indy-car trials detailed in the next chapter, Denny tested the new Ford-engined McLaren M7A Formula 1 car at Goodwood just after stepping off the overnight Polar flight from Los Angeles.

'I didn't like the car very much that day. Bruce was 2 seconds faster in the same car, which suggested that I needed a lot of miles in the car to get the hang of the handling and the characteristics of the new motor. During practice for the Race of Champions at Brands Hatch, I still didn't think too much of the M7A. It really needed a wider rev band there. As it was, everything started to happen at around 6500 rpm, which called for a lot of concentration and a delicate touch with the right foot.'

Denny qualified on the second row of the grid and about halfway through the race he started to come to grips with the new car and was satisfied with third, while Bruce scored a debut win with the new McLaren. They tested the car at Silverstone and then did 500 miles running on the new Jarama course near Madrid, before again testing the turbine car at Indianapolis. Back in Britain things started to improve when Denny won the sports car race at Silverstone in Sid Taylor's Lola on the morning of the International Trophy race and then started from pole and went on to win the main event in the afternoon! The win was not without drama.

'When the flag fell I got too much wheel-spin and got away slowly, but I wasn't too worried about that because the car was capable of staying with anybody out there, even after a poor start. Mike Spence got ahead of me in the BRM and I was planning to make a move on him when I came out on to Hangar straight on the seventh lap when a big stone came up from the BRM's wheel and hit me smack in the goggles! Luckily the lenses in my goggles are very thick and very strong. The impact knocked out the right lens, but there were no splinters. For a few seconds I couldn't imagine what had gone wrong so I slowed down and pulled over. It took about three laps before my eyes stopped watering and I was able to weigh up the situation. Should I stop for another pair of goggles, or keep going?

'My right eye was getting blasted by the air-stream but I decided to keep going because if I stopped for new goggles, I would lose any chance of winning. I crouched down very low in the cockpit down the straights to get maximum protection and soldiered on. The worst place for the wind was Abbey, where I just couldn't see properly. I managed to adapt myself to the situation, though I certainly wasn't enjoying it, but I found it was possible to get motoring again. I was down in seventh and starting to catch up, but when I got into the slipstream of a car in front there was a cloud of fine dust and grit trying to get into my naked eye. I had to choose my overtaking moves very carefully, but I was in front after 19 laps and stayed there to win.'

Denny was then in the air again, jetting back to Indianapolis, where he finished fourth in the 500 for the second year running.

'I suppose I shouldn't grumble, but the gap up to third was only 5 seconds and it separated me from an extra $15,000 in prize money. The Shelby turbine cars were withdrawn, but luckily Dan Gurney had a spare Eagle in his nest. It was a new car with a 4.2-litre 4-cam Ford engine, giving around 530 bhp and it was quite a bit different to the Eagle I drove at Indy last year. The car tipped the scales spot-on the Indy minimum at 1530 lb. The drive was taken through a Hewland 2-speed gearbox and the whole car was beautifully put together. Dan's car had the 5-litre stock-block pushrod Ford motor. I spent four or five days with my car before qualifying, but I was fortunate that Dan had set the car up for me. All I had to do was follow his style and it was the best style to copy, because Dan was really quick round Indy. I've no doubt that Dan would be faster than any other Grand Prix driver in the same sort of car simply because he knows Indy so well. And the secret? I'd say it's because he stamps on the throttle a helluva lot harder and sooner. That's where he makes up a lot of time on other drivers coming out of the turns.'

It seems hard to appreciate now in the new century when all Grand Prix drivers are millionaires with their own private jets, that drivers like Denny Hulme thought it was all in a weekend's work to practice for days at stupendous speed around the Indianapolis Motor Speedway in the middle of the United States, then fly to Monaco to practice for the Grand Prix around the tight street circuit, then back to Indianapolis for qualifying the following day.

'I didn't qualify at Indy the first weekend so I had to fly back and qualify between practice and the race at Monaco, and it didn't help that most of France was on strike at the time. Because of this I had to fly from Nice to Milan in a private plane in order to get a commercial flight from Milan to New York, but halfway to Milan the pilot of the private plane said we would have to turn back because the radio had gone wrong. I talked him into going on, and in the meantime the co-pilot decided he would take the radio out and try to fix it. But to get the radio out, the joy-stick had to be pulled right back and this meant that the plane went into a loop, so we flew around doing aerobatics while they tried to get the radio out. Eventually they got it working and I got to Milan with 5 minutes to spare!'

'It was at the time when I was getting the hang of things at Indy and lapping comfortably in the 165 mph bracket. Before that I was struggling to lap around 161 mph and I suggested to Dan that there might be something wrong with the handling. He jumped in and started lapping at 165–166 mph straight away . . . which suggested the answer was me and not the handling. Dan suggested that I was braking too hard, especially at the end of the two shorter straights. He told me that I didn't have to brake *at all* there and guaranteed that I'd still get round the turns. I thought of giving him an old-fashioned look but then remembered that Dan knew what he was talking about, took his advice, and immediately added 4 mph to my lap speed!'

The plan was for Denny to qualify for the 500 and get straight back on a plane from the mid-west for the south of France, but that was put on hold when the 'fourth engine' exploded in final practice. Gurney borrowed another engine from Gordon Johncock and by 4 p.m. that afternoon the Eagle mechanics were firing it up and Denny went straight out to qualify at 164.189 mph.

'It was a close call for time because a quarter of an hour later, after the qualifier's photograph had been taken, I was heading for New York at 600 mph, having lifted off from the Speedway to Indianapolis airport in a helicopter. The organisation of these flights was incredible. The pilot of the Lear jet asked for special let-down at New York in order to get me there in time and they let him jump the landing by 10 minutes and run me straight to the plane waiting to leave for Milan. This plane had already loaded its passengers and I scrambled on board at the last minute. It was all very neat and the pilot of the Lear never stopped his engines . . . I slept like a log on the flight across the Atlantic. A Cessna 411 was waiting at Milan to take me to Nice and I was in Monte Carlo before lunch! I had arrived there about the time I would have been getting out of bed if I had stayed at Indy and was feeling quite fit for the race.'

Denny finished fifth at Monaco on the Sunday and by 5 o'clock on the Monday afternoon he was back at Indianapolis. Three fuel stops were mandatory and they planned to start with only 30 gallons, which would give Denny an advantage in handling with a lighter car and also make it easier to stop or dodge if there was an early accident.

'This plan paid off well. I was running up in seventh place when I came in for my first refuelling stop and took on a full load of 62 gallons. When I moved off again I couldn't believe how heavy the car was and I had to wait for 20 laps or so before I could really stand on it again. After that I took on another 60 gallons at the second stop and then took on enough in the left-hand tank for the final run to the finish. With around 15 laps to go there was a crash and a wall of flame across the track, which put us all down on to the inside grass verge to get through.

'It was during this period that I must have cut a tyre on debris, because as soon as the lights went green I noticed the car was handling badly and I pitted to ask them to check the right rear tyre. The tyre looked OK and I shot back into the race, but when Dan lapped me he pointed to my left rear, so I rushed back into the pits. Unfortunately the pit crew were prepared with the wrong tyre and the wrong jack, so with the assistance of A.J. Foyt and Gordy Johncock and half a dozen of our crew the car was lifted bodily while they changed the left tyre! I had been lying third until I had this drama, but just as I rejoined the race, Mel Kenyon rushed past to put me back to fourth and with only four laps left there was nothing I could do about it. It made me mad thinking about the $15,000 I'd lost in those last laps . . . I was happy for Dan, who finished second. It was only the second time he had managed to finish the 500.

'Indianapolis took up a lot of time in May, but of course some of us had to squeeze in a couple of Grands Prix as well. For the Spanish Grand Prix my M7A was going pretty well, but I would have liked it to have been a little bit better. I was third in practice behind the 12-cylinder cars of Chris Amon and Pedro Rodriguez in the Ferrari and the BRM. It was a hard race for me because I got tucked in behind Graham's Hill's Lotus in second place, but the heat and the fumes made me feel woozy so I let him pull away for a time while I recovered my wits. Then I decided to have another go, thinking there might be a chance of squeezing through into the lead, but then I lost second gear and unfortunately it was the most important ratio at Jarama. So I settled for second place without second gear.

'I don't know what went wrong at Monaco. I simply couldn't make my car handle and I was down in ninth on the grid. A broken half-shaft cost me six laps and I came in fifth.'

Underlining the spirit of the sixties, when racing drivers raced just about anything offered, Denny had taken a phone call from Sid Taylor while he was at Indianapolis, with the Irishman offering him his Lola T70 for the Tourist Trophy race at Oulton Park the weekend after Monaco. Sid and Denny made an unlikely pairing, but Denny had already won two TTs for Taylor and would make it a third win, despite late-race gearbox problems.

'During that month I must have covered around 35,000 miles in the air and, of course, a few miles racing in between. Thank goodness I could sleep well on aeroplanes, but I did feel rather stiff for a few days after the TT. And there are some folks who think racing drivers have an easy life, what with all the foreign travel and posh hotels . . .'

After the first three Grands Prix, Denny was second in the world championship but 14 points behind Graham Hill, and the next race was the Belgian Grand Prix at Spa. 'Spa-Francorchamps is one of the fastest

Grand Prix tracks in the world and it poses quite a few problems not found on slower circuits, but we reckoned our M7As were already in reasonably good shape, so we carried out no special preparations before the race with things like wings or extra streamlining. The only concession to the very high lap speeds was a slightly taller screen on my car. We were more concerned with the durability of our drive shafts than with aerodynamic refinements, although we hoped we had solved that problem.

'For some reason we needed only a few laps in the first session to get down to a reasonably good time. We had consistently gone out and more or less set the pace but had then been unable to make much improvement on our times, while the opposition had been able to close up and gradually push us back down the grid. We were all surprised that we couldn't get down to the times set by Jim Clark last season. Most people had more power than last year and had not gone up much in that time, so the drag must have been pretty much the same. Personally, I think it was mainly due to a deterioration in the track surface during the past year. It was quite bumpy from the bridge at the bottom of the pit straight to the long left-hander at the top of the hill. If you were standing in the pits you could hear a sort of tremor in a car's exhaust note as it went up the hill with the rear wheels pattering over the surface.

'At the very end of the first day's practice my engine suddenly lost a couple of hundred revs and the only thing we could do was change engines. Then it tipped with rain all the next day and we couldn't do any serious practice or testing so I started fifth on the grid, hoping I could stay with the Ferraris of Amon and Ickx, and Surtees' Honda. That didn't happen and then Jackie Stewart arrived in the Matra and we raced together and Amon and Surtees dropped out and Ickx lost a cylinder, so we were racing for the lead. I reckoned I would sit back and wait until near the end before putting in the big effort and get into the lead, but a drive shaft failed again and I was out.

'It was doubly galling when Jackie stopped on the last lap, but that left Bruce out in front and he won the race in his own McLaren car, even though he had to be convinced that he'd won because he hadn't realised Jackie was out!'

They tested at Zandvoort before the Dutch Grand Prix but the race itself was run in a downpour and negated anything they had learned. Denny qualified seventh. 'The best I can say about my race was that it was reasonably brief. For the early laps I was running well back, for most of the time being half-blinded by a wall of spray. Then the engine's electrics became waterlogged and I lost several laps getting a dry-clean in the pits. I went back out again but by now I'd lost so much time that I wasn't going to complete 90 per cent of the race distance to qualify as a finisher, so parked it in the paddock.'

Before the French Grand Prix, the team experimented with wings, following the fashion started by the Brabhams and Chris Amon with the Ferrari at Spa. 'Although we had not had much success in the past trying wings on our 1967 sports car, we had a couple of wings hastily built up just before Rouen, based on a design by Robin Herd. We only had time for minimum testing in Britain but we were sufficiently convinced of their value to run them in France. The wings were lightweight affairs, built out of wrapped 20-gauge alloy sheet, and weighed only about two pounds apiece. The extra drag of the wing lost us about 150 revs on the straights, which means about 2–3 mph, but this was more than compensated for by the increased cornering power and stability and although the net gain in lap times was only about half a second on a circuit like Goodwood, the car was a lot more comfortable to drive. The effect was rather like a big extra shock absorber at the back, which had the effect of slowing down chassis movement. On fast curves it was much easier to hold the car in an attitude, because you got so much less pattering at the back as a result of the extra down-thrust that was being applied. This meant that at Goodwood it was possible to go through the long, very fast right-hander at Fordwater with your foot right in it, which was something we had not been able to do with the Formula 1 car, even though it had almost been possible to do it with the much more powerful CanAm sports car. I think perhaps we were just a little overinfluenced by our earlier experience with wings, and this made us hesitate before using them on our single-seaters.'

Denny managed equal third fastest time in practice, but as at Zandvoort, the weather ruined the race. The infamous 'Toto' Roche was the race starter as always for the French Grands Prix and Denny was expecting the unexpected. 'We were waved forward from the dummy grid and we all started to move up, but no sooner had the front row stopped than "Toto" dropped the flag and ran. I was still in first gear and crawling forward at the time on the inside of the second row, so I should think some of the back markers could hardly have left their places on the dummy grid when the race was suddenly on! Although it didn't affect me because I was more or less expecting it, the whole thing was plain ridiculous and it's high time someone explained to Roche a few of the basic facts of life . . .

'The track had been dry on the warm-up lap and all but two of us were on dry tyres and when the rain arrived it was too late to do anything. Those first laps were very unpleasant and by the time I had found some grip and sorted out the less slippery bits of the track I was running down in tenth place. Then came the horrible accident to Jo Schlesser, which brought a tragic end to a most unhappy episode involving the new air-cooled Honda, which in my opinion, and that of a lot of other people, should never have been in the race at all.

'One result of the Honda accident was that several of us punctured tyres on pieces of wreckage and I came in on lap 18 to change my nearside front, but it was now raining harder than ever so we changed all four wheels to wets. This completely transformed the car's handling and during the rest of the race I had a much easier time, managing to climb back from twelfth to fifth place.'

The British Grand Prix at Brands Hatch brought Denny a fourth place and the German Grand Prix in teeming rain on the Nürburgring saw Denny finish a drenched seventh. Denny spoke of this mid-season as a period 'in the doldrums'. They were getting ready for the CanAm series and testing to try to get the Formula 1 cars up to pace. 'I had done over 300 laps of Goodyear testing for three days at Goodwood and at the end of it all I was beginning to feel confident that we were getting competitive again.

'This was confirmed when we got to Monza and with a new type of Goodyear, we knew we were in business. We did all our practice on one set of these tyres and they showed virtually no sign of wear. I was a little disappointed not to get on to the front row of the grid, because I knew very well that at Monza we were in for a bitter slipstreaming battle and I knew that from the middle of the third row I would have to work hard if I wasn't to become detached from the leading bunch.

'During the final practice session, Bruce and I removed the wings from our cars and decided that this was the way we would race. To sum up, I would describe this year's Italian Grand Prix as a grand Formula 2 race. Everybody's engine seemed to be giving pretty much the same power. There were seven or eight of us circulating in close formation in the opening laps and if you did take the lead on one lap, you were likely to be dropped back to the end of the bunch on the next lap because of the determined slipstreaming. It was a terrific nose to tail battle until the ninth lap, when Chris Amon and John Surtees had their accident, which split the group. Then Graham Hill lost a wheel and I got left behind with Bruce.

'The Amon–Surtees accident happened extremely quickly. I think Chris just spun his Ferrari on some oil and John skidded on the same oil. The Honda nearly touched the Ferrari, which went over the guardrail, quite high in the air and backwards. I was worried for a moment, but I hoped the Ferrari would have landed on its wheels. Chris seemed to be going very slowly at the time. In fact, it all happened just like in a slow-motion film . . .

'Jackie Stewart and Jo Siffert were up ahead, but Bruce and I managed to catch up to them and then there were four of us trying to sort out the lead. A few laps later I was following Graham Hill through the second Lesmo when he lost his wheel. The first indication I had that something was amiss came when I heard Graham's engine screaming at very high revs. Then the wheel virtually leapt off the car and hit the guardrail. Graham kept the car under control, but the wheel followed him down the road right behind the car at the same speed, which I must say looked very strange. Graham managed to stop without trouble and the wheel went bowling down the road past him.

'It was rather difficult to shake off Jo Siffert in the Walker Lotus and Jackie didn't help me because he was making just enough of a group to keep Jo in tow. Jackie was very quick through the two Lesmo sweeps after I had towed him down the straights and when I eventually did break loose from Siffert I was able to pull away fairly comfortably at the rate of about a second a lap. I knew that once I did make the break I could get away from him.

'Without the wings on our cars it was easier to go motoring down the straights and save scratching to get round the corners. We were probably slower through the Lesmos because we didn't wear our wings, but we could make up heaps of time in a straight line. This made for much easier motor racing at Monza and it was a good race to win. It was a pity that Bruce had a bolt come out of the front of his engine, because he was really motoring, but all in all I feel that we have caught up with the opposition again.'

It was Denny's first win in his season as World Champion, in a race where the lead changed 15 times, with McLaren, Surtees, Stewart, Siffert and Denny all taking turns out front. Denny's winning average speed of 145.41 mph was faster than Jim Clark's lap record in 1967! The world title was still between Graham Hill, Jackie Stewart or Denny, with three races left.

The CanAm series was by now under way and Denny was a winner, but we will ride out the final three North American Grands Prix in the world championship and follow the sports car races later in the book.

The Canadian Grand Prix was at Ste-Jovite north of Montréal in Québec, a tough, bumpy circuit, partly because of the harsh winters. 'There was no really long straight, more a series of corners, some of them too slow to be of much use except to tire the driver and put extra strain on transmissions. The engine I had used to win the Italian Grand Prix was a really good one and when we checked it afterwards it seemed to be in such good shape that we decided to keep it in for the race in Canada. I intended to use it for the race if at all possible, and so as not to put too many miles on it beforehand I decided to do only the minimum amount of practice that was necessary to get my car properly sorted out. Having tried both the Weismann and ZF differentials and settled for the Weismann I got down to a decent time and drove the car back to the tent-type garage behind the pits to let the others fight it out for pole position. I reckoned that with 90 laps on this circuit, it was safer to spend less time wearing the car out in practice. That said, I reckon it was a fine effort by Jochen Rindt to put his Brabham on pole and a heroic effort by Chris Amon to equal it right at the end of the session in his Ferrari. I was equal sixth.

'Dan Gurney was using our spare car for the first time in this race and as we settled down in the early laps he was running a little ahead of me in a group working for fourth place, while Amon, Siffert and Rindt fought for the lead. I have to say I was surprised at how quickly the first bunch disappeared into the distance, even though I doubted that they would last the race. Sure enough, Rindt and Siffert dropped out before half-distance and as Dan had retired with a stone through his radiator and Hill was dropping back with loose engine mountings, I found myself running second to Amon but with no real hope of catching him. I reckoned that six more points from second place was a reasonable return for the weekend's work, especially as I could see some black rain clouds rolling overhead and I was on English-pattern Indy tyres, which were definitely not the thing to have between you and the track when it was wet!

'I was to have two lucky breaks. The first was that it remained dry and the second was that Chris's Ferrari broke its transmission at 72 laps, which put me in first place ahead of Bruce. It was tough luck on Chris, who must have thought he was at last going to win a Grand Prix, but I can't say that I objected to those 3 extra points! Bruce eased off and I lapped him just before the end and then out came the chequered flag and I'd won my second Grand Prix in a row and was now leading the championship, equal on points with Graham Hill. It was a good feeling.'

Next up was the United States Grand Prix at Watkins Glen and it was looking as though Denny had a chance of back-to-back titles.

'I spent the first part of practice checking out gear ratios and we made one or two changes to suit the circuit and to get me more revs down the two straights. Then, with the gearing right, I set about tyre tests on the new Goodyears. They certainly seemed an improvement, mainly because I found I could lean on them more in the corners because of their greater stability and I decided to use them for the race. I also elected to go with four-into-one exhausts, having tried both types, as I found I was getting more punch out of the corners, even though they didn't seem to give me any more revs down the straights.

'It was a reasonably uneventful practice and the only reason we made an engine change on my car was because I was keen to run the Cosworth V8 I had used at Monza and Ste-Jovite. It had been back to Britain for an overhaul and it arrived in time for second practice at the Glen. Although I was only on the third row of the grid, I was satisfied with my time as it was less than two-fifths of a second slower than pole time, which meant that we were pretty much on the pace. Everything went nicely from the start. Mario Andretti shot away into the lead, but Jackie got him under braking on that first lap and after that he was never headed. Graham, on the other hand, got away quite slowly and Chris slipped past into third place, while I ran sixth at first then overtook Rindt into fifth. On lap 11, fifth became fourth when Chris spun off in the Ferrari and then Mario had a pit stop to put me up to third, but on lap 16 it was my turn for a spot of drama. Someone had dropped a load of oil and I spun off into the dirt, damaging a rear brake-pipe. I made a pit stop where they sealed off the rear brakes and I carried on with front brakes only until I got the pit signal that they had found the parts to repair the brakes. By that time I had managed to break a plug, so that was replaced as well, but I had lost loads of time by now and although the car was really honking on, I'd resigned myself to no points.

'Quite a few people were in trouble towards the end of the race and as a result I was back up to seventh and that's where I thought I'd finish until I came past the pits for the ninety-third time and the world started going round in circles. I'd got a bit of a tweak on coming through the right-hander but the car straightened up, only to suddenly spin off to the left. I went charging backwards through a ditch, then hit quite a tall bank, which threw me high into the air before it all came down again with a sickening thump. I hadn't seen too much of the last part, because by that time I was well down in the cockpit, but I got away with only a scratch on my back. It seems likely that a drive shaft had let go inside the gearbox as I entered the corner. The car was a sorry mess and had to be flown back to England for a rebuild before the final race in Mexico.'

The Mexican Grand Prix would again decide the world championship, but for Denny to keep his title he would have to win while Graham and Jackie finished outside the first six. Denny qualified fourth.

'Jo Siffert, Graham and Jackie cleared off and left me, and I was running on my own with Jack behind, followed by John Surtees, Dan Gurney and Bruce. My drama started when the outer end of a front wishbone sleeve split as I came around the big banked loop similar to the corners at Indianapolis and the car suddenly leapt into one of the big guardrails. It flew up into the air and came down, by which time it was virtually minus the left-hand front wheel, while the rear one had got a puncture when it hit the guardrail, but it was still attached to the car.

'I came slowly across the track towards the pits, bouncing along on the front of the monocoque with sparks sheeting off. A petrol line broke and it caught fire just before the car stopped. I could see the flames in my mirrors. I managed to scramble out and then the pantomime really started. Fortunately the car had come to a stop in front of the pits and the fire did no damage at all to the car — it was just mainly petrol burning on the road, which made things look a lot worse than they were. By the time the fire people got there, hoses were unravelled and they'd found a big fire extinguisher. And all the time the police were trying to stop people from rushing up to put the flames out. Then when they turned on the extinguisher, the hoses were all tangled in a knot and nothing was coming out the end. It was a complete shambles . . .'

Graham won the race in his Lotus and the world title, while Bruce salvaged McLaren honours with second place.

New Zealand mechanic Allan McCall — popularly known as 'Maori', although he wasn't — had worked at Lotus with Jim Clark before moving to McLaren and Denny. He would recall years later: 'Working with Denny in 1968 was a completely different experience for me. Lotus was like going to school with the best team and one of the best drivers in Jimmy, but I was a pupil. At McLaren it was like I had graduated and got the best job. It was a privilege. The pay was great and you were made to feel like a partner in the team. Denny and I were given freedom to choose how we ran the car right from the start. For example, Denny liked a more positive brake so we ran 15-inch rims for an 11.5-inch brake disc. Bruce ran 13-inch rims with 10.5-inch discs. Denny ran Girling brake master cylinders and AP callipers; Bruce had an AP system. We also ran a higher front roll centre than Bruce. Denny knew what he wanted from a car and Bruce gave us all the freedom we wished.

'In 1967 with Team Lotus the rev limit on the Cosworth DFV was 9000 rpm. In 1968 Cosworth decided to let us run 9500 rpm. The first time we ran the car Denny said this particular motor really felt as if it wanted to go on revving, so we put a switch on the dash to turn off the limiter and ran and geared for 10,000 rpm. Later in the season Cosworth decided 10,000 rpm was good, so we went to 10,500 rpm. To my memory, Denny never over-revved or hurt a motor.

'The only thing he *did* hurt was the dog rings. I would take a look at the dog rings after every session and nearly always replaced them. When we got to Monza Denny was in top form. We removed nearly all the wings and nose ducts and Denny gave it a run. He came in and said, "Put it away. This car is a winner. We can't be beat!" He just sat on the pit counter and grinned and then he ran away with the race and the dog rings were perfect. The next race, at Ste-Jovite in Canada, was the same. He just ran away, with Bruce backing him. The Glen was a disaster, with the diff causing a huge shunt, and in Mexico he had another big shunt after a suspension breakage.

'Denny was always in contention for the championship in 1968. If we hadn't tried to run those dreadful Chrysler pot joint drive shafts that let us down at Spa and Monaco I think he would have had the title again. Working with Denny was definitely the most pleasure I ever experienced in Formula 1. With Bruce and Denny we were all mates trying to do our best ...'

Denny dipped out on the Grand Prix title but he would win a different championship that summer in the CanAm series.

13 Mystery Indy turbine trials

The first time Denny saw the Shelby Indianapolis turbine was in the rain at the Phoenix mile oval early in 1968. Denny was intrigued at the potential of the advanced new design from the pen of British designer Ken Wallis, whom Denny understood to have been a test pilot for Vickers and whom had been responsible for the turbine car which nearly won the Indy 500 for Parnelli Jones the year before.

He couldn't know the intrigue behind the designer, the car and the team. In hindsight we now know that the whole project was destined for the dustbin of racing history under a dubious cloud, but at the time Denny was in the driving seat experiencing a sort of amazing technical history being made on the race track and giving his personal expert commentary in his *Motor Racing* monthly column.

'The Shelby turbine was painted matt black when I first saw it, but it would later be painted in Carroll's blue and white colours. In effect, it's a refined version of the near-winner of the 1967 "500". It is powered by a General Electric turbine with a bunch of letters after its name, which in another life is used in helicopters. Of course, it has been modified to go into the car and also to suit the regulations, but I understand that GE have put their official stamp on the engine, which means that they guarantee it to run forever and a day. In fact, they reckon it should do four seasons of racing without taking it out of the car!

'It has an American-designed four-wheel-drive system which seemed good, but the rain prevented me from having any sort of go to discover anything about the handling. The whole car is amazing. The air intake was covered with a sort of rubber material, which looks as though it would prevent anything getting through, but in fact the air does get through very well and of course it reaches the engine nicely filtered.

'It was a curious sensation driving the car. From the outside it sounds like a normal turbine, but when you are driving it, it's just like it's in a big Boeing and waiting for takeoff. There is no rev counter. You judge your power on a percentage gauge, while keeping an eye on another gauge that tells you the temperature of the turbine blades. One of the problems is if the engine should become a runaway, but this is covered by a couple of computer devices, which keep an eye on this eventuality. The driver also has a convenient cut-out button.

'The form is that the engine winds up to 50 per cent on the gauge, you let your foot off the brake and away it goes, up to about 40 mph without touching the throttle. Nothing much happens with 60 per cent on the gauge, but at 75 per cent you hear the engine note change completely and at 80 per cent it's giving enough power to spin all four wheels in the wet. I gather the engine will pour on the power all the way up to about 220 mph!'

Denny kept calling the turbine 'the engine' . . .

'Driving the car will obviously pose problems and when it is raced the gauge won't go below 80 per cent and this will be tricky. When you lift off the throttle there is no braking effect from the engine — which is why they've given the cars really beefy brakes, set inboard back and front. It was a pity it was only possible to pootle around the circuit, but at least we are satisfied that it moves well and the next time I try it will be at Indianapolis.'

Bruce and Denny flew to Indianapolis late in April and spent two days there but only managed one afternoon running because of *snow!*

'An afternoon was definitely not long enough, but the Indy tests did give us an opportunity to try out the engine power, although so far they hadn't really turned up the wick. What the session proved to me was that there was a lot more to learn about using the power properly. The major disadvantage is the big time lag in the throttle response and this meant you had to do some tricky figuring at every corner.

'Driving the turbine feels so fantastic it was hard to credit. The acceleration was of the order of 1.5 G, which meant you needed a pad behind your helmet to protect your head. The engine kicks so hard that your head just smacks back unless you brace your head and neck really hard. As the engine was set up that afternoon I was only reaching around 185–190 mph on the straights, but the car gets up to 180 mph within 200 yards and that's where it scores.

'Getting around the corners properly is something of a teaser, because it feels like driving a normal car in neutral. This was particularly so because I wasn't able to control the throttle properly. You were watching a little power percentage gauge, trying to keep the needle in the 65–70 per cent bracket and also trying to keep an eye on the corner at the same time. The problem was that I didn't know exactly where the throttle was in terms of that percentage. In other words, it was difficult to decide by how much you should back off the throttle. At the same time you have to be ready to left-foot the brake pedal really hard in case you give the engine too much boot, because at about 80 per cent it gets pretty vicious. So this car demands a whole new driver-education programme. I reckon it will need several days just going round and round to get the hang of it through the turns. There is some indication of power from the noise of the compressor, but the only real answer to the problem is to keep working at the corners until everything becomes automatic. When we get to the proper pattern, it might be possible to put springs into the throttle system, to give a better indication where that 80 per cent comes in. There's no doubt that we were losing out around the corners, but we are as fast as anything there's ever been at Indy from corner to corner. There is still some work to be done on the brakes, but by the time we get back to Indy for the race I think we'll have something quite useful . . .'

The opportunity would never come.

By chance in 2005 I came across a photograph of Denny in this strange turbine car and I researched the story before I came across Denny's column on the car in *Motor Racing*. I worked with the assistance of the Speedway historian, Donald Davidson, and called the feature *The Indy Turbine That Never Was* and it fits well to reprint it here, linked with Denny's first-hand experiences with the project:

For the Indianapolis 500 in 1968, Goodyear invested millions to have a radical 4-wheel-drive Shelby Botany 500 turbine car designed for their Grand Prix aces, Bruce McLaren and Denis Hulme, but it was a project dogged by wild overspending and underdevelopment. It all ended mysteriously with an after-dark team withdrawal immediately after Mike Spence's fatal crash at the Speedway in the Lotus turbine.

Bruce McLaren became the first driver ever to take the rookie test at Indianapolis in a turbine car when he did his learning laps in the Shelby Botany 500 Special in 1968. This was a car shrouded in mystery, a high-dollar project that was doomed to failure. Two of these turbine cars were to be raced by Bruce McLaren and Denny Hulme. Goodyear was financing the team and paying the McLaren team $50,000 and Bruce was paid $20,000 for testing and racing, extremely good money for the day. Denny had a separate contract.

In his book, *Bruce McLaren — Racing Car Constructor*, George Begg wrote: 'When the new Indianapolis car was ready for testing in March and April, 1968, Bruce made four trans-Atlantic trips, first class, paid by Goodyear, to California. After he had inspected the car and met the people designing and making it, most of whom were aircraft people, Bruce was far from happy. Bruce could not help but feel more uneasy about the whole project, as when he inspected the factory, he was amazed to see that whereas the McLaren factory used Mini vans for day to day workshop transport, these people ran Cadillac Eldorados! The office was like something out of a plush film set and the toilet seats even had velvet seat covers!'

Begg quotes McLaren describing his first track experience with the turbine: 'Driving the thing is weird; you sit in it and press the brake pedal. They plug in a starter and it gradually winds up till it's whistling and then they flick some switches and it sort of goes *Booooo . . . woosh* and makes a noise like a Boeing. They pull the plug out, you let the brake off and it coasts out of the pit. You open the throttle and it still just coasts along . . . for about three seconds, that is, and then you've got 600 . . . 700 . . . or 800 horsepower, depending on how far they turned the wick up so to speak, all at once. It's like trying to write with a rubber pen . . . it's a little difficult!'

Ken Wallis, an Englishman who had worked as an experimental engineer at Douglas Aircraft in the early 1960s, had designed and built the first turbine car for Andy Granatelli's STP team and it came close to winning the '500' in 1967 driven by Parnelli Jones. Indianapolis historian, Donald Davidson, recalls, 'Jones was leading with 3.5 laps to go when a bearing went in the rear end. The turbine was still running but it couldn't deliver the power to the track.' A.J. Foyt went on to win in his Coyote-Ford.

That Granatelli project was funded by Firestone. Wallis would switch to the Goodyear-funded project immediately after the race in 1967.

Wallis was originally hired by Granatelli in 1966 to work on the veteran Novi in its final season at the Brickyard and he recommended that the heavy, old-fashioned engine be replaced by a turbine. The revolutionary new car was an elegant device of aircraft-type construction with an aircraft-type bulkhead. On the left-hand side was a capsule with a Pratt & Whitney gas turbine helicopter engine. The driver sat on the right. It was 4-wheel-drive and initially used an air brake flap as introduced by Mercedes at Le Mans.

The driver pressed the brake pedal and the air flap rose. It was considered to be an advantage, but there were complaints during practice and the device was removed.

There had been friction in the team with Granatelli claiming full credit for the turbine car and its pace-setting engineering and Wallis was quick to switch to the Goodyear-funded project. His new design was more conventional, with the turbine in front of the driver in a car that looked elegant but was fraught with problems. The brakes were poor and the car was well off the required pace. There were other unseen problems.

Denny Hulme tested the new turbine car at Phoenix. He said the car had enough urge low down to spin all four wheels on takeoff. It had a high whine when you stood watching it, said Denny, but when you were sitting in there driving alongside it, it sounded like a Boeing 707 lifting off from the tarmac.

The United States Auto Club had chosen to encourage turbine power as an option at the speedway, but when Parnelli Jones had been so dominant in 1967 the rule relating to the annulus air intake was reduced from 23.999 square inches to 15.999 square inches for 1968. This meant that the new Botany car was gasping for air and unlikely to make qualifying pace.

Intrigue now enters the equation. It was said that someone related to the project had developed a means of increasing the annulus inlet while the car was on the track but it was legal when parked in the pits. It apparently operated in the manner of an iris in a camera and could be activated by the driver. But the car was still well off the pace and running 10 mph slower than the new Lotus 'wedge' turbine cars that Colin Chapman had built for Granatelli to Maurice Phillipe's design. The Goodyear-funded project was also wildly over budget.

Salvation came in a bizarre fashion. It was said that one of the engineers 'in the know' on the Wallis team had been fired and he conveyed the information on the 'iris' to the rival Firestone team. This was passed on to the USAC technical inspectors, who planned a swoop on the Wallis cars on the evening of 7 May, but fate intervened dramatically.

Jim Clark had tested the new Granatelli Lotus turbine only a few days before his death in the Formula 2 Lotus at Hockenheim on 7 April. Graham Hill was already entered for the '500' and Jackie Stewart was to join him, but he had cracked a bone in his wrist and could not pass the medical. Mike Spence was drafted in, and was quickly up to speed, lapping faster and faster on that afternoon exactly a month after Clark had been killed in Germany. Davidson remembers: 'Mike Spence had been thrust into the limelight and he was in the car that Clark was supposed to have driven and he was going faster and faster and faster. The track closed each day at 6 p.m. and with about twenty minutes left Spence had run an unofficial lap at 169.555 mph — the fastest lap ever turned at the Speedway — and he was emerging as a real star. I was at the track, in the pits and all of a sudden I heard *Ka-Blom!* A huge *BOOM!* like a bomb going off and Mike had hit the wall in Turn 1. Later that night he succumbed to his injuries.'

At 7 p.m. that evening, an hour after the track had closed and while the USAC officials were involved with inspection of the crashed Lotus, the Shelby Botany 500 cars were withdrawn. Davidson said, 'The reason given was that in the interests of safety it was felt that the turbine cars needed more development and they would be returning for the race in 1969. The next day the team had gone, the cars loaded in the middle of the night and everything had just disappeared. There was a message in chalk on one of the blackboards with an official statement . . .

'I don't know what happened to the cars. Three were said to have been built, but I only ever saw two. One of them was on display in a Los Angeles museum for a while. As far as the drivers were concerned, a lot of car owners were interested in their services.'

In fact, Bruce and Denny were at Jarama for the 1968 Spanish Grand Prix when word came through that the turbines had been withdrawn and both were stunned at the news of Mike Spence's fatal crash, but delighted that they would never have to drive those turbine cars again.

Don Grey summed up the situation in *Sports Car Graphic*: 'The already tense situation wasn't helped when Carroll Shelby decided to use Spence's crash to cover the withdrawal of his turbine cars, saying, "After complete and intensive testing, I feel at the present time it is impossible to make a turbine-powered car competitive with a reasonable degree of safety and reliability." Issued only two hours after Spence's death, Shelby's statement caused considerable annoyance to the STP-Lotus-Firestone camp, because it appeared to refer to *all* turbine cars, rather than his entries specifically. The statement also skirted the fact that his cars — designed by Ken Wallis (ex of STP), bankrolled by Goodyear ($1.5 million), and powered by GE turbines — were grossly overweight, had inadequate braking, and the handling gave drivers Bruce McLaren and Denis Hulme the shivers. In a word, uncompetitive . . .'

14 A different championship title

The McLaren team gilded their CanAm lily by following Lotus Formula 1 fashion and using the new 7-litre 620 bhp version of the Chevrolet V8 engine as a stress-bearing part of the chassis. The team started running a test prototype of what would become the M8A in March of 1968. 'It was really one of last year's cars with lower profile tyres and the body cut down,' Bruce McLaren told me for a feature I wrote in *Road & Track* in 1969. I quote now from *Can-Am*, the series history by top American motor sports writer Pete Lyons . . . who in turn was quoting from original features I had written while I wrote columns with Bruce and magazine features. 'Then we tried a cast-iron 427 engine in it, a litre bigger than the engine we ran last year . . . The old chassis was cut in half and the engine became the rear of the car with the rear suspension hanging off a sub-frame. With this mobile test rig we tried a dry-sump set-up, wings, new brakes and all while the new M8A was taking shape on the drawing board.

'Hanging the engine off the back of the monocoque was pretty much my idea. Gordon Coppuck and I worked out the rear bulkhead, the suspension was a group effort, the front half of the chassis was largely Jo Marquart's work. And I worked out the body shape and general layout with Jim Clark of Specialised Mouldings.'

McLaren engine man Lee Muir told journalist Alan Lis about Bruce's first flirt with the power of the bigger engine. 'The first engine was a 427 with iron block and aluminium heads. It made 560 lb-ft of torque and 624 bhp at 6500 rpm. Bruce took it for a test drive and he came back with a grin from ear to ear. "Jesus Christ, there's never been anything like this! There's no way we can use all this horsepower." But within three weeks he was asking what we could do to get more . . .'

The McLaren team had always been built around Bruce, who took the good times along with the times when things weren't working to plan. Denny Hulme was a fellow Kiwi and team-mate who was to share the honours when and if they came. In the *Road & Track* feature, I described the new team-up: 'The pair get on well together, Hulme respecting McLaren's urge to design and build his own cars while reckoning himself to be a better driver than Bruce, and Bruce happy to acknowledge the point if it makes for a smooth running operation and lets him concentrate on new ideas.' It would be Bruce's last full racing season.

The first CanAm race was at Elkhart Lake and Denny was delighted with the power and performance of the new car. 'You don't realise the speed you are doing until you check the gear ratio chart. The way it gobbles the distance between one corner and the next is just fantastic. The engine is quite beautiful. The power comes in from 2000 rpm and keeps on right up to 6500 rpm. The throttle response is absolutely unbelievable, far superior to anything I have ever driven. It makes even the 3-litre Ford-powered Formula 1 cars seem sluggish. You just crack the throttle and it all works!'

Lyons captured the spirit of the McLarens in the fresh CanAm series, writing in *Autosport*: 'The impression made on onlookers was tremendous — if last year's M6As were advanced, the M8As are fantastic. The whole concept and construction is ultra-modern and the massive motors, topped by huge curved intake horns, are stunning — you can *feel* the power.'

Denny arrived at Elkhart Lake with a black eye. 'The previous Monday I'd been testing my Formula 1 car at Goodwood and had slammed a bird going down the straight. Fortunately I wasn't going full chat. There was a great smack in my face and blood all over the place. I simply didn't see it and I shuddered to think what it would have been like if I'd been doing 180 miles an hour. I was lucky to get away so lightly, but I had a lovely "shiner" for a week . . .'

The Gulf-orange McLarens filled the front row, with Bruce a tenth faster than Denny. But it was raining. 'Stirling Moss led the parade lap and he had his work cut out in a big American car, slithering around pretty desperately while we were idling along in second gear. He was hanging the tail out like fury and simply couldn't get any traction. I got into the first corner in the lead followed by Bruce and then Mark Donohue in his Sunoco McLaren. Mark had his throttle stick and he spun off, but I could understand his problem in the wet because even with the throttle just slightly open we were getting around 200 horsepower at the rear wheels.'

Denny led Bruce by 9 seconds on that opening lap and stretched it to half a minute. The rain stopped and the track was drying in the last half of the race, but Denny had a strong lead, which was just as well because with five laps to go, a valve gear rocker broke and the big engine lapsed on to seven cylinders. 'With a lap to go I noticed my oil pressure falling to zero, so I was rather glad when I saw the chequered flag and it was all over.' The McLarens finished a strong 1-2.

Next up was the bumpy Bridgehampton circuit in New York State and once again the front row of the grid was orange, Denny on pole this time. There had been oil-leak problems with the big Chevvy motors in practice and there would be major problems in the race. Bruce led early in the race and then Denny took over in front. Mark Donohue and Jim Hall in the Chaparral were coming on strong. 'I was closing quite quickly on Bruce late in the race but just as I was about to retake the lead my engine blew. More trouble was to follow. I had been right in thinking Bruce was in some sort of trouble because six laps later he parked his car with engine-bearing failure and Donohue went on to win the race from Hall and Lothar

Motschenbacher. Bruce had managed to get to the pits with his, but mine went up with a real bang that even bent the exhaust pipes! Morale was a bit low after the race as we prepared for a big engine-rebuild session. Some people were saying that we had made a mistake using the engine as a stressed member, but they were wrong. The root of our problem was detonation in the combustion chambers, which was knocking out the bearings, and the detonation was being caused by oil getting up into the chambers past badly seating rings. After Bridgehampton we fitted a new type of top ring and as far as we could tell at Edmonton two weeks later, this had just about cured our troubles.

'From New York to Edmonton, Alberta, was a full 2700 miles, which meant three and a half days of solid motoring for the lads, who had to trail our cars and all our equipment. Edmonton turned out to be a very prosperous town of about 400,000 and the whole town from the mayor down joined in to promote the race. They even stopped all the traffic in town for the afternoon before the race for a full-scale parade, with most of us riding in new Camaros. Being in the heart of the Prairies (and incidentally only a mile from the Arctic Circle) the circuit is dead flat, and they have managed to build in some great corners which are really tricky and they had obviously put in a great deal of thought in the way they've spent their three million dollars. The main straight is a 4200 ft drag strip, so there is no problem in passing.'

On the first day of practice both McLarens had problems, Bruce with a sheared metering unit drive and Denny with a wheel nut that seized on the hub and had to be chiselled off. 'After our Bridgehampton problems and then this setback I was starting to feel cheesed-off, so I went out for a real go in the final practice session and turned in a time worth pole and parked it. Then, right at the end of the session, Bruce had a big tweak and equalled my time, so once again we had an orange front row, with Hall and Donohue behind us.

'I went into the lead from the start and Jim in the Chaparral had got past Bruce, but after a few laps the Chaparral had a brake problem that cost him a long pit stop. It was just as well that the heat came off when it did, because well before half-distance I'd noticed my oil pressure fluctuating. We'd had this problem before and Don Beresford had rigged me up a pressurised one-gallon oil tank in the cockpit. All I had to do was turn the tap and the oil was forced into the engine and then scavenged back into the main oil tank. At the halfway mark I was given the "add oil" signal, but I'd dumped it in already, so I obviously had to watch the needle carefully towards the end of the race. With 15 of the 80 laps left, the needle started to surge again. I wasn't too worried because Bruce was about 20 seconds behind, so I eased up, but towards the finish the needle was staying on zero for about half a mile coming out of a corner and I was quite relieved to see the chequered flag with Bruce 12 seconds behind me.'

At the halfway stage in the series, Denny had a scant 1-point lead over Mark Donohue and he noted that while this was not quite as good as the previous season, when he had won three straight races and had 27 points in the bank, he had then gone on to strike out and not take a single point in the final three races.

The Laguna Seca race started rockily for the team, with both cars losing engines in practice. 'Early on race morning it looked as though the weather would be fine, but it changed and got progressively worse as the start time neared and it was obvious that we would need rain tyres. The hour practice on race morning enabled me to get in a few laps on the replacement engine and also to bed in new brake pads. We were aware after that untimed morning session that John Cannon was going to be quick in the wet with his original M1B McLaren. Bruce was on pole and I was behind him in third. Jim Hall had been second fastest in the Chaparral, but he had an engine problem before the start and his car was pushed aside. There were two warm-up laps in driving rain, probably in the hope that Jim could get the Chaparral started. I had been very careful with my goggles, rubbing soap inside the lenses to try to prevent them from fogging up. They seemed OK until we moved off and then they misted up immediately! It was so bad that I nearly came in on the first warm-up lap.

'So we splashed on in the race and after a very few laps I was rather surprised when John Cannon came by. I couldn't believe how much adhesion he was getting from the F5000 Firestone intermediates he was using. By this time it was steady rain and his tyres were working well, but when it started to pour down I started to catch him because my car was better through the big puddles than his. After about 20 laps I decided to put a bubble visor on and warned the pits that I was coming in. It made a difference for a few laps, but eventually the visor also fogged up. I didn't use the bubble from the start because I didn't think I would need it, but at least you could wipe a bubble when it started to mist. Bruce was having visibility problems, too. He said he was able to run for a long time with his goggles, but when he got behind someone in the heavy rain the cold spray steamed them up.

'Little did I know then that Cannon had taken his goggles *off!* As a result his eyelids eventually wouldn't stay open and he was holding one of them open with his hand. His eyes looked awful afterwards, but there's no doubt he was good that day and what a good-looking result it was, with McLarens in the first six places. In view of the conditions I couldn't be dissatisfied with my second place.'

Denny went back to Britain between the two Californian CanAm races, coming back with Greeta and Martin. 'We had two stabs at getting back across the Atlantic. On the first effort we got up over Iceland in the Boeing 707 when John Surtees' wife Pat said she could see smoke pouring from one engine! Eventually the pilot decided to turn round and head back to England, so that meant seven hours' wasted flying time and we didn't take off again until the next day.

'I eventually got to Los Angeles fairly late on the Thursday and went out to the track for practice on the Friday. My car was looking brand new and they had found a lot more beef from the engines — about 60–70 more horsepower than we had at Laguna Seca. Since it was obviously not going to rain at Riverside we felt in pretty good shape.

'Bruce really likes Riverside and always goes very quick there very early on, so I wasn't surprised when he was on pole position, with me beside him and Mark Donohue and Jim Hall on the row behind us. Most of the Ford-engined cars seemed to be having a lot of problems with oil — they were blowing it out everywhere. Mario Andretti turned up with a new Lola fitted with a 7-litre Ford and I think he just managed to complete one lap, but in the meantime oil was down round the whole circuit. Dan Gurney also had a 427 cubic incher; I don't know what his problems were but I'm pretty sure they were also oil-related. Lothar Motschenbacher had fitted a 7-litre Chevvy in his car and seemed to be going reasonably well, though he had an overheating problem and couldn't run with us at all. Both Hall and Donohue seemed to be having overheating problems on the desert circuit.

'Bruce shot immediately into the lead at the start and I followed close behind. We ran this way for most of the race. Hall passed Donohue after three or four laps and sat about 20 seconds behind when the race settled down. Bruce gradually got up to between 10 and 17 seconds ahead of me and didn't seem to be having any troubles. Neither was I until I came up to lap a back marker. There were about 24 laps left and I thought he'd seen me. In fact he hadn't, although he was away off line and just as I came up alongside him he decided to pull across in front. I bounced off through a bunch of marker tyres. The first lot of tyres I hit didn't seem to do much damage, but I spun and hit another lot on the other side of the track. It was this second hit that did the damage.

'I pressed on back to the pits with the body crumpled. Some of the aluminium panels were burst open at the front and dragging on the road. This was taped up at the pits and I went out again, but all the body started to blow off again and I made another longer stop to have it all taped down as firmly as possible. I went back out and eventually finished fifth. Naturally I was bit disappointed, because if I could have won at Riverside I would have clinched the championship. Bruce didn't seem to have a moment's worry throughout the Riverside race. He had a Thermos of iced tea in his car and sipped away at it as he went on his way to winning something like $21,000.

'Our extra horsepower came through doing a few little things like removing the gauze from the tops of the air intakes. The team were very happy about the whole result and this was one time when we really out-ran Jim Hall. We had the legs on him down the straight and everywhere round the circuit, which was encouraging for the final round at Las Vegas.'

As described in a previous chapter, Denny lost his world championship title at the Mexican Grand Prix on the weekend between Riverside and Las Vegas, but honour would be restored in the desert outside the gambling city. Denny's first visit to Las Vegas had been in 1966 when he drove a Lola T70 for Sid Taylor, and Sid's friend Jerry Entin told a tale of taking Denny to his first experience of gambling in the casino at the Stardust Hotel. 'Joe Louis, the former boxing champion, was the greeter there and when he learned who Denny was and that it was his first visit to a casino, he came with us while Denny tried his hand at various games — and won on each! I think he was up about $70 in 15 minutes and he was all smiles.' Entin retired for the evening, leaving Denny in the casino and he asked him the next morning whether he'd kept on winning. 'He said he'd lost it all and he didn't plan on gambling again unless he had Joe Louis and me with him . . .'

'The engines we used at Las Vegas had been checked and rebuilt. They were quite healthy, though not the best we'd had, but it's fairly difficult to tell if you are 30 to 40 horsepower up or down at a circuit like Las Vegas, which doesn't have really long straights where horsepower counts.

'On the first day's training I was on pole and Bruce was beside me after a tussle with Mark Donohue, who was the only rival we had for the title. On the second day, Bruce and I reversed positions, followed by Donohue and Hall. We didn't really have any practice problems, except that I seemed to be running through a lot of brake pads, I suppose because the circuit had three dead-stop corners per lap. Eventually I had to change the braking ratio to put more on the rear. This was strange, because the brakes had been fine at the other tracks. The result was that I spent half the second practice bedding in three sets of pads.

'The appearance of Chris Amon with the big new Ferrari created great interest and all the drivers were buzzing round it like flies. My view was that it wasn't at all bad, though it gave the impression of being on the heavy side, with one of the most complicated aerofoil systems I'd seen on a racing car.

'Poor old Chris didn't have much luck in his gambling at Las Vegas. In 1967 he got as far as the last lap and this year he finished his race on the first lap! The first-lap accident stemmed from the rather shambolic starting procedure. It began because Donohue had an electrical fault and didn't get away and possibly they were waiting for him to catch up. Bruce and I were leading the bunch on the rolling start lap behind Stirling Moss in the pace car and we suspected that we would have to do another lap before the starter gave us the flag. Behind us, the others were holding back in order to get more of a running start across the line. Well, the starter *did* drop the flag first time round and the others behind us were really rushing up on us. I had the best line into the corner and Bruce tucked in behind. Andretti, who had already moved up a couple of places, touched Bruce as they went round the corner and Bruce flew off into the dust. For those behind it was like driving into fog and Chris was one of those put out as a result.

'Bruce got going again because he had luckily spun out of the way of the other chargers. During practice I had tried a "birdcage" over the engine in my car to protect it from stones and fortunately I let Bruce have it for the race. The cage kept all the muck out of the engine but Bruce had to stop at the pits to replace the nose. We had brought spare tails and nose sections to cope with situations just like this. Unfortunately the replacement nose section wasn't fitted with wing mirrors and Bruce had to make another stop to have them pop riveted on. Despite this, he still finished sixth and so ensured himself second in the series ahead of Donohue.

'On the first lap I had a reasonable lead but I slowed down before the wreckage after the accident and Andretti started pressing until he retired a few laps later. Then Dan Gurney came storming through. He made the odd attempt to get on terms but found it wasn't possible and then broke a drive shaft.

'This left me with a lead of about half a minute, so I decided to slow down and go as gently as possible while keeping the others a safe distance behind. So it was a fairly uneventful drive . . . until the big shunt involving Jim Hall and Lothar Motschenbacher. There was a crazy heap of wreckage strewn across the track and I slowed down to a crawl to pick my way through, wondering whether my CanAm title hopes might be ruined by a puncture. I got away with that, but with a few laps left I got run off the road by another competitor. I'm sure the hearts of everyone in the McLaren pits were in their mouths. It was so close that the cooling vents on one side of my car were whipped off by the other car, while the vents on the other side were knocked away by a pile of tyres at the trackside. I thought for one awful moment that the series was lost for me, but fortunately I got back on to the circuit and went on cruising home to win the race and the championship.

'I'd lost my F1 title and won the CanAm sports car crown.'

15 Life at McLaren 1969–1970

Gordon Coppuck, the designer who had worked with Bruce from the early days of the team, realised that Denny had an input but that it was a different interpretation to Bruce's, rather in the same way that Denny held a golf club wrong-handed, with an unconventional, almost upside-down grip.

Interviewed for *Autosport* by Doug Nye, Coppuck said, 'Denny can come in and tell you what's wrong with a car and he's almost invariably right. But Bruce spoiled us, because he would come in and not only know what was wrong but have a solution already worked out! With Denny, we sit down and talk it over. But he's a very experienced race driver and really can set a car up to give the best it's got. With development work you have to go beyond that; you have to get it to give the best it's got, and then find a way of getting a bit more and then set it up to the ultimate all over again . . . it's a chain reaction.'

David Phipps, editor of *Autocourse*, summed up Denny's 1969 season, rating him as fifth and midfield in his First Eleven behind Stewart, Rindt, Ickx and Brabham and ahead of Amon, Hill, McLaren, Surtees, Siffert and Beltoise. 'The unluckiest Grand Prix driver of 1969 is undoubtedly Denis Hulme. Time after time he has been well placed or has done good practice times, only to be let down by unexpected mechanical failures. His record in CanAm racing shows that he is not a car breaker, yet he did not have a trouble-free Grand Prix from Zandvoort until Mexico when he scored a very convincing victory.'

The 1969 season started in the sunshine at Kyalami in March with Denny running his last-season's M7A, reskinned since Mexico with a rear suspension-mounted wing. He was immediately fastest overall, a tenth faster than Stewart's Tyrrell Matra on the first day and by the end of practice he was down to third but still on the front row beside Brabham and Rindt in the Lotus. By half-distance the order was Stewart-Hill-Hulme, with comfortable gaps, and that was the order at the finish.

Denny finished third again in the 1969 Race of Champions at Brands Hatch after having his race wrecked by the weather. He had tried the car with wings front and rear but finally settled for nose spoilers and a set-up similar to the way the car had run at Kyalami. 'The car seemed capable of going quick but it didn't seem possible to keep it going that way all the time. Perhaps it was something to do with the fuel load, because the handling was poor at the start of the race, good halfway through and then went off again.' He was grateful to finish third.

It was wet again a fortnight later at Silverstone for the International Trophy won by Jack Brabham. Denny's engine failed. 'It was probably the most expensive blow-up I've ever had. It was timed beautifully for the main grandstands because it happened right in front of the pits! It went pop and all hell broke loose. It just destroyed the crankshaft and I kept a few bits of the block as expensive souvenirs.' The weekend was not a total loss as Denny won the sports car race in John Woolfe's Lola T70, a car he had raced at Reims two years earlier when it was owned by Sid Taylor.

The Spanish Grand Prix on the Montjuich course above Barcelona would be remembered for the twin failures of the tall rear wings on both works Lotuses — Rindt and Hill were both injured in the crashes over the fast brow beyond the pits. Denny couldn't better fifth in the early practice sessions, started on the third row and would finish fourth.

At Monaco, following a meeting between practice sessions, the CSI controlling body announced that the tall wings would be banned forthwith, so the cars raced wingless. Stewart dominated practice in the Matra and Denny and Bruce were lacklustre in the McLarens, side by side back on the sixth row — no place to start on the streets of Monaco. Bruce finished fifth and Denny a distant sixth.

At Zandvoort Denny had been holding third place behind Stewart in the Tyrrell Matra MS80 and Siffert in Rob Walker's Lotus 49. 'I was rushing around thinking of 4 world championship points . . . until eight laps from the end when the engine suddenly went off colour. At least I thought it went off, though maybe I was only fooling myself, since I had spotted that the gauge was showing low oil pressure. In fact, a later investigation revealed nothing wrong with the engine, so perhaps it was the gauge that was at fault. Maybe we ought to throw the gauges away so that we wouldn't worry. That isn't as ridiculous an idea as it sounds and it's often been done at Indy . . .'

After the big engine failure earlier in the year at Silverstone, Denny eased back slightly and Chris Amon snapped past in the Ferrari, relegating Denny to fourth at the flag.

The French Grand Prix was at Clermont-Ferrand, a circuit Denny liked. He had raced on the five-mile Charade circuit once before in 1965 in his second Grand Prix and he finished fourth for Brabham. 'The car felt good and I was feeling fitter myself. I felt right at home from the start of the weekend. Practice went well and I managed to slip in a quick one just before the end of the last session to put myself alongside Jackie in the Matra on the front row. It certainly did a lot for my morale to be competitive again.'

Denny raised a laugh in the McLaren pit when he had his gearbox fitted with fifth gear lower than fourth. 'It was a sort of underdrive and I thought it would help me up the hill. It worked at that point, but made for some awkward shifts at other points round the circuit. So really it didn't work and I had the ratios put back to normal, but I thought it was worth a try.'

'On the warm-up lap I made a couple of practice starts, stalled the first time and then worked out the best pattern. When the flag fell I hung on a million revs and let it go in a cloud of rubber smoke. I think Jackie almost stalled at the start but he gathered it quickly and we went into the first corner virtually side by side. The Matra was quicker in the uphill section leading back to the pits, but I got right behind Jackie going into the final hairpin. Then he pulled away again up the hill after the start and I realised I would have to be content to stay second.

'My motor was sounding sweet and I never went over 10,000 rpm all day. In fact, I was *very* happy with the way things were going . . . until the tenth lap when the car suddenly started handling diabolically and I thought I had a flat tyre. It was wandering all over the road and felt terrible. I looked in my mirrors to see whether anything had come adrift at the back and then spotted the front roll bar was bouncing up and down in a way it shouldn't. I thought that maybe I could get used to the handling and carry on, but I gave the pit a warning signal as I went by and by lap 12 the car was almost uncontrollable.

'I came in next time round for a minor rebuild. The bolt holding the offside end of the roll bar had fatigued and broken. It turned out to be disastrous because we had to drill the bolt out before we could put another one in. It all cost me three laps and I came home eighth, while Jackie stayed out front and won.'

At Silverstone for the British Grand Prix, Denny picked up the pace with a front-row start and was running third behind Rindt's Lotus and Stewart's Matra when his engine went sour after 19 laps. He pulled in to the pits to check the ignition but retired with a broken camshaft. Denny seemed to favour complicated circuits and at the Nürburgring he started from the second row of the grid and was up to fourth late in the race when his transmission failed.

The Italian Grand Prix at Monza was looking good, with Denny on the front row beside Rindt's Lotus. *Autocourse*: 'Rindt was first away with Hulme almost alongside him, but Stewart shot through between them before the first corner and Hulme buckled his front nose wing against Stewart's rear tyre . . . on the sixth lap Hulme decided to see whether his car was capable of taking the lead and within the next five laps he moved up from sixth to first and back again; having satisfied himself of his car's capabilities he decided to take it easy and save the machinery . . . after 10 laps there was only a matter of 3 seconds between the first seven cars, in the order Stewart, Hulme, Rindt, Courage, Siffert, McLaren and Beltoise. Denny was the first to depart the group, dropping back without a clutch and a major brake problem and he finished seventh, two laps behind the leaders.'

At Mosport for the Canadian Grand Prix, Denny qualified on the second row beside the Stewart Matra, but he made a poor start, battled in midfield and was out on the tenth lap with electrical problems. The first practice session for the US Grand Prix at Watkins Glen was so wet that Denny didn't bother to go out, but he made up for it on the second day when the sun was shining — he was the first to better the 1968 Formula 1 record (he already held the outright lap record in the CanAm car) and pole was disputed between Denny, Jackie and Jochen. Rindt finally annexed pole, with Denny beside him on the front row.

Denny's drama started before the race. On the warm-up laps his gear-change went awry and his mechanics were working frantically on the dummy grid, battling time to the start, when police sirens started wailing and police motorcycles appeared on the circuit to tackle crowds that had broken through trackside fences. Denny was finally ready to take the start but not ready for the unconventional starting procedure of the colourful, lavender-suited 'Tex' Hopkins, who walked away from the field, turned, leapt in the air and flailed the green flag. Denny was taken by surprise on the front row and stammered off the line, while those behind tried to miss him. Andretti collided with Brabham, damaging the Lotus's rear suspension. Denny ran slowly on that first lap, waving the field past, and he stopped at the pits on the second lap for further gear-change remedy. He made two more laps and stops and then returned to have the whole gear-change mechanism replaced. When the car was behaving Denny ran a distant twelfth and eventually quit at half-distance.

Mexico would restore the Hulme confidence. 'Mexico City gave me my first Grand Prix victory of the season and it was not only satisfying in itself, but it proved what I'd felt for quite a while — that my McLaren M7A (basically two years old and twice rebuilt) was still a very competitive machine. It had given me front-row starts in South Africa, at Silverstone, Monza, Clermont-Ferrand and Watkins Glen, but unfortunately it had been dogged by a variety of troubles. You get runs of ill luck like that and unfortunately mine lasted a long time.

'The curious thing is that I seem to need slightly different tyres to other drivers. Maybe it's because I drive differently. Anyway, in Mexico I got just the tyre I wanted for the circuit, the Goodyear G20, and with a set of those, the car was definitely on top. It's always a good idea to have your troubles in practice and this happened to me during the second day's practice, when the engine popped. But our mechanics changed the engine in 1 hour 31 minutes, which must be some sort of record (our previous best was 2 hours 5 minutes) and which enabled me to put in a couple of laps before training ended. They fitted an engine chosen on the flip of a coin and it performed wonderfully in the race.

'I was fourth fastest on the grid, only slightly slower than Jack Brabham, Jacky Ickx and Jackie Stewart and I was pretty confident this time, because the car was handling so well. The night before the race we leaned off the engine quite a lot after some trouble with the metering unit, but when I tried a few standing starts on the warming-up lap, the engine stalled. So I decided, much to the disgust of the Goodyear boys and everyone else, to dowse the rear tyres with oil dragster-style, the idea being to get some wheelspin off the line and prevent the engine dying. The altitude at Mexico City brought our power down by about 20 per cent, and my car was not fitted with the special low bottom gear for the hairpin.

'I think the oil would have helped me (it quickly rubs off as you accelerate), but in fact I didn't really need it, since I had trouble starting the engine on the dummy grid and by the time I was moving up to my place the guy dropped the flag. It wasn't, in fact, a very well controlled start, because only the front row had stopped rolling when the flag went down. Anyway, I was about eighth into the first corner, but I managed to drive around three cars on the outside and tucked in behind Jochen Rindt. Frankly I was rather surprised myself that this overtaking was possible, but the car did operate very well round that corner. About the only other driver who seemed be as quick through that corner was Ickx. What I did was to let it roll into the corner in top gear with my foot on the brake, snatch back into third and then accelerate round. It certainly seemed to work.

'The car was clearly going like a rocket and I decided to get by Rindt on the first lap, tucking in behind Jack Brabham and tailing him for a couple of laps. Then I got by Jack at the end of the straight, partly as a result of streamlining. When Piers Courage and Jo Siffert had their little bit of nonsense just after the hairpin, Ickx took advantage of the situation to take Stewart's lead away from him in a rather dubious manoeuvre. Then Stewart goofed a gearshift on the straight and I got by him as well and closed up on Ickx.

'I couldn't believe that the car was running as well as it was. We had a switch to over-ride the rev limiter and I found the engine was running up to the limit in top gear. So I switched off the limiter and ran the race using a good 10,000 rpm every time, and sometimes a little more, trusting that it would hold together.

'On lap 10 I overtook Ickx, again at the end of the straight, and started to pull away without too much difficulty. The lap times at this stage weren't very exciting, but they were coming down progressively and I felt I was in command. Ickx fell back to 4 or 5 seconds behind and then cut the margin to around 3 seconds, but I managed to pull away again slightly and then, helped I think by luck in the traffic, I got 12 seconds ahead by lap 50.

'I thought that at that point Ickx was in some sort of trouble and so I eased off a little. Maybe I shouldn't have done this, because his Brabham started to creep up on me again, but I was pacing things and reckoned he couldn't catch me before the finish. In fact, I think I could have given it a little more time and gone a shade quicker if it had been necessary.

'Jacky Ickx had discovered a short cut behind a row of concrete markers on the corner after the hairpin and this was probably good for about a second a lap. I ran over these markers once or twice but I wasn't game to slip behind them, because I remembered damaging the car on some of these projections last year and I was worried about what they might do to the suspension.

'I can't claim that this was a victory which I had to sweat for. It was in fact a pretty comfortable race, but on this occasion Goodyear came up with the best tyre and the car was running like a dream. My M7A was still very competitive, particularly on the faster circuits (though Mexico is not super-quick) and it was great to be able to prove how good it was. It was also great to win a Grand Prix after failing to finish for so long — the last time was way back in June at Zandvoort!'

At season's end, Denny decided to rate the opposition: 'I'd say that the Matra was probably the best all-rounder [a safe decision, since Jackie Stewart had won the World Championship in the Tyrrell Matra] but we weren't really outclassed and Jack Brabham and Ron Tauranac clearly worked very hard indeed with tweaks to get their cars going well. The BRMs were never anywhere near and the Ferraris were very disappointing; perhaps the only time the Ferrari looked like doing anything was at Zandvoort. As for the

Lotuses, I feel that possibly the 49Bs were a little outdated and needed something of a rethink, though Jochen certainly pressed on with his at all times.

'Bruce set another record in Mexico, by breaking down for the second successive Grand Prix on the warming-up lap! A piece of bronze filing stuck under the metering unit relief valve and there was nothing to be done about it in the time . . . but he looked pretty pleased to see a McLaren go down with another win in the record books . . .'

Life was different three decades ago in Grand Prix racing. The morning of that 1969 race in Mexico we had breakfast in the apartment on the top floor of the Monte Cassino Hotel that Bruce and Denny were sharing. I reported the event for my column in *Road & Track*: 'It was one long laugh, interrupted by bacon and eggs. At one point Denny leaned his chair back on two legs and said, "You know, there isn't another team in racing that has such a good time as we do!" And he's right. He doesn't really want anything Bruce has, and Bruce is quite happy with what he's got. An ideal set-up. It's easier to win when you don't have to count your team-mate as one of the opposition and I know a few teams where that happens.'

Pete Lyons précised the Denny he knew as CanAm champion after he had taken the title in 1968 and it would stand handily as the Bruce and Denny Show set out into the 1969 series: 'Denny got results with any kind of car, but it was the big, heavy Group 7 cars that he seemed born to. Both his burly physique, built through years of filling his Dad's dump trucks with a shovel, and his keen mechanical sympathy — he was fascinated by mechanisms of any kind — helped him get the best out of the musclebound Big Bangers. Hulme didn't always seem to be working very hard; in fact, he sometimes looked to be a lazy old bear, and never missed a chance to take a nap atop a toolbox or a stack of tyres. Often, when all about him were chicken-littling about some car-preparation crisis or other, he'd settle nerves by calmly declaring, "She'll be right." And if she wasn't, he'd *make* her right, seizing a recalcitrant vehicle by the scruff of its neck and hurling it bodily towards the finish line. Watching Denny drive could drop your jaw . . .'

The M8B McLaren CanAm car was essentially a be-winged refinement of the car Denny had raced to win the 1968 series title. At the M8B's unveiling in England, the press was given a peak power figure of 635 bhp at 7000 rpm — 'an immense speed for an engine with pistons like bloody great flower pots and valves like small umbrellas' stammered *Autosport* technical editor John Bolster.

Rob Widdows grew up a mile from the Goodwood circuit and when Lord March launched his amazingly successful Festival at Goodwood House and later the superb Revival at the circuit, Widdows would mastermind the media side of the operation as the events established themselves, from nothing, on the international historic calendar. 'When I was a teenager my parents lived a mile from Goodwood, Dad having considerately moved there from the coast. From the bedroom window I could time the cars on the up-change out of the chicane. Every possible minute was spent hanging around in the pit lane for testing — and that was just about every day. The McLaren CanAm testing was a favourite — Bruce, Denny, Tyler and Robin Herd creating the car that became invincible.

'One day I just went up to Robin and asked him if I could have a ride round. Denny thought this might put me off ever wanting to ask again, so he agreed to take me. I climbed aboard (no seat, no belts!) and we did three breathtaking laps flat out! As we went down the Lavant straight at 160 mph I couldn't help thinking that just a mile further on, my mother was hanging out the washing, blissfully unaware of how I was passing my day. Denny was fantastic — grinning at me as I was pinned back against the bulkhead and then slammed down into the cockpit under braking. On one lap he looked at me coming out of Lavant corner, the eyes grinning, as if to say, "Well, you asked for it boy!" before blasting once more towards Woodcote!'

To nobody's great surprise the front row of the first round of the 1969 CanAm series at Mosport was all-orange, with Bruce on pole and Denny beside him. Dan Gurney would offer a challenge in his McLeagle conversion of a McLaren, but this ended with a broken rear upright. John Surtees, in his customer McLaren, raced with Denny in the works car, but the race shook itself out, as one reporter described: 'Now the McLaren boys settled down to enjoy their prowess, swapping positions again and again, playing with each other at 160 mph on the long, rising back straight.' Bruce won, with Denny tucked in his slipstream, but it had not been a comfortable race for him, roasted in the cockpit of his new car and demanding an improvement in the personal cooling department.

It was apparent that crowd numbers were falling, so Bruce and Denny, having commanded the front row again at Ste-Jovite, toyed with Surtees and Motschenbacher to make it look like a race for the spectators, but then Bruce got blindsided as John slowed for a yellow flag and Bruce slammed into him, needing a pit stop for repairs. Result: Hulme-McLaren.

Chris Amon turned up at Watkins Glen with a new Ferrari, so there were now *three* Kiwis commanding the CanAm headlines. The McLaren team now had a complete spare car 'and left it lurking menacingly under a cover but in full view. Some of their would-be competition couldn't manage to scrape up a spare *engine*.' McLaren-Hulme front row. McLaren-Hulme race result. In fact, it was McLaren-Hulme-Amon. The McLarens were then towed on a two-tier trailer on the long roll across the country to Edmonton. Hulme-McLaren front row, Amon third with a new 6.2-litre V12 engine in his Ferrari. The Kiwis swapped places until Bruce's engine failed, which meant Denny had to deliver. 'Revealing what he'd been holding back, he immediately began leaving the Ferrari behind at a second a lap. When the gap got to about 10 seconds he relaxed a little, but

Amon could still see him and kept pushing. As late as lap 68, Hulme still felt the pressure and pulled out the fastest tour of the day. Denny led the Ferrari over the line by just 5.1 seconds.'

The Mid-Ohio track appeared on the CanAm series for the first time, but the front row was still effortlessly orange: Hulme-McLaren. Bruce was trying an all-new front suspension from the Formula 1 car. Lyons: 'Imagine being able to borrow from your Grand Prix racer to fine-tune your CanAm. Imagine your mood if you couldn't . . .' Denny and Bruce commanded, swapping the lead, but with seven laps left, Bruce was in the pits with zero oil pressure. They decided to send him back out with crossed fingers and all held good for another Hulme-McLaren finish. Just.

Mid-point in the series at Elkhart Lake, front row: Hulme-McLaren. Once again the Kiwis played for the punters, with McLaren and Hulme tantalising Amon's Ferrari. 'Then, on lap 20 with 30 still to go, perhaps more to keep himself awake than anything else, The Bear stretched and went Zoom! In two laps he was back up on Bruce's tail and, as if to say, "Come on, let's go, I'm bored," he passed back into the lead. McLaren took the hint and with obvious ease the pair forged away by themselves. Amon soon found himself abandoned a quarter-minute behind. McLaren led across the finish line by inches.'

In his CanAm history, Lyons quoted Bruce on their command of CanAm in his 'From the Cockpit' column in *Autosport:* 'We were beginning to think that our domination of the series might have kept people away from the CanAm races — the only person it seems to have kept away is Roger Penske [that comment would come back to haunt, but sadly Bruce wouldn't be there to see the Penske Panzers take over] — but seriously, it seems to be reaching the Moss/Clark stage [for 2006 add Schumacher] where we are getting so much publicity that people are coming along just to watch us win. It's like elephants at a circus — there might only be one or two there, but you don't feel like going to a circus or a zoo and going home without seeing the elephants, no matter how many monkeys there might happen to be . . .' There was no comment recorded from the CanAm monkeys after they read that.

Bridgehampton really was the rub-it-in race. They ran the first qualifying session on Saturday morning, were both about 4 seconds faster than anyone else, and then the whole équipe packed up and departed. Lyons: 'So the Kiwis went water-ski-ing. At noon the McLaren team packed up and left the circuit. Hulme grumbled a bit, saying he figured it was all a plot to keep another pole out of his hands, but he readily went along with this ultimate of psych jobs . . . However, the "monkeys" left to their toil at the track must have thought they were witnesses to divine retribution the next morning . . .' Bruce came roaring in, shouting that a cylinder had gone, but the panic was relieved when it was found to be only a broken valve rocker stud. 'But memories brimmed up of how both the team's big Chevys had failed in this race last year. No such luck this year.' Result: Hulme-McLaren.

The race on the Michigan International Speedway used part of the banked section with an add-in road course and it was a one-off. Qualifying: Hulme-McLaren. Dan Gurney had been loaned the team's spare car and he started from the back of the grid but would finish third behind Bruce and Denny, simply underlining the ongoing total command of the Orange Elephants.

In California for the two rounds at Laguna Seca and Riverside, not a lot changed. At Laguna Seca, Bruce started from pole and won his second race in a row. Denny was second and second. At Riverside it was still all-orange, with Denny on pole. Lyons: 'Because Denny had never won here, it was understood that this race was his from the start. Ten events into the season and McLaren Racing still had that much of a grip on the 1969 CanAm. The happy Hulme, who'd just come from victory at the Mexican Grand Prix the weekend before, wanted Riverside and he took it.'

In his *Motor Racing* column, Denny wrote: 'The CanAm round at Riverside was one I had wanted to win for some time. Not only is it the richest race of the series but this was my fourth effort here and my previous best had been sixth last year after pit stops. This year they had resurfaced the whole of the track and altered turn 9, as well as modifying the Esses, so the circuit was faster. They had electric timing apparatus at the end of the main straight, really on a corner that is taken flat out in top and my car was timed at 198 mph!

'Because of past experience at Riverside, I set off at a cracking pace, wanting to build up a useful lead in case I had to make a pit stop. This time, though, the car ran like a train throughout and I managed to lap the whole field.

'The only time I slowed down was after Bruce had his big accident. His car just went to the right without any warning (we think that probably a rear wishbone broke) at about 150 mph, rushed up a bank covered with ice-plant and came back on to the track again. It all looked pretty nasty for a little while, but I figured that Bruce wasn't hurt because the wing was still on the car, which showed that it hadn't turned over.'

The final round of the series was on another new, banked course at Texas International Speedway near College Station, Texas. It was a last-minute replacement for the planned final on the Las Vegas Stardust, which had been damaged by a storm and also changed ownership. The team plan was that Bruce would win this last race and Denny would take second place in the race to clinch his second CanAm title. There would be changes in the scenario for this final round. Mario Andretti popped up on the front row in an older M6B McLaren with a big Ford engine, beside Denny on pole, with Bruce behind The Bear, on the second row for a change. Mario led for a few laps, perhaps with Denny's permission, but then Hulme moved out ahead, Mario blew up, and soon the race had settled back to 'normal', with Bruce through to lead and Denny running second as planned . . . until his engine died with 11 laps left, and with it his chance of becoming champion again.

Bruce took the race and the title with 165 points to Denny's 160; Bruce had won six races to Denny's five. Lyons: 'Looking back over the 11 races, it was not hard to pick out what Bruce McLaren had done to achieve his third successive success — nor how so many other would-be contenders had contrived to lose every race. The lessons were clear. Why couldn't anyone but McLaren learn them?'

16 Life after Bruce

'When I first heard that Graham Hill was pushing himself to get to the 1970 South African Grand Prix after smashing both his legs in the crash at Watkins Glen last season I thought he was crazy, but having been through a similar sort of thing, I can understand now. At the time I knew Graham must be in all sorts of pain but I also knew that when he sat in the car for the race there was no way you'd ever get him out of it. He was going to suffer anything, just to say he'd finished that race. He was just so determined that he was quite prepared to suffer for it, even if they had to cart him off to hospital on a stretcher after it.

'There are two ways of facing a problem like this. You can say to hell with it and give up. Or the other way, which is probably more natural with racing drivers or people in very competitive situations, is to be so determined that you'll do anything to get back, as bad and dangerous as it may seem.'

The reason Denny knew how Graham felt when he climbed into the Rob Walker car at Kyalami stemmed from the McLaren team's revisitation of their Indianapolis M15 design, which had been basically a single-seater version of the CanAm car. Their first visit to The Brickyard in 1969 had made them aware that there was more to the Speedway than 'just another motor race'. As a result, the new M16 for 1970 followed Formula 1 aero-thinking, with a wedge shape where the previous car had been chubby. New Zealand mechanic Allan McCall had been to Indianapolis in 1966 with the car he had built at Lotus for Jim Clark, and in 1970 he was at

McLaren to build and engineer a car for Denny. It was a typically McLaren arrangement and I think Bruce saw much of himself in McCall, who was building his own Tui single-seater — Bruce was always putting work his way to keep his funds up.

Over lunch in Auckland in 2006 Allan described the scene at the Speedway in May 1970. 'I built up Denny's car and looked after it at the track. The cars had Monza caps on the fuel tanks to make the fueling easier during testing and practice. Monza caps had an upright, spring-loaded lever that clipped over the cap when it was closed. The United States Auto Club scrutineers decided that our fuel caps need a bit of help to stay closed and they made us put springs 3 inches long by 0.25-inch diameter on both sides of the lever to make it stay shut. The first time Denny took the car out with the modified caps the car burst into flame on the warm-up lap.

'The fire trucks were right on the job, following the car, which floated off around turn 4 and eventually rolled to a stop on the infield, undamaged. Denny, on fire, was running after the car and the fire truck, trying to get their attention, and they eventually dealt to Denny and the car.

'Denny's Les Leston kangaroo-skin gloves and boots had shrunk with the heat to about a quarter of their original size and then split on his hands. I can't imagine how much that must have hurt.

'When we got the car back, the Monza fuel cap on the left-hand side was open. I was pretty upset, because it's not a good thing for a mechanic to try to fry his driver. By the frosty silence I received in the garage, I could tell that the general consensus was that the cap had been left open. I knew that wasn't so, but it didn't help.

'I repaired the car and got it ready for Carl Williams, Denny's replacement. I was warming up the car in the garage and decided to give the Offenhauser engine a few revs to see what would happen. At just over 8000 rpm the USAC springs started to vibrate and rotate. As the ends of the springs were attached to the chassis and the lever, only the centre of the spring could rotate. At just over 8000 rpm the two springs matched up their revolutions and flipped the lever open. I grabbed the scrutineers and gave them a demonstration. After that, we removed the springs and had no more problems but it was a painful and expensive lesson that we didn't really need to learn . . .'

Just before leaving Indianapolis for Monaco, Denny had worked Chris Amon's McLaren up to 167.9 mph — the fastest speed recorded during the first six days of practice for the 500. He returned to Indianapolis on Monday, 11 May, and the next day he was out in his own car when the fuel cap opened. Denny received second-degree burns to the backs of his hands and the tops of his feet and he was rushed to hospital. Don Grey reported in *Motoring News* that Denny left hospital briefly to watch the final day of qualifying. 'Although naturally slightly pale and with his hands swathed in bandages, Denny was very bright and chipper and obviously glad to be back in the swim of things. He was also very talkative about the accident.

'"I left the pits and did one complete lap, putting it into top gear going down the back chute. It actually pulls eight-four — that's what it had on the tach. At about the three marker I noticed there was fuel coming along the left-hand side of the car by the windscreen, and I remember thinking, 'Well, the fuel cap's open and the turn's going to be a bit hairy with fuel on the tyres.'

'"My hands were shrinking inside the gloves and I had to force myself to hang on to the wheel. I braked as hard as I could but every time I did so, this aggravated the fire because it sloshed more fuel out. I remember for an instant I tried to find the fire extinguisher, which had a manual control lever down beside the gear lever in front of the steering column. I don't remember actually hitting it, but I recall later that a lot of white sort of smoke came from somewhere, which indicated that it was coming from the fire extinguisher. It's carbon dioxide and comes out in freezing foam. The car seemed to cool, but only for maybe half a second.

'"At the same time I went past the first stationary fire-truck and realised I was going too quick to stop because I was already almost past him. I knew where the second fire-truck was and I thought I'd try to park beside it. The nylon tie-wraps that we had keeping the pipes and things down — they burned and created some black sort of smoke or something for a little while and then my vision disappeared . . .

'"I know it all takes a long time to explain this. But things were happening . . . it seemed like it took forever in the car, but if you actually timed it on a stopwatch I'd say it must have been 12 or 15 seconds, something like that, and these were the things I was thinking about. Things were really thrashing . . .

'"I thought, 'I've got to stop this thing and I'll get out as quickly as possible.' I bumped it out of gear and I tried to jump out of the cock-pit, but the windscreen was folding down in front of me so I knew it was still on fire. It was still hot, but the helmet was saving my face from any super heat.

'"I was actually feeling quite good. I knew what I was doing. I went to leap out of the car and I remembered I was still buckled in, that the belts were pulling me down, so then I had to talk really hard to myself, to convince me to undo that seat belt. And the hands . . .

'"I got that done and leaped out and I remembered. 'I must not jump out of the left-hand side because that's burning . . . it's got raw fuel on it . . . and if I touch it that'll set my overalls on fire, so I'm going out the right-hand side.'

'"The car was going round turn 3 in its normal groove, virtually on its own. I leaned on the roll bar and I thought, 'Now I've got to jump as hard as I can jump to clear the right-hand rear wheel because if that clobbers me it's going to do a lot of damage . . .'

'"I remember sort of jumping at 45 degrees, landing feet first and rolling around. And I saw — although I didn't know who it was at the time —

Ronnie Bucknum come around the corner and go by me. I turned and watched the McLaren going on down and touch the wall and I sort of thought, 'Geez, I wish I'd left it in gear,' because I knew it was out of gear and of course it wouldn't have touched the wall if it was in gear and I could have saved any damage.

' "It's funny because I was cursing the fire-trucks as they went down to the car, not thinking that I was still on fire because you can't see the alcohol flames. That's the part that annoys me and I wished they could do something about it, but apparently they can't. I ran down to the fire-truck and shouted to the guy. He came up to me and I knew then I wasn't burning because if I was, he would have backed off. I took my helmet off. I looked at the car and the front left-hand wheel was buckled and bent over. At the same time I shouted to the doctor to get my gloves off and he started zipping the left-hand one off . . . and then took me to the hospital.

' "So I knew what was going on all about me but it seemed like half a day . . . though I suppose it all took place in about 15 seconds. I was thankful for the Bell Star helmet but the gloves were of no use whatsoever. I'm not saying the gloves, the particular type I was wearing, were bad, but I just think that leather is not a very good fire protector. I guess the leather shrunk and probably the same with my leather shoes, transferring the heat straight through. There is no hair missing off the back of my hands but there sure is a lot of skin missing . . ." '

Denny stayed in Indianapolis to watch the Saturday race and returned to England that same night, predicting that he would be racing in the first CanAm race of the new season at Mosport. Bruce had flown back the following evening and the next day, 2 June, would be testing the second of the new cars for the CanAm series, the car he would be racing. A few laps into the test session, the rear body section came loose, lifted, and in the high-speed accident the car was destroyed and Bruce was killed.

Bruce's fatal crash at Goodwood had come so soon after Denny's

Indianapolis accident that he was hit doubly hard. He had handled the huge pain and shock of the Indianapolis incident in a way that we put down to Denny's toughness, and to a degree I think this was true. But when news of Bruce's death came through while Denny was in London having the burns treated by a specialist, even the traditional Hulme family courage wasn't sufficient. He broke down and wept helplessly when Greeta brought him to grieve with Patty at Bruce's Surrey home in Burwood Park.

In those two months his personal resolve was plumbed time after time, but he rose to the demands of the situation and personally led Bruce's team away from the suggestion of packing it in.

Motor Racing magazine had failed and I arranged for Denny to take over Bruce's column in *Autosport*. Once the awful sadness of Bruce's death and his own searing pain from the Indianapolis burns had eased, Denny was eager to commit his thoughts to paper. In a way, putting his feelings on paper helped to convince him that the Hulme way was the right way. The only way.

'I really do feel pleased to be back in racing, although I'd probably feel a lot happier if I could be on the front of the grid. In the eight weeks that I've been away I felt I might have lost something, but I haven't. I feel I'm still as competitive as I was before I got burned at Indy.

'When I was lying in hospital in Indianapolis with my hands all bound up and hurting like hell, I was telling everyone that I would be driving in the first CanAm race at Mosport on 14 June. The doctors just sort of laughed about it. I think they thought I was being a bit optimistic.

'Dan Gurney was going to go to Mosport in case I couldn't do the whole race in the McLaren M8D CanAm car, but I figured that if I got into that car there was no way Dan was going to take it over halfway through the race . . .

'Less than 10 days before the race at Mosport I couldn't bend either of my hands, but I really set to work on my right hand and within a couple of days I found that I could bend it with a bearable amount of pain. The left hand was a bigger problem because it had been burnt more seriously and it was taking longer to heal.

'The day after Bruce's accident at Goodwood I went over to the factory to have a chat with the mechanics and make sure they all realised how important it was now for us all to pull together, and I took a steering wheel round with me to try to get my fingers to bend around the rim. I could do it quite well with my right hand, but once again my left hand was the big stumbling block.

'I was a bit apprehensive about driving for the first time, but the day after I got back to England, I took my Ford Executive out on the road. Greeta reckoned I would be walking home and she would have to come and collect the car, but I managed. I must say it was difficult though — fortunately it was an automatic!

'The biggest problem was getting gloves on and getting any feel back through my left hand. My right hand had to do most of the work and fortunately the gearshift was on the right-hand side in both the McLaren CanAm and Formula 1 cars. I had to put my left hand on the wheel with the thumb above the spoke and sort of fold my fingers round the rim with the right hand, holding it like a claw. Consequently, in the races I did, I'd driven on rails and not done anything fancy, because if I took my hand off the wheel I'd have a reasonably hard job getting it back on again.

'I had to be very careful of the left hand because it was still a bit raw and sore and I had to watch that I didn't get sunburned to add to the problems I had already! I had to get bandaged up like a boxer and then put on gloves specially made for me by an American company. They are double-Nomex with a layer of Nomex foam in the middle and were quite thick and very spongy, but they had hardly any leather attached to them.

'Leather was my biggest worry after the way the leather in the gloves I wore at Indy shrank and burned onto my hands. Leather transfers heat through it so quickly that shoes are also a problem. If your shoes are reasonably tight you'll get heat transfer through them as well. I carried a do-it-yourself doctor's kit around with me so that I could lance any blisters that appeared with sterile needles and I had bandages and antiseptic and all that Doctor Kildare stuff.

'CanAm racing was probably easier for me because the racing wasn't as competitive as Formula 1 and I didn't have to worry about beating the whole field. That was why I decided to give the Dutch Grand Prix a miss and let my hands have more time to heal properly. I felt the field would be so competitive at Zandvoort that it would be too much of a strain.

'With the Formula 1 car you could drive it more with the throttle, whereas with the CanAm car you couldn't steer at all with the accelerator. It was either all on or all off and this meant you couldn't throw it around so much as the Formula 1 car. I would have liked to be able to throw the Formula 1 car around more, because that was the only way you could go really quickly. There was probably another second a lap available if I could hurl the car into the corners, but my hand wouldn't allow me to take it on and off the wheel all the time.'

Greeta remembers those painful days in the middle of the 1970 season. 'Denis used to bandage his hands and then pull on oversize gloves and then drive. I went to the races with him quite often to re-dress his hands and after he'd been driving in a race for 2 hours, he'd come in to the pits and nobody was allowed to touch him. He'd just sit there and ever so slowly edge that glove off and it was just back to raw meat again and I'd have to dress it all over again.'

The summer of 1970 had been sundered into two halves mid-season by Denny's Indianapolis fire and Bruce's fatal crash at Goodwood. Denny had started the season well with second place in the South African Grand Prix at Kyalami, then retired from the Spanish Grand Prix and finished fourth at Monaco. He would pick up his painful Formula 1 chase again in France.

The Clermont-Ferrand circuit had always been one of his favourites and he had been happy with his races there. It was something of a Grand Prix homecoming, getting to grips with a Denny-friendly track. 'It felt great at Clermont in that first practice session, setting third fastest time. I was happy in myself that the Stewarts and the Rindts hadn't driven off into the distance.

'I eventually qualified on the fourth row, beside Henri Pescarolo in the second Matra V12, and in the race Jack Brabham and I had quite a scramble trying to get around the Frenchman. When we got by I had an even bigger problem trying to get by Jack for what would have been third place. For lap after lap I drove right up his exhausts on the 5-mile switchback circuit, trying to find a way around the Brabham. Jack seemed to be able to adjust the width of his car as the race went on! Finally I started to feel a bit groggy — the seesawing up and down hill, gobbling up exhaust fumes didn't help at all and I eased back, feeling definitely off-colour. I started thinking about my hand and how much it was hurting and I lost quite a bit of time. Riding along in the fresh air soon brought me round, though, and I set off after Jack again to finish in fourth place right on his tail. My car was amazingly cool — so much so that I thought for a while that I had lost all the water from the radiator! Most times it was like sitting in an oven.'

Denny reckoned that he would have a harder race in the British Grand Prix at Brands Hatch because it was a circuit where the gear-shifting had to be done a bit quicker and it was usually done on a rough part of the track under heavy braking. At Clermont the braking areas were smooth, but at Brands Hatch he would have to hook his hand round the wheel even harder because the wheel would be vibrating more.

'My hands used to get blistered at the best of times, but since my burns my palm blisters hadn't been appearing, so I knew that I wasn't holding the wheel as tightly as I used to. Still, my problems were relatively minor ones — it just felt great to be in a racing car again . . .'

Denny had a few problems in practice and was not at all optimistic about his race chances, but he found that he was running fifth behind Ickx leading in the Ferrari, Brabham, Rindt in the new Lotus 72 and Jack Oliver's BRM. And when the Ferrari and BRM retired, Denny inherited third place, but it was a busy place to be. 'I was watching a big dice in my mirrors between Clay Regazzoni's Ferrari and Jackie Stewart in the March.

'With about six laps to go I was starting to feel a bit tired. The tip of one finger was very painful and I knew that it had started bleeding, added to which my left wrist was giving up. I figured I could summon just one more effort to stave off an attack before the end of the race.

'We were braking into Druids and I was watching the apex of the corner and just about to swing right when I heard the roar of the Ferrari engine. I looked across and Regga was right alongside me, going a lot quicker than I was! I turned away from him and he went straight on. I thought he was going to run off on to the grass and probably spin it and as I took off down the hill I watched him gathering it all up in the mirrors. He could have got away with it, but it was one of those classic mistakes — you think you can outdo someone who is already braking at ten-tenths and you just overcook it.

'I never imagined that he would make his do-, die- or bust effort at Druids and it was just fortunate that I happened to hear his engine alongside me.

'The finish was really a shame, with Jack running out of petrol so close to the line and Jochen pipping him. The championship should have been still wide open, but now Jochen had won four Grands Prix on the trot and two of those had been as a result of Jack's misfortunes . . . for want of a better word.'

At this time I was travelling with Denny to the Grands Prix in Europe one weekend and a CanAm race in North America the next and I was well aware of his discomfort, for all his tough-guy ways of covering his hurts. How he girded himself to climb into the cockpit and race, I couldn't imagine. On one flight I watched him cut his hand and draw blood . . . on the edge of a newspaper page. Somehow you don't think of a newspaper as being a lethal weapon, but his hands were *so* tender as the burns healed, despite Denny's determination to stay racing. Perhaps it was partly his way of 'doing it for Bruce', that fighting spirit that he had instilled in the McLaren team on both sides of the Atlantic.

During the 1970 summer, Denny also had two endurance races in the Porsche Salzburg 917, co-driving with Vic Elford. 'The main difference between the Porsche and the CanAm McLaren is that you get more wind buffeting and more wind and engine noise in the open McLaren, whereas in the closed Porsche, sure it makes a helluva noise, but you don't get blown about and it's more comfortable to drive. It doesn't feel like a sprint car, though. I wouldn't like to try to do 10 laps at ten-tenths in it, but I think Pedro Rodriguez and Jo Siffert probably did ten-tenths for the whole 6 hours at Brands Hatch! They certainly started out that way. We could qualify our 917 nearly as fast as John Wyer's Gulf-Porsches, but come race time and they just disappeared into the distance, going like the clappers. I'd like to drive one of the Wyer cars just to see where the difference is. I co-drove with Vic Elford and thanks to Vic, we finished fourth. They gave him the BOAC "Man of the Race" award . . . and I think it must have been for taking me along as a passenger!'

Elford remembered that race in his autobiography. 'Denny had one important weakness: he hated driving in the wet. At first practice and qualifying on Friday he said, "Vic, you know the car and the track, so you do all the set-up and qualifying; I'll just drive the three compulsory laps to qualify for the start." So I did and repeated the performance on Saturday. Sunday morning dawned grey and cold. It was raining harder than ever. Denny took me aside again. "Look, Vic," he said, "you drive the first three hours, then I'll take over for about 20 minutes while you take a leak and have a drink, then get back in again and do the rest." ' They finished second. Elford reckoned he drove for 6 hours of the 6 hour 45 minute race. Later in the season at Watkins Glen in a double-header Denny won the CanAm race and he finished fourth with Vic in the accompanying 6-hour race.

For the first time the German Grand Prix was at Hockenheim on the flat-out 4.2-mile blast out into the forest and then back into the huge loop of the stadium grandstand area.

'The Hockenheim track was quite smooth, but it was a much harder race for me than Brands Hatch. I could hardly take my left hand off the wheel to shake some life into it going down the straights. I needed it so badly through the infield section, but I just couldn't do a thing with it. I had started in sixteenth place on the grid and I'd managed to get by Emerson Fittipaldi in the Lotus, then Rolf Stommelen in the Brabham and Pescarolo in the Matra, but they were the only three cars I passed — as opposed to passing stopped cars on the side of the road — during a race where I finished in a fairly surprised third place!

'For a little while I could hold Pescarolo off, but then my hand got so bad that he could catch me quite a bit through the infield. Finally I let him past on the straight and I thought I would save myself for a big effort in the last three laps, but fortunately that wasn't necessary.

'The noise from the V12 in the Matra was just unreal. Coming up alongside it my engine was going flat out and his was simply screaming. From about 6 feet away the exhaust shriek was deafening — and you can't very well put your fingers in your ears through your helmet! When he was back in front he got wide on the dirt, but he gathered that up and then I heard the Matra dropping out of top gear. You could hear the engine revs zing up, he'd try the gear again and the revs would zing up again. Finally he stopped at the pits for a check and then I was in fourth place, but there was no way that I was ever going to catch John Surtees, who was way up ahead in his new car . . . and then blow me if I don't see John coasting to a stop at the side of the track. I was now third with only a handful of laps left, and I thought any time now I was going to arrive in the stadium and find myself in the lead!

'At Hockenheim you could really tell who had the good engines. During practice some of the other Ford-engined cars were passing me and they just kept going on by. Even if I tucked in behind them, I didn't seem to be able to gain ground. Another 10 or 15 horsepower would have made all the difference, but at least we still had ours at the end of the race when a lot of other people's horsepower had leaked out through holes in the block. I doubt whether we had 430 bhp, but I think some of the other Ford runners had nearer 445 bhp.

'Jochen Rindt's Lotus 72 certainly wasn't hanging about, although that chisel nose must have helped a lot on the long straights. He and Jacky Ickx in the Ferrari had a ding-dong go right from the start, but Jochen finally won by a few yards. I gather the cheering in the stadium — it held about 110,000 people! — was like a Cup final soccer match.

'I was completely worn out at the finish. I didn't even have the strength to fight my way through the crowd to climb up on the presentation dais with Jochen and Jacky. I just flaked out. I'm glad they're not all like that . . .

'Actually, my hands were improving all the time. I still had the problem of folding my left hand round the wheel rim, but the after-effects weren't so bad now. I used to get pins and needles in my hand for a couple of days after a race, but that gradually disappeared. One thing that did surprise me and the doctors, is that what we thought was a thick scab on the end of my left-hand index finger was actually bone sticking out the end! It wasn't giving me any trouble but I knew that if the skin didn't start growing over it, I would need an operation. But that could wait until the winter.

'I had never been to Hockenheim before, but I didn't think it was a bad idea to try a new track for the Grand Prix. The Nürburgring was an interesting circuit and it was a driver's circuit and it had everything that people said it had, but you couldn't overlook the fact that it was dangerous as well. They got a fantastic crowd for the race at Hockenheim and it must have been a good one to watch, and they will alternate the German Grands Prix between the two tracks.'

This third place in Germany helped Denny to third place in the championship, but Rindt was out of sight in the lead and Denny would be disputing second place with Jack Brabham and Jackie Stewart.

The 3.7-mile Österreichring was another fast new track on the championship calendar. Denny described it: 'It was built in the middle of nowhere on the side of a low alp with forest coming down the mountains, sheltering deer. I knew there were deer about because one jumped the safety fence and came charging up the road straight towards me during practice! Apparently it just about jumped Chris Amon's March as he went by ahead of me. I saw the yellow flags being waved although I couldn't see any cars about, but I knew something was up when I saw a photographer friend waving frantically at the side of the track.

'The deer — well, it was really only a little Bambi fawn, about 2 foot 6 inches high — ran straight at the car, did a panic handbrake turn and skated on its side. I was standing on everything trying to get stopped, because it would have made a nice old mess of the front of the car. To say nothing of itself. It must have worked this out too, because next second it was up and off again. I gather they had hunters with rifles stationed up in the woods during the race in case any more deer tried to get converted to venison the quick way!'

There were problems other than the wildlife and Denny had a race of high drama. 'It was just as though someone had switched off the light. Everything went black. I was storming along behind Jack's Brabham on the opening lap of the Grand Prix when suddenly there's oil everywhere and I couldn't see a thing! It turned out that François Cevert's March had blown up in front of Jack and sprayed us both with oil, but I didn't have time to figure that out in the instant it happened. I was too busy wiping my visor clear with my sleeve and the backs of the big Nomex gauntlet gloves that I wear. It didn't help matters when Cevert kept on driving, still pumping oil all over the place, but he soon got the message. We were down in the sixth and seventh turns when this happened, but at least we knew there was oil on that part of the circuit and the blokes in front of us didn't. Regazzoni just about backed his Ferrari through the fence and lost the lead doing so, and Jochen backed right off in the Lotus, thinking there was going to be an almighty accident. But that was as close as we ever got to the Ferraris. They just disappeared to a 1-2 win, with Ickx in front.

'As well as the oil and the Ferraris, we had another problem in the race — rocks. Some of the corners had so many rocks and stones spread across them that they looked like an English beach. It really was serious. Someone flung up a rock at Pescarolo's Matra that was the size of a couple of cricket balls and must have weighed a pound and a half. It lodged in his rear suspension, bending the shock absorber and he had to make a pit stop. I got a smack on the head from one stone that took a piece out of my helmet and another rock flattened the roll bar just above my head. After that I just put my head down and hung on when I arrived at the rocky bits! I had got as far up as sixth, but that only lasted a half dozen laps until the engine went GRRRRrrrr as I was going over the hill, and I banged the clutch in before it all went solid.'

Jochen Rindt was a country mile in the lead on world championship points, but he would lose his life in a huge accident during practice for the Italian Grand Prix at Monza. Denny was in his slipstream.

'It seemed as though it was all happening in slow motion and yet we must have been doing 150 miles an hour. I was only about 30 feet behind Jochen's Lotus 72 when he had his accident during Saturday's practice.

It felt as though I could have reached out and stopped him from doing it. Relative to one another at Monza we could have been standing still at 150 mph, but when something starts to happen, it happens at extremely high speed. While you're travelling with a slipstreaming bunch it seems almost slow. You get used to travelling at 190 mph — it's only when you break away from the bunch that you realise how fast you were all going.

'I had fitted a new engine after the first day of practice and we'd replaced the bigger wing on the back with a pair of smaller wings that we had taken off the nose. Jochen and I had been running together, but I made a bit of a mess of the second Lesmo Corner and pulled over to let him by so that he could take advantage of the rest of the lap. It looked as though it was going to be a quick one for both of us. We were doing about 190 mph down into the Parabolica and we normally brake just past the 200-metre marker.

'I saw Jochen start braking and I went onto mine at the same time. His car veered slightly to the right, then left, and right again. I knew he was getting a bit out of shape, but I thought it was just a Jochen-type demon late-brake for his good lap. Then it veered suddenly very sharply left and it was just starting to spin when it hit the guardrail. It didn't hit at a very acute angle, but it disappeared in a great cloud of dust and out of this came a wheel and a whole lot of bits and pieces and I was busy avoiding this and hoping that the car wouldn't bounce back onto the road.

'It's amazing how these things seem to happen so slowly and yet it must have been all over in less than a couple of seconds. By the time I'd turned the corner and looked back, the Lotus had stopped, but I could have sworn that Jochen would have stepped out practically unhurt. The news that he had died of his injuries was numbing. I can only presume that something must have broken and he had realised it but it got more out of shape the more he tried to cope with it.

'When we fitted the little nose wings on the back we also changed the braking ratio and fitted a higher top gear, because we had an extra

300 rpm to play with and I suppose we were getting around 195 mph on the straight, although it's hard to tell because the tyres grow at this speed.

'The down-thrust was tremendous, even with the little wings at Monza. There was a stainless steel tube between those wings and when I was following Peter Gethin's McLaren I could see the ends of the wings actually drooping and yet there was no way you could bend that tube in the pits!'

Denny's practice best was worth a spot on the fifth row, but he was not too worried. 'In the opening laps I knew that my engine was a real beauty. It was sitting on the rev limiter at 10,300 rpm on the straights when I was running on my own — was it ever singing along! Going up through the field I could feel a tow starting from a couple of hundred yards behind a car and by the time I was closing in, the rev counter was showing an extra 400 rpm.

'While Jackie and I were in second place behind Regazzoni's Ferrari he seemed to have a problem making any ground on us, but on one lap Jean-Pierre Beltoise squeezed the Matra V12 into second place and Regazzoni was on his way. By the time we had passed Beltoise again, the Ferrari was history. Long gone.

'On the vital last lap Jackie was just ahead of me and I planned to suck right in behind him and pass at the end of the straight. But then I spotted Beltoise in my mirrors, so I had to pull out from Jackie's March slipstream earlier than I wanted to, to avoid letting Beltoise get the jump on me. This meant that I didn't have enough steam to get by Jackie before the corner and Beltoise and I went in side by side. I'd been having trouble with the change from third to fourth and I muffed it while we were dragging out of the last corner behind Jackie. When he jinked to the left to try to shake me out of his slipstream (imagine him thinking I was going to do him on the line!) it left me out in the breeze with an engine struggling to get its revs up again. That's when Beltoise overhauled me and there wasn't a thing I could do about it. Regazzoni won in the Ferrari to the wild delight of the crowd with 6 seconds in hand on Jackie, with Beltoise and me crossing the line wheel to wheel in third and fourth.'

Denny was out of the Canadian Grand Prix when the flywheel came adrift and at Watkins Glen he was a distant seventh, two laps behind Emerson Fittipaldi, who scored his first win. Denny was impressed by the young Brazilian. 'He is 23, it was only his fourth Grand Prix and it was the first time he had raced the Lotus 72. It was the first race for Lotus after Jochen's fatal accident at Monza and I think he drove a sensible race to win at Watkins Glen. Of course, you've got to be fairly smart to win anyway, but during practice he turned in third fastest time behind Ickx in the Ferrari and Stewart in the Tyrrell-Ford and he'd never seen the circuit before!

'Emerson's win at the Glen means that Jacky Ickx can't get enough points to win the championship, so Jochen will be World Champion posthumously. Some people have said that this is a bit macabre, but I don't agree. He won five Grands Prix for his 45 points and that makes him a worthy World Champion in my book.'

The final race in the 1970 world championship was in Mexico and it would be a race with a threatening difference. 'The Mexican Grand Prix was the scariest race I've ever driven in. You can't imagine what it's like to drive flat out down the straight overtaking other cars with packed people sitting on the guardrails lining the bitumen! I was really glad when the race was over, nobody had been hurt and there hadn't been a riot. It could so easily have been a disaster, not only for the drivers and the 250,000 Mexicans who had all paid their 5 pesos to get in, but for motor racing as a whole.

'The start had been delayed for an hour before we were allowed out to do a warm-up lap to see just how bad the conditions were. The people were everywhere. I followed François Cevert in the Tyrrell March and he nearly clobbered a dog at the end of the straight. He was driving his car along the grass verge, waving and shouting to the people to get back, because they were lined along the safety bank quite oblivious to the danger of a car leaving the road. I drove alongside him and he threw his hands in the air as much as to say, "To hell with this, it's hopeless!" In French, of course.

'There was glass on the track where bottles had been thrown from the crowd and the mechanics were picking glass from the tyres of several cars after the warm-up lap. I don't think Ferrari team manager Mauro Forghieri was very keen to let his drivers start in conditions like this — I wasn't very happy about the whole thing myself! — but we had our choice of racing with glass in our tyres or facing a riot. With that sort of choice I guess a puncture was going to be a lot less serious than a punch-up with a quarter of a million people.

'The start was delayed by 80 minutes altogether and there was some arrangement made that if the drivers held their hand up going past the pits they would red-flag or chequered-flag the race and the results would be taken on standings at the time, but I wasn't very clear at which lap this was supposed to happen. I figured that if the race did get under way there was little chance of it being stopped. I couldn't imagine signalling that I wanted the race stopped if I was out in front. But then maybe that would have been a good idea . . .

'We'd had problems in practice and I was down near the back of the grid. When they finally cleared the grid and we went blipping up to the grid proper I reckoned they would only be watching the front row, so I started moving slowly up. Let's face it, the starter probably couldn't even see me from where I was on the seventh row! When he dropped the flag I was away down the outside of the grid and went nearly all the way down to the first corner in the dirt. I arrived there alongside Peter Gethin in the other McLaren and he was just about to carve me up when he realised that it was another orange car and he let me through.

'Our finger-crossing had paid off in the engine department and it was just as well that we had disconnected the rev limiter on the grid.

Down the straight for the first lap the engine was pulling 10,500 rpm, which is 500 more than we've seen before. I thought, if this is what a good engine feels like, what has Stewart got in the Tyrrell, because he could pass everyone else.

'I went by Graham Hill, who had something wrong with his car, then I took Pedro in the BRM and caught Chris Amon's March and got by him. Beltoise in the Matra was next on the list for passing and after 24 laps I was fourth, behind the two Ferraris and Jack's Brabham. Stewart had pitted with a steering problem and later hit a dog and he was out of the race. When Jack's engine blew up in a big way it put me up to third and the oil on the track let Chris sort Beltoise out. I didn't know where the Ferraris were up ahead. Regazzoni wasn't out of reach time-wise, but he was far enough ahead that I couldn't see him.

'With 17 laps to go I was 4 seconds ahead of Chris, but then my car started hopping out of low gear at the hairpin and not wanting to go into second at one of the corners, and I thought I'd had it. I haven't raced so hard in a long time. Chris was really giving me the message. I couldn't afford to let up or let either the March or the Matra get close enough to suck up in my slipstream, because if you have a slight horsepower advantage at Mexico in the thin air, you can pull past on the straight.

'Chris was right on my tail as we went into the last lap and in one of the corners I couldn't find any gears at all. Finally I grabbed one and legged it up to the last corner to a frantic Mexican waving a red flag with the chequered flag just down the road. I jammed on everything to get around the corner and found the road completely blocked with running people and all the other cars screeching to a stop. I swung over to the guardrail, switched off, unbuckled my harness and ran for the pits, leaving the mechanics to rescue the car from the mob.

'That crowd was unreal. There was a corner just after the sharp hairpin where you used a little bit of the verge as a buffer and the Mexicans were lying right out there. We must have been missing their heads by two or three inches and all they did was shield their eyes from the dust! In those sort of circumstances even a harmless spin would have been a tragedy.

'After all that hard work I was swigging down lemonade in the cool of the pit garage and realising that I'd finished third in the Grand Prix and fourth in the world championship, which I reckoned wasn't at all bad considering that I'd missed a couple of races in the middle of the season with my Indy burns.'

Denny was already on his way to winning the CanAm championship, 'winning it for Bruce' . . .

17 Denny wins for Bruce

The orange McLaren M8D CanAm car for 1970 was an evolution of the classic M8 design that had dominated the series in previous North American summers, but the man who put his name on the nose would not be racing again. Bruce's fatal crash at Goodwood 12 days earlier cast a pall on the grid for the opening race at Mosport in Canada. Dan Gurney would take his place and in true team style, qualify on pole, with Denny beside him.

In his CanAm history, Pete Lyons wrote: 'Every CanAm season had its own flavour. This one began bitter, and did not improve. There had been crashes and injuries in the CanAm, some of them very nasty, but no one had died before. In fact, in an era when death seemed to lurk around every corner in other branches of the sport, the full-bodied Big Bangers had seemed almost safe by comparison. Now it was no longer possible to see this as a bright, carefree game. Nor was Group 7 what it had been, a formula free of fetters, an invitation for the most innovative minds to explore their wildest fantasies. CanAm rules were still less restrictive than most, but aerodynamic clamps had been applied at the insistence of the FIA.'

There were to be no tall movable wings, no coupés and no aerodynamic tonneau cockpit coverings. 'As before, engines had to displace at least 2500 cc (152 cubic inches), but there was no upper limit, nor any restriction on the number of cylinders, camshafts, superchargers, fuel consumption, etc. Gas turbines were specifically banned.'

Denny drove into the lead from the start, with Gurney riding shotgun in second place. Denny's aim was to build up a cushion of a lead, which might afford his hands some relaxation later in the race, while Gurney coped with the opposition, stronger this year with the new Ti22 car built by former Formula 1 mechanic Peter Bryant and driven by Jackie Oliver. The Ti22 had appeared late the previous season but now it was fettled as Oliver showed by passing Gurney into second place, white meat in the orange McLaren sandwich. At half-distance the first three were covered by only 3 seconds, but trouble soon loomed when Denny was forced off course lapping a slower car and the steering wheel kicked back sharply. 'One could only guess at the pain in his hands,' wrote Lyons in *Autosport*. 'Immediately he was off his pace and Oliver passed him for the lead. His hands bleeding inside his bandages, and his engine running hot anyway, Denny waved Dan by too.' Oliver and Gurney disputed the lead until Oliver tangled with back marker Motschenbacher's McLaren and Dan roared into a lead he never lost. A battered Oliver came in second, while Denny was a distant third. 'But when it was all over and he was on his cool-off tour, The Bear saw the crowd pouring over the fences and lining the curbs to give him a huge ovation . . .'

At Ste-Jovite for the second round, Gurney was poleman again, with Denny beside him and Oliver and Motschenbacher, the Mosport adversaries, side by side on the second row. A mere three-quarters into the opening lap they crested a flat-out brow, and Oliver's car lifted in the slipstream turbulence from the McLarens and flipped backwards. 'Jackie Oliver walked away,' wrote Lyons. 'He was unhurt physically, but in his eyes was a long, deep, hollow look.' Dan let Denny through to the lead, but his engine was running hot again as it had in Mosport; after a pit stop for a water top-up Denny set fastest lap, but the engine was running rough and he pitted to retire, while Dan rumbled on to win.

The Watkins Glen CanAm race ran the day after an accompanying

6-hour endurance race and the track had suffered as a result. 'The track broke up really badly during our race. There were stones and pieces of asphalt flying all over the place and after the race I was almost tarred into the seat. My visor was pocked and ruined by flying rocks and the air intake in the nose was jammed full of road rubble. The track was potholed and we had a hard job keeping a line in the corners — it was more of a furrow!

'I used the "small" 7-litre Chevvy engine in preference to the bigger 7.5-litre motor we'd had overheating problems with in the first two races in Canada and in practice here. I didn't want to risk it. The traffic was really bad and it was difficult to lap some of the faster cars. The Porsche 917s were very quick down the straights and a lot of the slower CanAm cars wanted to dice with me in the corners. Some of the quicker CanAm cars were a problem as well when we came to lap them. They would leg you down the straights and then wave you onto the marbles while they braked like hell into the corners. As the nose started to get blocked with asphalt the temperature started to rise and I had to ease back. I was also getting a lot of understeer, because a smooth flow of air through the radiator helps to keep the nose down and with the airflow blocked, I was having a few problems.

'Jim Hall's new Chaparral, with Jackie Stewart at the wheel, caused a stir at the Glen but I've got mixed feelings about it. I reckon it must be worth a second and a half on lap times to have Jackie in it. Then they've got that great lump of an 8-litre engine. If they had built a conventional car like ours and put an 8-litre in it, it might have gone quicker, who knows? There are various ways of looking at it. Jim's come along and done it his way — we're doing it our way. Probably I'm just biased and I hope it doesn't work and beat us. I think it's just pretty complicated. Having to worry about one engine is enough, but when you've got *two* of them and one is a 2-stroke . . .'

Jim Hall had devised a system to suck the air from under the Chaparral, with the suction fans driven by the smaller 2-stroke that would prove to be an Achilles heel at the back of the car.

Two water stops dropped Dan to ninth while Denny won, the 917 Porsches of Siffert, Attwood and Vic Elford behind him. 'Those Porsche long-distance cars put on a great showing, but I'd put that down to the smoothness of those 12-cylinder engines and the ability of the drivers. I'd shared Elford's 917 the day before. We could use our sheer Chevvy power on the straights, but I couldn't really boot it out of the corners where the surface had broken up, because there was so much torque low down and it would just break the rear wheels away every time you got nasty with it.'

There had been a clash of sponsorship problem for Dan Gurney, and for the fourth round of the CanAm series at Edmonton in Canada Denny was joined by Peter Gethin.

'Peter didn't know until the previous Tuesday night or Wednesday morning that he was taking Dan's place, and by Thursday evening after a 14-hour flight he was in Edmonton with team manager Teddy Mayer. They were pretty clapped when they arrived. The mechanics heard of the driver change coming across the prairies with the cars, and as soon as they arrived they set about changing the cockpit for Gethin, who was only half as tall as Gurney. They changed the steering column, pulled the pedals back and put about a foot of padding into the back of the seat. Peter settled in very quickly. I had thought he might have a struggle, because the CanAm car is heavy to drive and it's different to anything he's been used to. I'd been telling everyone that he was a very good driver and would probably be as quick as Dan, and I think he was.

'In practice we both used the 7.5-litre Chevvies and experimented with ducting to try to keep them cool, but on the second day I switched to a 7-litre version for a back-to-back comparison. It pulled the same revs as the bigger one at the end of the straight, although it was down on power to the 7.5-litre, but it was running cooler. I don't think the overheating problem is serious — it's just that we can't pinpoint it. I was fastest with the small engine, 0.4 seconds ahead of Peter, with Motschenbacher third.

'Peter and I had a pre-race chat and I suggested that I would like to be first into the first corner, which was half a mile away on a straight drag strip, and I figured that with the extra torque from the big engine, Pete would out-drag me. It all worked according to plan, but it was noticeable with a full fuel load that the 7.5-litre engine definitely did a better job than mine on the fast part of the circuit. As the fuel load dropped, though, my car started going faster and faster and I took fastest lap seven laps from the finish. Peter lost part of the new ducting in the nose and his car started to overheat, but he still finished second behind me. I think he thought it was a fairly hard race. He hadn't done a 200-mile race for a long time and there is probably three times the effort involved, compared with the 100-mile F5000 races he has been doing.'

Denny won solid gold, as he had the previous season at Edmonton. 'First prize was a $12,000 gold brick, which we swapped for a cheque, because you're not supposed to bring gold into England. Imagine the Customs man's face if you showed him that as a paperweight!'

There was a one-month break before the next round at Mid-Ohio. Denny was fastest in practice, though slower than he had been for his pole the previous season. He put this down to the reduction in aerodynamics and the hot, humid weather in practice. 'Perhaps the lack of anybody pushing him played a role, too,' wrote Lyons. Gethin was struggling to come to terms with the tight, narrow track and decided he didn't much like it. He didn't much like being on the second row of the grid either, with Peter Revson in a T220 Lola-Chevy and behind Motschenbacher in the McLaren M8B. Denny was untroubled out front, using the bigger Chevy and winning by more than a minute from Revson.

A week later at Elkhart Lake it was Hulme on pole again, with Revson's

Lola beside him and Gethin back on row three. Denny had listened to the weather forecast and set his pole time on the dry first day. The rain came on the morning of the second day of practice and though it had stopped by the time practice started, the track was awash. I always rated Lyons as the best of the American racing writers and some of his pen pictures perfectly captured the moment. 'Gethin had claimed he enjoyed racing in the wet, but he'd never tried so much horsepower in so much wet. He came back in almost immediately. There was a vacant stare in his eyes. "There's no connection at either end! On the straights at 20 miles an hour I'm using *this* much lock! In the corners I can't get the front to come round, but when the engine just *ticks* over, the back is gone! Just gone! Can we take some plug leads off?" '

Lyons would write his *Autosport* report of each CanAm race late into the night and would appear at wherever our motel was as we were leaving. We would take his report back to a waiting *Autosport* person at Heathrow . . . and Pete would take over one of our beds to sleep until checkout.

Revson disputed the lead away from the line, but two laps later and the orange McLarens were 1-2 out in front. Gethin had started sixth on the third row of the grid, but he was happier in the sunshine and soon Denny had let him through for a taste of the lead. There was some high-speed hustling with Revson and then Motschenbacher, but Denny was putting his stamp on the race, roaring back to take the lead from Gethin. It didn't last long. 'I got tangled up with a back marker having a spin at the hairpin later in the race and because we switch the electric fuel pumps off after the start and run with a mechanical pump, when the revs dropped the fuel pressure died and the engine stopped. Marshals pushed me and I dropped the clutch to help the starter when the car was rolling. Peter Gethin had waited for me to get all that little lot sorted out and he followed me across the line in second place. Then I was disqualified.'

Denny was despondent, reckoning that the organisers should follow USAC Indy-car ruling on a push-start, which said you could be push-started during a race providing it was by a track official.

'So Peter had his first CanAm win and Team McLaren continued their line-up of 19 consecutive victories . . .'

The Chaparral sucker-car came back for the race at Road Atlanta in Georgia with Vic Elford as the driver, the same 'Quick Vic' who Denny had shared a 917 Porsche with at Brands Hatch and Watkins Glen. Elford was in his element and after a lap for lap battle with Denny during qualifying, Vic emerged on pole with Denny beside him. 'Watching Group 7 cars driven hard was always exciting, but the Denny Hulme versus the Chaparral Show at Road Atlanta in 1970 deserves to lie in the annals of motorsport for all time,' wrote Lyons.

The race was a different story and after five laps at Road Atlanta, Denny was 7 seconds ahead of the Chaparral and making ground. 'But then we caught up with the back markers and I ran into the back of one, demolishing the nose of my McLaren. While I was in the pits having the last rites read on the car, Peter Gethin arrived with the nose of his McLaren stove in. It seemed like a demolition derby out there and the race finally went to Tony Dean in the little 3-litre Porsche 908, because he had been able to tiptoe around all the debris!

'It doesn't say much for the CanAm series if you have to back right off and run at the pace of the slowest back marker to make sure that he sees you and doesn't run you off into the scrub because you've come up and lapped him quicker than he expected you to.'

Next up was the Donnybrooke race in Brainerd, Minnesota, and Denny was determined not to get involved with any tailend Charlies. Two races in a row Denny had been pipped for pole, Revson qualifying faster in the Lola at Donnybrooke. 'My "little" 7-litre engine had gone sick before I had a chance at prising Peter Revson off pole in his 8-litre L&M Lola, but unofficially in the morning I had been quite a bit faster, so I wasn't all that worried. I had also made up my mind that I wasn't going to get involved with any slow cars in this race, and if I thought I couldn't slip through, I would wait and lose perhaps 3 seconds in a lap rather than risk getting carved up and bounced off the track. In a Grand Prix you rarely lose more than a second getting by a back marker but with a CanAm sports car you can get hung up really badly . . .

'In the opening laps my car was really good through the sweeping right-hander at the end of the long straight and I was getting through there at 183 mph with a full load fuel load holding the car down. It was a fairly comfortable win for me, with Peter Gethin second, but he had a hard time of it with Chris Amon in the new March 707.'

At Legona Seca, the McLaren team drivers surprised themselves by qualifying with identical times. Denny was on pole, with Peter Gethin beside him, both on 1:00.6 for the 1.9-mile course, an average speed of 112.871 mph. That's the way the race started, but it wasn't the way qualifying ended. Chaparral had benefited from intense test and development work back at base in Texas and Vic Elford enjoyed the luxury of the super-sucker at Laguna Seca, turning a best lap of 58.8 seconds, which was faster not only than the 1970 McLarens, but also faster than Bruce's best ever the season before at 59.5 seconds. Denny didn't dwell on this episode in his *Autosport* column, but Pete Lyons described the end of the Chaparral's involvement in the race thus: 'After all the niggling troubles through the summer with the innovative auxiliary systems, it was the familiar old "big motor" that blew. Blew in a big way, scattering shrapnel and greasy fluids all over Turn 2 during the [race] morning warm-up. Changing it would take more hours than remained before show time. Abruptly, this CanAm was just another conventional sports car race. A good one, though.'

Jackie Oliver in Bryant's Ti22, now called 'Autocoast', was showing splendid form and taking the chase to the McLarens. When Gethin spun on oil and stalled, Oliver was squarely in Hulme's mirrors. 'This was such earnest stuff that it began to be frightening,' wrote Lyons. 'They were going so fast, slicing through so many slow cars. One slip . . . But they were Grand Prix drivers and both were showing all their stuff now. Denny was smooth, incredibly smooth, under the pressure. Toward the end, Ollie seemed to be just the tiniest bit ragged by comparison. That's when he set fastest lap . . .'

By winning at Laguna Seca Denny had clinched the CanAm championship. 'It was something that I really did want to do this season more than anything else — making it my second CanAm title and the fourth on the trot for the McLaren team.' It was also his fifth win of the year. He was 'doing it for Bruce'. Carrying the colours.

Two weekends later the teams were at Riverside inland from Los Angeles and once again Elford in the Chaparral 2J was showing startling form, out-McLarening the McLarens. Beating them at their own game. Elford's engine had failed at Laguna Seca before the start, and Denny's did the same at Riverside. 'Winning the Riverside CanAm race seemed like a nice way to round off the series. Mind you, 3 hours before the race started I wasn't exactly sizing myself up for the Datsun 240Z pace car that was included in the winner's prize!

'Vic Elford in the ground-effect Chaparral was 2.2 seconds quicker than I was when qualifying ended, so I didn't have much option but to treat the untimed practice on race morning as a gentle run to make sure that everything worked and nothing fell off. That was when I saw the big cloud of smoke in the mirrors. The oil temperature had gone off the clock and the oil pressure had slumped to nothing, so whatever problem I had was obviously a large and expensive one. I switched off and coasted as far as I could, because every minute was precious if we were to fit a new engine in time for the race. A tow truck picked me up and hauled me back to the pits and we all got stuck in to change the engine. It took just 2 hours from the time we started tearing the bodywork off until it fired the first shot.

'All that work was worth it in the race, because I led from start to finish, collected a shade over 20 grand plus the pace car, a cheque for $50,000 for winning the Johnson Wax Championship on points and all that added up to a total collect for the series of $161,091 (to the nearest greeny) after six wins and a third in the 10 races.

'My main ambition when the guy green-flagged the race from the rolling start was to lead the field on the opening lap. After that I figured the "vacuum cleaner" Chaparral would take over and there would be very little I could do about it. I was a little surprised to get the jump on him at the start, and even more surprised to see that Jackie Oliver in the Autocoast was also in front of Elford through the first corner. I thought perhaps Vic was "sandbagging" and hanging back to make a race of it, but by the end of the lap he had dropped even further back and was obviously in trouble. I hoped it was nothing trivial. Once again the little auxiliary engine on the back that drives the suction fans had let him down, and the race was between Ollie and me.

'Ollie had brake problems early on with a full fuel load (our McLaren is very good in this respect), but when the yellow caution flag came out after a couple of cars crashed and caught fire, he was able to catch up a lot of ground. The problem in a case like this is that slower traffic tends to go even slower, dawdling along to watch the fire crews at work, and you daren't pass any of them or you'll get black-flagged and hauled into the pits for an ear-bashing. It was just like being on one of the Los Angeles freeways when there's an accident on one side of the road and the traffic going the other way all slows to a jammed crawl to watch all the activity.

'Riverside is out in the desert just within smog distance of Los Angeles. It has a long fast straight and you need all the horsepower you can get, which immediately puts the works McLarens at a disadvantage, because we are running 7.5-litre Chevvy engines while our immediate opposition — the Chaparral, the Autocoast, Revson's Lola and Amon's March — all had Chevvy engines that were just over 8 litres. It was hot during practice in the afternoons and my engine was only pulling 6300 rpm, but when the temperatures dropped towards the end of the sessions the revs would pick up again to 6500 rpm, which was worth an extra 20 horsepower and this showed up on the stopwatches.

'The Chaparral was billed as some sort of super-car, but I wasn't convinced by any means. I reckon I could have equalled Vic's times using last year's McLaren with an 8-litre engine and the wing mounted on the suspension instead of on the tail, as it has to be now. All the drama about whether the Chaparral should be allowed to run with the fans and the suction gear hinges around the rules that were brought in to ban wings. I feel that if the anything-goes open regulations were brought back again, we could be at least competitive with the Chaparral, without all the complication and cost of the sucker system. If the Chaparral is banned, then the problem and the expense of developing a similar system doesn't arise. If the Chaparral is allowed to run, it means that the major teams will build similar cars within the regulations and the costs of CanAm racing will escalate even further, and the gap between the works cars and the private owners will become even wider than it is now. I'm not against Jim Hall, I'm just against the whole principle of the thing.'

A win was still a win, however, and McLaren cars finished 1-2-3 in the championship — Hulme, Motschenbacher and Gethin. 'Ten minutes after the race a flag marshal arrived in the pits with the money to buy the Datsun pace car, so team manager Teddy Mayer sold it to him! All in all, it was quite a profitable day . . .'

18 Rising rates, Indy spins and CanAm wins

The Hulme family holidayed in New Zealand over the Christmas period leading in to 1971, Denny spending time with Angus Hyslop (his Abarth co-driver at Le Mans 10 years earlier) on his farm. He was also recovering from the hepatitis that had weakened him at the end of the previous season. 'The most difficult thing I drove in New Zealand was the Hyslop combine harvester. It steered through little wheels away at the back somewhere and I never could work out whether it was oversteering or understeering — not that it mattered at three miles an hour!

'It was more important over at Ontario Motor Speedway, where even a trace of oversteer would have you hung on the wall before long. The new M16 Indy McLaren fortunately had the right amount of understeer inbuilt and as soon as we could coax the turbocharged Offenhauser engine to run properly — that took four days! — I did about 20 laps, and then turned one at 169 point something-something. And there was still plenty more to come.

'This business about understeer and oversteer is extremely important on the big ovals, where you are going so fast that your reactions just aren't quick enough to cope with any sort of oversteer when the back end gets loose. An understeering car is so much better, because you know you can apply a lot of power and the back end won't come round on you. It makes it easier to drive and gives you a lot more confidence.

'Confidence was something Leo Mehl, Goodyear's racing boss in Europe, didn't have when I took him for a few laps in last season's CanAm McLaren M8D at the Ricard-Le Castellet circuit in the south of France, to give him some idea of what tyre testing was all about from the hero's end of the operation. We slipped him into Peter Gethin's helmet and overalls and I told him I'd take it easy on the first lap. I gather Leo thought that I hadn't kept my promise and I'd done the opening lap flat out, but it took the second lap to show him that the first one had really been gentle! We only did three laps, but we were 2 seconds faster than the Formula 2 lap record!

'On my own I went 7 seconds faster than that to set an outright unofficial record for the track, 3.5 seconds faster than Chris Amon's best in the Formula 1 Matra V12. Leo couldn't imagine where the other 7 seconds came from in the CanAm car, because he thought we were going fairly quick — we were flat at 190 mph on the straight, but obviously not reaching the limit on the twisty bits or under braking. It gave him an insight into the problems that drivers have trying to pick a tyre that is only 0.2 seconds better than another tyre. If it impressed our tyre boss so much, perhaps it would be an idea to strap a few designers into the CanAm passenger's seat and show them the difference between their office and mine . . .

'When I drove the new wedge-shaped M16 Indy McLaren at Ontario a few weeks earlier, I said it was the best racing car ever to come out of the McLaren factory, but after a few test laps in the latest M19 McLaren Formula 1 car at Goodwood, I may have to revise my ratings. There's something about the first few laps in a brand new car that lets you know whether you're going to get along with it or not. We've got a completely new cantilever rising-rate suspension system on the M19 and I suppose I half expected to spend the first days of testing getting everything to point in the right direction, but it felt great right from the start. It felt as though it had run a couple of thousand miles and was really sorted, and yet it was brand spanking new.

'Last year's M14 McLaren never gave me the same feeling of confidence from the start and I don't think I really came to terms with it during the season. We've been able to spend more time and money on new designs, but of course this has meant finding the money in the first place and we're very pleased that our sponsors Goodyear, Gulf Oil and Reynolds Aluminum have shown their faith in our efforts by their continued support. It's all very well for the so-called purists to harp on about big money spoiling racing, but if there wasn't any big money about there wouldn't be any racing cars and there wouldn't be any racing. It costs quite a bit more to build and run a racing car than it does to buy and maintain a typewriter . . .

'It was weird driving the new Formula 1 car with the all-inboard suspension for the first time, because you could see all the cantilevers and rocking arms working up and down. On the conventional suspension layout there's not a lot to watch. As the load increases on the car the rate of the springs increases to counteract it, which means the handling stays the same as the fuel load is used up. It also means that the ride height stays the same in braking, acceleration and cornering. It doesn't roll and the nose doesn't dip or lift as much. Two quite heavy blokes totalling about 26 stone jumped on the front suspension and they couldn't make it hit the ground or touch the aeon rubbers, yet it's nice and soft to bounce up and down.'

Denny was in a confident mood on the morning of the South African Grand Prix at Kyalami, the first round of the 1971 season, even though he was back on the third row with Surtees and Ickx.

'The new car had gone really well once we got it sorted out. The new suspension system didn't seem to obey any of the traditional rules of setting up a race car. It was completely the reverse. We were cranking on more wing angle but this was making the oversteer worse, which was contrary to what it should have done. If you put on more wing with a conventional car it makes the back end stick better. It was getting more and more oversteer and we were putting on more and more wing, then it suddenly dawned on us that we were heading in the wrong direction. The rising rate suspension works back to front, so that when we eased the angle of the rear wing it reduced the oversteer — and oddly enough gave it less understeer as well. Ralph Bellamy, our Australian designer who came up with the new suspension, is trying really hard to get it sorted. We all started off pretty much in the dark and it's still a bit of a mystery. It's all too technical for me. I just don't understand all the different permutations of spring strengths and frequencies and rates and so on. At one stage in practice at Kyalami I was spending more time scratching my head with the rest of the crew than I was out driving on the track!'

Jackie Stewart, fastest in practice with the Tyrrell, and Chris Amon's Matra both made poor starts from the front row and Denny was able to make ground early.

'Jackie said his new 11-series Ford engine just seemed to take a big gulp of air and no fuel at the start and it kept doing this throughout the race. Chris was in power problems (lack of) and the fact that he was carrying about 20 gallons more for the V12 than we had for the V8s only added to his handicap.'

Denny always liked the Kyalami circuit and this gave him confidence out on the track. He was soon in front and pressing on to such good effect that the race seemed to be in his pocket — with five laps to go he was leading Mario Andretti's Ferrari by a couple of seconds. Surely enough to win.

'The Ferrari's fuel load had dropped and Mario was going quicker — he took fastest lap of the race just a few laps from the finish — but with the new suspension my car had been the same throughout the race, never altering from full tanks to empty tanks. I knew I was going to have trouble with Mario before the end of the race, but I was determined to make the McLaren as wide as possible to keep the red car behind me. It was going to be my race. All I needed was a few lucky breaks getting by slower cars, and maybe a tow on the straight, and we would have 9 points in the world championship to start the season.

'Then, going round Barbecue Corner, the McLaren started to wander a wee bit. I thought either I had a puncture or one of the tyres was starting to get some build-up on it. I had a quick look at all four corners, but everything was fine. I put it down to the jitters you get in the closing laps when you're out in front and praying that nothing will go wrong.

'But as I went down into Sunset Corner and braked, the car swerved across the road. I knew I was in big trouble. Mario had caught me, and as I was gathering up the McLaren he went whistling by into the lead. The rear wheel was wobbling and I didn't know exactly what was wrong, but I was determined to finish as high as I could. It was fine at 80–90 mph on a steady throttle, but if you got on the brakes or accelerated, the car wandered all over the place.

'When Mario came by to lap me just before the finish, he slowed along-side, looked across and gave me a little wave. He's like that. A brave, tough little guy with a big heart. When you're Italian-born, it's a big deal to be winning your first Grand Prix in a factory Ferrari, 20 seconds ahead of Jackie Stewart. It must have all seemed pretty good to Mario just then, but he must have known how I was feeling too. So near and yet so far. I trickled in sixth . . .

'I was pleased at the way the new McLaren felt exactly the same throughout the race — I wasn't a bit tired at the finish despite the fact that I hadn't done any racing for a long time. Fellow Kiwi Howden Ganley, having his first Formula 1 race in a BRM, had to drop out, completely exhausted. I can understand his problem — or part of it. You've really got to sit on the designers and demand that they put a lot of air ducts into the cockpit to cool the driver — after all, he's just as important as the engine and all the other bits and pieces that they go to some lengths to keep cool . . .'

Daughter Adele was born on 26 March 1971. Greeta remembers: 'I'd called her Alicia, but Denny wanted Adele! He got home about three days after Adele was born . . . Then it became a lot harder to travel with two babies, so I'd just work out which races fitted in best. It was good to go to Zandvoort with the beach and the supermarket downstairs and then we'd always go to Villar in Switzerland, where Bernard Cahier had his fun weekend in the snow. We took the Range Rover to Villar and Denny and Martin were up on the mountain on a ski-mobile when it suddenly clouded over and got really cold. The guide told them to get off the mountain as quick as they could. Denis didn't have his gloves and his burned hands were still bad and the nerve endings were really close to the surface. He had Martin in front of him on the ski-mobile and he was coming down the mountain and all the cold was coming on his hands, and when he eventually got back to the hotel he was a cot-case. He couldn't go to dinner and he had to go to bed, absolutely beside himself. He said if it hadn't been for Martin and he *had* to keep going, it would have been so easy . . . all he wanted to do was fall over and die with hypothermia . . .' The legacy of those Indy burns was still haunting The Bear.

The Race of Champions at Brands Hatch was a non-event for Hulme, his car dogged by an electrical problem. Over at the Ontario Motor Speedway for the second time that year, Denny was running the Formula 1 M19 instead of the Indy M16, on a road course in the infield that used bits of the speedway. Denny finished fourth in the first heat with brake problems and fifth in the second heat, which somehow earned him third behind Andretti's Ferrari and Stewart's Tyrrell on aggregate. However, the excitement had started long before the race began.

'The whole race was a well-organised package deal. The racing cars were all loaded into a freighter plane in England on the Tuesday before the race, and they were back in England on the Wednesday after it. That's the sort of time it usually takes us to go to and from the Italian Grand Prix at Monza, but Ontario in California was 6000 miles from the Colnbrook factory! The plane landed at the airport half a mile from the track, so it was all fairly cosy. In fact, the shipment nearly ran amok because something happened to the braking system on the plane and all the tyres blew out down one side as it touched down! They couldn't taxi back from the end of the runway, so all the cars had to be unloaded at the end of the strip.'

The month of May at Indianapolis was dominated for Denny by a giant 720-degree spin. He eventually qualified fourth on the second row, but he had been aiming for a front-row spot with the McLarens of Peter Revson and Mark Donohue. 'That spin a week before qualifying psyched me out and it knocked my confidence to hell. Another car dropped oil and it hadn't been signalled with the yellow warning lights. I hit it and took off. They say I spun completely twice and slid for 650 feet — although I didn't get out to measure it! — but I didn't hit anything and kept going to the pit lane. After that, if the car even looked like twitching I never knew what was going to happen and I couldn't bring myself to get back up to speed again. Earlier in the month I had been running 173 mph comfortably, but after the spin I couldn't get above 168. It was like a sort of barrier and I had to try to push beyond it. The only problem was that any twitch the car made scared me and I didn't want to push my luck in case I couldn't catch it. I might have been better off if I'd gone away and had a rest somewhere and just forgotten about the track, coming back later with everything fresh to start all over again.

'This barrier really exists, because when I went out to qualify late on the Saturday afternoon I knew the moment I'd gone through the barrier, and after my first lap at 174.351 mph I knew I had it made and just went faster, getting more and more confidence back all the time. The other three laps were 174.995, 174.858 and 174.439. Now I know that I can run at 174, I can probably go out at 172 or 173 and pick up from there, whereas before I was having to try to build up from much lower speeds.

'It was annoying that Donohue could smoke right out and rattle off quickies in the Penske M16 with apparent ease in practice — it was probably more demoralising than annoying and it must have been demoralising for our team when I just couldn't get myself back into the groove. But our team works so well that we could laugh and shrug these things off and say, "She'll be right on race day . . ." '

Denny had a comfortable knack of taking you with him in his *Autosport* column, but he was aware that you were a reader rather than a racer and he explained it as he went along, not too much to be patronising, but enough to make you feel you were one of his extended mates. Writing this now, 30-odd years after having taped it and written it in the 1970s, makes me appreciate how well Denny wanted to communicate with his readers . . . even if he wasn't as comfortable doing it one-to-one.

'Revvy snatching the pole was just great, I thought. Donohue would have gone quicker than he did, but they might have out-fumbled themselves a bit. Mark said the car was oversteering but maybe the engine was going a bit sour as well. I think Peter was so uptight after all the dramas with his engine that he just couldn't believe it when he saw the 176 board. After that there was no way of stopping him. In fact, the crew didn't believe his first lap time, which was 178.006 mph, and they showed him 176 in case they'd made a mistake. Pete showed them he wasn't kidding next time round at 179.354 mph, which was an all-time qualifying record at Indy to date! The crowd went mad. He knew he had the pole in the bag and he wasn't about to back off for anyone.'

The jump in pole speed was indicative of the design leap made by the new wedge-shaped M16 McLaren, its aerodynamics borrowed from the Lotus 72 in Formula 1.

'Unless someone shakes things up at Indy, nobody ever does anything drastic design-wise. They just carry on from year to year with the same basic lumps of machinery.

'How do you lap Indy at that sort of speed? Everyone keeps telling you that being smooth into the corner and getting the power on early is the answer, but that's hard to do when you're out there. You whistle down the straight so fast (over 200 mph) that when the turns come up they look like right-angle corners. I was backing off early but I wasn't hitting the brakes. I just let it roll in. It's hard to convince yourself that the car is not going to do anything nasty when you arrive in the corner and you surprise yourself by finding that it's all settled down and you can get back on the throttle so much earlier. Come race day we're going to be in good shape.'

Back in Europe Denny had finished fifth in the Spanish Grand Prix on the hilly Montjuich street circuit above Barcelona and he was fourth round more streets in Monaco the weekend before the 500 at Indianapolis. It was almost traditional at the Speedway that if you spun you went in to the wall and out of the race. During the month of May Denny had already spun twice and emerged unscathed — and there was more to come.

'A.J. Foyt told me he thought there was a turtle driving my McLaren as it went spinning down the track in front of him at Indianapolis on the fourth lap of the 500. "What was you doin' lookin' like a turtle out there?" A.J. asked after the race. "You pulled your head down and got out of sight. I couldn't see no head, man. Why didn't you stand up in that thing and look around?"

'I had just passed "Super-Tex" Foyt for fifth place and was getting into my stride when the back end started to slide a wee bit and suddenly the car took over at about 160 mph in turn 3. I stomped on the brakes and that set the car whistling round and round in the middle of the road. I must have gone round four times. Eventually the car ran backwards on the grass still going quite quickly, so I flicked the steering wheel to get it pointing frontwards, let the brakes off, and banged it into gear to see if I could revive the engine, which had stalled during my quadruple revolution.

'But I didn't quite make it. A tow truck dragged the car about 20 yards and it fired, so I drove to the pits to have all four wheels changed, because the tyres had flats where the rubber had literally been ground off during the spins. It seems to me that if you hit the brakes just as the car starts to spin, the car will spin in a straight line, because no one wheel is getting more adhesion than any of the others. But if you're halfway through a spin and you let the brakes off, one wheel might grip more than the others and send the car all over the place. That's the Hulme Rule for Survival when Indy starts going round the car instead of vice versa. This is the second time during the month of May that I've had the mother and father of all spins at Indy and both times the car spun straight down the road without hitting anything. Hitting the anchors seems to be the secret of it, but I'm not guaranteeing it . . .

'Indy is a race where waiting for the start is worse than all the 200 mph dicing once the race starts. You try hard to keep cool and you're conscious that you don't want to appear twitchy, but when there are 10 minutes to go and the balloons have gone and the marching girls have finished their parades, then you realise it's your turn to put on the show. You can't help but feel a bit apprehensive and your heart starts to pump away quicker than it really ought to.

'I was right behind Peter Revson in the other Gulf-orange McLaren on the rolling start and he had told me that we would be in second shifting up to third as the pace car pulled in. Our start wasn't what you might call a copybook operation, but we soon got sorted out. Mario Andretti had a go at me, but I out-dragged him down to turn 3 and then I set about getting by A.J. That was the prelude to the turtle trick . . .

'We had a third gear that was very close to fourth, the idea being to run in third after the car had been refuelled and was carrying more weight, using fourth as the fuel load was used up. I went zinging down to turn 3 on the first lap and the tacho was reading 9000 with a couple of hundred yards to go before I hopped on the picks. I popped it into top and it pulled strongly, so obviously we were OK in the horsepower department.

'After my pit stop I got back on the track and almost immediately Krissiloff, Mel Kenyon, Andretti and little Gordie Johncock in last year's McLaren M15 had their big pile-up. That slowed the race down under the yellow light and I was able to feel the car out at a steady pace and get over any jitters I might have had.

'Going down the pit straight I could read the race order off the tall scoreboard, so I knew when I came up under Al Unser that he was the leader. My number was so far down the board that I was out of sight! I found that I could hold Al comfortably and that gave me quite a charge. When you are lapping at 173 round Indy you really start to reel in the traffic. The other cars seem to be coming back towards you.

'I came up behind Peter in our other McLaren running quicker than he was and he gave me the signal to pass him, so I got on a big slingshot coming out of turn 2 and pulled by him on the straight. Alongside him I could see a build-up of black rubber dust on the back of the radiators and I worried that this would be happening to my car too and it would overheat, but the gauges said 110 water and 120 oil, so that was no sweat. I would have liked a bit more oil pressure, but when the yellow went on for a long time the temperature dropped and the pressure went up, so I knew I didn't really have a problem.

'But I didn't have long to wait for one. I'd worked my way up from thirty-first to eighth and figured I had a chance of finishing fourth or better when the first wisp of smoke came into the cockpit. Then it started a vibration, so I pulled round to the pits trailing smoke. Tyler Alexander checked it and said, "Forget it. It's all turned nasty and there's oil and water coming out all over the place." So that was it. Indy 1971. D. Hulme, seventeeth, retired.

'It was disappointing because I was feeling in really good shape physically. I'd had a problem with heavy steering on the car early in the month, but during the race the steering was fantastic. Peter had a problem here because his steering had become heavy and it was wearing him out. Five hundred miles is a hell of a long drive — you've got the G-forces from the four corners and you try to fight these forces by hanging on to the wheel. If the steering is heavy and you've got to work at that as well, it all becomes nearly impossible. You get mentally and physically very tired.

'When the final yellow came on after the Mike Mosley/Al Unser crash, Peter was second and closing on Unser, but he got caught up in the classic yellow light situation that I always dread, because it can go against you just as easily as it can go for you. Peter was hung up behind a bunch of slower cars that he wasn't allowed to pass and Li'l Al was starting to open the gap again, so we got permission (as Al's crew had done) from track chief Harlan Fengler, for Peter to pass the slower cars.

'Getting permission was the easy part — getting the message across to Peter was more difficult. We were giving him signals to go, but he wasn't going. Even Dan Gurney and Roger Penske were in our pit trying to work out a way of spurring Peter past the slower cars in pursuit of Al! But I knew Peter's problem. He was just beat and he was hanging on grimly to bring the car home in one piece and in second place rather than get involved in any heroics with back markers.

'He was whacked after the race. The problem at Indy is that during the month of May you hardly ever run more than 10 laps at a time, which takes about 8 minutes, and suddenly you're sitting there for more than 3 hours and it's a whole new deal.

'And so McLaren didn't win the Indy 500, but you've got to give us A for effort and a lot of credit for bringing along new cars that are just plain *quick*. Mark Donohue drove away from the field in the opening laps to nobody's great surprise in the Penske McLaren, but his transmission locked up and put him out after 66 laps. I guess Roger Penske wished Mark had parked the car just about anywhere else in the Speedway, because when Mike Moseley came flaming down off the wall late in the race he T-boned Roger's new McLaren and completely wrecked it. We'd been trying to work out ways of beating Penske and Donohue all month, but we never got round to thinking of anything quite as drastic as that!'

The remainder of the World Championship was a string of races Denny preferred to forget. Twelfth in Holland, retired in France, Britain, Germany and Austria, and Watkins Glen. Denny's fourth place in Canada was as good as the back half of the season got for him, but he would have probably preferred to forget that one as well. The Grand Prix at Mosport was run in downpour conditions and the driver who let everyone know that he *hated* racing in the rain set the fastest lap of the race!

I was running the media side of Gulf Oil sponsorship for the McLaren team in Formula 1, USAC and CanAm, and as we prepared for the opening CanAm round at Mosport I was delighted to find that the main Canadian television channel was running a full-hour feature on the way the McLaren team had been able to dominate the North American series. We set up driver interviews at the motorhome with plenty of Gulf identification in the background and Peter Revson went first. He was perfect. Lots of sponsor mentions. The interviewer and the sound man loved him.

Then Denny came out. I was standing beside the sound man, who had his headphones on and tape machine running. The interviewer asked his first innocuous opening question. Silence. Denny stared at him, then looked beyond him to me and said, 'Eoin — tell this c**t to stop asking such stupid fucking questions!' Then he stormed back into the motorhome, slamming the door behind him. The interviewer was in tears. The sound man looked as though he'd been slammed through his headset, which he probably had in word terms! I could see my Gulf contract crumbling as I hurried to the motorhome door. The Bear was sitting there tittering — it was the giggle he did when he was getting his own way. I told him he was personally ruining the whole television programme, but he just gave a big grin and said, 'Aw c'mon, Eoin, I was just getting their attention . . .' I assured him that he had certainly achieved that, and said would he now come out and do the interview. The interviewer looked as though he expected to be attacked, but The Bear had become a pussycat and Denny gave an excellent interview . . .

There would be a handful of Denny wins to come from the CanAm series in 1971. 'From my point of view the best thing about being overtaken by Jackie Stewart's new Lola in the opening laps of the opening CanAm race at Mosport, was that I had a close-up view of the oil that was spewing out the back of his car. I had led from the start, but we were moving through the back markers after only four laps and with 10 laps gone I found myself stonkered by a succession of slower cars. Jackie came up alongside, we crested a brow and there was a slower car dead ahead of me, so I had to back off and Jackie flashed past.

'The oil started spraying out after about five laps and I figured that there was only a limited amount of time left before he was either out of oil or out of the race, so I dropped back a bit. After all, I was the next car on the oil and I didn't want to do anything foolish.

'My mechanics must have wondered what was going on because they couldn't see the oil from the Lola as we blasted by the pits. They only knew that for some reason I was dropping behind yet giving them a thumbs-up signal. Very puzzling, it must have been. That's often a problem with signals that a driver gives from the car — when you're in the cockpit you just know that the signal is crystal clear in its meaning, but across there in the pits they're all scratching their heads and saying to each other "What the hell was that all about?"

'When Jackie was 6 or 7 seconds ahead I thought maybe I'd better not let him get *too* far in front just in case it was only his oil catch-tank that had filled up and was spilling over, because that certainly wasn't a fatal condition and could easily cure itself. I got up to within a couple of seconds but then he peeled off into the pits and I never saw him again. Apparently he had lost all the oil from the gearbox and the ring and pinion had quit.

'After that, there wasn't a lot to do except tool round and round until the chequered flag came out on lap 80. I would have been more than happy to see it after 40 laps.

'Peter Revson was behind me in second place with the other works McLaren M8F, running about 10 or 15 seconds away like an obedient number two. But then he started to get closer, and when the pit board showed that he was only 2 seconds behind and I could see him in the mirrors, I started to wonder what it was all about. I mean, team tactics are all very well but I'm never one to take chances. I had been lapping around 1:21, so I zapped in a couple at 1:19.4 and thought that would do the trick — if Peter was starting to get turned on to race me, he'd get the message that I'd only been sandbagging.

'Then team manager Teddy Mayer appeared out in front of the pits to slow Peter and a bit later he came out again to give me the slow-down treatment as well, so I figured he must have it all under control. Being the only Kiwi driver in the team now, I've got to keep an eye on what these Americans are up to, but my chief mechanic, Jim Stone, is a New Zealander too, so he keeps me posted. Can't have any of this racial discrimination in the ranks! I didn't hear until later that Teddy was getting poised to reinforce his slow-down signal by waving a large hammer if I didn't get the message quickly enough.

'Stewart's new Lola has the same 8.1-litre that we're using. The Lola looks stubby, but in fact the wheelbase is exactly the same as ours at 98 inches. It looks a smaller car because designer Eric Broadley has embarked on a different type of aerodynamic thinking to us, and the car has virtually no overhang at all, which concentrates the downforce in the middle of the car. We try to get the downforce out over each end of the McLaren.

'Surely it's about time that someone came along and beat us fair and square in CanAm racing, but we're going to make damn sure that it's hard work for whoever does it. You've got to finish the race before you can win and we have managed to get the reliability fairly well squared away over the past few seasons. Touch wood . . .'

Denny didn't touch it hard enough. He was on pole for the next round at Ste-Jovite, but he had Stewart's snub-nosed Lola beside him and the Scot was determined to take the race to The Bear. At three-quarter distance the Lola was in front and Hulme's McLaren was fading. ' "Why?" everyone asked of his neighbour,' Lyons wrote in his CanAm history. 'The engine sounded OK, there was no smoke, nothing was dripping or dangling. But Denny's pace was obviously off in the corners and on the straights he was lifting his visor to scoop in air.' Most of the race folk staying at the McLaren hotel — including the whole McLaren team — had been laid low by a flu bug overnight and Denny only just lasted out the race in second place. He stopped as soon as he took the chequered flag, and was so exhausted he couldn't remove his own driving gloves. Jackie Stewart had won with the Lola and suddenly it seemed that the axis of CanAm power might be about to change.

Denny had also suffered from personal overheating at Ste-Jovite and for the next round at Road Atlanta the mechanics punched holes in the seat back and ducted cold air to this part of the car. Denny set pole ahead of Revson in the other team McLaren and Stewart, but felt he could have gone even faster on that best lap but for an oil flag that appeared. 'I was shown the flag just as I crested the brow of a hill and I backed off. I was just a little bit annoyed to find the track perfectly clear and clean, because I had backed off and lost a few tenths on my lap time. I found out later that a snake had been slithering across the track, and they had shown me an oil flag because they didn't have a snake flag . . .'

Denny had been suffering engine problems throughout practice and on race morning a seized throttle cut into his set-up time. 'Peter swept into the first corner ahead of me and Jackie's Lola was tucked in behind me. By the second lap I realised that I had no brakes — the pads obviously hadn't bedded in properly in the brief practice run — and for the rest of the race I had to cool it, watching Revvy and Jackie racing for the lead.'

A puncture cost Stewart a pit stop and then a broken shock absorber put him out. And the McLarens regained their 1-2 finishing style. 'It was Peter's first CanAm win and his first big win of any sort in a fair while. I'm starting to get used to this second place slot.

'The service wasn't exactly scintillating in the restaurant at our motel, so team chief Teddy Mayer bought a barbecue and enough gear to stock a kitchen and set up shop out at the edge of the motel parking lot. The first night chef Mayer had something of a constructional problem with the barbecue, but once he had it built and fired up he was really in the catering business, with New York cut sirloins that melted in your mouth if you could get near enough to the grill to get them off!'

For Watkins Glen, Denny stayed with his usual 8.1-litre iron-sleeve Chevvy, while Revson stayed with the Reynolds aluminium 'sleeveless' V8. Lyons: 'Hulme's car lacked the revamped rear sub-frame put on his team-mate's to withstand "powerslide vibration". Denny's hadn't cracked, which was a matter of driving style, according to a team member's droll observation: "The only similarity between those two is they both hold licenses."'

Stewart started the Lola from pole, with Revson beside him and Denny back in third place on the second row. Stewart and Revson commanded the race, with the Lola in front until Jackie picked up a puncture and lost a lap. Revson then had an easy lead from Denny, with Stewart storming in an attempt to close on Hulme for second. Speed traps at the end of the straight showed Stewart at 194.6 mph, Revson a full 10 mph slower. It wouldn't last, though, and Jackie went out with serious vibrational problems.

Lyons: 'Through all this, Hulme had never turned a hair. Convinced his engine was soft and understanding that his team-mate was running the engine that was supposed to win anyway, he seemed content — if not happy — to trundle around way behind, all the way to the flag. But on lap 68, something happened to wake The Bear. The big orange Batmobile came storming in a cloud of dust down the pit lane; in seconds, the crew hoisted the front, swapped the left front wheel, and sent the car wheelspinning and fishtailing on its way.

'A puncture? No, all four spokes of the cast magnesium wheel had cracked. While he was stopped, Denny had seen Revvie roar by, and this alone of all the events this day seemed to switch him on. From a standing start in the pit lane, leaning on a cold outside front tyre, Denis Hulme went through the speed trap at 185.6 mph and completed his first lap in 1:06.083 — the race record! *That's* the Bear we knew. With seven laps to go, he unlapped himself, but kept driving as hard as he could. So there was a little life at the end, but it ended as a CanAm like most CanAms before. McLaren-McLaren-nobody. Nobody, though, knew better than the Kiwis how much of it had been luck recently. They were in a real fight.'

Jackie Stewart brought European élite Formula 1 concerns on safety to the CanAm series, which had thus far been a series unto itself where tracks were where you raced and racing was *supposed* to be exciting, wasn't it? Exciting and dangerous. Not to JYS. He demanded that trackside trees be felled and poles moved, and to counter the roughness of a country track, which was breaking and bending suspensions in practice, Jackie asked for the race distance to be shortened. The organisers refused. Jackie announced that he would drive . . . but he wouldn't race.

Denny was on pole, with Revson beside him, Stewart third fastest on row two. Lyons: 'Pacing the field under a bright sun, Hulme out-dragged Revson up past the pits, arced under the bridge into the fast first turn, and spun in the face of the onrushing pack . . . it was some kind of first turn! All that time-consuming qualifying; they might as well have drawn numbers out of a hat.'

Hulme: 'I accelerated off pole position into the first corner and as I touched the brakes a universal joint broke and the right rear drive shaft dropped out from under the car. With the rear brakes inboard this left me with brakes on three corners only and the car spun slowly in front of the pack. With outboard brakes I would at least have stood a chance of driving it clear without spinning and getting biffed about.'

Lyons: 'As early as the second lap, the decision Stewart made the day before became apparent. He was making no effort to stay with Revson. The McLaren went on alone.'

Revson had an easy lead. Easy that is, until the seventy-second lap, when his McLaren suffered an identical problem to Denny's.

Lyons: 'The flailing shaft made a mighty wreckage of the entire corner of the car, but Pete kept it all on the road and staggered on, with the body down on the tyre and smoking. He reached the pits before Stewart came in sight, but Jackie caught the excitement from the crowd and knew immediately that his strategy, this late in the game, had in fact paid off.'

Denny and Peter flew straight to Ontario Motor Speedway for qualifying with the M16 wedges, while the mechanics rebuilt Denny's car — with outboard rear brakes — in time for the Elkhart Lake CanAm the following weekend. Denny had problems at Ontario and made it back to Elkhart for the final practice session. 'Stewart and Oliver were fastest when I arrived but my third flying lap gave me third best time and my fourth flyer put me on pole position, which did nice things to my battered ego.'

In the race, though, Denny dropped from the lead with a broken crankshaft and Revson went on to win.

'The jinx about the pole winner not winning a CanAm race this season didn't bother Revvy at Donnybrooke — he just went out and blew the whole jinx right out the window!

'There was some talk at Donnybrooke that Revvy and I would be made honorary starters of the race next year after the good job we made of rescuing the start when the guy with the flag miscued and tried to flag us away a lap too soon! What a shambles. The steward of the meeting had told us all that we would do the customary lap behind Stirling in the pace car, then we would do a lap on our own, and *then* we would start. But when we came out of the last turn and Stirling peeled off, there was the guy with the flag waving it like mad. I looked across to see if Revvy was going to make a run for it but he had his hand up. I kept a gimlet eye on the mirrors to make sure that some hero didn't try running us over (the chief steward said he thought the whole field was going to be destroyed right there and then on the grid!), but Jackie Stewart and Lothar Motschenbacher were on the row behind us, so they were obviously going to be automotive cushions to protect us — whether they wanted to be or not . . .'

Jackie got the jump at the start but Revson took over the lead, Stewart pitted to check Lola handling that was feeling strange and Denny soldiered on. 'There was nothing I could do to reel him in because all the gauges on my car were pointing to an air-cooled Reynolds Aluminum Chevrolet. I had a 30-second cushion on Vic Elford and I backed off until I could see him in the mirrors and the crew kept me posted on his pursuit until he had a puncture and pitted. Peter and I finished 1-2.

'I understand that our team has sewn up the CanAm championship for the fifth year in a row, but now the big question is which McLaren will win the title — Peter's or mine. We used to have this thing about taking it in turns to win CanAm races, but I never seem to be able to get near enough to Peter to ask him about it! He's been on top form lately, while I've been having a strong run of either finishing second or parked.'

At Edmonton, round 8 of the series, Denny and Peter filled the front row, but on race morning 'someone' dropped a 3/8-inch bolt into a cylinder on Revson's Chevvy and it took a panic engine job to lift the head, retrieve the bolt and get Revvy into the race 11 laps after the start. Denny had run third in the early laps behind Stewart and Oliver and didn't look like a challenger. Late in the race he passed Oliver in the Shadow and when Stewart performed an uncharacteristic spin with 13 laps to go, Denny inherited a comfortable win. Stewart was a minute back in second place. Revson was twelfth on a flat tyre.

At Laguna Seca Denny was trying to sort unhappy handling and Peter was on pole, with Denny beside him. British driver David Hobbs had joined the series, replacing Oliver in the Shadow and immediately making his presence felt. Denny: 'At one stage he was up on the front row with Peter. 'obbs is a nice guy, but I don't like him *that* much . . .'

Revson and Stewart controlled the race, while Denny had a sick engine, later traced to a few broken valve springs, and he was grateful to finish third behind something of a comic opera at the finish. 'At the very end of the race, Peter's engine broke a valve stem and dropped the valve into the piston. He was comfortably in the lead when his car started belching out smoke. The officials threw a black flag at him but he didn't see it, then they forgot to put the chequer out to him when they should have on the next lap (after all, it was the end of the race!) and when they eventually got it out, they waited for Jackie and gave it to him. Pete must have figured that if he had made a pit stop (to have a door closed after he had been biffed by a back marker), run the last couple of laps on seven cylinders and still finished in front of the field, he was going to grab the money and run anyway! There was a big old hooh-hah, but they finally agreed that Peter could keep his win, they fined him $250 for being a naughty boy and I was third behind Jackie.'

Denny was into golf and he found it relaxed him as they prepared for the final race of the 1971 series at Riverside: 'Arnold Palmer doesn't have a problem with me yet! I'm having a problem with myself at the moment. Standing too close to the ball after I've hit it, and things like that, but I've found that golf is a great unwinder for me and maybe that's why I was able to get with the programme at Riverside. I had an outside chance of keeping my CanAm title if I was to win the race and Revvy finished lower than sixth. Before the race Pete and I got together to agree our race strategy. It wasn't all that difficult, because Peter didn't have anything to gain by making a banzai effort at winning — he had everything to lose in fact — so he said he would let me clear into the first corner and cool it while I did my thing out in front.

'My race was probably a lot easier than Peter's. He knew he only had to place above sixth and he could have done that with one hand tied behind his back, but you can't afford to back off too much because you lose concentration. And you also worry like hell about what might go wrong. You listen for every little noise that might indicate a problem. Like lying awake at night in an empty house wondering how big the guy must be that is climbing through the window downstairs . . .

'I could have pressed on harder than I did once I had built up a useful lead, but I wasn't pressing my luck. I had been winding a lot of revs out of the engine in the early stages, but it never faltered and never even ran hot. I headed Peter home by 46.62 seconds to round off another steamroller run for the McLaren team. The fifth straight win in the CanAm championship, Peter's title, and a race win for me . . .'

19 Winning and losing in '72

In 1972 Yardley sponsored the Formula 1 McLaren M19As, switching from BRM, and Denny was joined by Peter Revson. First race was the Argentine Grand Prix at the end of January and the McLarens were fast from the first day of practice, filling the second row of the grid behind Jackie Stewart on pole in the Tyrrell and Carlos Reutemann thrilling the home fans in the Brabham. Denny tucked in behind the Tyrrell and Brabham at the start, dropped to fourth when Emerson Fittipaldi took his Lotus past, but then picked up a safe second place for the rest of the race when Reutemann and Fittipaldi had problems. Denny had problems of his own, driving for most of the race without a clutch. Revson had been feeling unwell at the start of his first full Formula 1 season in eight years, and when a water pipe was dislodged after a spin, he retired with a tightening engine. Denny came home second, comfortably ahead of Jacky Ickx and Clay Regazzoni in the two works Ferraris.

At Kyalami Denny was on the second row again, this time beside Mike Hailwood in the Surtees. 'My fireball start off the second row of the grid in the South African Grand Prix took me into the lead before the first corner and if it startled me it must have really shattered Jackie Stewart, Clay Regazzoni and Emerson Fittipaldi, who were on the front row! The nose of my Yardley-McLaren was aimed between Fittipaldi's John Player Lotus on the right and Regazzoni's Ferrari on the left, and when the flag dropped I made one of those superb starts that you always dream about but seldom manage. The Ferrari barely moved as I dropped the clutch and for a fraction of a second I thought my engine would die, so I slipped the clutch and let it out again and did this four times while I just blew the doors off the front row with an enormous wave of acceleration. I guess it let the wheels grip, break into wheelspin and grip again as I dropped the clutch, rather than losing the bite in one big burst of wheelspin off the line.

'I'd disposed of the Ferrari before we reached the brow of the hill and I was well alongside Emerson when I spotted two guys running across the road 150 yards in front. I remember thinking if there were any more jay runners following that pair, there'd be a catastrophe, but suddenly they were gone and I was easing ahead of Emerson and there was the blue Tyrrell gunning up on the left-hand side. By this time I was running high in fourth and hadn't got into fifth and I was charging up the inside for the fast right-hander. I braked as l-a-t-e as I could, feeling the car locking up and wanting to slide straight on, but I made it through the turn ahead of Jackie and the pack.

'I wasn't kidding myself that I could hold Jackie off, because we'd been timing him in practice and he was up to half a second faster than us on the straight. He arrived into the hairpin before the long run down past the pits that ideal 30 yards behind me, so that he could close up going down through the right-hand kink and then slingshot by as we passed the pits. The gap at the hairpin was critical. If you were too close to the car in front you had to back off at the kink, which lost you pace for passing. In the following laps I was able to keep Emerson and Mike Hailwood's Surtees just far enough back to out-drag them on the straight and I held second behind Jackie until the water temperature started to climb because I had been running my new 12-series Ford-Cosworth hard at 10,500 rpm. I let them through after 17 laps and tagged on behind in fourth spot, running comfortably. I had asked for a higher top gear when the wind switched round on race morning to blow behind us on the straight, and although I was worried that I wouldn't be able to keep the revs in the power band on my own, I was able to run an easy 10,000 rpm down the straight in the slipstream.

'There had been a smell of hot oil in the air for some laps, but I wasn't sure which car it came from. It's odd how you can pick up something like that even when you're muffled to the eyeballs in mask and helmet. It turned out that a bolt had come out of Jackie's gearbox, draining the oil away, and his transmission was about to fry itself. So after 44 laps Emerson was out in front with no "rabbit" to chase and me in his mirrors some 5 seconds back. I think he was in some sort of handling problem with his car, but my Goodyears had settled down nicely thank you and I was somewhat surprised at the way I was able to close in and pass him and then pull away so comfortably that three laps later I docked my revs to 10,000 and towards the end of the race it was such a cruise that I was only running to nine-five.

'Not that I was sitting back and enjoying the sunshine by any means, because I remembered this race a year earlier, when I'd led to within spitting distance of the finish and then a bolt let go in my suspension and I was out. This time it held together and I won by 14.1 seconds from Fittipaldi, with my team-mate Peter Revson third in the other Yardley-McLaren. Peter had been trapped by slower cars at the start, coming by the pits on the first lap in eighteenth place, and it says a fair amount for his Grand Prix potential that he was able to stay on maximum charge and come through to third. If the race had been slightly longer or if he'd been allowed a better crack at the start I think he might have been able to pip Emerson for second place, and that would have been enough for a series of cardiac arrests in the directors' offices at Yardley in London!

'My car always seemed to be getting fitted with a new engine during practice —and the tyre testing we had run earlier at Kyalami — and my new race engine only arrived in the nick of time the night before the race. I tried it on race morning and there was oil leaking out the back of the crankshaft, but our mechanics had already cured a similar problem on Peter's engine so they were able to strip off the gearbox, clutch and flywheel and cobble up the oil seal, getting it all bolted back together just before race warm-up.

'Anyway, here I am way up on top of the world championship 6 points ahead of my new CanAm team-mate Stewart, after the first two races. It feels pretty good to be a Grand Prix winner again, and since we have just climbed up a long pile of bills into our new house (at long, long last) I may have to maintain this winning habit to keep my bank manager impressed. My young son Martin thinks Dad is pretty hot stuff. He was five on race day and he's sure I turned on a special effort for his birthday!'

The new Hulme home was a state-of-the-art dwelling built in a wooded area of the exclusive St George's Hill estate near to Weybridge and the old Brooklands motor circuit, which was the world's first dedicated motor racing facility when it opened in 1907. It closed for racing in 1939 at the outbreak of war, when it was taken over by Vickers and the old banked circuit was broken up in places.

Whenever Denny wasn't testing, racing or visiting the factory at Colnbrook close to Heathrow, he was working around the new house. I remember one epic modification he launched into after a wall just inside the door in the master bedroom had annoyed his sense of order. He couldn't understand why it was there, so he decided to remove it. With a chain saw. The reason it was there was because it housed the main wiring system for the house . . . and Denny carved through it, startled at the sheets of sparks and flame and then the house descending into darkness. The fact that the spray of oil from the chain saw blade links had splattered all over the bedspread and the wallpaper were very much secondary outcomes of Denny's chain saw massacre of his new house.

Denny had his Kyalami Cosworth refitted for the Race of Champions at Brands Hatch. 'It had been taken out of the car, dyno-ed and popped back in again, but it felt brand new. It's the latest 12-series and it gives you all sorts of confidence to have a nice crisp and reliable engine in there. In fact, it goes so well that I'm wondering whether it mightn't have been meant for Stewart and got muddled at the Cosworth factory. Can't say I'm about to check too closely on his behalf, though . . .

'I didn't repeat Kyalami form from the second row, but I was right there as we all peeled off into Paddock turn. Gethin had made a stormer of a start from the middle of the front row in the Marlboro-BRM, but Fittipaldi dived underneath him at Paddock, pushed him out wide, and that was the last we saw of the Lotus. He just drove away and won. I've got to give Gethin full marks for trying hard. He really deserved an A for effort and a Merit Star for bravery. He was trying so hard that I thought any moment he's going to throw this lot away up a bank somewhere. Mike Hailwood got fed up waiting behind me for Geth to have his accident, so he shouldered his way past the pair of us and set off after Emerson. "Mike the Bike" was scoring from the fact that his Surtees seems to pick up enormous momentum by the time it gets to the end of the straight. I noticed this at Kyalami too. It's nothing super at the beginning of the straight, but it sure does get after it by the end of the straight!

'Eventually, with six laps left I made a last-ditch run up inside Peter, reckoning to worry him if nothing else, and he missed a gearshift, which let me through and away. That was when I was convinced I had a puncture! All that work and here I've got a bloody puncture! The car started to wobble all over the place and I backed off, but I could see Gethin hurtling up in the mirrors so I couldn't afford too much back-offery. Brands Hatch is still very rough and when something like this happens to the car you immediately think of broken suspension first and then a puncture. In fact, it was neither. I realised afterwards it must have been oil on the track that took me by surprise.'

The Spanish Grand Prix was on the Jarama circuit outside Madrid and the Hulme Yardley-McLaren was in the middle of the front row for the start, between Ickx's Ferrari on pole and Fittipaldi's John Player Lotus 72. 'After my demon start in South Africa I felt obliged to do something special in Spain and I had a handy lead on the traffic jam in the first corner and I stayed out ahead of Stewart's Tyrrell, Ickx and Fittipaldi for four laps, but I was having all sorts of drama with the gearbox. I had to chase the gears up and down the box before I could find the one I was after, and I must have been in neutral when Jackie shot past on the straight looking across to see what the hell I was up to!

'A lap later and Ickx and Fittipaldi also went past while I was hunting for gears on the straight, but when I had reorganised my shifting procedure to try to cope with whatever the problem was, I was holding ground on Regazzoni and Andretti in the other two Ferraris.

'Then it started to rain. There had been official suggestions that the race would be stopped if it rained, because the slick tyres we had were hopeless in the wet . . . and it would also give the mechanics a chance to check my gearbox if the race was to be restarted. But the rain stopped. Fifth gear had gone completely and Mario was past me, but the oil spraying out the back of the Ferrari meant he wouldn't be around for too long. He wasn't.

'I was third, but my gearbox was getting worse and worse and when I could smell the hot oil I called it a day and stopped to watch the race from the pits. The gearbox pinion bearing had failed, which accounted for the woolly shift.'

Stewart spun and knocked the nose off the Tyrrell, so he was also a spectator and it left Denny in front of the title run, now equal with Fittipaldi, who won in Spain.

Denny was famous for his dislike of racing in the rain and Monaco in 1972 was high on his hate list. 'If the Monaco Grand Prix had stopped 20 laps before the finish I think everyone would have gone home a lot happier, a lot drier, a lot warmer and with a lot less damage done to various race cars. I don't think I've ever driven in such terrible conditions and I take my Bell Star off to Jean-Pierre Beltoise for his win in the BRM. He gets my vote for just staying on the road in that rain, never mind the fact that he had Ickx's Ferrari in his wake most of the time.'

It was all looking good when Denny qualified second fastest on the first day of practice, but it rained on the second day and he never bothered to go out. 'It wouldn't have proved anything, because you could get no idea of improvements on the wet track. We just hoped that it wouldn't rain in the race. Some hope!

'It looked as though it would stay dry for the race and we were told we would get a quarter hour of practice just before the race, but this was delayed and then everything happened at once. It started to rain just as they let us out — Princess Grace and Prince Rainier were still on their lap of honour with full motorcycle cop escort. It was Peter Ustinov's "Grand Prix du Roc" for real! A grid-full of guys all dead keen on trying out the track just prior to the Grand Prix and here's a bunch of motorbike cops trying to block us off! One tried to run me on to the pavement, but he looked the wrong way at the wrong time and I ducked the other side. What a shambles! Then the officials decided to stop all the cars in front of the new pits just below the chicane, instead of the original instructions, which were to form up on the dummy grid round by the Gasometer Hairpin. More chaos. Cars were howling out of the tunnel and over the brow of the hill to find the road completely blocked! The cars that had gone round to the proper dummy grid then tried to get back . . . and there was more commotion with the cops.

'In fact, the whole weekend seemed to be punch-ups. It all started when the car constructors signed an agreement with the organisers that they would start 25 cars, then the organisers decided they hadn't signed any contract, then the police impounded the cars on behalf of the organisers, and then the organisers denied telling the police to do any such thing . . . comic opera.

'Beltoise made a tremendous start off the second row in his Marlboro-BRM, leading Ickx into the first corner and staying in front for the whole race to win BRM their first points this season. He was OK because he had a clear track ahead, but the rest of us were running blind in rooster-tails of spray from the car in front. It was a case of follow-the-leader, because you simply couldn't see. It also proved the lie to those damn-fool red tail-lights. I guess about half the cars running had the lights on the back, but you couldn't see them until you were so close that you could see the rest of the car anyway.'

Peter Revson was over at Indianapolis for qualifying and his place in the Yardley-McLaren was taken by Brian Redman, who drove to an excellent fifth place, considering the conditions.

'I was running sixth early in the race with Brian tucked in behind and when my brakes started playing up and I went straight ahead up the escape road at the chicane, he followed me dutifully into the pen. By the time the traffic had splashed past and we were allowed out, we were running about sixteenth and seventeenth. Brian had had enough of being a dutiful number two, so he went sailing by (literally) as soon as we got back on the track. I was fully occupied just staying on the road and I ran out of *that* at one stage. Someone had dropped oil and if the track had been slippery before, now it was a joke. I could barely get up the hill to the Casino and diving down past the Tip Top bar to the Mirabeau hairpin it was very tippy-toe stuff getting slowed. A few heroes used the guardrails inadvertently as an aid to deceleration . . .

'And being a hero myself, I had a "moment" going into the Gasometer hairpin. There was more oil down and it seemed I was never going to get stopped. Then I saw this marshal ahead of me who obviously had his priorities scrambled because he was standing at the wrong end of the oil trying to warn us about it. At least I suppose that's what he was doing. It didn't seem like a very healthy place to watch the race from!

'I was convinced I was going to squash him against the Armco, but I slammed the railing just ahead of him and he went over it as though he'd been spring-loaded. Apparently he grazed his leg, but if that was the extent of his injuries, he was one lucky person — if he hadn't done that lift-off he might have been the only casualty of the race. I had bent the front wing during that bit of unscheduled action and I was classified fifteenth, unhappy at the low position but happy my race was over.'

The CanAm series started the following weekend at Mosport and veteran Formula 1 journalist Alan Henry remembered attending a test session with the new M20 sports car at Goodwood as a junior, a year before he was appointed to cover Formula 1 for *Motoring News*. 'I remember Denny saying, "You're a bit of a fatty," as I squeezed in beside him. I thought silently, "And they're right — you're a bit of an arsehole," but that initial frosty reception was soon dispelled. I liked Denny hugely. And I mean hugely. He bridged the gap between the inspirational figures who'd originally fired my imagination to be involved in motor racing when I was working at the bank, and the Hunt/Peterson/Lauda brigade with whom I would "grow up" once I was inside the business. When I covered my first Grand Prix, I was scared stiff of talking to him and to Jackie Stewart. Denny must have sensed that, because he edged up to me in the pits at the old Nürburgring and drawled, "How ya doin'?" So that was going to be all right, then . . . I could talk to Denny Hulme!'

Denny recalled that media day: 'To round off CanAm testing we invited a few journalists down to Goodwood to give them a first-hand impression of what racing cars were really like. As spectators it is difficult to really appreciate Grand Prix power and speed — it's a different world. The CanAm car is handy in this respect, because it's a two-seater with even more performance than a Grand Prix car. I think a lot of the writers were impressed at the way a big car like the Gulf-McLaren could corner and accelerate and stop. We had a blown head gasket on the big Chevvy, but it was probably still good for 700 horsepower and we were topping 180 mph on the straight, two-up!'

The Belgian Grand Prix on the new Nivelles circuit was next up and Denny was in good spirits, having just won the Gold Cup at Oulton Park in the Yardley-McLaren, but he had problems in Belgium. 'It was like watching a home movie when the screen suddenly starts to flicker because the sprockets in the projector are having a convulsion. Everything is a blur and it makes you feel weird just watching all the fractured motion. I wasn't just sitting back watching it — I was *in* it! Something must have gone haywire with the balance of the tyres on my car and my eyeballs were being whipped up like scrambled eggs. Really. I could see the track as a blur of grey, but I was relying on the continuous white lines at the edges and trying to stay between them. I was driving in my own private fog in the middle of a hot sunny day, trying to hang on to third place behind Emerson Fittipaldi's John Player Lotus and François Cevert's Tyrrell, and ahead of Mike Hailwood in the Surtees. I was getting no sensation of speed whatsoever, and going by the pits I had to steady my helmet with one hand and hope that my eyes would stop spinning in time to focus on the signal board. Normally you pick up three lines at once, flashing by the pits, but in this race I was having all sorts of trouble trying to read just one line. I knew Mike was behind me, but I had no idea how *far* behind.

'I found out later that Cevert and my team-mate Peter Revson had been having some problems, so all the more credit to François for his second place. It must have helped take a lot of pressure off Emerson. Poor Peter never really had a chance to get a slice of the action — he had all the action he could handle in the middle of the first lap when he was hit from behind and left to flail his way round to the pits with a puncture.

'My third place points put me up to second place in the championship with 19 points behind Emerson on 28. And even I can work out that a win by D. Hulme and a DNF by E. Fittipaldi in the French Grand Prix at Clermont-Ferrand will put D.H. and E.F. level pegging. I wonder how Brazilians handle switchback tracks like Clermont? I'm looking forward to it, because the Yardley-Mac goes well on a twisty circuit, but of course it also depends on things like engines and tyres — and whether you can fight off the strange motion sickness that often hits drivers, especially on the swooping, curving downhill section.'

The French Grand Prix would be harder work than Denny had hoped. 'I don't think I've ever driven so hard to finish seventh! Being a New Zealander seemed to be part of the requirement for getting on the front row of the narrow Clermont grid, because Chris Amon had taken pole in the new Matra — taken it away from me, as a matter of fact! — but I was sitting alongside him. The view back in the mirrors was giving us as big a charge as that nice, clear road ahead. There were seven different makes of car in the fastest seven spots and we had Jackie Stewart's Tyrrell and Jacky Ickx's Ferrari sitting behind us.

'When you're sitting around trying to look confident in those final minutes before the start and chatting away to people it usually isn't difficult to start programming yourself for the blast down into the first turn and to work up a bit of a psyche against the bloke you're supposed to beat. But how do you start working up a mini-hate against someone like Chrissey when he wanders across with that half-silly grin as if to say, "What the hell are two country lads like you and I doing up here, Hulme?"

'Working on the theory of all things being equal and that if they didn't change they'd stay the way they were, I had it figured that my chances were better than Chris's. If we were both going to be consistent, he didn't stand a chance of winning the race! We were both consistent — we both pitted with punctures!

'Chris powered the Matra off and held the inside line into the first corner, setting off into a lead that was doing good things for the French spectators round the five-mile course laid out like a mini-Nürburgring, switchbacking up and down round the domes of a couple of dud volcanoes above Clermont-Ferrand. In the opening laps I was hard on the heels of the Matra, my Yardley-Mac handling like a dream and sneaking in close to Chris when he'd lock the brakes on occasions and run wide with smoking tyres. But then my car started to get spooked after 10 or 12 laps. It wasn't anything I could put my finger on, but it felt like a tyre problem. I'm starting to be a tyrechondriac — every time the car gets loose, I blame the tyres. There was gravel strewn across the track in places where the edges of the road had broken up, but it wasn't normal sort of road gravel — it was razor-sharp volcanic rock and I had picked up a slow puncture. I let Jackie by going down the hill and hung on as best I could.

'Then on lap 20 Chris pitted with a flat and Jackie took the lead. A slow puncture is weird, because the change in the handling isn't consistent. On the fast parts of the circuit I suppose the centrifugal force was holding the tyre out so that the effects of gradual deflation weren't so noticeable, but on the slower parts — hoo boy! — I didn't have time to worry about drivers who take five weeks' holidays and then come back to dominate the race (Jackie had been convalescing with a stomach ulcer). I dived into the pits, took on two new rear tyres and went back out with a different car. Everything was sweetness and light again, except that my pit signals showed P11 instead of P2.

'I'm still trying to figure out how Amon and I could both stop with punctures and yet he finishes third and I get seventh! I think I understand part of it. With three laps to go Chris is pounding the Matra to make up time and he arrives behind Ronnie Peterson, who is fourth in the new March. Ronnie figures anyone in as much hurry as this blue car obviously has to be lapping him, so he moves over and Christopher charges by — into fourth place. And before the end of the lap he has done the same thing to François Cevert in the Tyrrell — for third!

'These young new boys are too polite by half when there are people like Amon in a hurry — it never happens to me like that. I get seventh . . . I had hoped to do a lot better at Clermont. I'm not disappointed, but it wasn't one of those happy days.

'Jackie's win vaults him up to second place in the world championship with 21 points, behind Emerson on 34. I'm third with 19 and Ickx has 16. It's early days yet, because the season is only half over, but it still looks fairly obvious that Emerson has to DNF somewhere soon before Jackie and I can start to look like the promising lads that we really are.

'These last few Grands Prix I've been on the front row, so I haven't had the problem of jamming the gear lever into low and your bravery into high and charging off into a world of flying grit, dust and smoke from exhausts and spinning tyres . . .

'I've been having a look at the bookmaker's odds for the British Grand Prix and they show betting on Emerson at 2-1, Jackie at 7-4, Ickx at 8-1 and me at 10-1. Now at 10-1 The Bear must be good odds the way the car is behaving now — to say nothing of the driver's new edge — so I may have to arrange a flutter. How do I do that? Call up the bookies and say I want to put 10 quid on my own nose?'

Hopefully Denny was careful with his cash and didn't invest in his own chances at Brands Hatch. He finished fifth.

Denny made an early exit from the German Grand Prix with engine failure. 'I had all my German excitement in practice following Graham Hill's Brabham back behind the pits at the Nürburgring. Suddenly he did a quick jink to the left and there was this rod coming through the air with something attached to it. I recognised it but had no chance to avoid it and almost by coincidence in the same instant my right rear tyre just abandoned the rim and flew up in the air in a cloud of smoke. The car turned sharp right into the guardrail where the mechanics were signalling and I eventually wrestled it to a stop relatively unscathed.'

In Austria the Hulme fortunes picked up again. 'I liked the bit where the World Champion waved me past into second place in the Austrian Grand Prix, right in front of the pits. It must have looked as though I was doing a real grandstander and out-accelerating Jackie in the Tyrrell, but he seemed to be in the grip of some dire sort of handling problem. He had scorched off the second row and led for the first part of the race, but then Emerson scratched by in his John Player Lotus and when I went by on the straight that put me up to second place, where I finished. Peter Revson came spluttering in third in the Yardley-Mac and I had taken the lap record — the first lap record I've set in a Grand Prix since I won the Italian Grand Prix at Monza in 1968! — so everyone in the team and the bosses from Yardley and Gulf Oil were delighted.

'The Grand Prix was run in heat-wave conditions and several of the cars had problems with overheating fuel. Fortunately we had our problems with the fuel system in practice and during the race my car ran beautifully. Peter was up to third in the closing laps but his engine was misfiring badly and he was concentrating on just finishing — never mind third place. His car cut out completely on the last lap, then spluttered into life just long enough to get him across the line and over the hill into the country on the cooling-down lap. Then it stopped. And there he was, marooned with his car in the centre of a swirling sea of wildly enthusiastic Austrians when the mechanics finally reached him! Peter doesn't mind adulation, but he must have been starting to figure the Austrians had designs on having *him* for a souvenir — not just his autograph or a readily removable part of the car!

'When the signal boards had started showing that I was about 4 seconds behind the leading pair I was starting to pick up the slipstream and that was all I needed. Emerson must have seen me coming up behind him, because he launched into a big scramble past Jackie on a downhill corner, which must have taken Jackie by surprise because there was smoke pouring off his tyres. It was an odd place to pass, but Emerson didn't really have much of a choice. Jackie held his second place for a couple of laps and then he let me by and it was D.H., number two and trying harder like Avis all the way to the flag. Fittipaldi told the media afterwards that he had been driving like an old woman in the closing laps to guarantee his win — and then he looked in the mirror and saw the Old Man! Some of these youngsters have no respect for age . . .'

When Emerson won the Italian Grand Prix at Monza and clinched the world championship, Denny was delighted for him. 'I think it's really great that a young guy like Emerson can come over from Brazil and win the championship just like that. I figure he's World Champion because he has matured so very well. He never makes mistakes, never goes out and wrecks his car and he really drives with his head. He deserves his success.

'After the first day's Monza practice, Jackie was on pole with me next up and we'd found that there was virtually no advantage in slipstreaming round there. The closer you tried to slipstream, the slower your laps, and the only improvement I could find was to run two or three seconds behind somebody and hope to close up on them.

'By the end of practice I had slipped down to fifth fastest behind Stewart, Amon and the two Ferraris, but on the grid Jackie was just in front of me. As the flag fell I made a good move only to find him sitting on the line with his engine revving like hell and no drive. His clutch had gone, and I just managed to squeeze left between him and the grass and away. By this time Emerson and Mario had blasted past on the clear side and they out-dragged me past the stands.'

Denny made an unscheduled trip down an escape road, which cost him nearly 20 seconds on the lead bunch and there seemed to be no way he could make up the time loss. 'Then Hailwood's airbox blew off the Surtees going by the main grandstands, and do these things *go!* It went up in the air like a cannonball, then just fluttered down again. I got these frantic signals from my pit and thought there'd been an accident beyond the pits, but when I looked round there was Mike's airbox in the middle of the road and I nearly clobbered it anyway!

'This slowed Mike down, leaving me around 8 seconds behind, and then Ickx stopped with engine problems, Chris ran out of brakes on the Matra and before I knew what had happened, Emerson was World Champion, I'd finished third and Peter Revson had pipped Graham Hill for fourth after Graham had had brake problems.'

Denny was happy being back up the front end of the Formula 1 races, with third place at Monza. 'Our Formula 1 Yardley-Macs have been getting faster and faster with each race and this is probably due to the fact that at last we've caught up with ourselves. We have plenty of engines now and we've also got a race-ready spare car, which takes the pressure off preparation of our race cars during practice. Being prepared also means that we are able to get to the track early and get in some pre-race testing, which has certainly paid off. We tested Goodyears at Mosport on the Monday before the race, dashing straight from the Donnybrooke CanAm race. We were able to tune the chassis and find the best tyres well before practice started. This meant we had a definite advantage and Peter qualified his McLaren on the pole, with me alongside him on the front row.

'I've always reckoned that this extra track experience helps. Even if you gain a few minutes on the others by being first out to practice, it means that you're that few minutes ahead for the rest of the weekend. It's like the approach of a good golfer — mind over matter, and practice, practice, practice.

'The Canadian Grand Prix was murder. Thick fog nearly caused the race to be cancelled and while we waited for it to lift, spectators had been traipsing mud all over the track, and on the warm-up lap a lot of us got dirt in the throttle slides. We washed my slides with petrol in the minutes before the start and thought we had it cured, but as the starter raised the flag I blipped the throttle and it stuck open, jerking me forward and putting me off my stroke for the start. I drove on the ignition switch for most of the first lap, having to switch off because I was unable to back off on the throttle. Eventually the fuel coming in on top of the slides cleared them, but by then the damage was done and my engine must have lost a good 10 horsepower. The tolerance on these Grand Prix engines is so fine that they simply won't digest anything other than air and fuel — a dirty track means that the throttle slides stick, the valve seats get peppered and pocked and the pistons and bores get scoured.

'I was well back in the pack when I eventually got the throttle situation sorted out and I started making up time and placings rapidly, getting by Amon's Matra and Tim Schenken's Surtees without a problem — until I arrived behind Carlos Reutemann's Brabham and I suffered the most frustrating race of my career. There was no way I could get by him and being down on power certainly didn't help. Finally I let Cevert through in the Tyrrell to see if he could make any impression on Reutemann, but he couldn't and I gained some small satisfaction to see that the Frenchman was shaking his fist in frustration as I had been doing. In the closing laps I was latched to the tail of the Brabham again and with a lap to go I heard his engine cough. I knew it was my only chance and that I'd have to take him next time his engine spluttered. On the last lap I seized the briefest of opportunities as his engine gasped for fuel and went through to third behind Jackie and Peter. If the throttle slides hadn't stuck and if I'd made a decent start, I honestly think I'd have been able to give Jackie a run for his Swiss francs out front, but then races aren't won on ifs. Unfortunately.'

Denny went to the final Grand Prix of the season, at Watkins Glen, in philosophical mood. 'It's been pretty much an Avis season for me. Number two and trying like hell all summer. Jackie and I went right down to the last race to decide which of us would be number two in the world championship, but he did the deciding by winning the race — and all those dollars! — while I finished third and had to content myself with third place on total points. It doesn't seem like five years ago that I won the world championship. Back in 1967 I was pretty much a rookie nobody rated, but now I'm one of the old-timers and just starting to be "noticed" by the press experts!'

The 1972 CanAm season started a few days after the end of the 1971 CanAm season and the world of North American racing was stunned. Teddy Mayer announced that he was promoting Peter Revson to drive in Formula 1 alongside Denny Hulme . . . and hiring Jackie Stewart to drive with Denny in the McLaren CanAm team. Soon after came the announcement that Mayer had been anticipating: Roger Penske was running a twin-turbo Porsche 917/10K Spyder in the CanAm series. For Mayer and Penske this was simply the business side of winning. The fans were outraged. They accused Mayer of castrating the series by plucking out Peter Revson, the first American to win the championship, and then hiring Jackie Stewart from the Haas Lola operation to take his place. The fun was fading, not that it hadn't always been business. Mayer, predictably, couldn't see what all the fuss was about. 'When Mercedes had Fangio and Moss everyone thought that was a wonderful thing and everyone was happy to see the two best drivers in the world running miles out in front . . . I really feel that some people are so attracted by the idea of someone beating the McLarens that they've entirely missed the point.

'The main reason we signed Jackie Stewart for the 1972 CanAm series was to have someone in our team to lead us against the Porsche opposition. We feel that Porsche, having gotten out of long-distance racing, will be concentrating heavily on CanAm and we need to take all steps possible to combat this opposition. With Jackie in our team, Denny and our whole crew will respond to Stewart's ability to rise to a situation. This will help Denny perform to his maximum and this may become important if

Porsche come up with the type of car that we feel they are very much capable of doing.'

If there were any concealed compliments to Denny in Mayer's statement, Denny was probably unable to find them. In fact, the situation resolved itself a few days before the opening round of the 1972 series at Mosport in June, when Jackie's doctor prescribed a month's complete rest to treat a duodenal ulcer! Revson was recalled to CanAm and the situation settled, but the Penske Porsche threat stayed and grew through the summer in North America.

Denny was philosophical, obviously aware that the total McLaren domination couldn't last forever. One waggish headline writer started his CanAm report of another Denny victory: 'Ho Hulme . . . '

'I kept telling people at Mosport that payday was Sunday. That was during practice, when Mark Donohue in the new turbocharged L&M Porsche was putting the psyche on the Gulf-McLaren team and I was third fastest behind Peter. I mean, who is this guy Donohue anyway? Doesn't he know that the McLarens are the masters of CanAm? He surely doesn't think he can come along and muscle into the series and take all that lovely money away from us . . . Well, you've got to give him a barrowful of credit for trying damned hard!

'Most of things we heard about the Porsche we didn't believe. Like 900 horsepower and 1:34 laps around Mosport. Unreal. Another Penske promotion, we thought. Until the first day of practice. There it was, all gleaming and white and red and turbocharged and 900 bhp . . . and fastest lap in practice.

'The new Porsche did one thing for us — it acted like a magnet for the journalists and photographers and kept our pits fairly clear during practice. Isn't it odd how opinion swings back and forth? For years we've been mopping up the CanAm races and people have been saying, "Oh God, if someone would only come and beat those damned McLarens —

they're ruining the series." But now that Mark has arrived with his L&M 12-cylinder, turbo Porsche with 900-count-'em-horses, suddenly the fans are coming by and saying, "Get out there and beat the Porsche — you've got to beat Donohue!" I seem to have been the bad guy for so long, I forget how you're supposed to wear a white hat!

'Anyway, folks, it's the end of the orange parades for the moment. In fact, what we're doing is mounting a very subtle psychological campaign against the Penske Panzer. We're letting them think that they're actually in a commanding position and getting pole position and leading the race, but then we bring in Plan B and give 'em the old one-two — Peter goes into the lead and then I win. It's a hell of a script and it felt good when it all worked out right, but the performance was a bit uncomfortable.

'I was on the second row behind Mark and I was just a mite bothered about how he would cope with the rolling start. I figured maybe if he had any lag from the turbocharger, Peter would get the jump on him and he'd block me off from chasing through that first turn. I needn't have bothered. In fact, Peter did get half a length on Mark sweeping down to the first right-hander, but suddenly the German horsepower clicked its heels in a burst of boost and Mark leapt ahead inside Peter and away into the lead.

'There was a faint vibration coming into my car as the race progressed and I figured it was probably just a wheel getting slightly out of balance and it wouldn't get worse. Wrong, Hulme. Mark's turbocharger got indigestion and he pitted to free a shaft that had jammed in the waste-gate, which cost him several laps and put Peter in the lead. I put on a spurt to close up on Peter, but the vibration was getting worse and worse and the tyres were getting crucified. At the end of the long uphill straight there were pieces of rubber lying all over the track and I was convinced they were off my tyres and this was causing all the vibration. I had a board meeting with myself to consider the wisdom of a stop to change wheels, but the motion was defeated. Half of me felt that the wheelnuts might seize and I'd be trapped in the pits while Mark flung his white racer round fast enough to unlap himself enough times to pinch my second spot. So I continued, with the vibration getting worse and a few extras to keep me amused like a throttle that started sticking and almost sent me up the anal passage of one back marker, and oil pressure which played tricks and flashed the oil warning light at me. Jimmy Stone, my mechanic, was flashing warnings at me every time I went past the pits, with signals that said Mark was peeling off 6 or 7 seconds a lap.

'It wasn't really fair. Here I was trying to bring the sick old girl home in one piece, scuttling along as fast as I dared, with Donohue bearing down on me like he wanted to win the race. There should be a law against this sort of mental cruelty to bears. It was hell out there. I'd figured that I'd be able to hold Mark off with a burst in the closing laps, but then I came down the hill to see the big skid marks and Peter's car tangled up in the fence! It meant I was in the lead, but it also meant that I had to do another lap because Pete had lapped me. The guys at the pit wall were waving me on, but I didn't need the encouragement. I was belting on as hard as I was able. Poor Peter. He had that $13,000 in his pocket and then his engine blew. It had seized solid and spun him into the catch fence. So we finished first and third and were warned that we'd have a month before the Road Atlanta race to find 200 horsepower from the engine . . . or 5 seconds a lap from the car!'

Denny was a canny driver. Accidents were something that usually happened to other people. There was the crash with Laurence Brownlie at Pukekohe in 1968, when he had come home with the Formula 2 car to celebrate his championship and started badly. There had been the fire at Indianapolis in 1970, but that wasn't his fault. Then there was the *huge* accident at Road Atlanta in the second of the 1972 CanAm races, when his M20 gathered air under the nose, reared up and flipped over backwards in the early laps of the race.

'There I was, upside down with nothing on the clock but the maker's name. Actually, I couldn't see that too well because that red Georgia dust was everywhere. When they dragged me out of the wreck and put me on a stretcher I must have looked like a red Indian with all that mud sticking to me! In fact, I don't remember anything about the accident on the fifth lap of the Road Atlanta CanAm race. I had started from pole position in the M20 and was out-dragged into the first turn by George Follmer in the turbocharged L&M Porsche, but after a couple of laps I figured I had his measure. I had been alongside him down the straight, and then when I saw Peter Revson disappear from my mirrors in the other M20, I thought I'd better get down to business. I can vaguely remember going round turn 7, but I have absolutely no recollection of whether I was about to pull alongside him as we crested the brow, or whether I was tucked up in his slipstream. With over 900 horsepower the big Porsche can afford to drag along acres of downforce and this means a big vacuum behind the car. Some spectators say the nose came off my car at that point and flipped it over on its back, but we'll have to wait and see. Whatever it was, I suddenly had no downthrust and my car went off like a big orange glider in a loop and skated upside down for 400 yards. From all accounts the car was too broad for marshals to turn over, so a dozen spectators hurdled the safety fence and eased the car right side up.

'At this point, handily placed as ever (talk about team-work!) Peter Revson arrives on the scene. He'd been doing a 10,000-mile check on his car just down the road when I did my stunt. A rotor arm had broken and he was busy replacing it with a spare he just happened to have taken along for the trip (I told you about the McLaren organisation — now maybe you'll believe it!). He said afterwards that he asked me if I could wiggle my toes and I nodded. That meant I didn't have anything vital disconnected in my personal chassis, so they hauled the steering wheel off me and dragged me out.

'A small fire had started in the back of the car from spilled oil or petrol, but fortunately it didn't come to much. The roll bar had done its job well and I came to in the track hospital completely unscathed from a 210 mph accident except for a couple of bruises and a headache. The first people I remember seeing in the hospital were team manager Teddy Mayer and Larry Truesdale, the racing boss of Goodyear. I knew who Teddy was, but I wasn't too sure who "Big T" was. I must have been woozy because I *always* remember *his* name — he's the guy with the money!

'The upside-down crash didn't frighten me because I didn't know I'd done it until I woke up in the hospital. I had no recollection of the shunt at all, but it certainly made me wonder whether the whole thing was worth it . . .'

It was ironic that Peter Revson should have been early on the scene when Denny had his accident, because Denny was there when Peter crashed and was killed in pre-race testing at Kyalami and it was his death that prompted Denny to make the decision to retire at the end of that 1974 season.

Denny's 'Behind the Wheel' columns in *Autosport* were expert 'name' comment on the news at the time, but they have become a record of motor-sporting history as lived by the driver they called 'The Bear'. I'm glad that I was able to have a part in crafting the columns then, and equally pleased to be able to use them now to convey Denny's life at that time. They were technical and accurate, but still had a touch of the Denny grin. You couldn't really get any closer to the action and the people involved. It was the next best thing to being there.

'The Road Atlanta race seemed to have been one series of heart-stopping shunts or accidents, although fortunately nobody's heart actually stopped during the action. Jackie Oliver had destroyed his Shadow when the throttle jammed open during pre-race testing and Mark Donohue had destroyed his Porsche also during testing. Mark's crash was a duplicate of Bruce McLaren's accident at Goodwood. The rear tail section on the Porsche opened up, jerked the rear wheels off the road, over-revved the engine, blew it, spun it, flipped him upside down into the guardrail and rolled him end over end. The car eventually came to rest the right way up minus the front wheels, with Mark sitting in what was left of the chassis, strapped to the rear bulkhead with his left leg bent at right-angles to what it says in the handbook. He had torn all the ligaments in his knee and although he was hobbling around on crutches for the first day of practice, he had an operation the next day and will be out of racing until October. That's a blow to a racing driver, but I'm sure Mark is thinking what I was thinking, sitting up in that hospital bed: It's damn good to be alive . . .

'My mechanics flew back to London to complete a new car for the next round at Watkins Glen and this will incorporate, as standard equipment instead of bolt-on goodies, all the new things we have been developing for the M20.

'François Cevert turned up at Atlanta for his first CanAm race in Gregg Young's second McLaren M8F and he seemed to thoroughly enjoy the whole CanAm way of life. We set up a barbecue at the motel and charcoal-grilled what must have been half a cow each night. François couldn't believe how relaxed it all was, compared with Grand Prix racing. I think he was probably more relaxed than he would have been if Ken Tyrrell had been along, ruling his racing with an iron hand . . .'

McLaren's way of CanAm life would soon be on the wane. After all the summers of total domination by the Orange Elephants, the tide was about to turn. The next race at Watkins Glen would turn out to be Denny's last-ever CanAm win.

'The fact that I won at Watkins Glen in the Gulf-McLaren was really a tip-of-the-iceberg effort and a tremendous credit to the team back at

Colnbrook, who built the car for me and had it on a plane to America in just under nine days! While I was unscrambling my brains after my Atlanta inversion the boys back at Colnbrook had already started work on the stripped skeleton of the prototype M20 we had used for testing. Under normal conditions it would have taken something like two months to build a CanAm car, but it was "all systems go" at the factory and at times there were 20 people working flat out — just to get D.H. on the starting line at Watkins Glen. Some of the lads even passed up the opportunity to go to the British Grand Prix, even though they had tickets. They worked straight through the weekend to finish the car. After an effort like that I felt obliged to go out and do something special, and Peter finishing second was the icing on the cake.

'Grady Davis, Executive Vice President at Gulf Oil, had been at the Road Atlanta race and he must have jetted home thinking we were a real bunch of clowns, with both of us sidelined before the race was six laps old. Teddy Mayer was pleased that Peter and I could revive the team reputation in front of Grady at the Glen — and it was kind of nice for Porsche to bring over a plane-load of German journalists so that we could impress them too. It isn't often that you get a re-run of the David and Goliath show with a Goliath supporter's club specially imported for the occasion!

'Not that we're kidding ourselves about this particular piece of Panzer-pasting. Follmer had a problem with the turbocharger, but between Porsche and Penske's crew they'll have it sorted for Mid-Ohio and Revvy and I will be working for our living again.

'When I drove out of the pits on the first day of practice at the Glen it was impossible to tell any difference from a car that had done a season's racing. The suspension settings had been done by guesswork and from the meticulous record that we kept on each car, and virtually nothing was changed all weekend.

'The effects of my Road Atlanta crash were still lingering, in that I had to make a conscious effort at first to brace my head against the G-force loadings on the car, and when you have to think about doing what normally comes automatically you tend to lose the razor-sharp edge you really need to go quick. All I needed was more practice, and during the race I hardly noticed it.

'Peter qualified his Gulf-McLaren on pole and I was beside him on the front row, with Follmer's L&M Porsche and François Cevert's McLaren M8F behind us. With 900 turbocharged horsepower on the row behind you, you become super-aware that your chances of being run over at the start are less than remote, so Peter wasn't taking any chances, and we were coming fast out of the last turn to the rolling start where Tex Hopkins waited with his lavender suit, big cigar — and the starting flag. George got the jump on us first time round and then we all had to shuffle back into order for another pace lap, but again we didn't get the start and this went on for four pace laps, by which time our pits were starting to worry about how much fuel we had aboard, because we measure our fuel consumption carefully during practice, add a few more pints as insurance, and set off. But we hadn't bargained for an extra 10 miles or so on top!

'When we finally got the green, Peter out-dragged me over the line, but I headed him into the first corner, which highlighted a peculiarity of the Glen where pole is on the inside of the track but the outside gives you a better shot at the first right-hander. I was in the groove, while Peter was inside on the rough and slippery stuff, so it meant I had better traction and better stopping power, and I led the pack out of the first turn and stayed in front for the rest of the race. Peter had a braking problem, but we stayed between 2 and 10 seconds apart most of the time, with the Porsche and the rest of the opposition receding into what we hoped was insignificance. Only François Cevert stayed on the same lap as us to finish third for a McLaren 1-2-3.

'Towards the end of the race our crew started getting concerned that the pace Peter and I were setting would be murdering our chances of finishing, so we were getting signals to cool it. Hell, I was all for cooling it, but I wasn't absolutely positive what was running through the mind of my old buddy in the orange shadow behind me and it seemed foolish to tempt his sense of friendliness to bears by backing off too much in case he thought I was saying, "After you, Pete," or something similarly unlikely . . .

'I thanked God and designer Gordon Coppuck for the side radiators at the Glen, because the temperature was up in the 90s and I would have been getting a slow bake if we'd still had the radiators up front. I couldn't even get to suck from my cooler of Gatorade because the tubes up into my helmet had become snagged and I never drank anything at all.

'At the end of the race I felt completely worn out. I wouldn't have worried if the race had gone on for a few more laps, because while you're out there rushing round you're far too busy concentrating on the car to worry about yourself. But when it was all over and I didn't have to worry about the car any longer I realised just how worn out and run down I was.

'With two wins from three races, I'm leading the championship, but there are six races left in what looks like being the toughest CanAm season yet.'

That could be looked back on as a prescient comment. Rain ruined the Mid-Ohio race for Denny. 'Rain showers made the event a series of catch-ups for me after making *five* pit stops for tyre changes. It wasn't Goodyear's fault, it was mine. Every time the weather zigged, I zagged, When it rained I was on dry rubber, when it stopped I was on wets. From now on, I'll leave the team management to Teddy Mayer. Someone said I was making as big a mess of management from the cockpit as Teddy would have made if he'd been driving under those conditions. I think that was meant as a knock to me, rather than Teddy, who must have been wondering what the hell I was playing at. Gilbert and Sullivan would have been hard-pressed to plot tactics like mine . . .' Denny was fourth and somehow took fastest lap. 'I'm hanging on to the championship lead by my fingernails — just two points ahead of George Follmer (50 to 48) who'd no doubt love to administer a manicure (with an axe!), and Milt Minter is third with 40 points in his Porsche.'

Trans-Atlantic jet-set travel had become part of commuting between the Grands Prix in Europe and the CanAm races in North America, but Denny found out that not all aviation was about comfort at speed. 'We had to leave a Goodyear party early after the race because we were due for a 4.30 a.m. call to catch a chartered twin-engined Piper Navajo to fly us to New York, connecting with the day flight to London. If it isn't compulsory, I'd just as soon not do that again. We ran through a thunderstorm for 20 minutes that must have added a good 20 years to our lives. I can still remember vividly the suitcases and cans of Coke floating up near the roof of the plane and seeing Peter Revson looking like I felt. If he was going through the roof he sure as hell was going to take the seat with him! White knuckles weren't in it . . .'

Denny qualified on pole at Elkhart Lake while some of the other top runners were qualifying for a USAC race on the Friday. It rained on Saturday. Denny led the early stages of the race, but Follmer fought through from a lowly grid start and when the McLaren suffered an electrical problem, Follmer won as he pleased. Revson's team car was a retirement with clutch failure. Double DNF.

'Trying to beat the 950 bhp Porsches with our 750 bhp McLarens has been like trying to shoot down a jumbo jet with a bow and arrow. In a valiant attempt to get competitive we managed to squeeze 35 more horsepower from the Chevrolet V8, but all we got was unreliable . . .'

It was an all-Porsche front row at Donnybrooke, with the two orange McLarens behind them. It wasn't all-Porsche in the race as Denny got up to second, taking the fight to Donohue and confident of a late-race charge but, as Lyons wrote: 'That's when the big 509-inch Reynolds block split, spewed out oil and water and the bright orange M20 was the head of a long, sad comet of blue smoke and white steam.'

For the race at Edmonton, McLaren tried a different tactic and actually de-tuned their motors in the interests of living for race distance against the Porsche power. 'This paid off unexpectedly well and I was able to lead the Porsches for the first 30 laps and eventually finished second behind Mark Donohue's Porsche and ahead of George Follmer, who had lost a lap with a puncture in the other Penske Panzer. For some reason the Porsches were bog-slow taking the flag from the rolling start and in the drag race down the long straight I took Follmer on the inside and in the mirrors I could see Milt Minter swinging across into second place behind me — and he had started off the third row in his 917. Milt didn't stay second for long, but he had made such a storming start that he was still in second place when he reached his pit where he retired with a disintegrated cooling fin on his turbocharged flat-12.

'I opened up a lead of about 10 seconds, wondering what sort of tactics the Penske team were plotting. I could only assume that they had started slowly with a heavy load of fuel (George had lost the race at Donnybrooke by running out of fuel on the last lap) and would soon start regaining their temporarily lost time. Unfortunately, I was right.'

The final round was at Riverside and the McLaren team had a secret weapon. 'In fact, it was *so* secret that nobody outside our team knew any-thing about it and yet because we knew and wanted to keep it under our hats, it seemed so glaringly obvious. Our engine men had been working on a giant version of the Chevrolet in the latter part of the season, but it wasn't until the last race that they managed to bolt one together that would live. We had been using 8.1-litre aluminium Chevy V8s, which give around 740–750 bhp, but "Big Bertha" arrived in from Detroit the night before the last day of practice, stroked out to a full *9 litres* with a special crankshaft and giving 800 bhp.

'It must be the ultimate Chevy. It had the extra 50 bhp all the way through the range and compared with our "little" 8.1-litre motors, this one had torque like a traction engine. And the delightful thing was that nobody knew we had it, least of all Roger Penske's Porsche crew. It gave the sort of extra lift off the turns that the Porsches must have been enjoying all summer, and towards the end of the session I started to stand on it, whittling my times down so suddenly that I had eased Mark's Porsche off the front row and looked like toppling George off the pole, before the Panzer brigade worked out what was happening.

'Unfortunately for me the engine had been little more than a morale booster with the life expectancy of a butterfly. We knew it was only going to last out the afternoon and that we'd have to go back to the regular engine for the race. I was under strict instructions not to rev over six-five (we ran the others to six-eight) and my target was Follmer's pole time of 1:31.7. With about five minutes to go my pit signal showed 1:31.9 and I knew I was "hot". The track was clearer than it had been, but I realised that the engine was starting to lose its crispness. Next time round I edged it to 6500 rpm but still the pit signal showed 1:31.9 and the guy was getting ready with the chequered flag to end the session. I tried all I knew to put together the perfect lap round Riverside on that final run, but according to Teddy Mayer's watches it was my third identical lap and the official times gave me 1:32.0.

'The next morning the lads had installed my normal 8.1-litre engine. I made a poor start, letting George get a ridiculous jump on me going into the first turn, but I was running a healthy second until the engine started to miss on the third lap, and after eight laps Mark came sailing by with Peter on his tail in our other McLaren. By now I was driving on the oil pressure gauge and getting depressingly slower and slower and being passed by people I hadn't even seen during the season. Finally the engine ate the top off a valve, which chewed its way through the piston, dropped into the oil system, the pumps gagged and it was all over . . .

'Milt Minter and I were having a casual conversation at the Riverside pit rail while we settled on being second equal in the championship and watched George Follmer winning in the L&M 917. Milt is a funny character. He had promised some friends at turn 8 that he'd stop and have a beer with them after the race and when he felt the turbocharged engine in his Porsche starting to run rough going through turn 2 he was determined to press on for that beer. All you would get if you stopped in turn 2 was tired trudging back to the pits. So Milt pressed on with the flat-12 getting all sorts of ratty. He finally parked it in 8 to get his beer — a can that cost him $60,000 as near as he could figure it. Porsche horses don't come cheap . . .'

It would be Denny Hulme's last CanAm drive.

20 Swedish success in '73

In Thursday's unofficial practice on the Autodromo Almirante Brown circuit at Buenos Aires, Denny started well in the previous year's M19 McLaren, second fastest to Jackie Stewart's Tyrrell, but the talking point was Regazzoni's instant form in the BRM after several summers with Ferrari. Denny had niggling engine problems and eventually started on the fourth row of the grid alongside Beltoise in the second BRM — Clay had put his on the pole! 'My engine was not super-healthy but Peter was going like gangbusters and running fifth until a small throttle linkage broke almost at the finish and I moved up to take over fifth when he dropped out.

'Regazzoni's drive in the BRM was the big surprise in Argentina, because we had all pretty much discounted the chances of the BRM team. He started off pole and led the opening laps until his tyres gave up. We figured he might do it again in the second round in Brazil, but he was baulked with a vapour lock that killed his engine as the flag fell and also choked the engine on Niki Lauda's BRM and my McLaren, leaving the three of us sitting there on the grid with not very much happening. I had been fifth fastest in practice at Interlagos, but I was twelfth on the first lap. After that I applied myself seriously to the job in hand and worked my way up to third without a whole lot of trouble, so maybe if I'd started off with the leading bunch I might have been able to run with them. But that's a debatable point, because the clutch packed it in just after I'd passed Ickx's Ferrari and this was a real problem because I was using first gear away from one of the hairpins and it became extremely difficult to slot it in. I tried

∧
Denny beats the Ferraris in Argentina in 1974. Niki Lauda (left) was second and Clay
Regazzoni was third.

PHOTO: DPPI, COURTESY HULME FAMILY COLLECTION

∧
A special birthday-present bear from his Marlboro McLaren team-mate Emerson Fittipaldi
in 1974.

COURTESY HULME FAMILY COLLECTION

∧
Denny in the 1969 winged M8B McLaren CanAm car.

∧
At Goodwood with the new M8D McLaren CanAm car before the start of
the 1970 season.

^
Denny does a pre-race check of the big CanAm Chevrolet engine with its giant inlet trumpets.

∧
Denny's CanAm team-mate in 1971 was Peter Revson.

PHOTO: DALE VON TREBRA, COURTESY EOIN YOUNG

∧
Peter Revson would win the 1971 CanAm title for McLaren and a rueful Denny writes 'Go Peter' in the oil on his wing after an engine blow-up and retirement.

PHOTO: PETE BIRO, COURTESY EOIN YOUNG

Denny at the helm of his new boat *CanAm* on the Thames with son Martin on the dock and daughter Adele in the front hatch. Sandra and Selina Young at rear, author Eoin Young in left-hand seat.

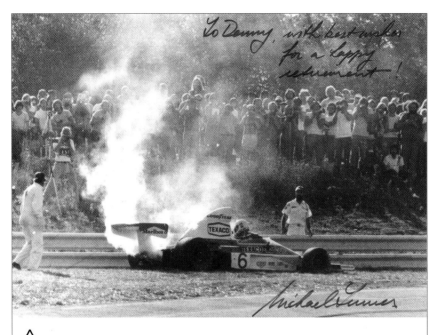

To Denny, with best wishes for a happy retirement —!

Michael Turner

∧

A poignant photo of Denny's final smokey retirement from his last Grand Prix at Watkins Glen in 1974. The message is from the motor-sport artist, Michael Turner, who took the photo.

PHOTO: MICHAEL TURNER, COURTESY HULME FAMILY COLLECTION

∧

Racing the controversial 'Golden Holden'.

COURTESY HULME FAMILY COLLECTION

^
With the TWR Jaguar team at Silverstone: Denny, Tom Walkinshaw, Armin Hahne and Win Percy.

COURTESY HULME FAMILY COLLECTION

^
Denny's helmet on his coffin on his final parade. Bearded Bill Bryce in the background, Greeta to the right of photo.

PHOTO: *NEW ZEALAND HERALD*, COURTESY HULME FAMILY COLLECTION

^
Denny with McLaren designer, Australian Ralph Bellamy, when the new M19 Formula 1
car was announced in 1971.   COURTESY HULME FAMILY COLLECTION

^
Jim Clark in the new Lotus 49 leads Denny in the 1967 Dutch Grand Prix at Zandvoort. Jim
won, Denny was third.   COURTESY EOIN YOUNG

using second gear to chunter away from the corner, but we were all worried about fuel vaporisation and if the engine ran too low on revs the fuel pump might quit and I'd never get the engine started again.

'As it turned out, this clutchless act was one of my lesser problems, because the heat was something else and I was getting more and more exhausted — from dehydration probably — with every lap towards the finish, and when the flag came out I was more pleased simply that the race had finished than that I'd finished third behind Emerson and Jackie.'

The South African Grand Prix in the thin air at Kyalami was one of Denny's favourite circuits. 'I came within spitting distance of winning the 1971 Grand Prix in South Africa when we first ran the M19 and I did the job properly to win with the car last year, so with a brand new M23 for 1973 we reckoned we'd be looking good. At least the car will be looking good. Different, anyway. It has already been nicknamed the Colnbrook Concorde, because from certain angles the droopy nose and the flare back to the radiators at the rear of the car make it look a lot like the SST. Our Formula 1 cars have never really been super-efficient when it comes to penetrating the air, but we hope the futuristic new shape with the sexy streamlined tail and airbox to round off the package will provide all the answers to aerodynamics.'

The new car did 70 test laps around Goodwood and it was then flown down to South Africa for pre-race tests at Kyalami a fortnight before the Grand Prix. 'On our first test day there we ran faster than we had ever managed with the M19, even after the thousands of test miles we must have run round there in the past two years. One of the most noticeable things about the new car from a driver's point of view is that you're sitting much farther forward because the majority of the fuel load is now between the engine and the cockpit. You are sitting with your feet up ahead of the centre line of the front wheels and you can almost lean out and touch them. It's less than 12 inches from the steering wheel to the steering box, which is now mounted just forward of the dashboard! This means that all the steering links and arms are behind the uprights, and the front bulkhead has suddenly become extraordinarily tidy, with only the brake cylinders and none of the steering gear normally stowed up there.

'For the first 10 laps or so testing, I found it very difficult to judge just where the rear wheels were and what they were doing. It was hard to gauge the amount of oversteer and when it would be coming in. Eventually I reached the stage where I could set it oversteering and control it to a far greater degree than ever I had been able to with the M19. When the M23 did oversteer the back stayed out and did not go back to neutral and oversteer, back to neutral and oversteer again as the M19 tended to do on occasions. The new car oversteers and stays out there in a nice comfortable slide and this may have been one of the reasons why it was so fast around Goodwood.

'Peter and I are going to revel in the lower cockpit temperatures of the new car, because the water radiators are mounted at the sides of the car back behind us. This was a big factor in last year's side-radiator CanAm car, because it meant that you never had to combat heat exhaustion in addition to everything else on the race track. Another aid to the well-being of Revson and Hulme backsides is that with the fuel and oil tanks repositioned between us and the engine, we will be effectively insulated from the heat of the engine.'

On the earlier monocoques the fuel went all the way to the front of the tub, which meant that the drivers were literally sitting in a bath of petrol, but with the new M23 only a very small amount of fuel was carried in the side of the monocoque and the tanks didn't go up as far as the driver's knees. This meant that most of the weight was central on the car and it wouldn't vary the balance as the race progressed and the fuel load dropped.

'We are following a modern trend in neutralising the polar moment of inertia by bunging all the weight between the front and rear wheels. I think it was Tyrrell designer, Derek Gardner, who defined a polar moment of inertia as an eskimo's tea break . . . Just think what they could do down at Tyrrell's wood yard if they were serious about all this!

'The cockpit on the M23 is the smallest we have ever had on a McLaren — so small in fact that we now have a detachable steering wheel. The reason for the slimline office is to bring the monocoque in very narrow and get the air passing back to the radiators. The car looks a lot wider than it really is, because the monocoque is shrouded by the bulky radiator cowlings. Another striking feature of the M23 is the list of assorted plumbing strung all over the place. It's extremely clean, especially around the back of the gearbox area, and this helped us to streamline the whole back end. The oil radiators are now mounted in behind the water radiators.'

There was drama aplenty at Kyalami and Denny was concerned, both with the seriousness of Regazzoni's fiery crash and Jackie Stewart's brush with track ethics. Denny's view on this is interesting, because he sided with Stewart on the safety side of racing, while other drivers may have been a tad more cavalier about the risks.

'The crash at Kyalami involving Mike Hailwood and Clay Regazzoni when Mike dragged Clay out of his burning car, and the incident when Jackie Stewart was protested for passing under the yellow caution flags, both point up shortcomings that we should address, and fast. First and worst was the fire. I know what it's like to be burned and I take my hat off to Mike Hailwood for actually catching his overalls alight, putting them out, and then going back into the fire to help a fellow driver. The fire-truck was too late on the scene — there's no question in my mind about that, and we should be thankful that the results were not much worse than they were. Communications have to be sharpened up and the fire-truck has to be armed and ready for an instant "go" signal throughout the race.

'Jackie's reprimand for passing under the yellow caution flags was withdrawn after an appeal, but as Grand Prix drivers I don't think we should put ourselves in situations where our integrity could be questioned by anybody, much less stewards and fellow drivers. If there is an accident anywhere on the track we should be racing in a "caution" situation and sure as hell not pressing on like tomorrow has been cancelled.

'The main problem is that racing drivers are racing drivers and we need a compulsory way of defusing the more volatile ones. How about putting the whole circuit under a yellow flag or yellow light with an automatic pacing system that is fair to everyone to eliminate cheating in this "cool it" period while the accident is being attended and the track cleared? I didn't see the situation where Jackie was involved and it might seem post-righteous to comment, but I don't think I'd have been trying quite that hard with the remains of a big shunt just round the corner.'

Denny was in storming form with the new M23, qualifying on pole position with Emerson beside him in the JPS Lotus, and young South African driver Jody Scheckter in a third works Yardley-McLaren on the outside of the front row for the first time in his home Grand Prix.

'The race was only two laps old and I was out front with the new Yardley-Mac M23 pulling away from the field when I saw the black smoke almost a mile away as I came down out of Leeukop in the downhill sweep past the pits. There were no yellow flags out so I thought maybe it was a car that had gone off and was well clear of the track, or that the fire had been put out and everything was all right. It was the reaction of the crowd that saved me from piling into the burning cars. They were waving programmes and handkerchiefs from the fences and the grandstands to get me to back off, so I was ready to stop when I got round the corner and found cars and people all over the place. I picked the most promising alley through the debris and team-mate Jody Scheckter followed me, thinking — correctly — that I would have cleared a path. Soon my car started acting a little weird and I knew I must have a puncture.

'Jody could see the big rear Goodyear going out of shape and as I slowed he went into the lead for a couple of laps of glory in front of his home crowd before Jackie went past him and off into the middle distance to win in the Tyrrell. Everybody went rushing by me as I limped to the pits, had the wheel changed, and set off again. It wasn't long before I noticed a most extraordinary thing. Every time I turned right a great plume of smoke would come off the left rear tyre. I couldn't imagine what it was, but whatever it was it wasn't right, so I stopped again and though it wasn't going down, I insisted that it was changed. I can only assume that there must have been fuel on the road and that the high temperature of the tyre was almost setting it alight!

'After my second stop I saw a signal that said twentieth and my spirits soared at least a millimetre. There doesn't seem like much point in continuing to have a look at it if you're going to be fed up with reading the race order before you get to your own name, but then I got embroiled with Jody and Peter Revson in the Yardley-Macs who were doing a great job in second and third places, holding off the JPS-Lotuses of Fittipaldi and Peterson. Peter went by Jody and at this point I had passed both Lotuses to give young Jody a bit of support from the rear. He seemed to be in a situation where his tyres were just starting to lose their bite and his energy was waning, so I went past him and out ahead of Peter to tow him away from the World Champion. As it turned out, we did ourselves both some good. I was able to clear the way for Peter and tow him up to some extra pace on the straight, so that he held his ground and just headed Emerson across the line to finish second, and my new interest in the race had brought me through to fifth, which pleased me a lot more than fifth usually does. Jody was a safe fourth when his engine took a dump only four laps from home and he was classified ninth.

'As we had hoped, the new M23 was fabulous. We expected some impressive practice pace after testing at Kyalami and I was able to hang on to pole position through the three days of practice. After the first day our

Yardley-Macs were 1-2-3! It must be a long time since any team has turned on a show like that in a Grand Prix with a new car.

'It was also the first time in my venerable career that I had been on pole position in a Grand Prix! It even amazed me when I realised that, but Austrian journalist Heinz Pruller is something of a statistician and he came to the Sleepy Hollow Hotel where we were staying, and presented me with a bottle of champagne that he has been toting around the world waiting for just such an occasion! Waiting that long, of course, it was vintage . . .'

The Circuito de Montjuich was a grand 2.35-mile course of public roads in a hill park above Barcelona. 'From some parts of the track you could look down into the busy streets with buses, cars, taxis and people bustling about, hundreds of feet below where we were racing. Weird. Before practice, I took our designer, Gordon Coppuck, round the circuit in a saloon car to explain the various aspects of the track and enable him to grasp some of the problems involved in getting round it quickly — to give him some idea of what's liable to happen where the car leaves the ground and the important role that wings, roll-bars and springs were going to play.'

Denny was first out to practice and set fastest time, which would stand for most of that session. Ronnie Peterson bettered it late in the day in his JPS Lotus, but Denny's comeback best would stand as second fastest for the rest of practice and give him a front row grid place beside Ronnie. The race started at noon so that, as Denny explained, it didn't interfere with late lunches, siestas, bullfights and the more normal Sunday afternoon activities of Spanish gentlefolk.

'I was quite happy to be in second spot, because Ronnie had the choice of position and left me with the side of the road I would have chosen for myself if I'd been on pole. So who needs to try for the pole when you've got a friendly Swede like Ronnie around the place? When the flag dropped, Ronnie made a drag start but then seemed to falter and I pulled ahead. (I discovered later that he had a very low gear fitted and when the

engine hit the rev limiter in low he semi-stalled as he changed to second.)
I nosed ahead until I tagged the limiter in second and he came alongside
as we crested the two brows, and he went just ahead for the inside line
on the drop to the first tight left-hand hairpin, but then out of nowhere
comes Jackie Stewart in the Tyrrell, looking like his braking point will be
the cathedral downtown. He must have thought the hairpin was a mile
or two farther down the road, because by the time he'd got it sorted out
Ronnie was through, I was on his exhausts and Jackie was motoring hard
behind us.

'My tyres weren't settling down, Ronnie was getting away and Stewart
was giving me all sorts of stick from behind. He went by me after three
laps and then I had François Cevert's Tyrrell and Emerson in the other
Lotus glued to my gearbox. I was starting to come right and pull away
when a wheel weight — three of them, in fact — came off the rim and the
vibration was unbelievable. I signalled the pit that I'd be stopping next time
round, but when I got to the bottom of the hill there were yellow flags
everywhere and Andrea de Adamich's Brabham was lying about all over
the place. A rear wheel had come off and he'd bounced off the guardrails,
leaving the other rear jammed in a guardrail and the original one careering
up the road on its own. So I used the yellow flags to pit on, just like Indy.

'The crew changed the right front wheel and I was back in business
going faster and faster . . . until I started to have problems with my *left*
front tyre. At that point I'd been keeping pace with Ronnie in the lead,
and if the car had kept going — the way things turned out in the race — I
could possibly have won, even after my first stop. The second stop creeked
everything. Ronnie's gearbox packed up when all the oil ran out, Jackie's
Tyrrell ran out of brakes and he packed it in, Cevert made a stop and Peter
was soldiering on in the other Yardley-Mac with a spark lead hanging loose
and one side of the exhaust system adrift, so the car sounded just awful and
it probably felt like that as well.

'When you're down below the big money Teddy Mayer doesn't seem to bother signalling who actually is earning all the bread up front, so I figured François must be in the lead and I was tagging on to him. I thought he was trying a bit hard for being in the lead, but I found out later that he had stopped too and was pressing on to make up time. I was all set to pass him when my engine coughed at the hairpin with just a couple of laps left and I knew I was in fuel pick-up trouble again and backed off to bring it home in sixth.'

Next round was the Belgian Grand Prix at the new Zolder track and Denny was still on top form with the new M23 on the front row of the grid, but he was not a fan of the new venue. 'They should have named it the Mini Prix, because there wasn't much that was Grand about it. The absurdity of the whole situation was that we were bulldozed into racing at Zolder — a track that even club racers had refused to drive on a few weeks earlier! — when the brand new Nivelles track where we raced last year was sitting idle only a few miles away. Why? Because the Nivelles track was in the French-speaking area of Belgium and the Zolder track was Flemish.

'But to the front row. Ronnie had bent a couple of Lotuses on the morning of the race, which probably didn't put him in the perfect frame of mind to do a whole lot about his pole position when the flag dropped, but he still made a better job of the start than I did. I just sat there with far too much wheelspin, but I finally got round the first corner behind Peterson, Ickx in the Ferrari who had made a stormer start gung-ho with national pride, and François Cevert in the Tyrrell. I'm sure there must be an in-built secret in those Tyrrells somewhere. They don't always qualify well, but when the flag drops they're on their way like someone's lit the fuse. François took Ickx and then Peterson and just drove away from the field as though the rest of us weren't trying.

'I was tucked in behind Ickx's Ferrari, but the pride of Italy was poking a bit of oil out the back and since I was nearest, I got the shower. I was wiping my visor twice a lap until the back of my glove got so oily it was a waste of time. At this point Jacky did a real job on the Ferrari, which dumped all its oil right in front of me going into the first corner after the pits. I felt my car starting to spin on the glassy surface and gathered it up, but by this time I was off the track into the sand and for a second the whole cockpit went dark as a great wall of sand went over me. The throttles were jammed with grit instantly and I scrambled back on to the track with a choice of peak revs or stalled, so I made it back to the pits on the ignition switch.

'I lost over two laps getting the bigger rocks out of the injectors, but when I went back into the race I discovered that my troubles were only just starting. The brakes were on the way out and then I lost third gear, so I was changing straight from second to fourth. Second was far too low for some of the corners and fourth was much too high, and I was soldiering on in seventh place as best I could when Jackie went past me in the lead and some time later François went by as well in second place — it surprised me that they weren't really running much faster than I was, but then they were obviously tiptoeing home and taking things very, very cautiously. The track looked like the dying minutes of a demolition derby.'

Monaco was always a course that Denny felt deserved the title of Grand Prix, although if the street circuit was suggested as a new venue today it would be laughed at and dismissed. It still has history on its side and is the most challenging race left on the international calendar.

'I was in all sorts of trouble during the first practice session because my front wheel rims were leaking air (nothing to do with the tyres — punctured *wheels* now!) but on the early morning Friday session I was in very good shape. That's when I should have sat on my fast lap until the very end. As it was, I went scorching out, set fastest time and then watched the message being flashed to Messrs Stewart and Peterson. It's always easier to go faster if you've got the goad that someone else has done it, so it must be possible.'

Stewart was on pole with Peterson beside him. Denny and Cevert were on the second row. 'My engine felt sour on race morning when we did a few warm-up laps, so I wasn't really feeling in Grade A shape as we formed up on the grid, sighting the road between the rear wheels of Stewart and Peterson. Not that it would have made a whole lot of difference, because we had changed engines twice in my car trying to find a good one. I'll use that as my excuse for the start I made. Cevert lit up from beside me and was storming away in front of the pack, taking Stewart and Peterson as though they'd been roped to a post . . . and I was getting myself sorted out down in eighth place.

'I was having to dip the clutch coming away from the slow corners to make the engine run clean and this was really bugging me when I was running in traffic and being baulked into these corners. Clear of traffic I was making good time, but Monaco isn't the best track in the whole world to be dodging traffic.

'When the race had settled down I found myself in fourth place behind Stewart and the brothers Fittipaldi, but as I was going down into the new loop that replaces the Gasometer hairpin, a bolt dropped out of the gear linkage and the rods came apart down at the back of the gearbox, which left me stuck in second gear. Fortunately, it was only a few yards before the entrance to the pits, so I went straight in and had a new bolt fitted, but this dropped me a couple of laps and although I came back in and pressed on, I couldn't do better than sixth.'

Denny had come back to Monaco from having enjoyed a different look at the Indianapolis 500 . . . from the pit lane. 'Just by way of a change I was to be part of Peter Revson's pit crew. I was number seven and officially termed "start". It was my job to jack up the right front wheel, check that the side radiator was free of rubbish, and then stand out front to give Pete the go signal when the pit work was completed. Not the most onerous job in the world, and as it turned out I didn't have to do it anyway, because the start was aborted with the Salt Walther accident, and I was on a plane back to England that night while everyone else waited around in the rain for a couple of days before they finally ran as much as they could of the race. They should call this year's event the Indy 332.5, because that's as far as it ran, what with Swede Savage's fiery crash and then more rain.

'I know enough about Indianapolis now, not to drive there any more. As Jochen Rindt used to say, "I don't need the money that badly . . ." Just because it's the oldest race in the business doesn't mean to say it can't be improved to handle modern traffic. I mean, tradition is one thing but if the 500 is to remain as the greatest spectacle in racing (and it *is*) they've got to clean their act up a bit.'

Denny was suggesting a 2-2-2 grid (the Hulme Ark Start) to replace the traditional 3-3-3 line-up, and positioning the starter in the tower where he could see the whole grid, instead of standing at track level and seeing only the front row. That was 33 years ago. Still no change at The Brickyard.

The next Grand Prix on the calendar was in Sweden and it would continue the cycle where Denny would win one Grand Prix a season until his retirement, starting with the South African Grand Prix in 1972. This was a significant statistic for a Grand Prix driver then, maintaining a standard where he could still rise to a win and set the occasional lap record despite the fact that he was one of the 'older guys' on the grid, and considering that most of his younger contemporaries would *never* win a Grand Prix.

'Martin and Adele probably thought Dad was going a bit far, wanting to win the race on Father's Day as a sort of party preview for his birthday (37, he adds in a whisper) the following day, but it all added up to a perfect weekend. We started off on the right note by motoring up to Sweden with Phil Kerr, joint MD at McLaren Racing; and John "Mac" MacDonald in his Rolls-Royce Silver Shadow. Very posh, we were, and very relaxed after the 25-hour ferry crossing from England to Gothenberg and the short 2-hour drive from the ferry port to the track. I was most impressed with the track and the people who ran the race. You could run virtually anywhere on the track without getting into trouble and there were kerbstones, catchfences and guardrailing exactly where it had been requested.

'Our whole team meshed in well from the first day of practice. We had decided that I would keep my engine in for the whole meeting, rather than play our game of "musical engines", which usually results in me being out-guessed, and the mechanics doing a lot of extra work. So that's how I started the race with "old No. 061" bolted in the back. It's a Ford-Cosworth we seem to have had around forever and although it never gives as much horsepower as the others on the dyno, it really works like a beaver when it gets into the chassis.

'There was one dismal stage in the Grand Prix when I just knew it was going to be another of those races where I would have to make a pit stop. The first part of the race had been a bit of a procession, with Ronnie Peterson and Emerson Fittipaldi out front in the black JPS Lotuses, followed by the Tyrrells of Jackie Stewart and François Cevert. I was doing my best to get by François when we came up to lap a group of slower cars and one of them put a wheel in the dirt and the whole lot missed Cevert's car and dumped down the trumpets of my engine. It looked like Zolder all over again, with throttle slides full of sand and the throttle jammed half open and immovable. In a situation like this you should either lift off and keep the throttle slides tight shut, or crack the throttle wide open so all the gunge goes straight through. It's often better to let the engine munch up a few rocks than have a throttle jammed on full noise at a tricky bit of track.

'I was hobbling round to the pits driving on the ignition switch, coasting round the corners on a dead engine and switching on for the straights, all the time desperately trying to free the jammed slides by tweaking the pedal. Amazingly enough this worked, the throttle freed itself and I was back on song again even though I was now about 16 seconds aft of the Lotuses and the Tyrrells.

'All my dramas had happened around half-distance and when I'd sorted it all out there were 21 laps to go. I knew at that point that I could make it. I wasn't convinced that I could win it, but I knew that I could be right up there, trying very hard. So I did, and on the way I collected the lap record. I was pulling François a second a lap and I was on the exhausts of his Tyrrell just as we came up to lap my team-mate, Peter Revson. Peter had been given the message that I was in a bit of a hurry and rather anxious to pass François and at the end of the straight there was an unexplainable curious sort of situation where François couldn't quite make it past Peter and I managed to slipstream past him while he was figuring it all out. Peter let me through and it was downhill all the way to Jackie's Tyrrell.

'It does your ego all sorts of good when you know you're reeling in these superstars at more than a second a lap. I was having no problems with any of the back markers and in fact I was collecting good tows from some of them, which fired me into the corners very nicely. When I arrived along, Jackie had his hands full of black cars. Ronnie was out front and obviously determined to win his first Grand Prix on home ground, regardless of how the battling champions felt about it. (I was a World Champ once too, so I include myself in there!) Jackie made it past Emerson on the inside going into the corner after the pits and I went under him at the next corner. Jackie was then trying everything to get past Ronnie, but Ronnie wasn't having any of it. Then Jackie's car quit on him with some sort of brake failure as we were going down past the pits and it was all down to D.H. and R.P.

'I made one attempt at doing Ronnie at the end of the straight, which was really the only place I could do anything about him. I switched off the rev limiter so that I didn't lose any split seconds when I needed them most, gave it the big stick up over 11 grand in every gear and came sweeping up on the right-hand side of Ronnie.

'Now, when you're a Swede and you look as though you're about to win the Swedish Grand Prix, you don't stand any nonsense from bears, so he came moving across to the right, just as I knew he would and that was the signal for the Fastest Bear in the World to go sailing back across his slipstream and slingshot down past the Lotus right on line for the corner at the end of the straight.

'After that, it was all over bar the shouting and I gather there wasn't a lot of that. The crowd had been pretty excited when Ronnie looked like winning, but having a New Zealander out front apparently doesn't do quite as much for local enthusiasm. Ronnie had a slow puncture, which wasn't helping him one little bit, and even though I was delighted to be winning, I did spare a thought for how Ronnie must have been feeling. I didn't let it slow me down, though.

'The weird thing was that because of all the excitement of the chase and the thrash in getting past people, I hadn't been paying a lot of attention to my pit signals and I thought I still had four or five laps to go. On the lap that I nailed Ronnie I came by the pits very pleased with myself and was more than just a little startled to see my pit board showing one lap to go! I'd done it just in time. If I'd waited another lap, Ronnie might have been able to hold me out.

'The car ran like a dream from half-distance after it had disgorged all those rocks and I reckon it's probably the best race I've ever driven. It was also very satisfying to think that I was the first driver this year to break up the Fittipaldi/Stewart lockout on Grand Prix wins.

'Rather appropriately, with even a suggestion of pre-arrangement, the winner's trophy was a beautiful hunk of iceberg-green glass and carved into the back of it as a main feature was, would you believe it, a big bear! Ronnie never stood a chance . . .'

The Rolls-Royce trip to Sweden had been the icing on the racing cake for Denny. But it was anything but stately progress on the way home. Phil Kerr remembers the dramas: 'We had to get back to Esbjerg on the Monday evening at 5.30 for the ferry back to England and we figured if we could be away by 8.30 a.m., it'd be a cruise. It was about 470 kilometres and, allowing for ferry crossings, we reckoned we'd be there by 4 p.m. — no problem. We threw the luggage and the trophies that Denny was so delighted with in the boot. The first sign of how the day would develop was when we came to close the boot on the Roller . . . and it just sprang back open. The boot lock had quit. We wasted about 20 minutes with a screwdriver, but without success. Eventually we found some wire and secured it that way. By now it was after 9 a.m., but we still had over 8 hours to get to Esbjerg. Mac drove and Denny decided he would lounge in the back. We had gone about 80 kilometres when Denny said, 'I think we've got a problem.' It was a wheel bearing on its way out, so we stopped at the side of the road and there was smoke pouring from the left rear wheel. And what were the chances of finding a Rolls-Royce agent in rural southern Sweden?

'We decided to drive slowly, with the winner of the previous day's Grand Prix now at the wheel, and we soon happened upon a small country garage where the owner's command of English was matched by the sum total of Swedish spoken by the crew of the crippled year-old Roller. We pointed to the hoist and soon the genial proprietor had the car raised to where we could examine it. This was where Denny was at his absolute best. He knew a proper fix wasn't going to be possible, but he got the guy to fetch a big drill and then announced that he was going right through the hub, guessing where the bearing was. He attacked the hub and told our new Swedish friend that he wanted a little grease nipple and lots of his best grease. He was going to stuff the hub full of grease and hope it would hang together.

'We paid the man some money, Denny signed his autograph book and then he drove fairly slowly to the ferry over into Denmark. By now we were well into the afternoon and our only option was to press on. Denny drove to start with, but then said maybe it was best for Mac to drive . . . in case anything went wrong . . . and he climbed into the back again while I got out the map and stopwatch and we were on a time/distance average, just like the good old days when we were rallying back home. We figured we'd just forget about the wheel bearing. It would either last or it wouldn't. Mac was driving absolutely flat out, cruising around 120 mph on the clock and never mind the fact that Denmark had strict speed limits. Past Odense there were lovely straight roads and we were doing 130 mph running level with an airport runway as a Viscount was coming in to land, and we went past it! About 10 minutes later there was an unbelievable crash on the windscreen — we'd hit a pigeon! How it didn't smash the screen, I will never know. There was blood and feathers everywhere.

'We were now right on the limit of time and distance and we said to Mac, "If the road is clear, forget traffic lights!" We were slowing down for the villages, but otherwise it was flat chat. On the outskirts of Esbjerg it was touch and go and we had less than 2 minutes. Every light was red and we drove through them all, screaming into the departure gate and handing the guy the tickets just as the loading ramp was being raised. They lowered it again and we'd made it. On the ferry I worked out that we'd averaged over 122 kph, which is probably still a record for a Rolls-Royce crossing Denmark . . .'

Ronnie might have missed out on his home win but his chance came soon when he won the next round, the French Grand Prix on the Paul Ricard circuit in the south of France, although it had looked like being a debut win for Jody Scheckter. Jody had been drafted in while Revson was racing in the Pocono 500. Denny thought Baby Bear had been shafted, but put it down to a racing incident that needn't have happened when Fittipaldi in the other Lotus tangled with the young South African late in the race. 'Jody was disappointed, but he's young and I think he's sensible enough to know he has a glowing career in front of him if he plays his cards right. It isn't every day you see someone with such raw talent. I take it almost as a compliment that they call Jody "Baby Bear" on the American F5000 scene.

'After the Swedish Grand Prix when everything went right, it seemed as though it was back to my jinxed dramas with engines and punctures and I seemed to be changing engines all through practice to start on row three, while Jody was in the middle of the front row with Stewart and Fittipaldi. When the race settled down Jody was out front looking as though he'd been a Grand Prix driver for years (it was actually only his third Grand Prix), with Peterson second, Stewart third, me fourth and Emerson fifth. Then I had my puncture. If this goes on much longer I'm going to see if Goodyear can make me up a set of solid rubber tyres instead of these things with air in them . . .'

Denny lost a lap with the stop, which dropped him to nineteenth. 'I clambered back to an eventual eighth — I missed out on seventh by a mere tick of the stopwatch — and two laps from the end I set a new track record.' Another Hulme lap record to prove his pace among the youngsters.

There were three Yardley-Macs for Denny, Peter and Jody at Silverstone for the British Grand Prix, the setting for one of the most spectacular race incidents anyone had ever seen. Denny had a box seat for the excitement.

'Baby Bear didn't need any help from Goldilocks to spill his porridge at Silverstone. From where I was sitting — about two lengths behind him through Woodcote at 135 mph — it looked as though there was going to be porridge and broken chairs all over the place. It was Jody's bad luck that he lost it in such a confined space and came back across the track right in front of the pits. If none of the other cars had hit him it would have been just a one-car accident. If he had lost it at any other part of the track it wouldn't have been as serious, either. I'm sure he will get a lot of stick for the accident, Formula 3 driver going too fast in Formula 1 and that sort of thing, but he probably felt he had to live up to the reputation that the press has been building up for him this season. I don't think it will affect his career — I just hope he doesn't take the praise or the criticism too much to heart. If you start believing your press clippings, you're in trouble.

'Jody could have semi-lost it because he had a very new tyre on one corner and he could have hit some oil or water on the grid as he went across it to accentuate his dire problem.

'I suppose you could say that the Yardley-McLaren men dominated the race from start to finish, what with Scheckter's effort at the start and Peter Revson's fantastic win to make him the first of the famous "Ditton Road Fliers" to bring off a Grand Prix victory. Way back in the good old days, Revvy shared a rambling old house in Ditton Road, Surbiton, with Chris Amon, Mike Hailwood and Tony Maggs, and Peter is the first of the four to break his Grand Prix duck.' He was also the *only* one of the famous fliers to win a Grand Prix. Denny was in the middle of the front row with Peter beside him on the outside. Jody was on row three.

'I reckoned I had made the best of the start initially when the engine just faded a fraction and picked up again, but by that time Ronnie was away in the lead, Jackie Stewart had come smoking up from the second row in his Tyrrell and Carlos Reutemann followed him up from the third row to be in third place as we rushed down to Stowe corner, where Jackie swept by Ronnie and took off into the lead. Jody was just behind me and I could see that he was catching up a fair amount on the approach to each corner, so I waved him by coming into Woodcote, the fast right-hander before the pits. I had changed over to a hard compound left front tyre and I was being a bit cautious, so I left Jody the normal line and then slid out behind him to cover his tail from Cevert's Tyrrell.

'As we went into Woodcote I saw Jody's car give a bit of a wriggle and I thought for sure he'd catch it, but the wriggle got progressively bigger each time he tried to twist the wheel. It seemed to get more vicious and eventually it seesawed out on to the grass and then there was this huge cloud of dust that went up as the car turned sideways and slid down the track. It kissed the pit wall backwards and then slowly rolled out into the track.

'I braked very hard, because I didn't know which way he was going to spin or whether he would hit the wall, but when I saw him clobber the wall and almost stop, I ducked behind him and François followed me through with Peter so close that he knocked part of his wing off on Jody's wing! Scheckter was sitting there with his arms up in the air, but after the first car hit him he ducked down in the cockpit and stayed there. Everyone was extremely lucky that the worst injury was Andrea de Adamich's broken ankle. It looked like Indianapolis all over again, but we had the edge on the Indy guys because of our regulations stipulating deformable structure around the fuel cells. There were nine cars knocked out in that one accident, but there was no fire.

'Meanwhile, Jackie, Ronnie and Carlos were thundering along out in front, unaware of the mechanical carnage behind them and Jackie stood on everything when he saw the red flag — his first indication of trouble — being waved at Woodcote. He parked his Tyrrell on the straight, unbuckled his harness, jumped out and ran like hell for the pit wall in case he was hit from behind, because there wasn't anywhere else to leave the car.

'The field restarted about an hour later in original grid order and this time it was Ronnie who made the best of it, followed by Niki Lauda in the BRM, who was soon nailed by Jackie in the Tyrrell, who latched on to Ronnie and tried to go down the inside of him going into Stowe. When I arrived at the corner, Jackie was still on the track but pointing out towards the wheatfield and then he seemed to accelerate into the wheat as though his throttle had jammed. All I could see of him was the tall airbox of the Tyrrell scything through the wheat like the periscope on a submarine! Very odd . . .'

Later in the race Revson moved into the lead and it started to spit with rain. Denny had handling problems and considered a pit stop, but as the fuel load dropped, the problems eased and he finished third.

Drama seemed to stack on drama during the 1973 season and the

Dutch Grand Prix at Zandvoort brought the tragedy of Roger Williamson's fiery death.

'We just don't learn . . . we just don't learn. We get the most horrifying kinds of lessons and yet we simply do not learn from them. After Piers Courage's fatal crash at Zandvoort in 1970 we said that something should be done about fire-fighting systems at tracks. We said it again when Jo Siffert was killed at Brands Hatch in 1971. To say it all again after Roger Williamson's fatal crash, as the fire raged unchecked at Zandvoort, seems almost futile.

'The Clerk of the Course should have stopped the race as soon as he realised the seriousness of the crash. There was a fire-tender standing 150 yards beyond the burning car, but it didn't move because the driver apparently had instructions not to drive the wrong way round the track. So a driver died. After Piers' accident and then Roger's accident on almost the same part of the track, you can't help but feel that the people in control at Zandvoort are less than competent when it comes to an emergency situation. It beats me how they could let themselves be caught out again in virtually identical circumstances.

'One of the problems may have been that the drivers were unaware of the seriousness of the accident. I certainly never knew that anyone was still in the burning car until after I had retired at the pits. When I came past the first time, I saw the car on fire and David Purley brushing flames off himself and my initial reaction was that he had crashed and managed to get out of the car OK. But when he was still there struggling two laps later I started to wonder. It never occurred to me that it was his car stopped on the other side of the road. I just presumed that it had been a two-car accident and that David had climbed out of the burning car. Initially the flame was small and the flame was low, blowing sideways as though a petrol line had severed and with the pump still on it was feeding flame out sideways like an acetylene torch. If Purley had had assistance as soon as he arrived, Roger could probably have been rescued. As it turned out, it was a complete disaster. The fire-truck took some 8 minutes to arrive after driving round most of the track, while the other truck stood 150 yards away and did nothing. I simply fail to understand it.'

Denny's race ended when his engine failed spectacularly and Jackie Stewart moved into the record books when his win brought his career total to 26 Grand Prix victories, moving ahead of fellow-Scot Jim Clark's score of 25.

Denny's German Grand Prix on the Nürburgring was dismal, with a fourth row start beside team-mate Revson. Team guest-driver Ickx was on row two and would finish third. Denny had his moments in the race, chasing down leader Carlos Pace at one point, but eventually pitting with a broken exhaust, which he said made his car sound like a Chevvy that had dropped an inlet valve, and he finished a lowly twelfth. After his spate of tyre troubles the team had attached a tow rope to the rear bulkhead and a tyre repair canister to the rollover bar . . .

In Austria, the Yardley-Macs of Hulme and Revson were fastest for much of practice, only to be pipped late in the last session by the Lotuses of Fittipaldi and Peterson. Peter's clutch failed at the start and Denny nipped into second place behind Ronnie. He was finding it easy to keep his pace, but then his engine went sad and he pitted to find it was a loose plug lead. He stormed back into the race a lap down, but then the lead came loose again — and again! — costing Denny a total of three pit stops and all chance of doing anything in the race. He was eighth.

At Monza the Yardley-Macs were still on the pace, with Revson on the front row beside Ronnie and Denny on the second row with Emerson. From the start Denny was tucked in the slipstream of the two Lotuses, but he had brake drama approaching the chicane on the eighth lap. Pete Lyons in *Autocourse*: 'Certain of the current Grand Prix cars are displaying a rare but disturbing brake malfunction; partway down through a braking area the pedal will suddenly go straight to the bulkhead for no discernible reason at all. Hulme had this happen in testing at Silverstone a few days before, and now as he was tucking in close behind the nearer of the JPSs it happened again — a quick pump restored pressure and there was just enough time left before committing himself, for Denny to think he could still make the swerve, but as he bent in the car took charge, made a lazy long spin and slid sideways on to the kerbing forming the right-hand side of the gate. The chassis took a nasty blow at the radiator line and bounced high in the air. It came crashing down slightly damaged and still mobile, but by the time Denny had backed and fiddled and waited for a gap to develop in the still closely bunched midfield, he had lost a hopeless amount of ground; in any case he prudently stopped to check for damage and dropped completely away from the race.' He was classified fifteenth, two laps behind the leaders. Peterson won the Grand Prix and Stewart clinched the world championship.

The Canadian Grand Prix was run in showers with safety car periods that confused the race order; and by the finish Howden Ganley might have been a winner in Frank Williams' Iso-Ford, and Lotus thought Emerson had won, but the laurels eventually went to Peter Revson in the Yardley-Mac. Denny suffered *three* punctures and pit stops and was classified a dismal thirteenth.

Denny had high hopes for the final race of the season at Watkins Glen. 'We had expected that the M23 would really perform well, but in fact we didn't qualify as fast as we did last year with the M19s! Last year we felt we were very competitive and this year we felt the car was even better, so it's all something of a mystery. Peter and I were back on the fourth row, with Jody on the fifth row in our third car. Peterson and Reutemann were on the front row. Ken Tyrrell had withdrawn his cars for Jackie Stewart and Chris Amon after François Cevert's fatal crash in practice.

'Up until about 10 seconds before the flag dropped everything seemed fine, but then Peter started to move forward and I thought for sure he'd be penalised for jumping the start, but either his clutch had given up or started to grip and there was nothing he could do about it. When the flag did drop, Peter just stopped there, stalled, with his hand up while everyone behind him went into a wheel-spinning swerving series of phenomenal avoidances to miss the stationary McLaren. I had talked to Jody on the grid and told him to take it easy in the race, because he didn't really need another coming-together on his short Grand Prix record, but he said he had planned to play it really cool this time. No heroics. I said that I'd probably make a cracking start down to the first corner and then ease it for a couple of laps after that, making sure that the tyres had warmed up properly before I started to stand on it. Sure enough, Jody slotted right in behind me from the start and in fact he could probably have overtaken me on the corner at the end of the long straight, but I moved over and blocked him off and we settled down to run nose to tail in fourth and fifth place behind Peterson, James Hunt and Reutemann after we had passed Hailwood and Fittipaldi. Jody said afterwards that he had really been working hard to stay where he was and it was probably a good driving lesson for him, because he didn't do anything daft and if his front wishbone hadn't broken, he probably would have finished ahead of me.

'I dropped out of contention when I started to feel a vibration that I couldn't identify, but I remembered a previous experience at the Glen when a front wheel started to break on a CanAm car. Each time I turned into a corner the car vibrated more, so I eased back and still managed fourth.

'Although the M23 has been rated with the Tyrrell and the Lotus as the top trio of cars for this season, I don't feel the M23 has been as competitive as it might have been. It's been good at some tracks but not so good at others, even though we have come out of the season with one Grand Prix win for me and two for Peter. At the Glen the car seemed unbalanced all the time, with initial understeer going into a corner and then violent oversteer at the exit, and it was very difficult to pinpoint the problem, because the track kept on changing to the point where if we were faster we weren't sure whether it was the change we'd made to the car or the track improving since the adjustment . . .'

At the end of the season, Denny was due to go on a family holiday in New Zealand. Before he left he was interviewed by Alan Henry for an article in *Motoring News*. Henry made the point before the interview started that Denny had been with the McLaren team for seven seasons, one of the longest stays any driver had had with a post-war team. Denny said that he felt part of the team and 'I don't know whether anyone would have me in another team. They seem to think that I'm so well stuck, so well glued to McLaren that they never approach me with offers. I hope I'll stay with McLarens until I give up motor racing.' I wonder if he realised how soon that would be?

Denny was remarkably forthright about USAC racing and the super-speedways. 'Surprisingly enough, providing the four wheels stay on the car, Indy isn't too dangerous a place. But it's a different world and you could get a little carried away. After 500 miles round the oval, the sheer speed feels like about 10 miles an hour. You just forget that you're doing 215 mph down the straights. The big thing is to keep out of anyone else's accidents and that's where the whole problem lies. It's so easy to get sucked into somebody else's folly at Indy. Just to go there and rush around on your own is probably no more hazardous than going to Silverstone and rushing round there on your own. But when something happens at Indy, boy, it happens fast and there's just no way you're going to avoid it. That's one of the problems that they're going to have to take a long look at and change; but I don't know how they're going to do it. I really don't.'

Bobby Rahal, winner of the 500 in 1986, would say at one of our Barley Mow pub lunches in Surrey: 'In downhill ski racing and the Indy 500, there's no such thing as a *small* accident . . .'

Speaking at the end of the 1973 season, Denny continued: 'Indy is such a big deal, it's really the biggest deal that's going in the world as far as motor racing is concerned, and you're inclined to forget the little problems it brings. Once you get out there in qualifying you just seem to forget about safety; you like to *talk* about it, but you know nothing can be done and you just have to cross your fingers for the whole month of May that you're there.

'It's a strange thing, but if you win Indy, then you're looking good for the rest of your life, particularly if you're an American. Even Graham Hill still gets some of the rub-off from winning at Indy and that's some time ago, but people still remember him in America for winning the 500. Indy is a very small place relative to somewhere like London and you can go shopping, but never without being stopped by people asking, "How's your car running?" or "Can I have your autograph?" because they live, eat and sleep motor racing. Everyone just talks about the 500, it's all everyone has to live for. The oval. And whenever foreign drivers go there, they'll always be remembered. You always make friends at Indy.'

Henry asked Denny how he coped with the track officialdom and the strict rookie tests for first-time drivers at the Speedway. 'It's one of the strangest phenomena of my life. But, as difficult as I may appear to everyone over on this side of the Atlantic, I change my attitude the day I arrive at Indy. Even to this day I still respect their system. They are organised. The press is organised. The whole of America is aware of what's going on at Indy for those 30 days in May. So I respect them and I change to suit their way of thinking, rather than expecting them to change to my way of thinking. It got to be my home for one month every year while we were racing there . . .'

21 Grand Prix finale 1974

The 1974 season started early in the boardrooms of Philip Morris, which owned the Marlboro cigarette brand, Texaco, and the Yardley cosmetics company. At season's end Philip Morris would host a dinner in the ballroom of the Carlton Tower in London to farewell Denny following his retirement from Formula 1.

Phil Kerr, Joint Managing Director at McLaren at the time, takes up the story. 'In 1972 and 1973 our cars were sponsored by Yardley and driven by Denny and Peter Revson, with an occasional third car entered for Jody Scheckter. When we did the sponsorship deal with Marlboro/Texaco for the 1974 season the two cars were to be driven by Denny and Emerson Fittipaldi. That was their preferred choice, with two World Champions in the team.

'I then had to sort out the arrangement with Yardley (delicate, as they still had a contract with us), who weren't prepared to increase the funding for a two-car team, which is why we had to go with Marlboro/Texaco. It was eventually agreed that there would be a one-car Yardley team and Peter Revson would drive it. Unfortunately, Peter wouldn't go along with this as he thought he might not get equal equipment, which wasn't the case but Teddy couldn't convince him. The result was that Peter left to join Shadow, with a very sad outcome.

'I then suggested Jody for the Yardley car, but politics entered the scheme with him being South African and Emerson wasn't in favour either. In the end I managed to sign Mike Hailwood and Yardley were in agreement

314

with this, as he was British with a high-profile name. All these negotiations were delicate and difficult, to say the least, but we finally resolved the issues and Denny drove the 1974 season in a Marlboro Texaco McLaren.'

For Denny the season would start strongly after a winter jetting between socialising in Britain and arranging a home in New Zealand, perhaps anticipating retirement before he had actually made up his mind. Or before fate had made his mind made up for him . . .

'For most of the winter I seem to have been lying around, relaxing and really enjoying it. After Riverside I went home to New Zealand for two or three weeks and only came back to England for the Doghouse Ball. Then I returned to New Zealand, where I wasn't so much lying around as getting myself organised with a house. Greeta and I have never had a home out there, we've never had any land of our own, so we wanted to find a piece of property, somewhere where we could be happy and perhaps look forward to living at some future time.

'Testing the M23 has largely been Emerson's job, because I went to Ricard just once. It wasn't a very successful day, so I went back to England. Emerson seems to like the car set up the same way that I like it, which is obviously good. He goes about testing a little differently from me, because he likes to change things. I tend to get myself fairly happy with the car, then change myself to suit the car, but he prefers to tweak it that final little bit so that it's perfectly adapted to his taste.

'The changes that are notable on the car this year are that it's 3 inches longer, and a couple of inches wider at the rear. Otherwise it's just been refined, tidied up here and there, and of course it's got a nice red and white paint job to suit the new sponsors. Until we get on some of the circuits where we ran last year I can't say what has improved, but I do know that it's quicker round Paul Ricard, and I was very happy the way it went in Buenos Aires.

'Last year I was affected by the heat in Argentina, and it was even worse at Interlagos in Brazil. This time I was much better and perhaps it's a psychological thing, because after spending four weeks in New Zealand I've been able to get some time in the sunshine. If I'm brown, then I feel fit, but apart from a bit of swimming, I don't do as much training as the team manager would like. Motor racing is my way of keeping up to scratch, and as long as I watch my diet I don't have any trouble.

'This year they decided to switch the Grand Prix to the long Number 15 circuit in Buenos Aires. It makes it a bit easier on the driver, because there's not much to do as you thunder down those long straights, but I figure the car has to work a bit harder. We might have performed better round the short circuit, but in the end it's the results that count, and for us the result was perfect!

'I just managed to scrape into the top 10 qualifiers, but I wasn't too worried about that. We tried the car with full tanks on race morning and it was pleasant to find that only Carlos Reutemann and perhaps Mike Hailwood in his Yardley-Mac were any quicker.

'Some of the guys got caught out at the start. But Fangio didn't mess about with the flag because he's an ex-race-driver, and he knows that those race engines get damn hot if they're not moving through the air. Even so, once we'd moved up on to the grid, I had time to take it out of first gear for 10 seconds, and then slip it into gear again and move off. Anyway, with a Latin-American start you've got to be prepared for anything at all . . .

'Nobody is quite sure what happened in the accident after the start. It would help if we could see a slow-motion film so that we could work out better what happened. From my point of view, I remember that Mike Hailwood made a good start from alongside me, and we set off together. Then I was semi-blocked-off for a fraction, and I had to make up my mind whether I could get around Clay Regazzoni's Ferrari. The Ferrari is difficult to get off the line as fast as a Ford because of all the extra fuel it carries and Clay was lagging a bit. But I didn't want to swerve past, because that might have squashed out someone alongside me. There were cars off all over the place, bouncing into each other.

'Then I found that I was sandwiched between Mike and Clay, backed out of that situation and at that moment, Mike and Clay came together. There was a great sheet of magnesium sparks, and it occurred to me that things were getting a bit desperate. Mike scrambled through, Clay swung to his left and I came through from behind him to find Peter Revson's Shadow turning sideways in front of me. Peter was heading for the infield, which is where I'd decided to go, and it seemed inevitable that I would run over his nose, but there was no thump or thud and I knew I was clear.

'There didn't seem to be anyone following when I looked in the mirror, so I thought there must have been an almighty shunt, perhaps another Silverstone, and that the race was bound to be stopped. There was no pace car arranged for this one and it all looked like being a shambles, but it had all been cleared up when we got back, apart from some debris and tufts of grass on the road. It was just a matter of pressing on.

'The accident had cost me a bit of time on the leaders, but I got most of it back through the Esses and the M23 seemed to be getting through the big fifth-gear loop at the end of the straight better than anyone else. By the time I got to the end of the next straight I was right with the bunch, and it was just a matter of picking them off one by one. James Hunt eliminated himself on the first lap by getting the hairpin all wrong, and all I could see of him was an airbox spinning through the long grass. He was a long way off the road, and there was no way he could get back on the track before the pack arrived.

'Meanwhile Carlos Reutemann had made a fantastic break and gone. I think I'll reserve judgement on the new Brabham until it gets to another circuit. Carlos went very well at Watkins Glen, I know, but remember that he was on the pole for the Grand Prix here in BA two years ago. It's his home track, after all, and this time he had a really good engine . . . I'm not knocking him, but let's see what happens elsewhere. For sure he had bad luck and the local papers gave Bernie's team a hard time on Monday, which maybe they didn't deserve.

'Ferrari has done a lot of useful homework through the winter, and the 12-cylinder seems to pick up well out of the slow corners. I've always had a lot of time for Mauro Forghieri, because he's such a practical person, and Niki Lauda has turned into a useful test driver. Clay, of course, just presses on.

'Peter Revson is enthusiastic about his UOP Shadow; in fact, he says it handles better than the M23 he drove last year. Peter's always been a tryer, and if he wants something, then the designer's got to go and do it. Perhaps this is what Shadow lacked last year.

'Tyrrell is bound to get his cars sorted out. The team has gone through a dramatic change and it'll take time before the drivers can get through to the designer what they need on the cars. Jody and Patrick Depailler are very young and they'll have problems getting designer Derek Gardner to understand what they want.

'Lotus had a bad day, but they'll get going again soon. We've got Emerson from their side and he's going to go like hell all season long. Obviously I'm going to try to go like hell too, and having Emerson on the team takes some of the load off my shoulders. Perhaps I give the impression that I don't care too much, but I do care and Emerson will help the whole team. I know I'm getting the same equipment as him and we're working well together. I don't know what would have happened if that plug lead hadn't come off on his car, but my car was good in BA and Emerson was enthusiastic about his.

'I benefited from a couple of plug leads coming adrift. Once when Emmo's engine went off song and he lost pace and then in the closing laps Carlos's Brabham lost a plug lead and as Pete Lyons wrote in *Autocourse* "... suddenly the Brabham was making the ugly sound of seven cylinders.

Rapidly Hulme loomed up behind . . ." It didn't sound ugly to me! It was a beautiful noise and I had won another Grand Prix.'

It would also be his last, but there was no way of knowing that after the first race of what would turn out to be his final season in Formula 1.

'Our team has split its efforts this year, but there's never going to be a problem between us and Yardley. That side was all sorted out some time ago and we have the staff and the facilities to run three cars. At the track we'll keep things separate, for the sake of the sponsor's identities, but all the equipment comes out of the same factory and we'll continue to swap ideas. Mike Hailwood is already going well, and I really can't see any difficulties in the arrangements.'

The Brazilian Grand Prix was something of a shambles, with rainstorms sweeping the area and eventually stopping the race, and the unruly, noisy crowds almost ensuring that it wouldn't start, throwing bottles and debris on to the track. Lyons: 'Denny, in his role as outgoing President of the Grand Prix Drivers' Association, and the boss of Goodyear racing, walked the length of the main straight on race morning and gathered pounds of rubbish. Hulme at one point straightened up to display a rusty nail, 3 inches long. Meanwhile, the swollen, restive crowd chanted and shouted and scrapped with good nature among themselves and doubtless wondered what the delay and the fuss was all about.'

Denny had his views on the situation: 'There was a frightening amount of glass on the track on race morning and there was a delay while Ed Alexander of Goodyear and I gathered as much as we could from the pit straight. We pointed out to the Clerk of the Course that glass on the track is the equivalent of a gun pointed at your head: pull the trigger and someone's going to be dead for sure. In South America the fans have difficulty controlling themselves and chucking bottles seems to make them happy.

'They'll only recognise the problem when someone threatens to cancel a Grand Prix. After all, the equipment we use isn't an earthmoving tyre that can cope with rocks and sharp debris, it's a highly sophisticated device which nevertheless resists punctures in many ways. The mechanics picked a dozen bits of glass out of Emerson's tyres on the grid, but I wasn't so lucky. A front tyre had picked up something nasty on the warm-up lap and it must have been big, because the air disappeared in a rush, which is very unusual. I had to change the wheel behind the pits and I didn't like the idea that there might be something in the other front, so I changed that one just in time to move up to the grid.

'I made such a bad start that I was fifteenth or sixteenth on the first lap and then I had huge tyre problems, with an enormous vibration at the front that shook the car about so much that I was just plain slow. The race was stopped when a devastating rainstorm hit the track and I was happy enough to finish, even if I was down in twelfth place.'

That weekend the GPDA had elected Graham Hill as the new President to take over from Denny. Peter Revson, Emerson Fittipaldi and Jean-Pierre Beltoise had all put their names forward for a job that had been hard to fill in 1973, when Denny had volunteered. 'Last year they couldn't give the job away and when they came round asking, I was one of the few guys who didn't refuse. I'm glad that there is so much interest inside the GPDA itself, because the job is not a rewarding one to do. Everyone who has done it has come under heavy fire, from Jo Bonnier through Jackie Stewart and latterly me. Now Graham's going to be the target and his satisfaction will be to see that something is really being done about circuit safety.'

Denny's stand on circuit safety had changed through 180 degrees since his quote to Denis Jenkinson in *Motor Sport* after his win in the 1967 German Grand Prix on the Nürburgring, en route to his world championship that summer: 'Strange that the winner of the German Grand Prix is not a member of the Grand Prix Drivers' Association. He says he doesn't want to join "Bonnier and his lot". Grand Prix racing is all right as far as he is concerned.'

Fate stepped in with horrifying suddenness during practice for the very next race. 'Peter Revson's crash in pre-race testing at Kyalami inevitably points the finger at the guardrailing he hit. What was regarded as good enough in 1968, or whenever the guardrailing was put in, is simply not good enough now. That sounds like a pretty bald statement, but the fact is that we're all going so much faster now that the tracks tend to change their aspect. The corner where Peter crashed certainly wasn't flat five or six years ago but if you're going quick now, it's got to be flat. It's the sort of corner that you don't take quite flat on the first day of practice, but you work up to it so that by the time you're doing your quick laps towards the end of the final session, you're whistling through there either flat or lifting just a whisker.

'I maintain that it wasn't the fact that Peter's car hit the guardrail, it was the fact that something must have broken on the car to trigger the accident in the first place. If it had happened just about anywhere else on the track Peter would probably have got away with it, but the combination of factors defeated him.

'Peter and I had been chatting on the pit counter that day and he sounded quite pleased with the way the car was going. His "tweak" last year was to run with very little angle on the wing and he was doing that with the Shadow at Kyalami. He said it was a bit loose round the back, but it went like hell down the straight. This season was going to be Revvy's year. He was determined to win the world championship and on the occasions when his car was running properly this season he was turning in really good times. What a damn shame . . .'

Denny was back on the fifth row beside Ickx's Lotus on the 2-2-2 grid, but his engine lost its edge early in the race. He battled on and with sixteen laps to go he was sitting behind Scheckter's Tyrrell and working out how he could get past before the finish. 'He was faster on the straight, but I figured that if I could get right up his chuff as we went out on to the straight I could probably gnaw past him before the braking area. I chose the Esses to do my closing up, but the back started to come round and I over-corrected to wind up on the edge of the track pointing into the weeds. I had a choice between bouncing over a shallow ditch or driving up behind some catchfences and across a boggy piece of ground to get back on to the track. I chose the long way round to avoid dragging anything off the underside of the car on the ditch, but by then I was history. Or even more historic than I had been. Reutemann came by to lap me before the finish and I followed him until he finally took his first Grand Prix chequered flag. I was ninth.'

The rain in Spain caused confusion in the Grand Prix at Jarama. Or rather, the fact that the rain stopped early in the race when all were on wet tyres caused concern. 'We had arranged that we would signal for permission from our pit when we wanted to change tyres, but every time I went past asking to come in, I kept getting the signal to stay out. Eventually I was running slower lap times in the dry than I had been in the wet and it wasn't until after the race that I discovered the delaying tactics were because Emerson's car was getting a 10,000-mile service and they didn't want two cars in at once. Emerson's engine was running sour from the start, so they changed the plugs while they were changing tyres and discovered a water leak down one of the plug holes, which had been shorting the plug. He went back into the race with a healthy engine and eventually finished third.

'My race plan was to play it very cool away from my fourth row grid position because of the rain. I was going to use a modest amount of revs and start the race as though I was leaving the traffic lights in my Jaguar XJ6, with a fair amount of decorum. I let the clutch in with about 3000 revs on and it gripped so I shot straight into second and I was up between

Arturo Merzario and Reutemann on the third row when I suddenly realised I was bear meat in a Latin sandwich with a lot of bumping and banging and wheel grinding going on. I thought, "Gawd, any minute now I'll get flipped up in the air and this could all turn to rubbish right on the start line," so I hit the brakes hard and dragged myself back from between the two of them and was consequently passed by everyone else in a hurry. Then I realised that the car was bottoming badly going down the straight and I thought maybe the bumping together at the start had broken the rear beam and it was all going to settle down on the road at an inopportune moment. I figured it was better to be sure than sorry so I made a pit stop to check. It turned out that it was a combination of running smaller-diameter wet-weather tyres, a large amount of rear wing and shockers that had been cranked back for a Cadillac ride.' Denny made another stop to change to dry tyres and eventually finished sixth.

In Belgium Denny was sixth again after a troublesome midfield run, while Emerson won. At Monaco Denny qualified down on the sixth row beside Beltoise in the BRM, but he was a main player in a shunt on the opening lap. Lyons in *Autocourse*: 'A few days before the race Denny had said, "If you can get round Ste Devote and then get round the Station, you'll be lookin' good." Denny did make it round the first corner all right, but 100 yards later, surrounded by a flood of racing cars pouring uphill towards the Casino, he felt a sudden blow against one wheel. His and Beltoise's cars had come together. It was enough to create a log jam in midstream. The front part of the race flowed on ahead. The middle part splashed like crashing surf in all directions. Hulme's car was left parked in the road, hard against the left-hand barrier halfway up the hill, a yellow flag stuck into its mechanism. A little above, pulled into a backwater out of the way, were the crumpled remains of the cars of Merzario, Pace and Redman.'

Sweden was no victory repeat for Denny. He was down on the sixth row again beside Mike Hailwood in the Yardley-Mac and a row behind Emerson in the other Marlboro Texaco Mac, but Denny was out just after half-distance with a broken bolt in the rear suspension sub-frame. Scheckter and Depailler finished 1-2 in the Tyrrells.

At Zandvoort it was the Ferraris of Lauda and Regazzoni finishing 1-2, with Emerson and Mike 3-4 in the McLarens. 'It must be simply a matter of horses for courses. In Sweden our McLarens and the Ferraris were nothing special, while the Elf-Tyrrells were absolutely brilliant, but in the Dutch Grand Prix the Ferraris came back super-strong, our cars were good, but the Tyrrells had lost that dominating edge. We really can't put a finger on why our McLarens should be up there again, because we didn't do anything magic to them. Obviously Ferrari found some sort of demon tweak and we know that Ken Tyrrell always tries hard wherever he goes, so I can only think that some courses suit some horses better than others.' Bears too. Denny qualified on the fifth row beside Ronnie Peterson in the JPS-Lotus but went out while in eighth place late in the race.

Pondering the performance of the Ferraris versus the McLarens at Zandvoort, Denny wrote: 'Apparently our Marlboro-Texaco sort of red doesn't work as well as that Italian Ferrari sort of red. It must be something to do with the horse painted on the side and not a little to do with the horses inside as well . . .'

Denny's father Clive was a popular team guest in the paddock at Zandvoort and *Autosport* ran a photo of him giving a demonstration of water divining to Emerson.

The French Grand Prix at Dijon featured a parade of historic racing cars and prompted Denny to write: 'You get a revised idea about how old is old when you are asked to drive a Grand Prix car in the historic demonstration as well as in the Grand Prix itself! Marlboro had done a tremendous job in assembling old cars and drivers who had won or featured well in past French Grands Prix and I was tagged on the end driving the Repco-

Brabham I'd used in 1967, when I won the world championship. It seemed like stepping out of a time machine, switching from the big roomy cockpit of the Brabham into the tight, tailor-made fit of the McLaren for the "real" race. I couldn't believe how different the Brabham felt and how slow by comparison with the present-day 3-litre cars. It was only seven years ago, but it was nowhere near as fast as our cars are now and it made me realise why Denis Jenkinson said we didn't need guardrails in those days, but if you live in that era and haven't progressed, you don't realise how important guardrailing and catch fences are as safety measures now.

'I didn't realise how strange it would feel, going back to the Brabham. There was plenty of room, the long nose out front, no wings . . . it was seven years old and it seemed like a vintage car. It was easy to steer, very light to drive and not a lot of horsepower, but the engine was probably feeling its age. Unfortunately, I had no real chance to have a go on the demonstration laps because the battery went flat and the fuel pump stopped — just like it used to do in 1967!

'I'm sure a lot of the old-timers wondered how the hell they ever managed to hump those cars around the circuits as fast as they did, because they must have found it was all much different to what they remembered. I went along dressed for the part in my old Esso overalls, my 1967 crash helmet and goggles, but some of the old drivers had come dressed in their original gear as well and that was really impressive. Louis Chiron had the same overalls, cloth cap, shoes and even the same socks that he wore when he used to race the Bugattis. It was a fantastic sight to see drivers like von Brauchitsch wheeling the big supercharged 1938 Mercedes round the Dijon track, Prince Bira in the little blue Gordini, Lang in the streamliner W196 Mercedes and Stirling Moss in the 1960 Cooper-Climax. Stirling looked quite young and boyish alongside the pre-war brigade!

'The Dijon track did nothing for me at all. It was just over two miles round with a straight and a wiggly section before you came back on to the straight again. If you were in with a chance you had to be lapping under 1 minute, which is ridiculous for a world championship race.'

Denny finished sixth and was awarded the Jo Siffert *Prix Rouge et Blanc* for his efforts. 'With about 15 laps to go the engine started to cough on almost every lap so I switched the rev limiter off, switched the oil pump on and gave it the big stick, hoping that my engine wouldn't do what Emerson's had done and blow itself apart. It's not the engine going wrong internally. It's just that the fuel system gets a vapour lock or something and every so often it digests a big dollop of air. And it doesn't run very well on just air . . .'

At the British Grand Prix at Brands Hatch Denny qualified way back on the tenth row of the 2-2-2 grid, but clambered back as far as seventh. Jody Scheckter won for Tyrrell, ahead of Emerson.

'I know I only saw Niki Lauda briefly at Brands Hatch — that was when he lapped me in the Ferrari! — but I know what he must have been thinking when he felt the handling change after collecting a puncture five laps from home and comfortably in the lead. You don't have much of a choice. You either press on and try to keep it all together to the flag, you back off and try to keep it all together, or you head for the pits and hope you were right about it being a puncture, because if it wasn't a puncture, Mr Ferrari will have your head delivered to his office on a plate.

'Your natural reaction is to try to keep the machine going as long as possible. Niki's mind must have been crammed with calculations: how many laps to go, how far is Jody behind, will they be ready in the pits, how much time will I lose? Finally, the tyre shredded itself and he had to stop with a lap to go, the crew were ready for him, and he was ready to go racing again in super-quick time. Then there was the downer with all those people and cars blocking the pit exit road and he must have seen his world championship points slipping through his fingers. I'm sure Niki was boiling and it makes me mad just to think about it. People in the pit lane are one of my pet hates. When can we ram it into their thick heads that the pit lane is part of the race track?

'Being a strictly partisan sort of Bear, however, I shouldn't be making too much of a show for Niki, because his slide down the leader board brought one Denis Clive Hulme up to sixth place and a championship point. The Ferrari people protested that Niki should have been given fifth or sixth place, but our manager Mayer was in there using all the tricks of his old lawyer's trade to keep Denny in the points and pennies. I feel that Niki deserved to get the money for fifth or sixth as a sort of consolation prize for his tremendous efforts during the race, but I don't think he should have had the points on a straight legal sort-out. You just can't say that Niki would have certainly finished fifth or sixth if he'd been allowed to complete the last lap, because anything could have happened which would have resulted in him not making it to the finish. A wheel might have come off, he might have crashed, the engine might have quit, he might have run out of petrol . . . What if somebody had been leading the race with five laps to go and a dog ran out in front of him, causing him to spin, stall and lose the race? Are you going to award that guy first place because the dog (like the people and the cars in the pit exit road) shouldn't have been there? I think Teddy's reasoning was right in this case, however much you might feel that Niki was robbed. Two points would have kept Niki in the championship lead, but you've got to remember that the 2 points he didn't get have pushed Emerson into the lead . . . and underneath all that Texaco and Marlboro paintwork there's a McLaren.'

The German Grand Prix was another race Denny would have preferred to forget. He found himself in the results as not one, but *two* retirements. The first retirement happened during the start, when Emerson couldn't find first gear. Or any other gear. Lyons in *Autocourse*: 'The next car behind [Emerson] in a direct line was team-mate Hulme's. Denny got off with everyone else but as he realised Emerson's machine was stationary he swerved to the left to go by between it and the guardrail below the grandstand. Ickx, however, had made a perfect getaway, and was already heading for the same slot. There just wasn't quite enough room for them both. Hulme thought he was going to make it through, just, but didn't. The one M23 grazed the other, rear wheel to rear wheel.

'Denny carried on with the momentum of his start, but his rear wheel was wobbling like a drunken thing round its broken upright and he had both his hands jammed on to his ducked head waiting for someone to smash him up the back. By great fortune everybody else streamed around, including Fittipaldi, who had found the shunt had cured his gear selection problem if nothing else and he set off after the others. Denny pulled over to the pits side of the emptying grid and climbed out of his bent No. 6, leaving others to push it on its wobbly way down to safety, while he approached the team's spare car, which was sitting there all ready to go, wearing No. 5T. It was too much temptation. He was strapped into it, and about 6 minutes after everybody else had gone, he drove away to join the race — in his second chassis since the flag fell!' Two laps later and Denny was black-flagged into retirement.

At the Österreichring Denny bounced back with a surprise second place in the Austrian Grand Prix. 'With trackside temperatures up over 100 degrees, sitting on a beach made much more sense than being cooped up in the cockpit of a Formula 1 car. But upwards of 180,000 spectators had decided the Österreichring was the place to be on a day like that and my second place at the end of the afternoon's drive more than made up for the hot ride.

'A computer had worked out the results of the race before it started and it had me pegged at seventh. When the race started I was seventh and I figured I'd been fixed there by some sort of electronic omen. But then I went from seventh to third and finally second, so you can think what you like about computers. They believe every word you tell them. When the

P2 boards started coming over the pit rail late in the race I didn't even know who was leading except that he was 35 seconds in front of me; it was bloody hot out there, and I wasn't about to start reeling him in. Whoever he was. Towards the end of the race I was pointing back over my shoulder because I wanted to know who was behind me. If my oil pressure dropped off, if I saw an oil flag, an accident, or if anything happened, I wanted to be able to back off, and take it nice and easy. But I could see our mechanics all nice and happy, jumping up and down and giving me "P2". There was no sign of nail-biting, so I reckoned there was no drama. Eventually they told me that James Hunt was behind me, but as I could see him around one part of the circuit I was able to gauge my distance on him. I suppose I could have gone harder, but it's nice to finish, and by staying on the road we nailed a pretty handy placing.'

Denny was nineteenth fastest in qualifying at Monza, back on the tenth row of the grid and he struggled home sixth, while Emerson had been strong all race in the other works M23 and finished on the exhausts of Peterson's winning JPS-Lotus.

In the Canadian Grand Prix at Mosport he was sixth again, a fading force while Emerson was on pole and race winner. At Watkins Glen for the final race of the 1974 season, Emerson finished fourth behind the Brabhams of Reutemann and Pace and Hunt's Hesketh, but there were points enough to clinch his second world championship and the constructor's championship for the McLaren team. Denny qualified back on the ninth row of the 2-2-2 grid. Lyons in *Autocourse*: 'The luck of the day caught up to Denny Hulme first. After but four laps his engine blew up. He packed his bag and, with the race still going on all sides, hustled himself over to a helicopter. He left no message, no statement, but a photographer intercepted him on his way. "Denny, what about it? Tell us." "Yeah," said Denis Clive Hulme over his shoulder, "I'm retired." The photographer said he was smiling broadly . . .'

Bye-bye, Bear.

After Denny's final Grand Prix at Watkins Glen, I sat with him and recorded a tape for his column, as we always did after a race. This wouldn't turn out to be one of those insightful, witty columns written literally from the cockpit, where Denny shared with his eager readers his true feelings about what it was really like out there. This was Denny talking about his decision to retire. It ran as a feature in *Autosport* on 17 October 1974, and I am reprinting it here because of the honesty in Denny's views, which I felt so accurately captured the aura of a World Champion stepping down.

'Grand Prix racing is a selfish ego trip where the winners take the spoils and satisfy their ambitions. The also-rans satisfy lesser egos merely by being involved, by being part of the élite international scene. Being a Grand Prix driver is as near as many will ever get to being a Grand Prix winner and their greatest triumphs will be to retire with their life. To retire wealthy is a bonus, but retiring alive is the goal for most. And knowing *when* to retire is probably the most important decision a Grand Prix driver ever takes.

'Denny Hulme built himself a granite reputation as a tough individual, a craggy Kiwi who couldn't care less about the human side of racing, the cares and the worries at home, the elation of winning or the gloom of defeat; it was all the same to The Bear. But Denny Hulme had worked hard to build a wall around his private feelings so that very few people really knew him away from the race track, or knew that he and his wife Greeta had discussed retirement shortly after the death of his great friend and team-mate, Bruce McLaren, and decided that Denny would race for only two more seasons. Those two seasons stretched into a third, but a series of accidents determined Hulme to hang up his hat at the end of the 1974 season.

'We started this interview a week after the 1974 Italian Grand Prix, when Hulme had run a dogged sixth in the race in a performance that could scarcely have impressed the racer who won the World Championship in 1967 and came close to winning it again in 1968. He skirted the subject of impending retirement without actually mentioning it, but when we began talking about racing accidents and how they affected other drivers, all the Hulme concerns for racing came flooding out along with the reasons for his decision to retire.

'He had been close behind Jochen Rindt when his Lotus crashed at Monza in 1970. Did an accident like that have an effect on him? "Jochen's crash was just a big shower of dust and rubbish and wheels flying everywhere . . . no, it didn't affect me, because at the time I had the spirit to keep going and I wanted to keep going, but after François Cevert's accident at the Glen . . ." He sighed, and then settled down to the real and human reasons why a racing driver doesn't want to race any more. "Most of the drivers were kicking themselves that they hadn't stopped at Zandvoort to try to save Roger Williamson, so at the Glen they stopped to see if anything could be done. The whole thing was just a mess, the car hadn't caught fire so some of the drivers had gone right in. This affected Jody very badly and he said straight afterwards that he was going to quit, no way was he going to continue, he was too young for that sort of nonsense. Then you began to wonder. It had all happened so damned quickly and there was another driver and it was all very sad, and I went over to Paris for the funeral and I thought, 'Oh Christ, can it all be worth it?' and I made up my mind that I'd do one more season and that would be it . . ."

'The 1974 season started well for Hulme when he won the Argentine Grand Prix, but then in South Africa the spectre came back with the Peter Revson crash during the pre-race testing. Hulme was one of the first on the scene. "I saw all the shambles and I thought well, bugger it, that's it . . . I just can't wait for the end of the year to get it all over with."

'And for the rest of the summer, Hulme was a turned-down racer, staying out of trouble on the race track, admitting that his career was over but going to the races to fulfil contractual obligations. "That probably wasn't the right attitude from the team's point of view, but I don't really think the team suffered because Emerson was way up there in the Championship and I was the block at the back. If I'd been up there with him, I'm sure things would have been really hectic and they would have had to divide their attentions. I think . . . I *hope* they won't be disappointed after the Glen. Sure, I won Argentina. I was lucky because Carlos dropped out, but I was happy to win. So I've had a win and a second place and finished sixth what seems like a dozen times . . ."

'Hulme is 38 and he candidly thinks it's too old to be racing. "You have less worries or cares when you're young. But then you take time out to think *am* I doing the right thing . . . you've got a family, responsibilities and here you are thundering around a race track like an idiot . . . I don't think that's the right attitude for a man in his mid-thirties. I still enjoy what I'm doing, but I basically know it's not right for me to be doing it. And for Graham Hill to be still racing . . . I think that's pretty foolish, because for sure he doesn't *have* to do it. Jackie made the right decision to finish when he was at the top."

'When Jack Brabham decided to try his hand at retirement in 1965, Hulme took his place in the Brabham team, but for 1966, with Jack back in harness and new Repco engines for the 3-litre formula, Hulme was his regular number 2. That was Jack's year to take the title. In 1967 it was Denny's championship and he won the Monaco and German Grands Prix on the two toughest tracks of the season, having led in South Africa and Canada. Although presumably satisfied that one of his cars had won the world title, Jack would have preferred to do the winning personally. Hulme felt Brabham might have tripped himself by experimenting during the season with new parts for the engine. "If the experiments had worked they would have been an improvement, but they let him down. Maybe he should have finished higher, but he was always trying something new while I had a nuts-and-bolts engine . . ."

'There was tension in the Brabham team and tension is something

Hulme has never really been equipped to cope with. When he was offered a CanAm McLaren at the end of the 1967 season he thoroughly enjoyed the new atmosphere as the "Bruce and Denny" show began its domination of the CanAm series. Bruce won that year and Denny won in 1968 and 1970. In 1968 Hulme had switched to the McLaren team in Formula 1 as well and looked like retaining his World Championship right down to the last round in Mexico City, but a suspension breakage put him into the wall and out of the championship chase.

' "I can now realise that it was bad of me to go away and leave Jack after winning the Championship in '67, but I think I did the right thing, because Jochen Rindt drove for him in '68 and they had a disastrous season, whereas the McLaren was running like a dream." Hulme won two Grands Prix that season, in Italy and Canada.

'One of Hulme's happiest racing seasons was the dreamy summer of 1968 driving the M8 winged McLaren-Chevrolet. "We were so far ahead of the opposition in those days that we went water-skiing one afternoon when we should have been practising." He won three of the six races and the championship.

'That M8B McLaren was Hulme's ideal as a motorcar and he would like to buy one of the ex-works cars to restore it. "People can't understand why I don't have a Boxer Ferrari or a Lamborghini or something like that . . . it's just that I've driven what I consider to be one of the best cars ever made, and I'm probably one of only a dozen guys who have ever driven one. Nothing else measures up. It's like going to the moon. There are only a few guys who have ever gone up there, and I'll bet they're pleased too . . ."

'Hulme was very much the reluctant champion when he won the title in 1967, but he looks back on it with no regrets at his lack of grace. "It put me on the map, right? I won the World Championship, but I don't think 1967 was my happiest year. Sure it was exhilarating building up to it and the chances that you'd win the title, but you were also on tenterhooks wondering if you'd do it and you only needed a couple of things to go wrong and it wouldn't have happened. OK, we scraped through and got enough points to win, but I felt a lot happier the following year with Bruce . . ."

' "It was more enjoyable being CanAm champion those two years than it was being World Champion in 1967. I knew when I won the World Championship that I'd have to do this and do that, make speeches and give interviews, it was something that I still dread to this day. I'm not so bad when I actually get there, but it's the thought of having to do it, preparing myself to go to these places. As far as I'm concerned I'd rather stay at home, but I know you're obliged to go out and do these things. When I won the CanAm series there was only the prizegiving at the end of the series and that was it. We'd won the series, had a good time, a lot of fun, met a lot of people, but there was no big deal afterwards, which suited me just fine. When I won the World Championship I was forever making speeches and wondering what I'd let myself in for.

' "It's nice to win the World Championship, sure, and I felt everything as justified once I'd done it. I'd justified my family's decision to let me go racing and justified my own ambition to try to press on and do it. Once I'd done all that I was quite happy within myself but then I had what was, from my point of view, the aggravation of going and doing all the things that a World Champion is supposed to do, and that's what I shunned. I really hated it. I suppose I was lucky to get away with it as well as I did without being ridiculed and people saying what a right bastard I was . . ."

'Bruce McLaren's death in 1970 caught Hulme at a very low personal ebb, still recovering from severe burns to his hands when the M15 McLaren caught fire during practice at Indianapolis, and it was at this point that Denny started to seriously consider his future. Until then accidents had been things that happened to other people. His 10 days in hospital at Indianapolis gave him time to dwell on the shortening odds.

'There was always the chance element, the chance that it wouldn't happen again. But it did. In the opening laps of the Road Atlanta CanAm race in 1972, Hulme was tucked into the slipstream of Follmer's turbo-Porsche, shaping up to pass, when his McLaren flipped over backwards and skated to a halt upside down. A flash flame was immediately extinguished, and the heavy car was manhandled back on to its wheels. It was more food for thought. He could so easily have been killed in a crash he knew nothing about, a crash he had escaped from with only a bump on the head. "Then I realised you could be wiped off the face of the earth without really knowing it. I was following Follmer and I don't remember anything to this day except coming to in hospital . . . it was an indication that you could be snuffed out painlessly without even knowing you'd been killed. It could have caught fire or destroyed itself, but fortunately the car stayed intact and there was no damage to me except a bump on the nut. Then you start to realise how easy it is for it all to go wrong . . . just too easy . . ."

'Hulme says this experience with the vagaries of aerodynamics snatching control from a driver had an effect on his racing from then on. "It stopped me from racing right close to people, trying to dice and frig about with them. If I couldn't run clean or get past them cleanly I wouldn't bother to get too close to them. I think that had an effect on me in Formula 1 as well. I do not like running close to anyone in Formula 1 cars . . . not right up their exhaust pipes. Ever since that Atlanta flip I've worried that something is going to lift and the car will skate out.

' "Ronnie said in Austria this year that he tucked in behind me on the first lap and his car just washed completely out across the road and nearly hit the guardrail . . . I *know* that's what it's going to do — I don't need anyone to tell me what's likely to happen . . . so I don't run within cooee of anyone for that reason. Maybe I don't race as well as I used to, but I know how easy it is to get yourself sucked in and flung off the road. It's just one of those things. The older you get the more you begin to realise that it's more difficult than it looks. All right, it might never happen again, but I'm just not prepared to take that risk, sucking right in behind and hoping to dive out at the end of the straight and go by. I'd probably dive out but I know I'm only faking because I know I'm nowhere near enough to go past them under braking unless they make a mistake . . ."

'Just what does Denny Hulme plan to do with himself now that he has retired? Frankly, he doesn't know. He says he has saved enough money to live comfortably for the rest of his life without having to work again. He will eventually take his family back to live in New Zealand and he talks vaguely of a small farm, a comfortable home, enough land to keep the neighbours at bay and be self-sufficent. A few cows, perhaps. Some sheep. A garden where he could grow enough vegetables to be self-sufficient . . . independent.

'Hulme's fierce disapproval of regimentation and officialdom in its many forms at race tracks met its match at Indianapolis. The Speedway survives in its adherence to rules and principles that could have been drafted at the time of the Civil War and administered by men who look as though they may have taken part in it. When Denny Hulme arrived at Indianapolis he was a very small cog in a large machine and was constantly reminded of it. Instead of rebelling completely, he actually came to like and appreciate the weird rites of Indianapolis. But it was a type of racing that out-paced him. In 1967 he was fourth in the 500 driving for Smokey Yunick, in 1968 he was fourth again, but this time in one of Dan Gurney's Eagles. In 1969 he was up to second when the clutch failed on his Eagle. In 1970 he missed the race recovering from his burns and in 1971 with the new M16 McLaren he qualified fourth but dropped out with engine failure. Peter Revson started off the pole that year in a car identical to Hulme's, and that was enough for Denny. He never raced at Indy again.

' "I stopped racing at Indy because it was very, very difficult for me to qualify. I could race all right, but I couldn't qualify like those guys who

^
Denny with his Eagle after qualifying at Indianapolis in 1968.

∧
In the M23 Yardley McLaren in the 1973 South African Grand Prix at Kyalami.

∧
In the M19 at the 1971 Spanish Grand Prix on the Montjuich circuit.

Denny with Adele, Martin and Greeta at Heathrow airport.

∧
In contemplative mood on the CanAm series in North America.

∧
Denny in 'The Dipper' at Bathurst in the Holden Monaro he shared with Larry Perkins in 1988.

∧
In the TWR Rover at the Österreichring in Austria in 1986.

∧
Promo postcard for Denny's Eta Ripples Scania racing truck.

"There comes a time when all good bears should be in bed."

Friday 25th October 1974
Ballroom,
The Carlton Tower,
London.

∧

The Pooh Bear menu for Denny's farewell dinner in London, signed by Denny to his goddaughter, Selina Young, in October 1974.

∧
The Hulme/Miles Ford at Le Mans in 1966.

∧
The final Bathurst laps in 1992. Denny in the BMW M3 he was racing when he succumbed
to a heart attack.   COURTESY HULME FAMILY COLLECTION

∧
Less than two months before high wings are outlawed, Denny takes the be-winged McLaren
M7A to third in the Race of Champions at Brands Hatch.   COURTESY EOIN YOUNG COLLECTION

could tweak themselves up and get a good quick time just for four laps. When the race starts they're all right, they're in the race, the pressure's off and they go round and round to try to pick up the money. I enjoyed the race, but I didn't enjoy the first three weeks at Indy trying to get up to speed and qualify. It just became a big problem and I figured I was better off without all the aggravation so I thought, 'To hell with it.' I didn't want to go back and the team arranged a better driver so it was a good arrangement: I didn't go back and they picked up Gordon Johncock."

'If 38 is too old to go racing, what is the right age? "If you could plonk your bum in the seat of a Formula 1 car by the time you're 20, that's the time when you get the best feel for a car. I don't say you'll win then, but you'll get the feel and in a few years you'll have the feel, the technique and the whole works put together that will enable you to win races. You might win a couple when you're 21, but you'll only do it on sheer guts, no brains, that sort of thing. After a while you get the technique and it works for everything, brains, feel, guts and the whole thing . . . you understand it much better.

' "It's important to get the breaks, of course. If you're an unknown with no persuasion and have to buy your own car and go through the whole rigmarole, you're going to be 30 before you're in Formula 1, but if you're lucky and can find a good talker and a good sponsor, you'll get in younger with a much better opportunity."

'It comes as no surprise to hear Hulme talking about Jody Scheckter as the driver with most potential, because it was Hulme who acted as coach and mentor to the impressionable young South African when he began his Formula 1 career with the McLaren team. He was a young colonial as Hulme had been when he first arrived on the European scene and Denny was giving him a break, the benefits of his experience. Another driver might have been content to let the young charger find out for himself. Other drivers made a point of it, but Hulme took Scheckter under his wing.

' "I think without a doubt, Jody is the driver with the most potential, although I think on the day Ronnie is the guy who can screw himself up the most, who can pull out the extra little bit. I know that Emerson is very quick, but he drives very much within himself, he's racing at 9.75-tenths, with just a fraction in hand. I know Ronnie steps over the limit and goes ten-tenths or more and Jody does on occasions, but not that often. I think Jody backs off a wee bit as well. Most of the others drive right on their limit, but it's generally a limit that is lower than the guys I've mentioned."

'Boredom is one of the factors that could prompt a racing driver to put off retirement, but Hulme has never been a jet-set socialite, flitting between the bright lights as a member of an international celebrity group. He almost gives the impression that race weekends intruded on his lawn mowing, or pottering around in the gardens of his modern new home in St George's Hill, the wealthy private park near Weybridge in Surrey, where the address can double the price of a dwelling. "I don't think I'll be bored. I know I'll miss a certain kind of life that I've semi-enjoyed, but I've never been overawed by grandiose things. Staying at posh hotels and having flunkies open the door bothers me more than it makes me happy. I'd sooner hump my own bags into the hotel, get my own lift, and do things for myself. I guess I grew up different to other people. I just can't accept that these guys aren't spongers . . . most people think that that's their job, but to me they're spongers . . ."

'Denny drives a 4.2 XJ6 Jaguar, the economics of a V12 confuse him and he's happy with the 4.2 six. He may get a Range Rover for New Zealand; something to tow a boat. He has tracked down and bought back the MG TF he first raced and plans its leisurely restoration. He is trying to buy the first of the M23 Formula 1 McLarens, as well as an M8 CanAm car to form the basis of a small private collection and he talks of equipping a small machine shop to help with his hobby.

'Steam shows in England have taken his fancy recently and stationary engines, steam or petrol, from the early 1900s look like being a hobby soon. He already has a 1912 Amoco stationary engine, bought on a summer trip home two years ago.

'The record shows that Denny Hulme has raced in 112 Grand Prix in 10 years of Formula 1 competition. He won eight of these, set seven fastest laps, yet started only one Grand Prix from pole position — the South African Grand Prix in 1973. He was Rookie of the Year at Indianapolis in 1967. He won two CanAm crowns and a total of 22 wins in the McLaren CanAm cars. His father, Clive Hulme, had his bravery on Crete in the Second World War recognised by the award of the Victoria Cross. Courage obviously runs in the family, because it certainly takes courage to take the decision to retire from Grand Prix racing.'

In the October of Denny's final season in 1974, Philip Morris Europe put on 'A Dinner Party in honour of Denny Hulme, Racing Driver, given by his friends on his retirement' at the Carlton Tower in London. The cover art of the menu shows an E.H. Shepherd Pooh Bear heading into the sunset, titled 'There comes a time when all good bears should be in bed.' My wife Sandra found a copy of the menu while I was writing this book, made special because Denny had signed it 'To Selina with best wishes, October '74.' It was special because Selina was our daughter . . . and Denny was her godfather.

22 The appeal of Africa

Perhaps it was the similarity to home in New Zealand, plenty of sunshine and an outdoor approach to life, but Denny always enjoyed his time in South Africa.

Paddy Driver was a South African charger of similar age to Denny, and he had come up through motorcycle racing. Four years after his retirement from Formula 1, Denny and Paddy shared the drive in a Ford F100 pickup truck for the Total Trans Kalahari Road Race in 1978, an overland event covering 1000 kilometres in two gruelling 500-kilometre sections. The invitation came at short notice, but Denny looked forward to getting back into a new kind of competitive excitement and after the event he wrote about it in *Autosport* with his usual enthusiasm.

'Paddy Driver — with whom I get along very well — built up this truck from scratch three years ago and he had been improving the thing all the while. The 6-litre Ford V8 has a Paxton blower on it, pumping 5 lb of boost at 4000 rpm, which in the higher altitudes gives it a good performance. The gearbox is a heavy-duty Ford Type C6 automatic with an American B&M hotrod conversion. The conversion is primarily like a manual box in that the particular gear you select stays there, and to change gear you just bang the lever like a motorcycle gearshift; it then selects the next ratio up or down automatically. In this case, the gear lever was mounted high up between driver and navigator, because most of the time the navigator was swapping the ratios while the driver was wrestling with the wheel and left-foot braking. The driver called out the different numbers of the gears he wanted, but after a while this wasn't necessary, because we knew exactly what was needed. After spins and stalls, the navigator made the necessary "N" shift and used the key to restart the engine; all the instruments were located his side of central, high between the seats. And written across the dash was the legend *Hang on to your nuts* . . .

'The truck had enormous strength and tremendous ground clearance, fitted with 1100 x 15 American off-road tyres. I only drove the truck for about a kilometre and a half outside Paddy's front gate (for a press photo-call) before Paddy and I flew in his own Mooney to Gaborone, the capital of Botswana, where the event was to start.

'After clearing customs, Paddy filed a local flight plan and off we went on a two-hour jaunt following the so-called "roads" and cattle tracks we were going to be driving over in two day's time. From the air, you couldn't see all the washouts and so on, but I could see the lay of the land and got the message loud and clear that if you broke down, you didn't wander off for help but waited for help to come to you . . .

'It was going to be compulsory to carry at least two gallons of water, sleeping bags, food, matches to light a fire for a cold night and (in the final instructions) malaria tablets for the mosquito bites. There is also a little cattle tick which can suck the blood, and you come up in a type of boil, accompanied by a headache and nausea. The temperature in the afternoon is 25–30°C and, at night, zero. Hence the sleeping bags and matches . . .

'A friend of Paddy's set off the night before the start with spare wheels, shocks, axles etc, plus a tent, and he camped out halfway towards the overnight halt — commenting afterwards about the noises of all the animals, especially the restless hyenas. His truck was a 3-ton International 4-wheel-drive vehicle, with a tank winch on the front and compressors, electric drills, showers — in fact, you name it, he had it. His son was also competing. He is a person who goes walk-about in the desert just for kicks with his rig. When he gets to a river he will choose not to cross by the bridge but to drive the truck across, winching it through if necessary; it wastes hours but he enjoys every minute!

'It was hot, even for winter, when we landed the Mooney again. Gaborone can only have a population of 12,000–15,000 and the whole of Botswana has only about 800,000 inhabitants. After completing the 1000 kilometres, I still don't know how they did an accurate count, because the place is just a desert.

'The race truck was driven up from Jo'burg by another friend of Paddy's, along with another F100 (also Paddy's) full of more spares — and fuel. The race truck used aviation gas, 70 gallons in two tanks. An extra 20-gallon tank had been added for this event because we were going to do the whole of the first 500-kilometre section without a stop, although there was a fuel depot at 250 kilometres for the smaller cars and bikes. Of the 159 vehicles entered, 21 were motorcycles.

'To determine starting positions, a huge old cotton field was used with a one-lane 4-kilometre track bulldozed right round it. The competitors were set off at 30-second intervals on this track, and the time they recorded gave them their starting positions. The start itself was a Le Mans start, believe it or not. We were all to line up diagonally parked on the right-hand side of an 8-kilometre straight stretch of dirt road before the cattle tracks started.

'Paddy and I did several high-speed runs down this dirt road, and several runs for about 8 more kilometres of the track which followed. So we knew the first few miles of the route pretty well. On these runs, the engine would miss at about 130 kph, so we changed the electrics. That didn't help, so we fitted bigger jets. The bigger the jets, the faster we went: 150 kph, then 160 kph. We figured that was good enough, since there weren't going to be many places where we could do that kind of speed, and anyway the fuel consumption would get a bit frightening — about 8 kilometres to the gallon!

'At 7.30 a.m. on Friday morning, 12 May, we all lined up. We were in thirty-first position at the start, although I questioned our qualifying time, because by our stopwatch I figured we should have been much higher up the grid. Five minutes before the gun, I cleared all the big rocks down the left-hand side of the road, way out onto the grass — we were going to have our own track! Paddy was to drive the first 500 kilometres nonstop; if we made it to the night stop, I figured that then I would know how it all worked.

'The gas canister gun went off, and we went straight from the right-hand side of the road to the left, blocking anyone behind, slid 50 yards, and there — in the track I had cleared earlier — was a buggy on its roof. Apparently this guy had jumped the gun and someone had pulled out and hit him, rolling him over. I spoke to him after the event; he told me he was absolutely petrified, because he had seen me clearing the rocks, and when he found himself on his head, he remembered that a two-ton Ford would be using that very lane . . . We were, but we managed to miss him and everyone else.

'At the end of the 8-kilometre road we were running about ninth, weaving from right to left and back again at 140 kph in a total blackout caused by all the dust. At the first of the big "yumps" on the cattle track, we landed on the tail of a buggy: nudge, nudge, seventh place . . .

'Paddy doesn't have a reputation quite like Parnelli Jones, but how can you argue with a 2-ton truck?

'After about 190 kilometres we were second, flattening trees, and we had one big moment when we failed to take a corner, went up an anthill, came down sliding sideways, up another bigger hill — and by this time we were all ready to roll. Paddy had both hands on the roof and both of us were hanging in the belts, but luckily the steering decided to unwind the correct way (all eight turns of it); Paddy, driving in shorts, got two lovely wheel burns on his legs, very close to his privates . . .

'We set off again after Bobby Olthoff, who was in the lead from the pole in a turbocharged Chevrolet Nomad (a local South African vehicle). At the next control we were 3 minutes behind, but 20 kilometres later we overtook him on a section which is all huge, sharp, white marble rocks. We were in the lead for about 2.5 seconds and BANG — we stuffed a front tyre. So we had to do a very quick, unrehearsed tyre change (if you can reckon changing truck tyres quick — it took about 3 minutes). We were back to third place.

'We had to park off this cattle track to let the other competitors through, and the country is covered in a bush called Wag n' Bietjie (pronounced Vuk in Bikkie), which translated means "wait a bit" because you literally have to stop and detach yourself.

'Then, on the fuel stop, Bobby was there refuelling, so we flashed by, back into second place. But we got lost 200 yards from the control, screwed up on the sheet and lost 5 or 6 minutes. We went back to the control and asked directions (politely) and then took off on a 20-kilometre straight, a 100 kph rough section. Then the engine stopped. Out we got, lifted the hood, and for no reason swapped the wires on to the other coil. The engine started off again after about 90 seconds, but we were in third once more.

'Later we passed the buggy stopped, and then Olthoff with his hood up, his blower pipe having blown at the intake manifold. We were first again!

'Out of the wilderness, we now came to this fabulous three-lane highway. It's dead straight for 100 kilometres, and made with a compass and 'dozer. We only used a portion of its length; it's 100 foot wide, with three deep sets of tracks down it about 18 inches deep (no cars use this road, only 4-wheel-drive vehicles and cattle trucks). Less than one mile down it, at 140 kph, the Ford jumped the tracks and we cleared all three lanes, ending up in the boondocks. The engine stalled, and you know what hot V8s are like to start after flooding. Olthoff sped by, but we were soon in pursuit again. Another mile at 145 kph, and what did it do? The same bloody thing, only this time 10 times more frightening, clearing all three lanes and ending up on top of a big tree-cum-bush — some performance, these V8s! We backed out, but talk about difficulties in the soft sand to get across into the correct lane again!

'Then we switched on the extra 20-gallon tank pump, and it didn't work — and the gauge on the 50-gallon tank said empty. We only had 8 kilometres of this road to the finish, and this was also where the Ford was going to kill everyone dead. What happened? It suddenly became the Total Economy Run. Mind you, I was much happier at 90 kph, then 80 kph, then 60 kph. We passed Bobby with a blowout, but he overtook our snail again, and a buggy also passed us. We managed to reach the last control with about 1.5 gallons in the big tank and 16 in the 20-gallon tank, so the pump must have worked for a while; we found a wire had come off the Bendix pump. We arrived at the control and overnight stop very relieved, 92 seconds behind Olthoff.

'The overnight stop was at a place called Kue Pan ("pan" is an area that floods when the rain comes). This one was quite big, and looked like a wheat field with sand holes in it; when we had flown over it two days before, it had had eight ostriches on it.

'All the drivers were reliving their experiences, and there were people telling tales about crashes, rolls, punctures and so on all over the place. Some were checking in after only 250 kilometres and I didn't envy them that extra 250 they still had to do — it would be dark by the time they finished. And talk about dust! We were clean compared with the open buggies. The first bike in (Keith Rivers' KTM) did the section 14 minutes quicker than the cars, and you had to take your hat off to the bike competitors (I also had a trail-ride bike in New Zealand now); no navigators and no route sheet, which they all leave behind, but they started two hours after the cars so they could follow the carnage and the tracks.

'Other than fuel, the truck was in good shape. A hot shower and a tent were rigged up while we checked the truck. The womenfolk of the Gaborone Four-Wheel-Drive Club had a big tent and a huge barbecue ready at 6 p.m., we had a good feed and then climbed into the sleeping bags. Talk about cold! There was a frost, so I slept in my Nomex gear, with the sleeping bag right over my head. And we were inside a tent — what about the guys missing? Sleeping bags were taken to the overnight stop for the bike competitors too.

'Next morning we were up at daylight and had bacon and eggs, toast and coffee. As it was Paddy's birthday, we were really hoping for a win.

'After the 9 a.m. start, we were going to run the first 250 kilometres in the same direction as the day before, then the second 250 backwards to home. This time we started as we finished, at the same intervals up to the first hour, then those after that time left at 20-second intervals; the fastest bikes left with us.

'For the first 5 kilometres, I widened their so-called roads. We could look back in the mirror as we went through the thorn bushes at 85 kph, and watch the bushes come out of the back like confetti. I also wanted to know how Paddy felt, because he hadn't even seen me drive the Ford. He just grinned and said, "Hoch mon, just send it!"

'After 20 kilometres, we caught up with the buggy, then the quickest bike, and then Olthoff. We were first again. We were running 100–110 kph on this 50-kilometre rough section, opening 25 kilometres in the air and 25 kilometres deep into the sand; they all said they could see our diff's marks all the way.

'When we approached the end of the section, Paddy said he thought the chassis was stuffed, because the rollover bar behind the cab was now banging it! So, steady does it over this rough veldt (no more roads).

'Then the bike passed us, and we were back onto the three-lane road. I told Paddy to tell me when we got to 100 kph, as I thought that would be quick enough, and a spin would waste so much time. I had no instruments facing me except the fuel gauge and ammeter, and what does Paddy do? I say what's our speed? He says 90, so I go faster. What now? Paddy says 100.

I try a bit more. Paddy says 105, so I settle for 105–110. I found out at the end he was docking 20 kph off the clock, but we made it all the way with no serious leaping out of the rails.

'At the Kue Pan control we were 8 minutes in front. We overtook the bike, which had stopped for fuel. He caught us a short while later along with a film helicopter, hovering just above us; we just jumped out of this very deep sandy rut and let the bike go through. In the confusion we missed a right-hand turning on to the veldt, so we travelled another 6 kilometres to a turnaround and went back, our hearts in our mouths in case there was someone else doing the same. Half an hour later, there was a big accident there when the bike that had passed us before and a mate were coming back onto the course, and had a head-on with a buggy which had also wrong-slotted. One bike (Keith's) leapt off the track, the other didn't. It took 5 hours to get a helicopter to the scene to take the injured rider to hospital at Gaborone and then on to Jo'burg the next day.

'Anyway, we lost about 10 minutes, which of course would have put us 10 minutes down the other road, so that was like 20 minutes lost. We decided the best thing to do was to take it a bit steady, get closer to home, and then go for it. By this time the chassis was completely broken on the driver's side, and all the time the gap between the cab and deck was opening and closing 3 or 4 inches. We imagined the cab and the rear tray and wheels parting any time, and we hadn't arrived at the rocks yet! We took it very easy over this section, and at the next control we were in second place again, 9 minutes behind a Toyota Land Cruiser, which had started 30 seconds behind us at the morning start.

'The next incident came when I hit a rock in a thorn bush and blew another front tyre. We had a quick change this time, but at the next control we were 2 minutes behind. Then there was a peculiar smell in the cab and a noise like a tyre rubbing on the chassis. We couldn't identify the smell, and at the finish we found that the radiator had broken and dropped onto the very expensive Kevlar glassfibre fan, which instead of 8-inch blades, now had 4-inch ones! Paddy used to use a steel-blade fan until this same thing happened, caught the rad and stuffed it, so the glass blades paid off.

'We still had two high-speed sections to go where we could stretch the Ford's legs. It was still good at high speed, so 170 kph, and the tyres at that speed were like gyroscopes, so she ran quite straight. Towards the end, the front shocks took a bashing, so the old girl was like a bucking bronco, bending in the middle and just bounce-bounce-bounce. After the final 20 kilometres, including two small rivers and 8 kilometres of flat-out straight, we finished a very welcome second, 15 minutes behind the Toyota Land Cruiser of Tibney and Beswich. They were both local people, and they were tremendously popular winners. They ran the Toyota in four-wheel-drive all the time, for the trouble with two-wheel-drive was that if you ever stopped in the sand, that was almost the end.

'I was really impressed by the bikes. The riders spent half the night digging out thorns (which were like barbed wire, even giving car tyres punctures). I couldn't believe the riders' hands and shoulders, with thorns right through fingernails! Then there was the Peugeot two-wheel-drive pick-up that finished — Peugeots always seem to do so well in darkest Africa, and this 404 won its class.

'Everyone asked me whether I would come back. You know what they say about banging your head against a brick wall — it's great when it stops. But I could take some aspirin, and I just can't wait to go back to Botswana for the Total Trans Kalahari.

'I almost forgot. Did you hear what the hurricane said to the coconut palm tree? "Hang on your nuts — this is going to be no ordinary blow . . . !" '

Denny's affinity with motorsport in South Africa meant his curiosity was piqued by an entry of classic cars under the 'AFRICA Racing' banner at a Pukekohe race. He strolled over for a chat. Which part of South Africa did they come from? They looked at Denny curiously. Didn't he know what the acronym stood for? Denny probably didn't know what an acronym was, so he asked. It stood for 'Another Fucking Race I Can't Afford' . . .

23 The Bear goes home

Michael Clark

Denny and Greeta had always planned to raise their family back in New Zealand. What they hadn't planned was that their holiday home, constructed in the early 1970s, would remain their permanent residence. The home was built on an idyllic water's edge site at Lake Rotoiti that they'd discovered almost by accident while back in New Zealand for the Tasman Series of 1967.

Lake Rotoiti is a half-hour drive from Rotorua, the 'thermal wonderland' in the Bay of Plenty in the North Island. The general area was well known to both of them and both sets of parents lived within 70 or 80 kilometres of the location by the time Denny and Greeta returned for good.

In Maori, Rotoiti means *little lake*, an indication of its size relative to the larger Lake Rotorua. On a summer's day drive around the lakes from Rotorua, Greeta and Denny happened upon this little piece of paradise. Denny could launch his boat *CanAm* at the end of his property and then power to Rotorua in a quarter of an hour.

Greeta was pregnant at the time and the purchase of the property was concluded after Denny had headed off for the South Island races. Martin Hulme was born in Tauranga Hospital while Denny was racing at Longford in the final round of the 1967 Tasman Championship. Greeta was induced so Denny could see his son before returning to England to commence what would be his world championship season.

The original Hulme plan was to build a house in Tauranga, an hour's drive north from Rotorua, on a site that overlooked the harbour and was close to Greeta's parents. For various reasons they never got around to it and the 'weekender' at Lake Rotoiti became home. It remains a 'weekender' to Greeta, daughter Adele and her husband Michael, a local doctor. They still have the site over at Tauranga and will probably build there one day. However, in 1976, as the Hulmes settled back into life in New Zealand, the property soon became one of 'Denny's projects'.

Greeta: 'We used to go over there and mow and mow — it was a horse paddock. There's a steep bank down to the railway line and Denis got someone with a bulldozer to make a track. In the summertime we'd be over there toiling — Denis would be busy with a motor-scythe (known in New Zealand as a noisy "weed-eater"). We planted lots of fruit trees — kiwi fruit, grape vines, and citrus.'

Part of the reason for not building at Tauranga immediately on their return to New Zealand was that Adele, by then five, had just started at the local school. Martin, who was eight, had gone off to board at the exclusive Southell school in Hamilton. 'It was about an hour and half drive and he was terribly worried about ever seeing us again. To make it worse, he had quite a posh Pommy accent and got teased about it.'

When he had any energy left after dealing to his property over at Tauranga, Denny took it upon himself to help out around the community — even if no one had actually asked him to do so, as Greeta recalls: 'Denis volunteered to help rebuild the hot pools — he was such a practical chap. He also did a lot of work around the area, mowing lawns of people he didn't know — almost as if it was his duty to do it. The first part of Rotoiti that people driving around the lake would see was overgrown with flax, so Denis took it upon himself, him and I, to clear it up. We had a winch on the front of the Range Rover and we winched all these flax bushes out and cleared it. One day a Department of Conservation guy stopped and asked what we were doing. Denis told him, "I'm not doing this for my sake, I'm just making it look a whole lot better than it is — the public should be able to see this lake and enjoy the view." '

Some top-level sportsmen play golf in their retirement; Denny Hulme became a self-appointed beautification crusader.

Greeta: 'He also got into trail bike riding for fitness, but his big love became all these stationary engines up the back in the shed — he'd notice where these things were rusting in fields — he had them earmarked all over the countryside, then he'd go back with a trailer, he'd pay a minimal amount to the farmer and then bring it back and restore it — they were just rusty old bits of junk.

'In England we used to go to traction steam fairs and he loved to see them mowing from one side to the other on a big wire rope. So he started at Pongakawa [the tiny settlement where Greeta and Denny grew up], where a neighbour had a stationary engine to cut his firewood.

'We came home one Christmas, the old chap had died and the engine was just rusting away. Denis salvaged it — this was his first one, it's still up in the shed . . . He'd get all the magazines so as to get all the colours right. The older the better. Funny really — at one end of the shed were all these old traction engines and at the other end of the shed was his McLaren M23! Such a contrast to Formula 1!'

Angus Hyslop, the 1962–63 New Zealand Gold Star champion, was one of Denny's oldest friends — since before they shared the class win at Le Mans in a Fiat Abarth. Greeta recalls a weekend with the Hyslops at their farm in the Hawke's Bay: 'Gus's neighbour had a stationary engine on a carriage that used to run a shearing shed. It was kept under a canopy, so it was never out in the weather. He said Denis could have it, so we took the race car trailer over to their farm and loaded this "thing" onto it. It hadn't run for years, but in no time Denis had it going. I went out to tell them dinner was ready and he and Gus just stood there with huge grins on their faces. They were in heaven! All they could say was, "Look at that." They were absolutely over the moon.

'He used to get so much pleasure — Denis hated to think of scrap metal going off to Japan — this drove him to "save" these contraptions. He's got one of most things. I suppose it was a hobby bordering on obsession!'

And so, in his fortieth year and within two seasons of retiring from the front line of professional motor racing, Denny was working his land, undertaking odd voluntary jobs around the area he lived in, playing with his traction engines, boating on *CanAm* with its aluminium big-block Chevrolet engine, and fettling with his racing cars — his first and last. His last racing car was the McLaren M23, a gift from the team when he retired. It was his 1973 Swedish Grand Prix race-winning car, chassis M23/1, in the Yardley colours.

The first car Denny raced — the MG TF — had also joined his stable. He was 19 when the little red convertible was acquired in 1955, and at the end of 1988 he completed its restoration after he'd repurchased it nearly 20 years after first taking possession.

Not long after the Hulmes returned to settle in New Zealand, Phil Kerr decided that he'd had enough of Formula 1 and also came home. A few months later Mike Hailwood and his family arrived, deciding to immigrate permanently. The Hailwoods settled close to Kerr on Auckland's North Shore and during the course of 1976 they hatched a plan to contest the Benson and Hedges 500 — a 500-kilometre race for New Zealand-assembled cars. The race had been dominated by the Chrysler Charger since 1972, but Hailwood and Kerr reckoned the new four-door Holden Monaro could break the stranglehold.

Phil hadn't raced for years, but in 1958 he had been one of three finalists for the inaugural New Zealand Grand Prix Association Driver to Europe scheme. As Phil recalls, three decades on: 'Denny became our fan club. He thought it was just hilarious, the two of us wallowing around in this big saloon car with no brakes. We didn't win, but we had a marvellous time — Denny thought we were quite mad . . .'

The Chargers won again in 1977 and for 1978 the rules were altered to include slightly modified imported cars of up to 2 litres. Phil Kerr reckoned a Ford Escort RS2000 would be the way to go for himself and Hailwood. He recalls: 'Denny was back as our cheerleader and one day, while we were testing at Pukekohe, I asked if he wanted a go.' Denny did and from that moment Kerr slipped into a more managerial role as both Ford and race sponsor Benson and Hedges rejoiced in having not one but two World Champions in the race — and in the same car! The Escort was painted near enough to 'McLaren orange', with the drivers' surnames in large lettering on the side panels.

Kerr: 'It was a quick little car and before long, they were in the lead. Sadly, a stone went through the radiator causing major overheating problems and they retired — but this seemed to whet Denny's appetite.'

A few weeks later he had the chance to race again, thanks to an invitation to compete in a celebrity support race at Macau. The event, around the streets of the Portuguese colony, was Macau's annual motor race and a chance for future stars to put their name in lights back in Europe while motor racing was on hold during the winter. By the late 1970s the 'Grand Prix' category was Formula Pacific (similar to Formula Atlantic, as it was known in North America and Britain); however, the stars of the 1978 event were not Grand Prix drivers but the contestants in what was billed as the 'Race of Giants'.

A quality field of legends of the sport was assembled by British-born Hong Kong-based entrepreneur Bob Harper, including Prince Bira, Jack Brabham, Emanuel de Graffenried, Dan Gurney, Mike Hailwood, Hans Hermann, Phil Hill, Denny Hulme, Jacky Ickx, Innes Ireland, Stirling Moss, Roy Salvadori, Jackie Stewart and Bobby Unser.

True to his word that he would never race again, Jackie Stewart took one of the identical Ford Escorts out in practice . . . and promptly rolled it! Ickx comfortably won the race, while Denny finished in the wheel tracks of his old boss and team-mate Brabham in sixth, having qualified fifth, one place ahead of Moss.

In 1978 Denny involved himself in an LPG company, set up by former racing mechanic Grant Duncan who had a service station at Kopu on the Coromandel outside Thames. Grant had met Denny on the European circuits. 'It progressed from getting Denny involved financially to the point where the company was re-named Hulmegas,' he says. His sister-in-law, Paula Duncan, designed the special flame emblem that was patented and registered. 'The plan was to have our own company, with the gas coming from the Maui field and being put to automotive use. We were importing kits from the US and Holland, and converting cars.' Grant eventually sold his shares but said that Denny stayed involved and the company expanded into bottled gas, with a delivery service of Hulmegas trucks around the Coromandel Penninsula. Grant and his wife Tina went on to establish the prestigious White Tie Catering company in Christchurch.

Denny raced in the Benson and Hedges 500 again in 1979, this time partnered by none other than Stirling Moss. The venerable Chrysler Charger had won again in 1978, despite the fact that production of them had stopped some years earlier and the rules had changed to encourage more competition. For 1979 the field was limited to 2-litre cars — the obvious contenders being the Volkswagen Golf Gti (choice of Hulme and Moss), Alfa Romeo GTV, Fiat 131R and BMW 320i. One of the drivers pitched against the Hulme/Moss combination was Jack Brabham, who was sharing a BMW with Ross Jensen. Another Golf GTi won the race, but Denny and Stirling were second after endless tyre troubles.

Greeta: 'He had the bug back and wanted to go racing again. He had spare time, probably too much spare time, but he found that he enjoyed it. He had tried to keep himself busy, but he didn't have enough to keep himself occupied. The motor racing fire was certainly re-ignited by that trip to Macau. That got the group going . . . it was our first chance to socialise with a lot of our old friends.'

And was Greeta concerned that her husband was returning to the dangerous world of motor racing? 'I was pleased actually. At home he'd come supermarket shopping with me and he'd be putting things back on the shelves saying, "Why do we need this?" — he didn't like spending money — and I thought, "How can I live with this?" '

The timing of Denny being rebitten by the motor racing bug coincided with the introduction of the New Zealand Benson and Hedges Production Saloon car series. Whereas previously there was just one race for such cars — the 500-kilometre race at Pukekohe — from 1981–82 there would be a championship that even attracted Australian touring car legend Peter Brock. Brock, in fact, won the 1982–83 title with former open-wheeler ace David Oxton. The 1983–84 championship was also won by Holden's new SS Commodore model, but the backgrounds and level of racing experience of the two drivers involved — Denny Hulme and Ray Smith — could not be more different. And the car was painted gold . . .

Ray Smith's involvement with motor sport started as a sponsor, not a driver. By no means a motor racing enthusiast, the bronzed and golden-haired Smith had started the Auckland Coin and Bullion Exchange. He did very well and by the early 1980s had become a major player in the local gold market. One of his friends was Jonathan Gooderham, the then manager of Colin Giltrap's 'Coutts' prestige car firm in Auckland. And one of Gooderham's friends was Australian Greg 'PeeWee' Siddle, who just happened to be the manager of racing driver Roberto Moreno.

After dominating a star-studded field to win the Australian Grand Prix for Formula Pacific cars at the end of 1981, Moreno was brought to New Zealand to contest the 1982 summer series. There was just the matter of a sponsor needing to be found to finance the racing . . .

Enter Gooderham and Ray Smith. The pair met Moreno and his manager at a barbeque and did enough to get Smith interested. In fact, he was sufficiently impressed to do the deal and, in return for NZ$4500 in gold Krugerrands, his company's name adorned the cockpit surround of the Ralt.

Moreno won the championship without having to contest the final round. He'd won three of the four other rounds, including the prestigious New Zealand Grand Prix at Pukekohe, and the Lady Wigram Trophy. Smith was delighted with the coverage his firm received for his investment.

Later that year Gooderham suggested to Smith that perhaps he'd like to try *his* hand at racing. A Golf GTi was the agreed weapon of choice and the pair entered the Benson and Hedges 500. In his autobiography, *Where's the Gold?*, Smith wrote: 'Jonathan took me around the circuit a couple of times and scared the hell out of me. He then did about 10 laps and I went for a drive. By the end of the morning session I was consistently faster than Jonathan and the only other GTi at the meeting. I wasn't terribly surprised. I knew I was a good driver . . .'

After feeling he'd mastered the Golf, Smith turned his attention towards the front of the field: 'I was now keen to have a serious attempt at motor racing and I knew I needed a competitive car and co-driver.' He purchased Neville Crighton's successful Commodore and approached Denny to assess his ability '. . . or lack of it. At least I knew I sadly lacked experience and was keen to learn. Denny decided I had some potential and he was unlikely to be disgraced, so our partnership commenced.'

Denny not only became Smith's driving coach but also took over the testing, sorting and setting-up of the Commodore. The series was run over three races, the first at Bay Park near Mount Maunganui, not far from where Denny and Greeta grew up, followed by Manfeild near Palmerston North, and the finale at Pukekohe, just south of Auckland. Rumours and accusations of dodgy crankshafts and other dirty tricks flew amongst the leading contenders, as the team ordered a new Brock engine. Smith recalled the situation in his book:

'One of the conditions Denny had made when I asked him to drive with me was that he would not tolerate cheating and he was always very careful that we complied with the rules.' The Commodore that had won the opening round won again at Manfeild but was later disqualified, meaning that the gold Commodore was elevated to second and still in with a chance to take the title. The gold Hulme/Smith car actually ended up winning quite comfortably at Pukekohe and so the series was theirs. Smith: 'That was the only year the whole race had been televised live and the Auckland Coin and Bullion Exchange car received massive coverage. Business boomed.'

The introduction of Group A in 1982 put some order into European touring car regulations. Australia adopted the Group A rules in 1985 and the range of cars expanded to include the Holden Commodore and Ford Mustang. In the northern hemisphere the European Championship had been fought out between the BMW 635CSi and Jaguar's XJS, with growing pressure from the unlikely looking turbocharged Volvo 242. The British championship, meanwhile, had a 3.5-litre limit and was largely ruled by the slippery Rover Vitesse.

In 1985, when Ray Smith made his Bathurst debut, local contenders had emerged in the form of the Holden and Mustang — both 5.0 litre V8s — and the leading drivers were longtime rivals Brock and Dick Johnson.

Prior to the first Australian Touring Car Championship held under Group A regulations, New Zealand hosted the inaugural Wellington street race — the Nissan Mobil 500. It was televised live and resulted in massive enthusiasm for motor racing in New Zealand. If New Zealand could afford it, Group A looked like the way of the future, not just for saloon car racing, but for local motor racing generally.

Denny had made his Bathurst debut in 1982 driving for his old mate

Frank Gardner's JPS-sponsored BMW team in a Group C 635CSi with Stephen Brook. He joined the team again for the 1984 race, this time partnered by Prince Leopold von Bayern. They finished fifteenth overall and second in the Group A class.

In 1985 Denny went back to Bathurst with Ray Smith. Greeta recalls Smith clearly: 'He tried to sell us some gold bars but Denis said, "No way" — not unless he could take them away. He was very generous. Of course, he was living on Denis's fame so he could achieve something he'd never be able to do otherwise. We were at Bathurst and he gave me so much money to go shopping — I don't know how many hundred dollars — Denis was horrified by how much money he'd given me to go shopping. Denis wouldn't have given me half as much, let alone letting me loose downtown! We all had black shirts with gold logos. He was generous but really a "wanna-be".'

Prior to the 1985 Bathurst 1000, the pair entered the Sandown Park round of the Australian Endurance Championship to speed their learning curve. They were impressed with the presentation of the Commodore and surprised with its speed. They were the fourth fastest Holden and finished seventh. Smith was one of 11 Kiwis making their debut at Bathurst in 1985 — this high number coming as a result of the Group A formula.

Not surprisingly, Smith was slower than Denny, given it was his first look at the daunting Mount Panorama. The gold Commodore got steadily quicker and eventually qualified a highly respectable fourteenth, the fourth fastest Commodore. Denny was up to ninth after the first lap and held eighth at quarter-distance. They lasted until lap 146 (of 163), when the crankshaft disintegrated. They were running thirteenth at the time.

Soon after Bathurst, run on its then traditional first Sunday of October date, the New Zealand series was due to start at Manfeild. This event was a turning point for at least two drivers, and one of them was Ray Smith. Even before he entered motor sport, Smith was a close friend of Kent Baigent, a respected and talented touring car driver, who had also made his Bathurst debut in 1985. The introduction of Group A gave not only the Kiwis, but internationals too, the chance to see how quick Baigent was.

As usual Denny started the car at Manfeild and some 30 minutes into the race Baigent tried to put his BMW 635 past the gold Commodore at Higgins — a tight and tricky sharpish right-hander that leads onto the back straight. Smith takes up the story in *Where's the Gold?*: 'They were side by side coming down the back straight with neither prepared to give an inch. To enter the sweeper before the pit straight it is necessary to be on the left of the track. Kent tried to force his way in between Denny and the car in front, but Denny held his position. By this time they would have been travelling at close to 140 mph. Denny gave Kent a nudge at the critical moment. Kent's BMW flipped and bounced, flying probably 50 metres through the air, right through a display hoarding 6 metres high and landing in a field next to the track.'

It was one of the worst accidents witnessed in years in New Zealand and there were murmurings among some fans about the similarity of this incident to the Laurence Brownlie crash during the 1968 New Zealand Grand Prix. Some of those who had been prepared to give Denny the benefit of the doubt in that accident started to ask questions about just what sort of racer this guy Hulme was. Those who clearly did not view this as a racing accident were bandying about terms like 'ruthless'.

There had already been some history between the two, as Smith states in his book when talking about the start of 'the Great Race': 'Denny started for us and on the very first lap, Kent Baigent, racing a BMW, almost pushed him off the track at Forest Elbow, just before pit straight. Denny was furious. When he came in and I took over the driving, he confronted Kent's manager. Denny was angry because, in his opinion, Kent's manoeuvre on the first lap of a six-hour race was stupid and dangerous. He had almost been forced into the wall and couldn't move because he was being held up by slower cars . . . Denny was angry enough to issue Kent a warning: "Play games with me again laddie and look out." (That threat was not idle, as I found out to my dismay one month later.)'

Baigent was rushed to hospital with serious head injuries and in a critical condition after his helmet had exploded off his head after the first impact. Smith: 'I too was in a dreadful state. My car with my partner at the wheel had executed a dreadful payback on one of my best friends. I drove a terrible race and immediately it had finished I rushed to the hospital. Kent's wife Erica was there and we were both appalled at his injuries. Kent was unconscious and there was some doubt he would survive. I confronted Denny afterwards. While he said he was very sorry that Kent was badly injured he was quite remorseless. His last comment to me on the matter was, "Better he get the message now, than after he kills one of us."

'Without doubt, Denny was the most experienced driver in our series. He never bent the car and was always in the top two or three. You don't get those results consistently unless you have enormous natural talent. But they didn't call him "The Bear" for nothing. Kent was absolutely fearless and a very good driver. I was unable to clear my own mind whether Denny was annoyed at being beaten by Kent or was really concerned at his aggressiveness. Racing lost its glamour for me after Kent's accident.'

Also losing its glamour for Smith were the costs of Group A, as he explained in *Where's the Gold?*: 'During 1985, a meeting was held to decide if the competitors in saloon car racing wanted to stay with current regulations. They required unmodified New Zealand-built cars, or certain imports if imported in large enough quantities, [and] to use road rubber . . . The alternative was Group A . . . Denny was the only negative voice at the meeting — "None of you realises what Group A will cost you. You will destroy saloon car racing in New Zealand for all but the very wealthy." He was dead right but out-voted.'

Smith's accountant advised him that he'd spent over $400,000 on motor racing in the previous 12 months, so he decided to retire and sold up.

Baigent's situation improved and he was soon back racing. He remains a wealthy and successful businessman. Smith's life since retiring from motor racing has been far from a fairytale. His company, Goldcorp Holdings, collapsed, leaving some 1600 investors out of pocket and more significantly, out of gold. Was it a Hulme premonition that he didn't want to be paid in gold unless he could take the bars home with him, or simply Denny's adherence to the old adage that 'cash is king'. You can be assured Denny Hulme wasn't one of the 1600 unhappy investors.

The Bathurst that had seen Smith's debut had been won for Jaguar by TWR (Tom Walkinshaw Racing), but after that Tom decided to focus on the other Leyland product that was a contender in Group A — the Rover Vitesse. Walkinshaw was as good a touring car driver as he was a businessman. A shrewd and tough Scot of sturdy build, he'd started out in open-wheelers — initially a Lotus Formula Ford and then a Hawke, in which he won the Scottish championship. Formula 3 and England beckoned and in 1970, at the age of 23, he headed south — seriously under-financed but full of determination and steely resolve. After breaking his legs in a works March and abbreviated forays into Formula 2 and Formula 5000, he settled in saloons, being hired by Ford for their Capri attack on the 1974 British Touring Car Championship.

He formed TWR in 1975. The business grew from touring car preparation to both road and racing car development, design and construction. TWR was variously associated with BMW, Mazda, Jaguar, Rover, Aston Martin, Ford, Holden, Volvo and Porsche. Such was the reputation of the group, that it was not uncommon for Walkinshaw to be working with two or more manufacturers at any one time.

TWR had involvement in sports-prototype racing as well as touring cars and in 1992 Tom himself was employed by the Ford-backed Benetton Formula 1 team as 'engineering director'.

In 1986, though, the Rover Vitesse was about to be phased out, but Tom figured that, in Group A form, it had another season left in it. In 1984 TWR had run the Rovers alongside the Jaguar XJS in the European Touring Car Championship, with Walkinshaw himself aboard the leading V12-powered 'big cat'.

After Jaguar's withdrawal at the end of that year, the focus shifted to the Rover programme for 1985, which faced a growing threat from the 2.0-litre turbocharged Volvo 240, and the omnipresent BMWs. After 14 rounds the Volvos prevailed by a whisker — seven wins to six — from the TWR Rovers, while BMWs sole win came in the Spa 24-hour race.

The 1986 European Touring Car Championship was effectively a watershed, it being the last year when Group A remained something of a lottery amongst four or five manufacturers. In 1987 BMW introduced the M3, and Ford the Sierra-Cosworth. After that, the identity of the winning car became far more predictable.

Of course, Denny wasn't to know the historical significance of 1986, in touring car terms, when he, fellow Kiwi Neville Crighton and Australian Ron Dickson headed to Europe to be part of a TWR off-shoot known as 'South Pacific Racing'. Crighton and Dickson were to share one Rover, while TWR stalwart Jeff Allam would partner Denny.

Allam's father was a Vauxhall dealer in Surrey and young Jeff raced a homebuilt Viva while he was still a teenager. Although he'd started in karts, his career had been entirely in touring cars and after starring in Ford Capris in the late 1970s he joined the Rover programme in 1980, winning the British Grand Prix support race in July.

Twenty years on, Allam recalls being advised by Walkinshaw that his co-driver for the second half of the 1986 season would be the craggy 1967 World Champion. 'I felt very privileged — he just fitted in so well and not only did he and I become good friends, but he was a great family friend as well. My kids just adored him . . . good old Denny.'

Denny Hulme's return to racing in Europe took place on 4 May 1986 at the Misano circuit on Italy's Adriatic coast, where he was partnered by Crighton and Dickson in the fourth round of the championship. They finished ninth but were disqualified due to pitwork irregularities. BMW won from Volvo, while the Walkinshaw/Percy entry was a lap down in third.

For the next round in Sweden Denny was moved up to the 'Texaco' car, with Allam. He was familiar with the Anderstorp circuit for it was there, 13 years earlier, that he'd given the soon-to-be-legendary McLaren M23 its debut victory. In fact, in the very car (M23/1) that was sitting in his shed back in Rotoiti.

The locals won on the track in a Volvo-Rover-Volvo-Rover-Rover finish, but the Swedes were disqualified for using illegal fuel and so, months later, the fifth of Allam/Hulme became third. Amazingly, it was Volvo-Rover-Volvo-Rover-Rover again on the treacherous Brno circuit in Czechoslovakia on 8 June, with Allam/Hulme again fifth and that's how it stayed, as there were no disqualifications.

Denny spent the weekend immediately prior to his fiftieth birthday racing on the Österreichring in Austria, but despite qualifying fifth they had a range of problems and finished well down.

The Allam/Hulme Rover was absent from the next round on the new Nürburgring as they focussed on the Spa 24-hour race and their attempt to break the stranglehold BMW had on that event. The duo was joined by Armin Hahne. They qualified well in third, behind the lead Rover of Tom Walkinshaw/Win Percy/Eddy Joosen and a BMW in which Emanuele Pirro joined Roberto Ravaglia and Gerhard Berger.

It is a race that Allam remembers not for anchoring the first non-BMW spot (they finished sixth) but for another example of Hulme ingenuity and his loose attitude to sartorial elegance. Allam: 'It was bloody hot and of course even worse in the car. We couldn't believe it when Denny turned up with the bottoms of his overalls chopped off. It was a hilarious sight — we all just fell about. We thought he was taking the piss but he wasn't — that's how he drove . . . three-quarter length overalls and an open-faced helmet. That was Denny, he didn't care what people thought, just as long as he was comfortable.'

The next round of the championship was the Tourist Trophy at Silverstone on 7 September, a race Denny had won in Sid Taylor's V8 Chevrolet-powered Lola T70 in 1966. Two decades on, he was driving a very different sort of car in a series that was at its best in terms of the variety of machinery capable of winning.

Allam recalls the lead-up to the TT: 'Tom [Walkinshaw] had a new development engine but wasn't confident to run it in the race as he and Win Percy were on target for the title. I suggested he put it in our car and he agreed.'

They qualified fifth. Forty-four cars faced the starter for 107 laps of the 2.932-mile circuit. The winning car would travel 500 kilometres and was expected take just over 3 hours to do it. The pole-winning Rover of Gianfranco Brancatelli and Hahne was an early retirement, as was the quickest Sierra and a leading BMW.

Allam: 'Our car ran strong all the way through. We'd had a mixed season until then, but the Tourist Trophy was such a special race to win. Probably my biggest career win, now I come to think about it.' Only three cars finished on the same lap, a Schnitzer BMW between the winning Rover and the Walkinshaw/Percy entry. Their Istel-sponsored car had won by nearly 50 seconds.

Allam had driven about three-quarters of the race but, perhaps not surprisingly, the winners were presented to the waiting media as 'Denny and Jeff', something the 1967 World Champion was quick to put right, as Allam recalls: 'He said, "No, no, it's Jeff and Denny" — it was a nice touch, something he didn't have to do, but I'll always remember it. There was no ego with Denny. He just slotted into the team so well and we became great friends. It was a great privilege to be partnered with him.'

Denny went out on a high, as the Tourist Trophy was his final event in the campaign. His next race was back at Bathurst a month later. Silverstone was not only the last round of the 1986 Championship won by Rover, it was the last for the marque at the top level.

However, this wasn't the end of the friendship or connection between Allam and Hulme, as they would cross paths many times in New Zealand and Australia over the next few years. But as Allam recalls: 'He never changed. We'd still catch up for a meal and, just like back in Europe in '86, he'd always be wearing sponsor's giveaways — almost always a shirt with a logo, sometimes a jacket. On one occasion I remember him coming downstairs to leave for a restaurant with red trousers and a yellow top. I asked him, "Denny, are you seriously intending going out in public dressed like that?" And he said, "They're all clean!" He was such a simple, non-materialistic man.'

For Bathurst 1986 Denny was down to share a 2.3-litre Mercedes 190E-16 with Austrian skiing legend Franz Klammer. Born in 1953, Klammer had not only won the gold medal in the downhill event at the 1976 Winter Olympics at Innsbruck, but also largely dominated the event in the mid to late 1970s.

There was no way a 2323 cc Class B car was in contention to win, and given that the pole-winning Nissan Skyline was also in Class B, even winning the class would be a tall order. The Skyline qualified with a time of 2:17.159, compared with the Mercedes-Benz's 2:23.19, which was quicker than one of the two Volvos also in Class B. Denny and Franz ran strongly to finish ninth overall and second in Class B.

During the course of 1986, Denny had already raced four different Group A cars, in the form of the Smith golden 5.0-litre Holden Commodore, TWR's 3.5-litre Rover Vitesse, the Mercedes-Benz and a BMW 325i owned by his old mate and fellow Kiwi Billy Bryce. A month on from Bathurst and he was reacquainted with the TWR team, but not in a Rover.

In November 1986, Denny drove a Jaguar in the Fuji 5-hour race when Walkinshaw decided to give the XJS Jaguars one last outing — or in fact, three outings, as the Group A races in New Zealand were also part of a 'Big Cats' farewell tour — around the streets of Wellington in late January, and at Pukekohe a week later on 1 February.

The Fuji 5-hour race was held on the 4.4-mile Mount Fuji circuit, which Denny had not driven before as the first Japanese Formula 1 Grand Prix was run two years after he had retired. Also new to him was the large green V12 coupé he was to race with Armin Hahne. The Walkinshaw/Percy car secured pole position, with the Hulme/Hahne car third fastest. In the race their differential failed just before half-distance, but they at least lasted longer than the sister car, which was out after only six laps.

For the Wellington race, Denny was again partnered by Hahne. They qualified the big green V12 XJS third quickest behind the Skyline of Australians George Fury and Glenn Seton, and the Holden Dealer Team Commodore of Peter Brock and Allan Moffatt. In the other Jaguar Win Percy and Tom Walkinshaw were down in tenth spot on the grid, but neither Jaguar finished.

A week later and the situation was much different. Denny had been drafted into the Larry Perkins team to share the bespectacled Australian's Commodore, while Percy and Hahne piloted the lone Jaguar. Revelling in the greater power of the Perkins VK Commodore, the pair dominated the 500-kilometre race with the Enzed Fluid Connectors-sponsored car. Second place went to Percy and Hahne in the XJS.

Denny was by now arguably New Zealand's best known saloon car driver, notwithstanding that the first two Australian Touring Car Championships for Group A cars had been won by Kiwis.

So, for a 50-year-old who'd retired a dozen years earlier, he'd proven there was life in the old dog yet — he'd never really raced saloons or touring cars before, but had shown that, not only had he adapted quite easily, he could be more than competitive. As Chris Amon recalls: 'It was as if Denny was having a second childhood.'

Denny was back in the Perkins Engineering VK Commodore for the 1987 'James Hardie 1000' at Bathurst, but he never got a chance to race as Larry crashed out on the second lap after qualifying a brilliant eighth.

Bathurst was Round 8 of the World Touring Car Championship and a week later, on 11 October, Calder hosted Round 9. Things went better for the Perkins/Hulme car, which finished sixth and was the first V8, but they were off the pace a fortnight later around the streets of Wellington, qualifying twelfth and finishing eleventh, 10 laps in arrears.

If the Commodores had been losing ground to the turbocharged Sierras and nimble BMW M3s in 1987, the gap simply widened in 1988. With Brock having defected to BMW, Perkins and the newly created Holden Special Vehicles équipe, a joint venture between General Motors and TWR, was the leading team running locally built product.

The top 10 qualifiers for Bathurst in 1988 saw the defiant Perkins/ Hulme Commodore in eighth, albeit some 5 seconds off pole pace. The 5-litre V8 couldn't handle the Sierras and BMWs and expired with only 15 per cent of the race to run.

Things went better for the HSV Commodores at Adelaide, supporting the final round of the World Championship Grand Prix in a year dominated by McLaren in a fashion reminiscent of the 'Bruce and Denny show' in the CanAm series two decades earlier. One by one, the Sierras dropped out — the mercury still high despite the late afternoon running — and the HSV Commodores ran 1-2, to the delight of the partisan crowd. The dinosaurs finished in that order — Perkins from Hulme.

24 Countdown to a career

Michael Clark

Witnessing the performance of the 52-year old former world champion at Adelaide was his 21-year-old son Martin. Sadly, it would be last time they attended a Grand Prix together. Greeta: 'Denny was so proud of Martin, because he'd just completed his bachelors degree from Waikato University. For someone like Denis, who had very limited education, this was a fantastic thing. His friends, who hadn't seen Martin since we left England, couldn't believe how tall he was . . . Denis was really proud.'

Martin, due to return to Waikato University and study for his Masters in Earth Sciences, had taken a Christmas holiday job as the interim caretaker at the Manupirua Springs, a hot-pool complex near the Hulme property that could be accessed only by boat. Greeta: 'As Martin was on duty at the hot pools, we decided we'd all take Christmas dinner over to him. Mum Hulme [Rona] and Anita's family would travel to the Springs on their boat and Denis loaded up *CanAm* with tables, chairs and the food.'

Greeta recalls Anita telling her children not to swim straight after Christmas lunch. Martin was helping to entertain the younger children as his parents, aunt, uncle, and grandmother relaxed after lunch. Greeta: 'Martin dived into what was the shallow part after running up the jetty towards land. Anita was wiping down the tables and could see Martin face down in the water. The other children thought he was all right but, try as we might, we just couldn't resuscitate him.'

369

The passing of nearly 20 years since the diving accident that claimed Martin's life that day has not eased Greeta's pain. She recalls the speed at which Denny piloted *CanAm* back to the house with Martin's body on board, on what she frequently refers to as 'an awful, awful day'. A family day of celebration had turned out disastrously and it affected the entire family at what was a very delicate time in Greeta and Denny's marriage.

Greeta remembers a standard saying of Martin's: 'I'm a happy chappy'. 'He was always so very positive and content. He had a girlfriend and life was looking really good for him. He liked motor racing but didn't seem to have any desire to get involved. He'd happily go along with Denis, but I don't think he ever saw himself racing.'

It was early in 1989 that Denny stopped living at Lake Rotoiti permanently. Greeta: 'I seemed to be the only person who didn't know Denis was having an affair and that it had been going on for some time. You go through all these emotions — jealousy, revenge — you just torture yourself. I thought, "I can't help you". I needed my own resources to survive Martin. It was an absolute mess. But I just had to let him go. He had to find out for himself — it was awful, awful, awful.'

The woman who was the focus of Denny's affections was Auckland-based motoring journalist Sandy Myhre — a divorced mother of three sons. Although he'd left Rotoiti Denny would still sleep there from time to time in the self-contained downstairs area. Sometimes he would stay with his mother, but he spent increasing amounts of time at the home of Myhre.

Greeta: 'He'd pop back and would go out into the shed and work on his stationary engines. One day Adele said to me, "Mum, what's that noise?" It sounded like an injured animal, but it was Denis, sitting out there bawling his eyes out.' Adele, also struggling terribly with the loss of her brother, went out to the shed to try to pacify her dad but, as she recalls all these years later, 'it just wasn't possible'.

Greeta: 'Denny would spend hours at Martin's grave and he eventually gave up trail bike riding . . .' Trail bike riding was a pastime Denny and Martin had enjoyed doing together. For Denny it was a fitness regime, Hulme-style, but after Martin died, as Greeta says: 'He'd sit on his bike, up in the bush that he and Martin used to ride in, and just cry. He self-destructed. It was never the same for him without Martin.'

With the benefit of hindsight, Greeta believes Denny's 'bad behaviour' had been brewing since about 1986. 'I wondered if it was me, was I having a mid-life crisis? Or was it his male menopause? I just kept busy with the kids, playing badminton. I just hoped he was going through a bad patch.' Greeta eventually got herself a job, encouraged by her girlfriends, and also started to play golf. 'I tried to keep things as normal as possible. My emotions were all over the place. Something would trigger them off and you'd have to work through them all over again — it was not good.'

At the 'Shell Spectacular' in late January 1989, barely a month after Martin's accident, Denny was not surprisingly withdrawn and less approachable than normal. This classic racing car extravaganza was held at Ardmore — the first time the spiritual home of the New Zealand Grand Prix had been used for years. Chris Amon was there, reunited with his Maserati 250F, and can recall the struggle Denny was going through.

Three months later, truck racing came to New Zealand, specifically to Pukekohe. It is unlikely the track ever had such a big crowd, even in the heyday of the Tasman Championship when the New Zealand races were run in early January and featured 'stars' in the form of McLaren, Amon, Jim Clark, Jackie Stewart, Jochen Rindt and Graham Hill. The trucks had an obvious novelty factor, unlikely giant racers spurting great clouds of dark grey smoke as they lurched around the circuit.

Denny was in the thick of this truck revolution. Late in 1988 he'd been invited to Australia to race a truck along with other top drivers, and it was enough to convince him that, not only could he handle one of these leviathans, but also it was a lot of fun.

Leading Kiwi contender was the hugely under-rated Avon Hyde from Christchurch, Auckland speedway racer Calven Bonney, and Denny Hulme in a Scania. The event had been in the wind since trucking magazine publisher Trevor Woolston and speedway driver Bonney made a trip to Calder Raceway in Australia to witness truck racing first hand. The pair realised the potential for such an event in New Zealand, particularly if the top Australians were invited to compete.

It occurred to Woolston and Bonney that to best promote the event, a 'name' was needed. A few big names were kicked around, but it was to Denny Hulme that they kept coming back. As a youngster, Bonney had been part of the Hulme pit crew (an opportunity that arose because Bonney was doing his apprenticeship with an old mate of Denny's, Merv Mayo, who had been a finalist, with McLaren and Kerr, for the first New Zealand Driver to Europe scheme) when the recently crowned World Champion brought a F2 Brabham to New Zealand for the summer series, so he had a 'lead'.

Denny was approached and was sufficiently interested to accompany Woolston and Bonney back to Australia to race. In addition to being a top-flight speedway driver, Bonney was a member of one of Auckland's most successful trucking families — in short, a natural for this newfangled form of motor racing. He recalls Denny saying to him, 'You'll have to teach me to drive a truck' to which Bonney responded with 'Only if you teach me to drive around a track'. Bonney honoured his part of the bargain, but when it came to Denny showing him how to drive a circuit, the response was, 'You'll be right!'

Bonney recalls with affection that 'There were no airs and graces with Denny. He was one of us. Hard but fair. There was a time when we agreed to put on a bit of a show, swap the lead a bit and then race to the flag. He just shot off and afterwards I said, "That wasn't fair." Denny just laughed and said, "It wouldn't have looked good if I came second." '

In addition to Bonney, another early leading Kiwi contender was Avon Hyde. There are drivers like Avon Hyde throughout history, racers who, with the right breaks, would not have disgraced a Formula 1 field, yet, in real terms, they achieved comparatively little. Hyde was a natural and took to truck racing immediately. He can recall a meeting at Manfield where he raced smoke-stack to smoke-stack with Denny's Scania.

Hyde had obviously earned The Bear's respect: 'From that day on, we became real good mates. He was just happy to be one of the guys . . . although it did annoy me that some people treated him too casually. He didn't want to be worshipped, but he certainly deserved respect — more respect than he got from some.'

Hyde and Hulme shared the championship in that first year of truck racing and, years on, the surviving joint winner is full of Denny memories. 'He organised a film evening one night in Te Puke, his home town, before a meeting at Bay Park. We all went along to watch videos of truck racing from Europe and Australia. Can you imagine some other World Champions bothering to do that? He was a straightforward bloke, old Denny — you can't be anyone you're not, when you come from Te Puke . . .'

Hyde also recalls watching with awe whenever he went up to Wellington for the street race. 'He was quick. I mean he was *magnificently* quick.' There is no doubt that Hyde is particularly proud of the way he came close enough to Denny to have The Bear pour his heart out to him. 'We were both down at Dunedin, at a classic meeting on the old road circuit. We chatted for ages and he told me about his personal life and about how the death of his son had affected him. I've thought about that chat a lot since. I've often wondered if he only went truck racing to get his mind off Martin.'

Among the many new friends Denny made through truck racing was Don Wright who, at the time, was a Scania dealer. Don talks of his introduction to the new world of truck racing: 'Trevor [Woolston] came to see me, all enthusiastic about truck racing and that we should get involved.' Wright wasn't particularly interested, but Woolston persisted and kept throwing the names of potential drivers for a still non-existent Scania racing truck. Eventually Wright said that, if he had a choice, he'd be prepared to run with Denny Hulme. Not long after Wright took a call from Woolston: "It's all on! Denny will come and see you." Wright had his team start work on rebuilding a Scania 111 from a wreck and, as promised, one day Denny walked in and said, "Where's this truck I'm going to race?" Wright pointed to the incomplete project in a corner of the workshop and the 1967 World Champion quizzically said, "Really?!" '

Although he'd never met Denny before, Wright and The Bear were soon close friends. 'He used to treat my office as his own. He'd just arrive and ask if he could do anything to help progress on the race truck. He was convinced we'd never have it ready on time but when it was done he simply said, "I didn't think I'd see it but, OK, let's go." He really was a joy to work with.'

There was still the matter of running costs to deal with. 'Denny made a call to someone at Shell, but we didn't get all that we needed. Then we went to see Eta. Denny's name just opened doors. The deal was simple; we met two fresh young marketing graduates and sold them on what we could do for them. They could see Denny was a real guy — there were no pretensions with Denny.'

Both Avon Hyde and Calven Bonney remember Denny's Scanias as 'beautiful trucks'. Wright: 'It had all the good bits. The second Scania we ran had been racing in Europe and Denny had gone and raced a couple of times over there — once with a backup Scania at Silverstone and then later in Germany.' Wright, too, is certain that Denny's enthusiasm for truck racing was, in part at least, to fill the void left by the death of Martin.

'He told me once that he and Martin used to go trail bike riding together, but he just couldn't do it anymore without Martin.' Denny tried to talk Wright into going to Bathurst in 1992. 'I'd never been to Bathurst and had always wanted to. I was out in the garden and came inside to watch the television. I grabbed my "Denny Hulme Eta Ripples" T-shirt, and would you believe that was what I was wearing as I watched him pull over on Conrod . . .'

Of the 112 Formula 1 Grands Prix that Denny contested, 85 of them were powered by the famous Ford-funded Cosworth DFV V8. Six of his eight Formula 1 wins were with the DFV and of course there was one sitting in the back of his McLaren M23 in the shed at Rotoiti. Given that he never intended to race again, he could never have imagined racing with Cosworth power again, but at Bathurst at the end of 1989 that is precisely what happened. After two years of battling with the venerable stock block V8 Commodores against the state-of-the-art Sierras, Denny decided to join the turbo ranks and reunited with his former Formula Junior sparring partner and old mate Frank Gardner in his Benson and Hedges-sponsored team of Sierras.

Denny was partnered with another former World Champion — Allan Jones — and their yellow coupé qualified ninth, albeit nearly 5 seconds slower than the pole-winning Sierra driven by Peter Brock and top English touring car driver Andy Rouse. Putting this in perspective, the Larry Perkins VL Commodore just missed the top 10 cut-off in the unique Bathurst qualifying format.

The former World Champions were joined by 1988 winner Tony Longhurst and finished fifth, at that time Denny's best result at Bathurst. Denny was partnered with Jones again for the 1990 event in the second yellow Benson and Hedges Sierra, but this time they were out of luck and dropped out after 65 laps. They'd qualified tenth, ahead of the Sierras of Kiwi youngster Paul Radisich and Jeff Allam, who finished second between a pair of HSV Commodores.

After two years of sampling Sierra-Cosworths that never quite had their wicks turned up as high as others, Denny got a ride again with Frank

Gardner's team when the expert one-liner traded the fragile Fords for the generally bulletproof BMW M3 Sport Evo, which, at 2.5 litres and normally aspirated was giving away many horses to the Sierras, which in turn were lagging behind the Nissans in the power stakes.

Denny was well used to the M3 and had become a regular feature on the New Zealand touring car scene with BMWs owned and run by his mate Billy Bryce, who sadly passed away in 2003. Denny shared the BMW drive with Peter Fitzgerald, and they qualified nineteenth with a 2:20.88 lap. The best Sierra set 2:14.89, while the other M3 set a time of 2:17.80.

The Longhurst/Jones M3 finished its race after 138 laps with an engine problem, but Denny and his co-driver had a dream run, their fifth place finish on the track becoming fourth when a Sierra was disqualified.

In 1992 Denny was again contracted to the Gardner-run team of BMWs, this time partnered by young hotshot Paul Morris, while Venezuelan ace Johnny Cecotto shared the lead car with Longhurst. The race was run in appalling conditions and was eventually red-flagged on lap 143, but this was over 100 laps after Denny had suffered a heart attack on Conrod straight.

Frank Gardner remembers Denny on the radio saying that he was having vision problems, but they thought his screen was misting. They couldn't know their driver was dying. He maintained control and on the television news footage that was later repeated over and over again, the BMW is shown gliding down the guardrailing to a stop. He was dead by the time rescue crews arrived at the scene.

Reflections

Denny was born under the astronomical sign of Gemini. Interestingly, both authors of this book are also Geminis and, although self-analysis is always difficult, it would seem Denny portrayed the commonly regarded 'split personality' more dramatically than most. Many people interviewed for this book have made mention of his Jekyll and Hyde tendencies from time to time.

Chris Amon, sole survivor of the unofficial Kiwi 'trio at the top', admits that he got to know Denny much better after they'd both retired to New Zealand than when they were facing each other on a regular basis in Formula 1 and CanAm. 'Most people in New Zealand can't appreciate how well known the three of us were. Because we went to so many places, we were better known than, say, the All Blacks — especially in the States, where we were almost household names. Not only did the New Zealand media not give motor racing much exposure at that time, I rather suspect it was downplayed.'

To some it seemed Denny had a chip on his shoulder about the lack of recognition that he received in New Zealand, although some wonder if this was connected with his annoyance at missing the really big money in Formula 1. Perhaps, as an illustration of a trait, it seemed that part of Denny wanted a red carpet — but only a short one and only on some days.

For reasons that seem unfathomable 14 years on, when the New Zealand Hall of Fame was launched it was deemed that only one racing driver should make the first group of inductees. Denny was brought on stage to accept the induction of his pal Bruce McLaren. It was an embarrassing episode and was made worse when the 1967 World Champion and two-time CanAm champion was himself finally inducted to the Hall of Fame in June 1993 — one year after he had passed away doing what had brought him and his countrymen so much pleasure throughout his life.

Postscript   Sir Jack Brabham

Denny Hulme came to race in England early in 1960. He was a friend of Bruce McLaren and Phil Kerr, who was my manager at the time. I gave him a job in my commercial garage, but I was unable to help him with his motor racing ambitions until 1962–63 when I started building cars myself at Motor Racing Developments.

Our first car was a Formula Junior and Denny came to Goodwood when I was doing early testing. I gave him a few laps and he showed such clear talent straight away that we offered him some drives and he was soon winning on a regular basis.

Denny was a man of few words but when he did speak it meant something. Denny's father was awarded the Victoria Cross, which was won by confidence and determination and Denny was out of that same mould.

Honda wanted me to drive their little 600 sports car at the Nürburgring in 1964, but as I had Grand Prix commitments we sent Denny to drive it. He won the class and gave Honda their first international success.

In 1965 he joined me for the Honda Formula 2 programme for 1965–66 and although we had some success in 1965, things came right in 1966 when Honda built a new engine for us. We won every race except one, winning Honda their first World Championship.

At the end of the 1965 season, Dan Gurney left my Formula 1 team and as Denny was doing a great job in Formula 2, I put him in the Formula 1 team with me. This turned out to be a great combination. I won the

World Championship in 1966 and Denny won it in 1967, a worthy World Champion in our Grand Prix car.

Denny's ties with New Zealand and with Bruce McLaren were strong and Denny drove with Bruce in the CanAm series with great success. In this book, Eoin Young has highlighted Denny's successes as no one else could. Denny was a great driver and enjoyed racing anything on four wheels, from karts to trucks. Racing was his whole life.

'70 M14A McLaren F1

Cooper-Climax

'71 M16A McLaren Indycar

'70 M8D McLaren CanAm

'67 BT24 Brabham-Repco